ESSENTIAL
BUSINESS STUDIES

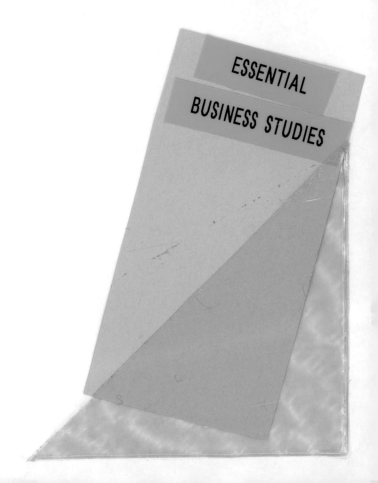

Also in the HarperCollins Essential Series

Essential Psychology
G.C. Davenport

Essential Government and Politics
Jim Cordell

Essential Marketing
Tony Proctor

Essential Accountancy and Finance
Bijon Kar

Series Editor: Roger Gomm

ESSENTIAL BUSINESS STUDIES

Stephen Barnes B.Sc. (Econ.)

CollinsEducational

An imprint of HarperCollinsPublishers

Published by
CollinsEducational Ltd
77–85 Fulham Palace Road
Hammersmith
London W6 8JB

First published in 1993

British Library Cataloguing in Publication Data

A catalogue is available on request from the British Library

ISBN 0–00–3222640

Typeset by Ellis Associates, cover design by Ridgeway Associates
and printed in Great Britain by Cambridge University Press, Cambridge.

Contents

Foreword

Every book in the Essential Series is designed to put you in control of your own learning.

In using this book, you will not only cover the key elements of your course but you will also benefit from the author's use of modern teaching and learning techniques, with the result that you will make the best possible use of your time.

Each chapter in this book has:

• a clear statement of the objectives at the start. This gives you information on the content to follow while setting clear goals to be achieved in terms of your understanding and learning
• frequent advice on making your own notes as you work through the material
• suggested activities which help you to get involved with the ideas explained and to relate theories to practice. Most activities are case studies or exercises, but some involve personal research
• notes in the margin of the text. These may highlight a topic or provide additional material. They are intended to add clarity and interest to your study
• a summary and comment section at the end. This will briefly restate some major themes and provide you with some points for the evaluation and integration of what you have learned – vital to reaching higher grades in your examination.

At the end of the book is an important section on revision and examinations. Read this carefully but well in advance.

Successful use of this book will involve some serious work. However, as well as achieving exam success, you may gain a lasting ability to understand and enjoy the business world.

Author's preface

This book is sub-titled 'a guide to success'. As a good guide, it should keep you company in both your coursework and in your preparation for exams. I have written with direct and recent experience of teaching students on post-16 Business Studies courses, and intend that it should be practical, thorough and friendly from your point of view. As a book though, it is more than a sequence of examination topics. By this I mean that it has an underlying pattern or paradigm. Business activity is about the human effort to make the best use of scarce resources through adding to their value in consumption. In a market economy the reward for success is profit. However, I hope students will – like this book – ask searching questions about social responsibility, the environment and ethics.

Learning to enjoy a subject is a fast route to examination success. As a teacher, my goal has always been for students to find pleasure and excitement in their studies. Much depends on a lively sense of enquiry. There is a tremendous amount to be discovered about business through everyday life: in the street, at work, in shops and cafés, on television, in newspapers and in magazines. Keep asking questions. Talk to teachers, write letters, make phone calls, argue with friends, challenge yourself.

Essential Business Studies is primarily designed for students on A level and BTEC courses. At A level it is particularly suitable for the AEB, Cambridge Modular, London and JMB syllabuses. However, it should also be valuable for students on first year university courses who need a secure foundation in the subject before tackling more advanced work. In addition, it will provide a thorough overview of the business world for those on courses leading to professional qualifications in banking, accounting, insurance, marketing and personnel. I hope, too, that it will be useful to the general reader who wants a better grasp of the issues in business and economic affairs.

Acknowledgements

The author and publisher would like to thank: Young and Rubicam Ltd for the use of their Cross Cultural Consumer Characteristics market segmentation model; the Department of Trade and Industry for permission to reproduce the map of Assisted Areas and Urban Programme Areas; the Hulton Deutsch Collection for permission to reproduce their picture of Adam Smith. The publisher has been unable to contact the copy-right holders of Figure 12.1, but will be happy to include an acknowledgement in future reprints.

The author particularly wishes to thank: Kidsons Impey (Chartered Accountants) at Brighton; Jane Champ at American Express; Peter Tyson at Body Shop International; Nicholas Bray for advice and word processing; Martin Taylor and Clive Maunder for advice and help; Maria Bailey, Keith Brumfitt, David Lines and Nancy Wall for criticism and suggestions; David Middelton for help on accounting and finance; John Rowland for ideas and encouragement; my Business Studies A-level students (class of '91) at Brighton Hove and Sussex Sixth Form College and Julie Barnes.

1 Business, market forces and entrepreneurship

Chapter objectives

After working through this chapter, you will:

▌ understand the real meaning of business enterprise

▌ appreciate business activity as a network of relationships

▌ be able to classify production sectors and the national work-force

▌ be aware of the importance of investors

▌ understand the meaning of the market and market forces

▌ know how the price mechanism operates

▌ appreciate the significance of profit

▌ be able to analyse how and why resources are reallocated between firms

▌ know the meaning of the following key terms: market, price, surplus, consumer surplus, demand, expenditure, utility, revenue, incentive, economic democracy, optimal allocation, specialization, money, resources, consumer, producer, ownership (direct and indirect), production sectors (primary, secondary and tertiary), entrepreneur.

BUSINESS STUDIES

Business studies is a kind of backstage pass. It may or may not take you into the Levi's jeans factory or the workshops at Coventry where Jaguars are made. But it will take you into the world of these and many other products, so that you can see and experience the extraordinary excitement of making good products that people want.

Making notes

In following this course you will need to make two kinds of notes. One kind is for key ideas and definitions of key terms. The best way to make these notes is on card index cards, which you can file alphabetically or in some other logical way. You can retrieve these and add to them as the occasion arises. In this book important terms are always listed at the beginning of each chapter and are printed bold when they are first mentioned in the text. These terms are suitable for entry on to index cards. For example a term

Learning skills

Getting organized: Information

Find out at the start of your course:
• how long it is, both in hours per week and in total
• what the content (syllabus) is
• what homework and coursework you will have to do
• how you will be assessed
• what the deadlines are for any assessed coursework, and what the dates of the final examinations are.

Getting organized: Time
• how much time will you need?
• how will you fit the course into your existing commitments?
• analyse how you use your time now
• identify your best times for study – a few hours study a day is usually more effective than twelve hours on Sunday.

Getting organized: Place
At home establish a place for working. This needs to be no more than a chair and a table. After a while, just sitting in that place will trigger the work reflex in you.
Do not try to study on the sofa where you usually watch TV or in bed where you usually sleep.

Getting organized: Equipment
The minimum you will need is:
• A4 size paper, bought in a ready punched pad
• ring binder files, so that you can store your notes subject by subject
• a pen you find it easy to write with
• a pencil and rubber
• a ruler with a good edge

- card index cards
- your textbook(s)
- a scrapbook or plastic wallets for storing news cuttings.

Media Watch

To get the best out of a business studies course you must keep abreast of the business news. This means a regular reading of the business pages of a quality newspaper or one of the specialist magazines such as *The Economist* or *Business Week*. Radio and TV programmes are also important sources of information. At the time this book was printed the following were regularly broadcast.
Saturday
Radio 4 12.00pm *Money Box* (personal finance)
Sunday
BBC2 6.35pm *Money Programme*
Radio 4 6.30pm *Eurofile*
Radio 4 7.00pm *In Business*
Monday – Friday
Channel 4 12.30pm *Business Daily*
Monday – Thursday
Radio 4 9.45pm *Financial World Tonight*
Friday
Radio 4 11.45pm *Financial Week*

Figure 1.1

► A modern economy depends upon the principle of specialization and exchange involving money.

which appears in this chapter is **Production Sector**. A suitable card for this would look like this:

> **Production Sectors**
>
> PRIMARY: extractive industries (mining etc.), agriculture and fisheries (declining importance in advanced economies)
> SECONDARY: manufacturing and construction (declining relative importance in advanced economies)
> TERTIARY: service industries (services to people, finance etc.) (increasing importance in advanced economies)
>
> See Chapter 27 in Lockheed and Bigby Modern Economics

You will also want to make notes on other matters, and every now and again this book will suggest when you should. You can make these notes in the form of ordinary text or in the form of pattern notes. For example if you wanted to make a pattern note covering this chapter it would look something like this:

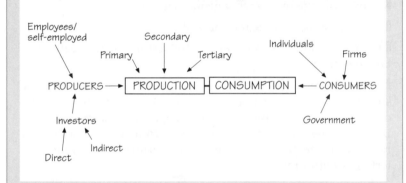

You will notice that advice on notemaking is usually given at the end of the relevant section of text. This is because you should always scan a text to see what it contains **before** making notes.

To give yourself interesting up-to-date examples, collect news cuttings and add them to your notes.

The Business Network

Because modern society is based on such intense specialization, almost nobody is capable of meeting all their own needs. Today, people exchange the value of their specialized output for the goods and services that they require. The key medium of exchange is **money**. Modern currencies are worthless in themselves, but they represent **resources**. Money acts as a kind of go-between among consumers and producers. Thus the specialized work of one person can be exchanged for the equally specialized output of another. For example a doctor earns money seeing patients in the surgery, while his/her car is repaired at a garage, which will accept money as payment for its services. In a modern economy people and companies relate to each other in a **business network.**

People are involved in **business activity**, either as **consumers** or as **producers**. Everyone is a consumer, and almost everyone is a producer, at least for some part of their lives. The network of relations between consumers and producers makes up the business world.

Consumers

Every individual is a consumer, because they are certain to consume the products of business activity. All firms are consumers because they consume the products of other firms. The government and local councils are also consumers, depending as they do on the products of ordinary firms.

Statistical analysis of the size and changes in consumer groups (see Chapters 5 and 6) provides vital information to firms in attempting to match their output with likely sales.

► The government collects statistical data through censuses on households and firms.

Producers

Firms are the major producers, but also significant are the government (e.g. Department of Health and Social Security), local councils (e.g. education departments), and other public organizations (e.g. the Forestry Commission).

Production may be classified by sectors:

- **primary sector** includes all extractive businesses engaged in the production of raw materials, e.g. farming, mining, oil production
- **secondary sector** includes all manufacturing and construction businesses that transform raw materials into finished products, e.g. the motor industry, electronics, textiles
- **tertiary sector** includes the production of all services, e.g. transport, banking, health.

Producers have two important identities:

- people who own a business: **investors**
- people who work for a business: **employees.**

In some small firms these people or groups of people are one and the same. However in most large firms there is only limited overlap between owners and employees.

Employees

The country's working population is defined as all those aged between eighteen and sixty/sixty-five who are available for work. Its size depends on such factors as:

► Employees

- population trends
- the school-leaving and retirement ages
- women seeking work
- student numbers.

Subtraction of the unemployed and those occupied in the armed forces from the total working population, gives the total in **civil**

employment. A key variable here is the **unemployment rate**, which varies with the overall level of business activity. This in turn depends on the strength of demand from consumers. Governments can influence total demand (see Chapter 33), but only to a limited extent.

Investors

► Investors.

Investors are broadly those who provide finance for a business. This may be by direct investment, in owning a business outright, or in owning shares in a business (see Chapter 3). Or it may be indirect through a savings plan, such as a pension fund or a life assurance policy. These funds are then invested in business by specialist managers. In addition, part of people's savings in banks and building societies are lent to firms, but these investments are not equivalent to ownership, and are rewarded by interest rather than profit. Finally, it is also possible to 'invest' in the government by buying fixed interest stocks called **gilt-edged securities.**

MARKET FORCES

The Meaning of the Market

► Adam Smith (1723-1790) His book *The Wealth of Nations* was the first to explain the action of market forces. He argued that the competitive desire for profit was turned by the **invisible hand** of the market into the overall public good. He also warned that firms will try to obstruct competition which would be contrary to the public interest.

Figure 1.2
Adam Smith

► Markets enable buyers and sellers to communicate and agree a price. Markets include traditional markets, shops and shopping centres, warehouses, offices, mail and telephone ordering, commodity and finance markets.

► Transactions can occur in a market when the buyer enjoys a consumer surplus and the seller makes a profit.

Imagine a large market square, sellers on one side of the stalls and potential buyers on the other. There is continual bargaining over price. Seller and buyer confront each other. Each side has a secret. The seller knows how much the product cost in terms of manufacture, overheads, etc. and will not sell it for less. The buyer knows how much the product is worth to him or her and will not pay more. The game is to strike a

price on which both sides agree. Provided that the buyer's valuation of a good is higher than the seller's cost, bargaining can occur. The finally agreed price must fall within this bargaining zone and will provide a **surplus** for both sides. The seller makes a **profit** defined as the difference between the cost price and the selling price. The buyer enjoys **consumer surplus** which means the difference between the buyer's valuation and the actual price paid. A transaction has taken place. A product has moved from seller to buyer while a sum of money has moved from buyer to seller. Both sides are satisfied. The seller can direct finance to the production of further similar products, while the buyer is motivated to earn money to finance further similar purchases. This picture is highly simplified, but it represents the essential dynamic of the market.

Figure 1.3
Market forces and the price mechanism

This diagram is worth understanding since it explains how the market really works. Start at the consumers box. Consumers have wants, which we call **demand**. If supported by money, this demand becomes **expenditure**, in the purchase of a product, at a price. This product should yield satisfaction – which is called **utility**. The consumer will only make the purchase if the value of the expected utility exceeds the price. Think about this carefully. You are considering the purchase of an ice-cream at 50p. The maximum price you would pay for it is 60p. In other words, you estimate the value of its utility at 60p. The price is less than the utility expected, and a purchase takes place. You, the consumer have made a 'profit' of 10p – which is called consumer's surplus. This surplus will encourage the consumer to make further purchases in future, unless a better product can be found.

Now look at the producers box. The reasoning is an exact parallel. Producers will potentially supply goods or services. This supply incurs business costs. However the product's sale should yield **revenue**. The producer will only make the sale if the revenue exceeds the cost. The minimum price that he/she would accept for the ice-cream is 40p, since this was its cost to the firm when all outlays are included. The actual price at 50p is greater than the costs, and a sale takes place. The producer has made a profit of 10p. This return will encourage the producer to continue output in future, unless a more profitable product can be found.

The Meaning of Profit

Profit is an **incentive** to put forward capital (from savings or with a loan) to finance **business enterprise**. The risk of failure – and losses - is counterbalanced by the prospect of success - and profits. Business activity is essential to the creation of wealth. Profit therefore acts as a motor in driving the forces of wealth creation.

Under market forces, the consumer is often said to be king. Every product from every firm must face the test of the marketplace. In their every potential purchase, consumers assess the likely surplus of utility over expenditure. Products that keep failing this test experience falling sales, falling profitability, and the progressive withdrawal of resources from their production. By contrast, products that find consumer approval see rising sales and profitability, attracting new

► Economic democracy.

► Profit acts like a directional beacon channelling resources to their optimal (best) allocation. This must be the use in which consumers find the greatest utility and firms find the greatest profit.

resources to expand their production.

This pattern suggests the idea of **economic democracy**. Every purchase of a product is in effect a vote for its continued production. The firm receives the sales revenue and corresponding profit, so ensuring the continued use of resources for output of that product in the future. Products that are rejected in the market are starved of revenue and profit; this leads by stages to their complete withdrawal from production.

Profit and Resource Allocation

Birmingham Biscuits and Coventry Cakes
Birmingham Biscuits Ltd and Coventry Cakes Ltd are two firms of roughly equal size, with products in the same broad market sector. A change in their sales and profitability could be caused by a shift in consumer tastes, or by a change in relative costs. In this case events are triggered by a change in consumer preference, from biscuits to cakes. The consequences unfold as follows:

	BIRMINGHAM BISCUITS		COVENTRY CAKES	
	Resources	*Finance*	*Resources*	*Finance*
1	Demand for biscuits falls	Sales fall	Demand for cakes rises	Sales increase
2	Unsold stocks build up	Profits fall	Stocks run down	Profits rise
3	Output is cut back	Investment reduced	Output is increased	Investment increases
4	Machines are sold, staff made redundant	Capital withdrawn	New machines bought, more staff employed	Capital injected

Look carefully at the link between resources and finance. It is very important to realize that finance only represents resources. What happens to the real resources is therefore mirrored in the corresponding financial events.

► At Birmingham Biscuits, demand, sales and profits fall, and the firm's hold on resources rapidly weakens. Meanwhile at Coventry Cakes, demand, sales and profits rise, and the pull on resources rapidly strengthens. If the trend continues, Birmingham Biscuits will close and the resources released may be re-employed at Coventry Cakes.

In reality the pattern will be less neat. A firm like Birmingham Biscuits may react to changed demand and alter its product range. Both decline and expansion are often quite gradual. Rarely are resources so directly exchanged, and in practice there is always a pool of capital and workers seeking more rewarding employment. Often, too, neither capital nor labour are particularly mobile, and firms may limp on long after market forces have turned against them. But in the end the market wins. Every day countless millions of consumer spending choices are made, and the invisible messages reach firms in their detailed accounting data. Firms and industries are always expanding and declining with the corresponding changes in their power to attract and retain resources. We are looking at market forces in action.

THE ENTREPRENEUR

The creation of wealth, which people tend to take for granted, depends on the forces of enterprise and the ability to compete in the markets of Britain and the world.

Individuals who are willing to accept the risks of business enterprise are called **entrepreneurs** (from the French word *entreprendre* – to undertake). An entrepreneur is a person who commits resources (their own or others') and provides the 'guidance system' within a business enterprise. The entrepreneur's challenge is to engage with market forces and to win: to develop the enterprise that takes the custom, makes the profit, re-invests and expands.

In some ways, enterprise is a state of mind. There is a certain ability to recognize the needs of people that are not being met, and then imaginatively to think how they might be met in a practical and cost-effective way. The entrepreneur is self-confident and believes that things can be done better. He/she sees everything as possible, and never takes 'no' for an answer. He/she thinks positively about how something might be achieved, and pursues an idea with energy and determination.

As a company grows in size and complexity, the role of the entrepreneur often becomes less clearly focused on one person. In a company the capital is divided into shares which are owned by a number of shareholders. These shareholders elect a board of directors, who make business decisions on their behalf. In a smaller company the directors are normally also the larger shareholders, and form a group of entrepreneurs. In a large national or multinational firm, the directors' proportional shareholding may be quite small, and the entrepreneurial functions become very diffuse or scattered. In practice the careers and often the salaries of directors depend on their firm's success in the market. The transmission of the profit motive through a firm's hierarchy (i.e. levels of seniority amongst employees) is very important in achieving efficiency and customer satisfaction. Some firms will deliberately foster a profit-driven sense of enterprise in the firm through profit-sharing schemes or staff ownership of shares (see Chapter 29).

► Profit is the reward for efficient use of resources to generate consumer satisfaction. The enterprise that creates the most satisfaction for the fewest resources (lowest costs) is rewarded by the highest profits.

► In the early 1980s there was a widespread belief that the spirit of enterprise was not sufficiently strong in Britain. The government was anxious to encourage an 'enterprise culture', and offered incentives to people starting in business or running small firms. The thrust of government policy has been to make even large firms more responsive to market forces. There has also been growing emphasis on the need to value business and industry more highly.

 Two cycle manufacturers are located in the East Midlands. Centurian Cycles is a traditional Nottingham based firm making a conventional range of family and sports models. A reputation for quality does not alter a growing consumer perception of the bicycles as dull and unfashionable. Sales are steadily declining.

Twenty-five miles away in Leicester, Golden Eagle Ltd is a new and innovative producer of all-terrain and mountain

 You will see this sign where I have suggested an activity for you to carry out. Sometimes it will be an investigation, sometimes a case study with questions, sometimes a short piece of written work.

bikes. As well as catering for specialists, the range has been skilfully adapted to enter the urban cycling and children's markets. Sales are steadily increasing.

Explain carefully how market forces are acting on the firms and their resources.

Summary and comment

• in theory the operation of market forces ensures an optimal distribution of resources. In reality too, market economies seem to be more dynamic, productive, and consumer orientated than any other economic system

• many imperfections exist in markets. Firms may try to reduce competition through monopoly power, or other tactics to fix price and restrict consumer choice (see Chapter 27).

• the economic democracy does not provide equal voting power. Both incomes and wealth are very unevenly distributed and resources are often directed to the production of profitable luxuries for the few, rather than basic necessities for the many

• markets tend to consider only the short-run profit. The long run is given a very low value, and thus important investments for the future may not be made where short-term profit is the main goal

• the market has encouraged ever increasing consumption without adequate regard for the environment, or for the ecosystem on which all life depends (see Chapter 44).

• in small-scale business the entrepreneur is the risk-taking owner or major shareholder, whose use of resources to satisfy consumer demand is rewarded by personal profit. In larger firms the entrepreneurial function exists only nominally with shareholders, and is transmitted into the firm's management by the elected directors

• profit is fundamental in motivating talented people to accept responsibility for managing resources and to inject their creative energy into the generation of wealth.

2 # Sole traders, partnerships, cooperatives and franchising

Chapter objectives

After working through this chapter, you will:

▌ understand the opportunities and problems of being a sole trader

▌ know how a partnership operates

▌ understand the principles of a cooperative

▌ know what is meant by franchising

▌ know the meaning of the following key terms: partner, ordinary partnership, limited partnership, producer cooperative, consumer cooperative, business format franchise.

Media Watch

For useful background to this chapter you should watch the news and follow the media for examples of the problems faced by small businesses, many of which are sole traders, partnerships and franchises.

SOLE TRADERS

An idea and a small sum of starting capital are all that is necessary to start a business. No permission is needed, no forms need to be filled in. Of course, the enterprise is more likely to succeed with some market research, some business expertise and an adequate sum of starting capital. The one-person business or **sole trader** – is the simplest and most common form of business enterprise. Essentially the individual provides the capital, takes the risk, and is rewarded by the whole of the profit (or loss).

Sole trading, as a pattern of business organization involves few formalities. Financial records must be kept for tax purposes, and VAT registration is required if annual turnover exceeds £50 000. The sole trader will also be subject to all normal business laws, such as those relating to employment or health and safety.

Sole traders have great flexibility. They can discover and meet their customers' needs without reference to any head office or set of rules. The product range, marketing and hours of business can all be adjusted to suit local needs, and the response to changing demand can be immediate. Customers can be provided with a high degree of personal service, which may be preferred to the more anonymous service of large firms. Overheads such as office space and administration costs are usually low, so that price can be very competitive. Sometimes a greater variety of products may be offered, that a larger competitor would be unable or unwilling to stock. Finally the sole trader is highly motivated since profit is the direct reward for success – and loss is the penalty of failure.

However very real problems are faced by the one-person enterprise.

► Typical business formats for the sole trader include:
• small scale retailing, e.g. grocers, newsagents;
• building traders;
• transport services;
• personal services, e.g. child-minding, gardening;
• restaurants, cafés, guest houses;
• arts and entertainment providers;
• smallholdings.

Starting capital is usually limited to the owner's savings, and loan capital will be limited in availability, and often secured on the borrower's home. Liability for debts is unlimited, so that in the event of business failure all debts must be settled, even if this means selling the family home and most of its contents. Expansion is therefore difficult, and ploughed-back profits are often insufficient to take full advantage of any business opportunities. There is little chance of specialization in the management of the business. For example, few sole traders will have the advanced marketing skills that could increase their sales. Similarly the effective interpretation of accounts needs training and experience. A major drawback faced by all small firms is the higher cost of goods or materials when buying on a small scale. Similarly, marketing, transport and borrowing on a small scale all tend to be proportionally more expensive (see Chapter 15). Finally, to keep the enterprise running continuously can be difficult. The owner may need to make a trip away from the business to market the products, or may simply want a holiday. Equally there is a risk of the business collapsing if the owner falls ill or dies.

► Many sole traders have a high average cost base.

PARTNERSHIPS

Under the Partnership Act (1890) any group of two to twenty people may jointly finance and operate a business enterprise. The rights of the partners, including their share of any profits, are stated in the Deed of Partnership. Unless specified to the contrary, each **partner** carries equal weight in decision making and management. A sleeping partner can choose to contribute capital and share profits, but to take no part in running the business. **Ordinary partnerships** carry unlimited liability for debts, but a **limited partnership** is possible (Limited Partnership Act, 1907) where sleeping partners have their liability limited to their capital input. However, at least one partner must always have unlimited liability.

► Partnerships are common in retailing, building, farming and consumer services. They are particularly popular in providing professional services such as accountancy, law, architecture and medicine.

By contrast with sole trading a partnership combines greater financial resources with an enlarged pool of business ideas and expertise. Partners are able to specialize and make different contributions to the business. There are fewer problems with continuity, as an absent partner's duties can always be covered by colleagues if necessary. Nevertheless many of the limitations affecting the sole trader remain. The ability to raise new finance is still restricted, and all ordinary partners have unlimited liability for all debts. Since the decisions of any one partner are the responsibility of all the partners, a high level of mutual trust is necessary. There is much potential for conflict in decision making, especially if business declines. A partnership can be dissolved voluntarily, or necessarily by bankruptcy or the death of any partner.

► Partnerships depend on trust and cooperation.

COOPERATIVES

Producer cooperatives are owned and controlled by the workforce who elect a team of managers and share the profits among themselves. Most producer coops in Britain are relatively small, with an average of ten employees. As businesses become larger and more complex, it is difficult to run them in a genuinely cooperative way.

Consumer cooperatives are owned by their customers who join the cooperative society by purchasing at least one £1 share, with a maximum holding of 1 000 shares. The society functions under the democratic control of the members who elect a management committee. Dividends are paid to members according to the value of their purchases over a period of time. The only major example of a consumer coop in Britain is the high street retail 'Coop' stores. However, few members participate actively in their management, and trading stamps or price cuts have replaced members' dividends.

► There were about 1 600 producer coops in Britain in 1990 employing about 18 000 people.

► Membership of consumer cooperatives has fallen from 13 million in the 1960s to around 8 million today. Mergers have reduced the number of societies to around 180.

 Read the folowing case study and complete the tasks.

The impact of computer technology on newspaper printing was sudden and dramatic. Among the many who had found themselves made redundant were ten of the present owner-workers at Primrose Printers. It was back in 1986 when they had legally formed a workers' cooperative, each member contributing £10 000 as start-up capital. The premises in Primrose Hill were cramped but the volume of business had expanded rapidly and membership increased to fifteen.

Management meetings were held on a weekly basis with everyone attending – and increasingly long agendas. Problems began to emerge in 1990 when the recession began to bite into orders.

Stuart Leigh, the marketing manager, urged increased spending on advertising and sales. This proposal met sharp opposition from Martin Cummins, the accountant, who believed that some serious cost cutting was required.

'It's no good being romantic about this business. We need a freeze on wages for everyone. And there's too much waste. I'm afraid that some members believe that what belongs to everyone belongs to no one.'

Wages too were a source of conflict. The policy of equal pay for all was popular at first, but now dissatisfaction was surfacing as some members felt that their effort and skills were not being properly rewarded. Lengthy discussions of these issues in meetings led other members to complain that time was being wasted. Moreover, quite small business problems could take an hour or more to resolve. The idea was to avoid voting and reach decisions by general agreement. But as Steve Hursthouse, the computer expert said,

'Nothing ever gets decided. Our service to customers gets slower. Orders go to commercial rivals. Where will it end?'

1 Summarize the problems being experienced by the business.

2 How far are these the result of being a cooperative?

3 Can you suggest changes which might alleviate these problems?

► Wimpy, Pizza Express, Tie Rack, Body Shop and the British School of Motoring are all examples of franchising.

FRANCHISING

A **franchise** literally means a contractual licence granted by one person (the franchisor) to another (the franchisee). The traditional franchise agreement simply meant one firm granting certain rights to another concerning the manufacture or sale of its products. For instance Heineken lager is brewed under licence by Whitbread. The modern **business format franchise** was developed in the USA during the 1950s. The concept involves development of a clearly defined business formula by one firm, and its expansion, by granting licences to other entrepreneurs, who operate the same formula under the terms of a contract.

Key features of the franchise business format include:

* a contract stating the obligations of franchisor and franchisee
* the business is owned by the franchisee, who provides a major part of the initial investment
* the franchisee gains exclusive rights to the use of a business format, including a trade name, and benefits from associated goodwill
* the franchisor provides the necessary training and advice for the launch of the business
* the franchisor supplies permanent support for all aspects of the operation; e.g. marketing
* the franchisee pays the franchisor for the rights obtained and for future support.

Taking up a franchise is a means of starting a business with a much reduced risk of failure. The franchisee has a large measure of independence, but also enjoys a great deal of direct and indirect support. The eight major advantages are:

1 Successful Business Formula
The franchisee is launching a business format that is known to be viable. A valuable reputation and well-known name exist from the outset. Access may be gained to various patents, copyrights and trade secrets.

2 Start-up Assistance
Often the franchisor has options on key high street sites, and is sure to provide intensive assistance at the start-up stage.

3 Finance
A franchise often requires a smaller capital investment at the outset than the equivalent independent operation. Bank loans are usually more readily available and less costly for a franchise.

4 Training and Support
Lack of experience is made good by the franchisor's training and continuous management support. The permanent backing of an expert and sophisticated head office organization is always valuable, but vital when problems arise.

5 Marketing
Franchisors will often provide a national advertising and marketing effort that far exceeds anything possible for a small business. They will also carry out in-depth market research.

6 Economies of Scale
A franchising system is able to achieve major **economies of scale** (see Chapter 15) in purchasing, marketing and distribution.

7 Territory
The franchisee may be allotted territory within which no rival units of the same franchise will operate. This zoning is designed to ensure that each unit has the potential market base to be fully viable.

8 Research and Development
The franchisor will have the resources to carry out research and development, so ensuring that the product and allied business format are as advanced and up-to-date as possible.

Despite these substantial advantages, the franchisee will inevitably encounter some problems. Five typical difficulties are:

1 Controls
The franchise agreement will specify the rights of the franchisor to exercise some control over the business.

2 Dependency
There is a danger of becoming over-dependent on the franchisor, and failing to take the necessary initiative and responsibility.

3 Conflict of Interests
The franchisor's greatest financial concern may be to increase turnover, i.e. the rate at which stock is sold and replenished, in order to maximize growth and fees received. The franchisee will naturally be more concerned with profit.

4 Franchisor Judgement
Any strategic errors of judgement by the franchisor could seriously affect the franchisee (e.g. excessive speed of expansion or inadequate product development).

5 Other Franchisees
All franchisees are mutually dependent to some degree. A serious error by one could damage the business of them all.

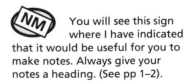

► The British Franchise Association (BFA)

The BFA is the central organization for companies engaged in trading through franchise agreements. It has a strict ethical code of practice with which members must conform. It provides for exchange of information and expertise among members. It produces publications giving advice to both franchisors and franchisees. It represents the interests of franchising to the media and the government.

 Make notes illustrating the advantages and disadvantages of sole trading, partnerships and cooperatives. Summarize the benefits and difficulties of becoming a franchisee.

You will see this sign where I have indicated that it would be useful for you to make notes. Always give your notes a heading. (See pp 1–2).

 As a business franchise format, the Soft Shop offers a wide range of computer software for home and office use. UK sales have been increasing on average at twenty-five per cent a year over the past six years. There are now twenty-five outlets concentrated in major urban areas, including two owned directly by the franchisor. The start-up capital required is £100 000 of which £12 000 represents a management fee.

You are considering becoming a franchisee of the Soft Shop and running your own branch. List the key questions to which you would need answers before signing an agreement and risking £100 000.

 Many real franchise opportunities are advertised each week in *Exchange and Mart*. Send for details of one such opportunity and assess its advantages and disadvantages, under the headings listed above.

Summary and comment

• on the principle that only some acorns grow into oaks, plenty of acorn-sized (i.e. very small) enterprises are necessary for the health and growth of business in society

• sole traders and partners are very direct entrepreneurs, and often represent a pool of energy and ideas essential to an enterprise culture. Such firms may pioneer new products, and nurture new business leaders

• in many markets the advantages of large scale operation are too great for the very small firm to survive. But gaps in markets may be small and/or local. These are niches that sole traders and partnerships can profitably hope to fill. Such businesses may be effective in opening new markets that are still too small for the commitment of large firms

• the pattern of such business opportunities changes with time. Food retailing has been squeezed by supermarkets and multiple stores, but inexpensive computer technology is providing new opportunities, for example in desk top publishing

• neither consumer nor producer cooperatives are easy to run on cooperative lines if they grow beyond a certain size and both have found it difficult to attract investment capital from outside without control passing to large investors or creditors

• franchising offers an opportunity to start a business with limited capital, based on a product or service which is already commercially proven, and with support services provided by the franchisor.

③ Limited companies

WHAT IS A COMPANY?

The term **company** means an organization set up in law to carry on a business with the objective of making a profit. The assets (e.g. land, buildings, machinery) of this organization are owned by a group of people (company) who each hold a share of its capital. These shares are subdivided for convenience into small units, for instance £1 or 50p shares. Shareholders in such 'joint stock' companies carry rights to vote at meetings and are entitled to a corresponding proportion of profits.

This form of business is the foundation for the great majority of business activity in Britain and other market economies. There are two essential concepts involved:

1 The company has a legal identity that is separate from that of its owners.

2 The owners' liability for indebtedness is limited to the value of their stake in the company.

Private Limited Companies

A **private limited company** is one whose shares may only be sold privately to family, friends and business associates. They are often called family firms. The sale of shares to the general public is prohibited, as is their resale on the Stock Exchange. Often a family or other small group owns most or all of the shares, and this arrangement may

▶ The earliest joint stock company dates from 1553 when merchants subscribed £6 000 in £25 shares to finance a voyage to discover a new trading route to the Far East. Modern company law emerged through several acts of parliament between 1844–62.

▶ **Limited Liability** was introduced in the nineteenth century to encourage investment in high-risk capital projects such as railway building.

▶ In 1991 there were 1 141 000 private companies in Britain. Most were small to medium sized companies.

be protected by the requirement that an investor wishing to sell his shares must offer them first to the other shareholders. The company and its investors enjoy the full privilege of limited liability (indicated by Limited or Ltd in its name). Each year the company must supply the Registrar of Companies with its accounts and other information concerning business activities and organization.

The advantages of forming a private company are clearly those of limited liability and access to greater sources of finance through the sale of shares. As a legal entity the company is also more assured of continuity regardless of circumstances affecting individual shareholders.

However the actual amount of finance raised depends on the investors available and their readiness to supply risk capital. There is the added complication that many private companies do not wish their shares to be held outside the inner group of directors, in order to avoid any dilution of control.

Public Limited Companies

The shares in a **public limited company** can be sold direct to the public or to financial institutions (e.g. pension funds). They can be readily resold on the Stock Exchange, where their price is publicly quoted. This encourages investors to purchase shares, since they know that they can recover the market value of their holding whenever they wish. With a public limited company there must be at least £50 000 in issued share capital, of which twenty-five per cent or more must be fully paid up. In practice the sums involved will be far larger. Limited liability is automatic for all shareholders, and the company's name must include the letters plc. Before a company may 'go public' it must submit further details of its affairs to the Registrar of Companies, and face a careful check by the Stock Exchange Council in order to protect potential investors. The whole process is quite expensive.

A public company has potential access to unlimited amounts of capital, and is likely to be able to obtain loans more cheaply and more easily. It is a common form of organization in industries where the scale of operation must normally be large: for instance oil or banking.

1 Make notes on limited liability and the advantages this has over sole trading or trading through a partnership.

2 Set up a two column table: one column for private limited companies and one for public limited companies. Make your notes on the two kinds of company in this format.

Forming a Company

A new company – private or public – must register with the Registrar of Companies. This involves providing two key documents:

1 **Memorandum of Association**
This deals with matters of **external** status. It gives the company's

► Companies Acts 1948–85. These brought about laws designed to protect investors and to ensure that the right of limited liability is not abused. Significant breaches of company laws are a serious offence, while fraud and misconduct by directors can lead to heavy penalties.

► Memorandum of Association

name, registered office, trading objectives and capital structure (this is the maximum amount of capital that may be raised plus the nominal value of the shares).

2 Articles of Association

This provides details of the company's **internal** rules. It will specify the arrangements and rules for: the sale of shares, shareholders' rights, company meetings, the election and powers of directors.

There are then various statements and declarations to be made, after which the Certificate of Incorporation is issued.

▶ Articles of Association

Share Capital

The Memorandum of Association states the company's authorized capital – the maximum face value of shares that it may issue. The company usually chooses to issue (sell) shares to a lower total value, leaving scope for expansion. When they are first issued, it may not be necessary for the buyer to pay for them in full. For instance, 50p on £1 shares may be payable with the purchase application, forming 'partly paid' share capital. The outstanding 50p may not be 'called up' until a time many months in the future, when the issue will be 'fully paid up'. This device gives the directors a useful source of promptly available capital which they can request when necessary.

The majority of a company's share capital is usually issued as **ordinary shares** (also called **equity**). In a very real sense the ordinary shareholders are part-owners of the company, and face the risks involved of being in business. They normally have full voting rights on a 'one share, one vote' basis. Any profit, after payment of tax, is divided between **retention** in the business (money ploughed back), and payment of **dividends** to the shareholders. The amount of dividend may fluctuate widely from one payment period to the next. Meanwhile the market (i.e. resale) value of the shares may rise or fall – often unpredictably .

▶ Ordinary shares (equity).
Preference shares.
Debentures – a means of financing a company through fixed-interest loans often secured against company assets (stocks or bonds).

Some companies issue **preference shares**. These involve less risk than ordinary shares, but carry no voting rights. Holders receive a fixed percentage rate of dividend – if sufficient profit has been made – before any payment is made to the ordinary shareholders as preference shares are given priority over ordinary shares. **Cumulative preference shares** have the advantage that any unpaid preference dividends are carried forward, and remain payable as soon as profits permit. **Participating preference shares** allow the holders their fixed rate dividends, and then to receive an extra dividend if profit is still available after the ordinary dividend has been paid.

Debentures are not shares, but IOUs or certificates of indebtedness. The holder receives a fixed rate of interest, and is a creditor rather than an owner of the company. The interest payment on debentures takes priority over all other types of dividend, and secured debentures have their repayment value attached to specific assets in the company. If the firm is unable to meet its debts, then these assets can be sold in order to repay the secured debenture holders. Debentures of public companies are traded on the Stock Exchange, and are repayable by a stated date, or earlier.

Look at the financial pages of a quality newspaper. Identify examples of companies raising capital through ordinary shares (flotations and rights issues), preference shares and debentures (stocks/bonds).

Ownership and Control of Companies

A sole trader personally owns his/her business. In a private company the few major shareholders are usually directors who make the decisions and manage the firm. A public company is often different. There may be numerous shareholders, large and small, in Britain and abroad. The directors of the company are elected by the ordinary shareholders, and have a duty to act on their behalf. All voting shareholders are invited to the company's annual general meeting, where they can propose and vote on resolutions. In practice the directors are in a strong position. Most shareholders do not attend meetings and have no interest in voting. They may have little knowledge of the company's affairs, and will usually vote as recommended by the directors. Only in circumstances of extreme mismanagement would they be likely seriously to oppose, or in exceptional cases, to dismiss the directors.

Institutional Investors

Large blocks of shares in public companies may also be owned by financial institutions such as pension funds, insurance companies and various investment and unit trusts, in which case they are known as **institutional investors**. Usually, these professional investors play little part in the control of the company so long as performance is satisfactory. Thus a real gap exists between the ownership and true control of a major plc (public limited company). Nor do shareholders and directors necessarily have the same interests. The shareholders seek maximum profits and growth in the value of the enterprise. By contrast, so long as return on capital is 'reasonable', the directors may be more concerned to maximize the size or prestige of the firm and the consequences of this for their earnings and career prospects.

► The shareholders or owners, of most public companies exercise little effective control over the affairs of a business.

 Look at the financial pages of a quality newspaper for articles on shareholders' meetings. These are often only reported if there is dissatisfaction with company performance.

What is reported as happening at the meeting, and what was the outcome? Remember that if the story describes a 'crowded meeting', this will still only mean that a tiny minority of shareholders turned up. Usually what happens is determined by holders of large blocks of shares – on the whole these will be institutional investors or holding companies (see an explanation of these overpage).

Holding Companies

Since the shares of plc's are freely traded, it is possible for one company – called a **holding company** – to gain control over other companies through owning fifty-one per cent or more of their voting shares (less than fifty per cent may still provide effective control). Shares in the holding company may be offered to the shareholders of another larger company, together with some cash incentive. The finance necessary to gain control of the target firm may only be a fairly small percentage of its market value. This device opens the possibility of **pyramiding**. The holding company takes control of fifty-one per cent of the voting shares in the other company. These enlarged assets are then used to obtain control of the voting rights in a still larger company – and the process can continue. Control of a relatively small company can lead to real control of a far greater business empire.

Management Buy-outs and Management Buy-ins

Management Buy-outs
When the managers act to purchase part or all of a firm, the process is called a **management buy-out**. The negotiation and financing of the deal can be very complex, but the basic idea is straightforward. The managers come to believe that they could run the enterprise more profitably if it were directly within their ownership and control. Often it is a division or subsidiary of a larger firm that managers hope to buy. Since the price will be far beyond the managers' private means, they must obtain support from banks and financial institutions. These outside investors will assess the proposition and, if satisfied, will put up the finance to enable an offer to be made for the business. The banks and institutions involved often hold a proportion of the shares in the new company (an **equity stake**), as well as supplying the loan finance. Later, if the enterprise is successful and it becomes a public company, then the investors may sell this stake on the Stock Market.

Why do Buy-outs Occur?
Since the 1960s many very large firms have merged, often carrying into single ownership numerous smaller subsidiaries. Inevitably some of these subsidiary concerns will perform less well than required by the corporate budgets of their owners. The local managers of the subsidiary may decide that they could achieve greater success if operating independently. Even if subsidiaries are sufficiently profitable, the directors of a large business grouping may wish to concentrate on particular types of products or markets. Thus they will be keen to sell off any activities that do not fit their strategic plan.

Doubt has been growing about the 'big is beautiful' view held in the 1960s and 1970s. Large firms have found that expected economies of scale (advantages of operating on a bigger scale – see Chapter 15) have been far less than predicted. Trying to manage tangled strings of factories or shops can prove very difficult. Top managers may feel a lack of effective control. Local managers may feel ignored, and

► Management buy-outs are also sometimes made to avert a hostile take over bid.

become poorly motivated. A fertile situation then exists for a management buy-out.

The backers of buy-outs are often international financial services and banking firms (e.g. Investors in Industry, CitiCorp), who specialize in providing **venture capital** (risk capital to business). As a bought-out business is revitalized, the value of their stake may grow in value far faster than the return on a normal business investment. Such investment firms are vigorous in marketing their 'packages' of assistance for achieving management buy-outs.

The advantage of a management buy-out is that more entrepreneurial attitudes will flow through a business. Profitable investment may be possible that would not have been allowed before.

 Draw up a two column table headed 'advantages and disadvantages of management buy-outs'. Use the text above to list the advantages and the text below to list the disadvantages.

Problems for a Buy-out

Most buy-outs are achieved with a high or very high financial **gearing**. This means that they are financed by a small proportion of share capital, and a high proportion of debt. It is therefore essential for the buy-out to earn enough profit to meet heavy interest payments. Any rise in interest rates makes this burden even greater.

The institution which has provided the necessary finance will expect to influence management policy-making, and if it holds an equity stake, it will require its own business directors to be on the board. Conflicts of interest may arise between the institution and the management: for instance the institution may want quick financial returns at the expense of longer term goals.

Given the high level of indebtedness, a buy-out may not be able to raise necessary further funds for investment projects. This problem may contrast with the large scale investment finance previously available when part of a large group.

Lower level managers and staff in a buy-out may feel that their career prospects have been reduced by leaving a larger organization. They may also feel less secure. Unless adequate incentives are offered, some key staff may leave.

A buy-out can be affected by lack of specialist management services. For example management accounting or operations research may be well funded in a major public company, but prove more difficult to provide after the buy-out.

► In 1990 there were 480 buy-outs worth £2 525m.

The buy-out may also cause some dislocation to markets and customer networks. The newly independent firm will need to prove its reliability and permanence if the customer base is to be retained and expanded.

Northern Lights Ltd is a Yorkshire-based chain of fifteen shops selling lighting equipment and accessories. The original owner had sold the business to Sheffield Electrical in 1987, a company itself sold out to Hounslow Holdings, a London company with a sprawling empire of fast-moving consumer goods. Sales returns from Northern Lights branches are increasingly disappointing to Hounslow Holdings and high staff turnover is badly affecting the service offered to customers.

Mark Dickinson, the manager of Northern Lights in Leeds, and John Pilgrim, the Harrogate manager, conceive a plan for a management buy-out with subsequent expansion of the business into lighting consultancy and hire services for the entertainment and tourist industries. The likely value of Northern Lights is £1.5m. but the managers' combined assets total only £125 000.

What arguments could the managers use to persuade a large City bank to provide the financial backing for a buy-out to take place?

Management Buy-ins

A new team of managers is brought in to purchase and lead a business. This is most likely when a potential buy-out situation exists, but the existing management team is weak.

Financial institutions may introduce outside managers, with known expertise, to a target firm and arrange the necessary loan and equity finance, with negotiators to assist in clinching the deal.

► In 1990 there were 111 buy-ins worth £648m.

INSOLVENCY AND LIQUIDATION

Solvency means having the ready funds to meet financial obligations. The creditors of a company that is unable to meet such obligations may take legal steps to force the company into **receivership** and **liquidation**. A firm may also announce this step on a voluntary basis. The affairs of an insolvent company are taken over by the **Official Receiver**. His/her task is then to liquidate the firm's assets. This means turning them into cash in order to meet all debts, which are then settled in order of legal obligation. Any funds that remain will be distributed among the shareholders. Often, however, the shareholders will receive nothing, but they will remain protected from indebtedness by the privilege of limited liability. Thus some creditors may simultaneously find that their debts are worthless.

► An alternative to receivership is an **Administration Order**. Under the Insolvency Act of 1986 a firm in difficulty may be placed under the control of an external administrator giving it a period of protection from claims by creditors. The aim will be to re-establish the firm as a going concern.

Read the case study and answer the questions below.

'Too risky,' snapped Malcolm Taylor. 'If we chase off up-market and fail, then we endanger the whole traditional customer base. All that we've achieved will be on the line.'

Duncan Cole, the marketing director, studied his papers.

'I'm sorry, Malcolm. The evidence is there. Our traditional market is crumbling. Look at the market research. Luxury holidays are the future.'

Geoff Taylor looked up. He spoke quietly.

'I think he's right, Malcolm.'

Malcolm Taylor snorted.

'Value for money. That's what our customers expect, and rightly so.' He glowered down the long mahogany boardroom table. There was silence. 'Just who's running this company?' He growled.

Back in 1956 Malcolm Taylor had driven an old battered coach to Paris with his first fare-paying passengers. More trips and better vehicles followed. In those days, he remembered, Brussels and Luxembourg had seemed like exotic destinations. The holidays were all-inclusive, cheaply priced and very popular. As a sole proprietor he made his own decisions, risked his own capital and would find every gap in the market with all the flair of the natural entrepreneur.

Taylor Tours Ltd was formed in 1964 in order to enter the air charter market. Package holidays to Spain and Italy soon pushed coach tours into second place. The shareholders were Malcolm's brother, Geoff, and three other business friends. They became a strong team, although the Taylor brothers retained the controlling interest and Malcolm as managing director always made the final decisions. Expansion was rapid and by the late seventies the firm had over a hundred employees. Turnover passed first £5m. and then £10m.

► For smaller younger firms, the unlisted securities market (USM) was founded in 1980 to give wider access to public share subscription. The conditions for membership are less demanding than those for the main market.

In 1985, with some misgivings, the decision was taken to 'go public' and launch the company on the unlisted securities market, enabling Taylor Tours to issue and sell new shares direct to the public. The price for this injection of capital was a dilution of the directors' control. Additional directors were appointed and soon an insurance company had become a major share holder.

It was a slump in turnover and profits that promoted the present board meeting.

1 Why would Malcolm Taylor be called an entrepreneur?

2 ' ..the Taylor brothers retained a controlling interest...', What does this mean?

3 Why did 'going public' mean 'a dilution of the original directors' 'control'?

4 'Just who's running this company?' How would you answer this question?

Summary and comment

- the principle of limited liability is the foundation of the modern company. Very few investors would be willing to put forward risk capital if they faced unlimited liability. In effect the company's identity is detached from its investors. Creditors only make claims on the assets of the company, not on the private assets of the owners
- shares in a company are sold on a permanent basis. In normal circumstances the company will not accept their return, or refund the investor. Yet shares are still a **liquid asset** (they can be turned into cash) because of their second-hand market value. The Stock Exchange is a vast market in the second-hand shares of plc's. It is the option of resale that makes investors willing to purchase shares
- 'going public' and obtaining a Stock Exchange quotation achieves access to greatly enlarged sources of finance. However it also means that the ownership of a significant part of the company becomes mobile and unpredictable. Institutional investors may become important shareholders with their own particular interests, while others may build holdings as a platform for hostile take-over bids (see Chapter 27)
- a public company finds that it must satisfy City opinion and maintain sufficient confidence in its prospects to keep the share price at reasonable levels. Given the ways in which companies and their shares move in and out of fashion, this can be a frustrating experience
- in most private companies, ownership and control are very closely related. For public companies the link may become largely indirect, and in the practical affairs of business management the directors are virtually autonomous (act on their inclination and judgement). From the point of view of the board, the shareholders are simply one interest group among others
- management buy-outs bring ownership and control more closely into line, since the managers are themselves major owners. Buy-outs of a public company usually involve its being converted into a private company at least temporarily. However the heavy loans required for buy-outs put great pressure on managers to succeed, and give creditors considerable power over them. Buy-ins involve bringing a new management team in as owners. Management buy-ins have increased sharply in importance.

4 Public enterprise and privatization

Chapter objectives

After working through this chapter you will:

▌ know the arguments for and against state ownership in British industry

▌ understand the case for and against privatization

▌ be able to describe and assess privatization in practice

▌ know the meaning of the following key terms: public sector, central government, local government, nationalized industry, quangos, contracting out, deregulation.

► The public sector includes those organizations owned and controlled by central or local government.

THE PUBLIC SECTOR

The **public sector** has four main forms of organization:

1 **Central government**, which is divided into departments or ministries: e.g. the DSS (Department of Social Security), M.O.D. (Ministry of Defence).

2 **Local government**, which includes county councils and metropolitan councils, plus district or borough councils for local areas within counties.

3 **Nationalized industries**, which are state-owned business enterprises.

4 **Quangos**, (quasi-autonomous-non-governmental organizations), such as boards, committees, commissions etc., which are organized and funded within the public sector, yet have considerable independence in their activities; for instance the Universities Funding Council or the Forestry Commission.

► Total UK government expenditure in 1991–2 was £205 bn (including £53 bn to support local authorities) representing forty one point three per cent of national income. Government expenditure reached its highest ever peacetime percentage in 1988 and has fallen back a little since then.

The activities of central government are financed by a wide range of taxes and duties, including:

• income tax (twenty-eight point nine per cent of total taxation raised)
• value-added tax (VAT), charged at seventeen point five per cent on the sale of most goods and services, and excise duty (thirty-two point three per cent of total)
• corporation tax charged on company profits (nine point two per cent of total).

Local government receives about forty per cent of its income from central government, with the remainder raised through the community charge or poll tax (this will be replaced by the council tax).

Nationalization

Nationalization is the legal transfer of a private sector industry to the ownership and control of the state.

Before the Second World War, broadcasting was already owned by the state through the British Broadcasting Corporation. Electricity generation had been government-owned since 1926. State ownership was further extended to include London's buses and underground in 1933, and an airline (later part of British Airways) in 1939.

The scale of the 1945–50 Labour government's nationalization programme was very ambitious, and involved:

Industry	Year
Bank of England	1946
coal	1946
railways (and road haulage)	1947
electricity	1948
gas	1949
iron & steel	1951

Nationalization in the post-war period caused a fierce political controversy, which reached a climax over the steel industry. However the only denationalization carried out by the next Conservative government was of steel and road haulage in 1953. New enterprises to develop independent television and atomic energy were also established under public ownership in 1954. The reasons advanced for nationalization were:

- natural monopolies (i.e. industries like electricity where only a single supplier is practical) should be state-owned to avoid exploitation of the consumer
- economies of scale could only be fully realized if the industry formed a single enterprise
- adequate investment could only be ensured through the use of government funds. This was thought important due to the investment backlog after the War
- social benefits may be achieved through state ownership. Prices of essential goods and services could be restrained; redundancies could be minimized; unprofitable but socially valuable services could be maintained
- industrial conflict was considered less likely when the profit motive had been replaced by the public interest and state planning
- economic management by the government would be more effective if is was coordinated with the policy of major basic industries
- strategic interests could be safeguarded if industries vital to the nation's defence were in public hands
- democratic control through government ownership of key industries *could* be considered politically desirable.

The debate over state ownership has run from the 1940s to the present day.

Industries were nationalized by act of Parliament. The relevant

► The Royal Mail first provided a public postal service in 1635.

►The steel industry was nationalized by the Labour government in 1951, privatized by the Conservatives in 1953, re-nationalized by Labour in 1967 and privatized by the Conservatives in 1988.

minister sets broad policy, and appoints a board with a chairman to be responsible for day-to-day management. The boards are often required to pursue an imprecise mix of commercial and social objectives. Financially, they are set a target rate of return on capital, and must achieve a five per cent real rate of return on new investment ('real' means after allowing for inflation). Socially they are expected to operate in the public interest, and must often provide unprofitable services to meet social need (e.g. branch railway lines in rural areas). Both their pricing policies and investment programmes are subject to government control, which can distort business aims.

Heavy losses were made by many of the nationalized industries, with only a few achieving private sector levels of return on capital. However some of these loss-making industries were facing inevitable decline as foreign competition intensified (e.g. the demise of British shipbuilding), or underlying markets changed (e.g. the shift from public to private transport). Management difficulties were also caused by the sheer size and unwieldliness of some industries. This is a problem of scale rather than ownership (see Chapter 15).

THE CASE FOR PRIVATIZATION

► Lord Stockton (former British Prime Minister, Harold MacMillan) called privatization 'selling off the family silver'.

Privatization means a transfer in the ownership and use of resources from the public to the private sector. The new Conservative government of 1979 was determined to launch a policy of privatization as a key political commitment. Its most obvious aspect has been the sale of nationalized industries to private shareholders, but also important has been the **contracting out** of public sector work to private firms (e.g. refuse collection), the **deregulation** of industries subject to state control (e.g. allowing bus companies to compete) and the sale of council housing to tenants.

► Look out for news stories about contracting out.

The arguments for privatizing state owned industries are:

- market forces are a greater source of efficiency and value for money than government direction. Increasing competition will lead to better use of resources, and more vigorous efforts to satisfy the customer
- labour relations should improve when unions and workers recognize that they owe their jobs to the market and not to the government. Management will be motivated to change outdated work practices, and to ensure higher productivity
- wider share ownership will be achieved through the sale of shares in privatized firms, both to employees and to ordinary people
- government finances will benefit from the proceeds of share sales, reducing the need for state borrowing. There will be less need for subsidies to support unprofitable industries
- the political objectives of reducing state ownership, and handing back more responsibility to private firms and individuals.

In view of these arguments, a major programme of privatization has been in progress:

1979	BP	1987	British Airways
1981	Cable & Wireless		Royal Ordnance
	British Aerospace		Rolls Royce
1982	Britoil		(aero engines)
	National Freight		British Airports
1983	Associated British Ports		Authority
	British Rail Hotels	1988	British Steel
1984	Sealink (ferries)		Rover Group
	Jaguar	1989	Water Authorities
	British Telecom	1990	Electricity supply
1986	British Gas	1991	Electricity generation
1986–8	National Bus Company		

Proposed from 1992:

Trust Ports		Regional airports
British Rail		British Coal
Post Office		

► Note that some sales have been by stages: the years quoted signify the government stake falling below fifty per cent – and in many cases to zero.

The net proceeds from privatization rose from £370m. between 1979 and 1980 to over £5 000m. between 1987 and 1988. They are estimated at £8 000m. for 1992–3. Most privatization measures have involved large scale share offers, to the general public as well as to institutional investors. Others have involved management/employee buy-outs (e.g. National Freight), or direct sales to other firms (e.g. the Rover Group to British Aerospace).

The Case Against Privatization

The Conservative Party remains committed to privatization measures continuing well into the 1990s. Although any future Labour government would only be likely to consider limited re-nationalization, the arguments against privatization remain active:

- public utilities such as gas, electricity, water and telecommunications are still monopolies with little or no consumer choice available. They may make excessive profits at the expense of their captive market
- social objectives are less likely to be served by private enterprise. The social costs and benefits of production (see Chapter 44) may be ignored
- public service has been a distinctive ethos of the nationalized industries. Although prone to inefficiency, they have shown integrity and responsibility in attempting to serve all customers. Market forces respond to buying power, not need. Privatized firms may be unresponsive to individuals and communities with low buying power
- wealth and income transfers through privatization are broadly away from the whole society towards those who are most powerful and privileged. Shares can only be purchased by those with surplus funds, while privatization issues have often yielded large capital gains. Dividends will tend to be received by those consumers who

already enjoy the highest incomes
- government finances have been distorted by privatization. The government treats the process of asset sales as income, when they really represent liquidation of capital. As the flow dries up, taxes or borrowing will have to increase. Arguably, taxation levels have been cushioned by privatization – again to the advantage of higher income groups.

 Set up a three column table. Head one column 'In favour of privatization' and one column 'Against privatization'. Make notes for and against privatization in this format. Head the third column 'Privatization in Practice' and add to your notes as you read on.

Privatization in Practice

It is still too early to judge conclusively the performance of privatized firms, but observations include:

- **financial performance** has quite strikingly improved following privatization. In most of the companies, both return on capital and sales per employee increased substantially. For example:

company	British Gas	Cable & Wireless	British Telecom
year privatized	1987	1982	1984
return on capital			
• in year privatized	22.7	25.9	18.3
• in 1989–90	23.4	20.0	21.3
sales per employee (£k) real-terms			
• in year privatized	86.2	32.9	34.9
• in 1989–90	90.1	61.4	43.0

However the general business climate also improved strongly over this period, and industries remaining in the public sector also improved their performance
- **customer service** is even more difficult to assess. Real improvements in quality have been achieved, at Jaguar and British Airways for example. There is patchy evidence of more customer-orientated service from the utilities such as British Gas and British Telecom. Equally, the bodies set up to regulate these industries (e.g. OFGAS and OFTEL) have recorded a rise in consumer complaints, and are themselves argued to be ineffective
- **labour relations** have generally improved in the privatised firms, but this is also true across the whole economy. Major disputes arose at British Telecom in 1987, and at Jaguar in 1989

- **wider share ownership** both for employees and the general public has been achieved. In 1983 only five per cent of the adult population owned shares, while by 1991 this figure had increased to twenty-five per cent. However, three quarters of all investors only have small numbers of shares, while many sell them to realize a capital gain

- **privatization offer prices** have been widely criticized for being too low. The government argues that the prices were right given the need for successful flotation and the support of smaller investors. The steep and immediate rise in the value of some privatization stocks does suggest underpricing.

The debate will probably continue. But the radical shift in balance from public to private sectors is likely to be permanent, and may well be extended further.

 As a candidate for privatization, British Rail is a difficult case. Its sprawling but closely interrelated network of services is not easy to break up into sensible units. One possible solution is to have a national track authority that leases train running rights to competing firms. Another approach is to sell separately BR's existing business sectors, which include:

  InterCity mainline long distance passenger

  Regional secondary passenger

  Network South East commuter lines around London

  Freight

  Parcels

plus BR's property holdings, research and engineering interests. Again some track authority would be required.

The issue is complicated by the government subsidies for unprofitable but socially necessary services paid to Network South East and the regional sectors. These are very low by European standards but represent an effort to contain road congestion in the South East and provide suburban and rural public transport elsewhere. Also InterCity and Freight were both back in the red by 1991 due to the general recession.

1 What might be the general advantages of privatizing British Rail?

2 Suggest possible arguments which might be used to oppose privatization.

► Eight months after British Airways was privatized (1987) only thirty-six per cent of the original shareholders remained.

► In 1984 BT shares increased in value by eighty-eight per cent on the first day's trading.

► Look out for news stories on the debate about BR privatization and use them to illustrate your notes on privatization in general.

Summary and comment

• nationalization reflected a belief that public planning can maximize the benefit of business activity for the community as a whole. It aimed to assist a more equitable distribution of income and influence in society

• the nationalized industries can be seen as a vehicle for government efforts to pursue democratically agreed economic objectives

• privatization has often left monopolies practically or wholly intact. Though breaking up such monopolies prior to privatization would increase consumer choice and competitive pressure, this has to be set against the risks of losing economies of scale (see Chapter 15) and of reducing the total sale value of the nationalized industry

• the ultimate business argument for privatization is the effectiveness of market forces in ensuring that producers address the demands of consumers. Profit is the reward for efficiency in the use of resources to match the needs of the market

• nationalized industries have tended to be **product orientated organizations** rather than **market orientated enterprises** (see Chapter 5)

• The management of nationalized industries has been broadly biased towards a policy of caution and low risk. Political restrictions on funding can depress investment. Privatized firms may be more innovative, and will invest according to commercial opportunity

• social responsibilities may be as effectively met in the private sector as they were under nationalization. The leading edge of social responsibility in business has been well represented in the private sector (See Chapter 44)

• there is a worldwide trend away from state ownership towards private enterprise. Privatization is occurring in many other countries, including France, Germany, Japan, Eastern Europe and the former Soviet Union (now CIS states).

5 Market orientation and market segmentation

Chapter objectives

After working through this chapter, you will:

▌ understand the concept of market orientation

▌ understand the concept of segmenting markets

▌ know the typical segmentation criteria

▌ be able to apply the technique of market segmentation in simple examples

▌ know the meaning of the following key terms: marketing, product orientation, market orientation, marketing mix, market segmentation, market niche.

WHAT IS MARKETING?

Production is a dynamic process, converting resources into goods and services. Consumption is also a dynamic process in demanding, purchasing and using goods and services. **Marketing** means every activity in a firm that aims to join these dynamics together and achieve maximum profitability through the flow of completed sales.

Most larger firms have a marketing department led by a marketing manager or director. This has a range of functions which include those of the traditional sales department. **Market research** is used to identify the potential for new products and the need for the modification or relaunch of existing products (see Chapter 6). Sales are **promoted** through advertising, branding, packaging and point-of-sale displays. Price levels are set for strategic profit maximization. An optimum range of distribution channels is maintained and filled by a trained and motivated sales force. These elements of activity combine to form the **marketing mix** (see Chapters 8 to 11). Marketing management must coordinate this mix to fulfil corporate objectives. These will be expressed in financial terms through the sales budget (see Chapter 23), which will have been negotiated with the marketing department.

▶Marketing is **not** another word for sales.

▶ 'Marketing is the management process responsible for identifying, anticipating and satisfying customer requirements profitably.'
(*Institute of Marketing*)

'Marketing is the process of determining consumer demand for a product or service, motivating its sale, and distributing it into ultimate consumption, to the continued satisfaction of the consumer, on a realistic profit basis.'
(*Marketing*, Unilever)

 Make a check-list of the elements of the marketing mix.

Product and Market Orientation

When a firm starts its decision process with the **product**, and works from the product to the market, then it is **product orientated**. If another firm starts its decision process with the market, and works from the market to the product, it is said to be **market orientated**.

> ### Product and Market Orientation
>
> Consider two companies that manufacture garden tools. Firm A aims to maintain its traditional business. It believes that it makes excellent rakes, forks, spades, trowels and so on. Its future therefore depends on the demand for quality garden tools. Firm B does not think that its present products are necessarily its future products. It believes it is a business in the outdoor leisure market, with expertise in garden products. Its future depends on matching its resources to the demands of profitable markets.
>
> Firm A is product orientated: firm B is market orientated.

 Test yourself on the concepts of product and market orientation. Use a grid like the one below to enter a product or a market view of what the industry is selling:

Industry	Product view	Market view
Royal Mail	Selling stamps; collecting parcels and letters; sorting and delivery.	Business communication; the excitement of receiving a letter; good news; old friends.

1   Hi-Fi manufacture.
2   Banking.
3   Domestic heating oil.

MARKET SEGMENTATION

► The division of a market into sectors according to the characteristics of its customers and their usage of the product is called **market segmentation**.

In any market every consumer is distinct. Your reasons for buying a product will always be different from anyone else' s. Each individual has his/her own circumstances, personal motivation, and level of income. In this sense everyone is a kind of micro-market. Given that the marketing mix is an attempt to achieve an optimum 'fit' between the efforts of producers and the needs of consumers, it follows that ideally a firm would use a separate mix for each single customer. In reality, this is usually only possible in industrial markets (where goods are often made to a given customer specification), or for very expensive products. However it is possible to identify distinctive groupings of consumers within a market.

► Segmentation by consumer characteristics.

Segmentation in the Market for Holidays

Harmony Holidays have completed a market research survey which suggests the following customer types:

A families with children
B couples without children
C retired couples
D older single people
E 18–30 single people
F schools and organized groups

Each of these customer groupings forms a **market segment,** each with its own specific needs. For instance the all-night disco might appeal to segment E, but not to segment C! This approach is segmentation according to **consumer characteristics**.

► Segmentation by consumer characteristics.

Research also shows that the main attraction for consumers taking a holiday with Harmony varies widely, and includes:

- sunbathing and swimming
- social life
- rest
- relief from housework
- sightseeing
- walking and climbing
- pleasure for children.

Another whole range of market segments is opened. This approach is segmentation according to **consumer responses**.

► Segmentation by consumer responses.

Market Coverage Strategy

The use of segmentation depends on the **market coverage strategy**. Firms may choose to:

- aim a standard product at the centre of a mass market, so maximizing sales by satisfying the largest proportion of consumers
- create a product range designed to target different segments in the market
- concentrate on the demand of a single segment, and market a correspondingly specialized product.

Segmentation is becoming increasingly important due to the **fragmentation** of the traditional mass markets. Holidays are one example, groceries sold through supermarkets are another. Early supermarkets of the 1960s tended to sell mass-produced foodstuffs and household goods as cheaply as possible, and to regard all customers as a single group. Now the targeting of supermarkets includes luxury markets, convenience markets, health markets, vegetarians, one-person households and large families.

► Market fragmentation tends to happen most when incomes rise rapidly as in the period 1985–8.

Types of Market Segmentation

There are many different criteria for identifying market segments. Often consumer characteristics are the basis. These include:

sex	male/female
age groups	0–4, 5–15, 16–24, etc.
household size	1, 2, 3–4, 5–6, etc.
family life cycle	young singles, married with young children, etc.
socio-economic groups	A, B, C1, C2, D, E
education	unqualified, GCSE, A Level, etc.
residential neighbourhood	ACORN system
geographical region	London and the South East, Midlands, etc.
lifestyle	e.g. 'mainstreamers', 'aspirers', 'succeeders', etc.

Segmentation by Socio-economic Grade

GRADE	Head of household's occupation
A	higher managerial, administrative or professional
B	intermediate managerial, administrative or professional
C1	supervisory, clerical, junior managerial, administrative or professional
C2	skilled manual
D	semiskilled and unskilled manual
E	state pensioners, casual and lowest grade earners.

This grading system is the most widely used in Britain. It combines social and economic status, although in reality they do not always coincide. However grades A, B and C1 are broadly middle class, while grades C2, D and E are broadly working class.

Segmentation by Residential Neighbourhood

A recent development is the ACORN (A Classification Of Residential Neighbourhoods) system of neighbourhood mapping. The population is divided into eleven neighbourhood types and thirty-eight sub-types. Clusters of 150 addresses to cover every household in Britain are classified by their ACORN code. The system can enable marketing activity (e.g. direct mail) to be targeted with pin-point precision.

Segmentation by Lifestyle

A lifestyle means a way of life. It describes how a person's needs and goals are expressed through their work, leisure and social life. Its origins are social and psychological. Its outcomes in business terms are purchasing decisions. The measurement and

► Computer technology has made the analysis of point-of-sale and questionnaire-based research much faster and cheaper.

classification of psychological needs and corresponding lifestyles is called **psychographics**. A well known classification system has been developed by Young and Rubicam (a London marketing agency), and is called Cross Cultural Consumer Characteristics, or '4 Cs' for short.

Cross Cultural Consumer Characteristics (4 Cs)

The system uses research by Abraham Maslow (US psychologist) who developed his famous 'hierarchy of needs' (see Chapter 34). In each person one of these needs (from the heirarchy) is seen to be dominant, and becomes the key factor in determining their lifestyle. For example:

- **main-streamers** have security as their greatest need, and are the largest group, forming the foundation of society. They need to be seen as good citizens, and do not want to stand out from the crowd. Their homes are neat, tidy and conventional. They buy the products of multiple stores and favour well-known brands (e.g. Ford or Vauxhall cars, Marks and Spencers' clothes, Heinz baked beans)

- **aspirers** have status as their greatest need. They need to be noticed and admired by others. Their homes are modern, with plenty of fashionable and technological luxuries. Money is very important, they have a fascination for credit cards and cash. They like exclusive shops and designer products (e.g. Porsche cars, Gucci shoes, Rolex watches, high-tech hi-fi)

- **succeeders** have a dominant need to control. They are affluent but traditional, ambitious in their careers, and autocratic in their need to control organizations and people. Their houses are comfortable, stylish and fairly formal. They buy up-market and reputable products of good quality (e.g. BMW or Jaguar cars, Barbour coats, Wilton carpets)

- **reformers** seek self-fulfilment in their lives. They emphasize quality of life rather than material wealth, and find it important to contribute towards the improvement of society. Often highly educated, they are adventurous and ready to pioneer new markets. Their homes are often refurbished older properties, with stripped pine and natural materials in the decor. They tend to buy natural and healthy products with a mix of good value, good design and innovation (e.g. Volvo cars and buy groceries from Sainsbury's or Waitrose, and furnishings from Habitat.)

► About 40% of the population might be classed as 'mainstreamers'.

Alternatively, segments may relate to the product:

FACTOR	SEGMENTATION CRITERIA
benefit	convenience, indulgence, gift, etc.
attributes	size, colour, features, etc.
loyalty	total, partial, nil
usage rate	daily, weekly, monthly, etc.

Harmony Holidays – Market Segmentation

After careful research, Harmony Holidays decide to relate preferences for sunshine and activity on a holiday:

Three major sectors emerge:

A **Sunbathers** who want an easy undemanding holiday mainly on the beach or in the hotel area.

B **Middle-of-the-roaders** who want a mix of relaxation and moderate activity. Such a segment might be interested in coach tours from their resort.

C **Activists** who place great emphasis on stimulating activity with or without sunshine. They may favour sports, walking and climbing, or sightseeing.

Figure 5.1
*Market segmentation:
preferences for sun and
activity*

► Most major car manufacturers now offer a range of variants on each model designed to appeal most within different market segments.

Many individuals and families will not fit easily into any one category, but such groupings still form a very useful analysis when setting the marketing mix. Product features and packaging can be adjusted to fit the target customer type. Advertising can appeal to their dominant needs. Distribution can be directed towards optimal outlets.

 Nine ways of segmenting markets have been dealt with above. Take each one in turn, and make notes using examples taken from the holiday business.

Firms have always recognized some limited segmentation in producing, for example, luxury, standard and economic models of a given product. Today, sophisticated segmentation methods open a new and powerful marketing potential. Firms can develop and position products at the centre of their target segments. It follows that the total marketing mix should be highly flexible, and capable of fine-tuning according to segment needs.

In many cases new and highly profitable markets are revealed through segmentation. For example, Harmony Holidays may develop specialized sightseeing or walking tours for which customers in these segmented markets may pay a premium price.

Market Niches

A subsection of a segment is called a **market niche**. In terms of its defining characteristics, no segment has a regular shape. Equally no product can have equal appeal to all parts of its target segment. The areas of a segment that are partially or wholly untapped by the main producers become niches that offer specialized business opportunities.

Holidays in the Business Market

The diagram Figure 5.2 below, shows a market segment for hotels attracting business clients. The major chains have targeted the segment's central area, offering luxury and a limited degree of character. The niche represents business clients who want only moderate luxury but considerable character. This specialized market is not considered sufficiently large to be worth exploiting by the major chains. However with a well targeted marketing mix, the niche will support a profitable smaller business.

► The first Habitat shop opened in 1964 selling innovative designs in household goods. The firm developed this niche into a major segment and by the 1980s had virtually created a new mass market.

Figure 5.2
The market segment for hotels attracting business clients

The shape of market segments is never static. Rapidly changing patterns of consumer demand cause new niches to appear and others to contract. The components of **niche management** are intensive market research, a tight marketing mix, and a rapid response to shifts in demand. No niche is owned by its business occupant. Niche-based firms must always be on their guard against competition from firms positioned in the major part of the segment. Business honey pots attract predators.

► The Sock Shop was highly successful during the 1980s, but faced growing competition as large stores improved their ranges and merchandising of socks.

 Read the following case study and answer the questions below.

Sherwood Shoes Ltd design and manufacture footware for a mainstream market. Their reputation is for comfortable, practical and reasonably priced shoes. A new market research survey maps consumer priorities when buying shoes.

Figure 5.3
*Sherwood Shoes:
segmentation map*

1 What conclusions might the marketing manager draw from the diagram above?

2 Do you foresee any dangers in your answer to Question 1?

3 What other forms of segmentation might the marketing manager attempt?

Summary and comment

• inability to understand and respond to market changes has caused the failure of many firms with good products and reputable brands. Take over bids are now often based on the claim of superior marketing ability

• ultimately market orientation must relate not just to the customer, but to the source of satisfaction in consumption of the product. This means attempting to understand the customer's conscious and subconscious 'world' (see Chapter 9)

• effective market orientation is carefully guided. Its translation into profitable sales requires management's understanding of the firm's **distinctive competence**. This means identifying areas of excellence in the firm's capabilities and coupling these to known consumer demand

• sales is not another word for marketing. Sales orientation means a focus on **pushing** the product towards the customer, who is assumed to be reluctant to buy. Market orientation means building production around the market to such an extent that sales are only the final act in meeting the customer's needs

• changing the name 'sales department' to 'marketing department' does not make a firm market orientated. This is only achieved as a complete philosophy, emanating from top management and infusing every operation of the business. The market becomes the touchstone of all decisions

• market orientation means that the firm's organizational structure must be capable of tracking its market, and adapting rapidly to change. This realization is speeding up the abandonment of rigid hierarchies in favour of more flexible structures with fewer layers of authority, and more emphasis on personal and team initiative (see Chapters 33 and 37)

- the intensity of a firm's market orientation depends critically on the commitment of its managing director and senior management. Many managers have risen through the ranks in non-marketing business functions, and lack a thorough understanding of market orientation as a total business culture
- the marketing mix for consumer goods used to be on the 'blunderbuss' principle: i.e. a heavy discharge of activity aimed in all directions. In the 1990s the trend has been towards increasingly accurate targeting of markets and a far more discriminating mix that is adjusted for each market segment
- effective segmentation depends on the use of sophisticated market research techniques. Computer technology has made the detailed analysis of markets cheaper, faster and more accurate
- segmentation of markets has its counterpart in production where new technology is making possible a wider range of products and product features at a diminishing cost. It is likely that the product mix will follow the marketing mix in becoming increasingly flexible
- the most extreme form of segmentation involves analysing the special demands of each customer and offering a product to meet precisely their needs. This customization will tend to become more important with advancing production technology, especially in industrial markets
- segmentation must be seen as a dynamic analysis. Segment boundaries and patterns are constantly changing, requiring a more adaptable marketing plan
- some market segments are highly innovative in their readiness to experiment with new products. In the 4Cs model of lifestyle segmentation, the 'reformers' are only a small percentage of the total population, yet highly influential in establishing new markets
- by cross-classifying a range of segmentation variables, it is possible to identify very large numbers of possible segments: e.g. 'middle class, male, single, 16–25, central city neighbourhood, aspirer lifestyle'. A danger is excessively fine segmentation which identifies markets of inadequate size, and targets them at excessive cost.

Market research

Chapter objectives

After working through this chapter, you will:

▌ recognize the scope and importance of market research

▌ know the main objectives and types of market research

▌ be able to apply basic research techniques

▌ understand the use of forecasting

▌ know the meaning of the following key terms: market research, quantitative information, qualitative information, secondary research (desk research), primary research (field research), samples (random, stratified, quota, cluster), interviews (structured and unstructured), questionnaires, scaled responses, consumer panels, forecasting (quantitative and qualitative), scenario planning.

► A firm needs information about its customers and non-customers, their perception and use of the firm's products, the response to its marketing effort, and consumer needs that it does not presently fulfil.

Market research is the systematic effort to obtain that information which will guide the resources of a business most accurately towards the profitable fulfilment of consumer demand. This implies a strategy of continuous market analysis.

Marketing the Grand Hotel

The Grand is a large 150-room hotel situated on the seafront of a major Devon resort. The following type of information would be valuable to the management:

the guests
- numbers?
- business or pleasure?
- singles, families, children, groups?
- occupations?
- income groups?
- home address by region/area
- type of transport?
- number of nights in hotel?

the facilities
- occupancy rates by room types?
- meals taken? assessment of quality?
- use of bars, games room, discos?
- care of children?
- conference facilities?
- other services?
- special likes/dislikes?

the marketing
- reaction to brochure?
- use of holiday or hotel guides?
- AA/RAC registration?
- perception of price and value for money?
- use of discounts?
- recall of advertising?

the competition
- other local hotels used?
- competing price rates?
- facilities offered?
- food and furnishings – quality?
- rival publicity?

the business environment

National
- national economy: recession or boom?
- transport improvements?
- growth in incomes?
- inflation?
- interest rates?
- overseas visitors?
- exchange rates?

Local
- planned transport improvements?
- shopping developments?
- quality of beaches?
- local events?
- weather statistics?
- local council publicity?

The inset shows just a few of the factors that should be informing the managers of the Grand Hotel. Almost any line of research could split into many more specific enquiries. For example, use of the hotel brochure could be explored in detail. How was it obtained? What other brochures were obtained? Which parts were useful? Was the cover effective? Was there enough information? What image of the hotel did the brochure convey?

It is information of this type that enables management to shape its product to fit demand, and to target its marketing plan accurately.

The scope of market research embraces every variable that could affect present or future sales. The main areas of enquiry are:

► Central to market research is the identification of market segments (see Chapter 5).

- **consumer research**, which analyses market size and market characteristics, making breakdowns by age, class, income, locality, lifestyle, buying habits, attitudes and values
- **product research**, which assesses performance in use, variety of uses, use of allied products, after sales and maintenance needs, psychological perception of product, rival products
- **promotion research**, which includes advertising impact, packaging and image perceptions, response to displays and special offers, brand awareness, sales breakdown by territories and sales teams
- **pricing research**, which examines sales relative to price, value for money judgements, perceptions of price, effects of income changes, pricing of substitutes
- **distribution research**, which explores the breakdown of sales by distribution channels and types of outlet, effects of transit, warehousing performance

• **business environment research**, which analyses economic trends, foreign competition, market structure, changes in the law, demographic trends, cultural patterns.

 Take each of the six categories of research above, and list them with examples of research which might be done for the Grand Hotel.

Information from each of the above areas should feed into the decision process at every level of the organization. Generally, the more strategic the information (e.g. changes in customer average incomes), the more it will be the concern of the board and senior management.

► Cadbury's spent three and a half years and £10m. On **Project Gift** – a programme to create new chocolate assortments for the 1990s. One result was 'Inspirations'.

MARKET RESEARCH OBJECTIVES

Market research is expensive, and must compete for limited resources in the marketing budget. It must therefore work to clear objectives to ensure maximum advantage. The type of enquiry may be:

• **specific**, where an answer is required to a particular problem: for instance why did sales in East Anglia fall by twenty-five per cent during April?
• **general**, where the firm wants to monitor broad trends: for instance the average age of first-time house buyers.

► **Specific research** forms a discrete project. The terms of reference are set, the research methods are decided, the results are analysed, and the decisions are taken. **General research** is a continuous activity, with reviews at regular intervals that may prompt specific research projects.

Data gathered must be **relevant**. Information technology has made data collection and processing much quicker and cheaper. However this can cause **information overload**, where managers disregard data because of its excessive quantity. For a busy manager, one sheet of A4 paper may be far more powerful than a stack of computer print out.

► The need is for research goals to be well-focused. The timings and degree of accuracy required in the presentation of the findings must be decided.

Types of Market Information

• **quantitative information** answers questions about magnitude. It is usually expressed in numerate form. What percentage of families buy the *TV Times*? How many cans of Orange Fanta are sold on an average day in August?
• **qualitative information** answers questions of judgement and meaning. What is the image of Woolworths? Why are more women than men vegetarians?

► Desk or secondary research.

Desk or **secondary research** means the use of information that has already been collected and made available in some form. This may be from **internal sources** such as sales records (by product, area or sales representative), pricing data, or customer payment records. More qualitative information will be found in the experience and reports of sales staff, distributors and public relations personnel. Many **external sources** exist, such as trade and employers' associations, specialist journals and government publications. Market research agencies also sell their own specially collected data.

Field or **primary research** means the collection and collation of original data. This is far more expensive, and will usually only be undertaken for a particular purpose (e.g. to test the market regarding a potential new product). In its research the firm will be seeking the answer to specific questions, and may use personal or telephone interviews, direct or postal questionnaires, or a panel of potential consumers.

FIELD RESEARCH TECHNIQUES

Sampling

Few surveys can include the whole of a relevant population, as it would be too large. Usually a **sample** must be selected that is **representative** of a given population. There are various sample types:

- **random samples**: this means that every member of the population has an equal chance of being selected. Provided that the choice of respondents is genuinely random, then its statistical validity can be precisely calculated. However respondents may be widely dispersed, making interviews expensive
- **quota samples**: to use this method, existing data about, for example, the age and sex structure of the population must be available. The researcher identifies the number of respondents in each category who must be questioned if the sample is to be representative. For example, data may be available to tell the researcher that thirty per cent of biscuit assortment purchasers are women aged 45–60. In 250 interviews the quota for women in this age group will be thirty per cent or seventy-five. The interviewer finds the right number of respondents to fill each category until the quotas are filled
- **cluster samples**: to reduce financial and time costs, a defined cluster of the population may be used as a unit for sampling. Examples could include selected counties, towns, neighbourhoods, firms or colleges. The proportion of the selected population consulted can then be much higher. The distribution of population types within the cluster must be known, and allowances made accordingly.

 Make a list of the various kinds of sample with a few words of explanation on each. Then add the advantages and disadvantages of each kind.

Data Collecting Techniques

1 Interviews

Personal interviews may be **structured** and based on a printed questionnaire in which respondents are asked a series of questions, perhaps in a shopping centre location. Answers are recorded on

► Field or primary research.

► Firms with limited in-house resources will use a market research agency. Very large firms will have their own research teams, and prefer the greater guarantee of confidentiality that this allows.

There are 350 market research organizations in Britain with a combined turnover exceeding £350m.

►The survey methods selected will depend on the population to be surveyed, the cost, and the level of accuracy required.

paper or portable computer, the interviewer often using a range of given responses from which the consumer is asked to choose. **Unstructured** personal interviews encourage a broader discussion, and are often taped.

Telephone interviews

These are more popular in the USA, but are also used in Britain. Short structured interviews can be conducted quickly, cheaply, and with a geographically dispersed population. However low income groups without a phone are out of reach. It can also be difficult to gain the cooperation of respondents.

2 Questionnaires

The design of a questionnaire is vital to its value. Opening questions are normally for **classification** of respondents (by sex, age, occupation etc.). The main questions relate to the subject matter. All questions should be as brief as possible, in number and format. Their phrasing must be simple and very clear. The questions should be inoffensive, and answers should not rely on calculation. Bias must be avoided in the wording.

Layout should be spacious, clear, and organized for easy collation. A range of graduated responses may be offered for a question. For example:

I consider the catering service to be
excellent ◯
good ◯
adequate ◯
inadequate ◯
very poor ◯

Closed questions are those offering a choice only from a fixed range of options – for instance 'yes, no, don't know'.

Open questions invite a unique personal response – for instance 'what made you choose brand X toothpaste?'

In a **postal questionnaire** polite letters are sent to the sample population with a questionnaire enclosed, together with a prepaid reply envelope. Instructions must be very clear, and some incentive to participate is usually offered: for instance a small gift, or entry in a prize draw. Questionnaires may also be attached to periodicals or made part of a guarantee form. The response rate to postal surveys can be quite low.

Questionnaires can also be distributed direct to respondents to be completed on the spot. Where customers are detained, questionnaires may be placed in prominent positions, for instance in a room of a hotel or on seats of a train, in the hope that they will be filled in.

► When the respondent is likely to be less than honest, disguised questions may be used. For example the question 'why do you visit a pub at lunch time?' becomes 'why do you think people visit the pub at lunch time?'

3 Consumer panels

A small sample of consumers is asked to provide information over a period of time. Vouchers or gifts are often provided as a reward. Panel members may keep records of their purchases, usage of products or choice of radio/TV programmes. Panels may also test new products, or discuss their attitudes to products and brands. The method provides valuable in-depth data, and helps to reveal trends over time.

 List the various ways of collecting information, given above. Go back to the example of the Grand Hotel and against each information collection device in your list, write down an example of the kind of marketing information which could be collected using it. For example, for what purposes would it be appropriate to use a questionnaire with closed, graduated questions and for what purposes would it be appropriate to use a consumer panel?

► Continuous market research is necessary to ensure a prompt to changes in consumer preference.

Forecasting

No matter how good the quality of desk or field research, it can only relate to the past. Managers, however, need to anticipate the future.

Quantitative Forecasting

Subjective forecasts are those based on opinion. Sales staff are asked for their estimates of future results; customers may be asked about their buying intentions; panels or 'juries' of experts inside and outside the firm may report on likely projections.

  Published forecasts include government macroeconomic data, which may vitally affect the level of demand. Some universities and various other institutions also publish their own economic forecasts.

Qualitative Forecasting

This usually attempts to predict how the social, political, economic and technological environment for business will change.

  Scenario planning involves exploring the future implications of changes in a key variable: for instance the price of oil. A plastics firm might consider likely, optimistic and pessimistic scenarios based on corresponding projected oil prices.

  Delphi methods ask a panel of experts to make individual forecasts without consulting. A summary of these views is then provided for each member, who then gives a reconsidered opinion. Repeating the process then creates a converging picture.

  Value profiles try to predict changes in social values that affect patterns of consumption: for instance if marriage becomes more popular, more household goods will be purchased as wedding presents.

► Qualitative information is vital in setting longer-term strategy.

List the kinds of forecasting techniques available. Go back to the example of the Grand Hotel. Against each of the techniques listed note down how it might be used for forecasting in market research for the Grand Hotel.

 Read the following case study and answer the questions below it.

A large town and its surrounding villages are served by two local newspapers (excluding free, fixed circulation titles): *The County Gazette* and *The Weekly Courier*. The average combined circulation of these titles in 1990 was 42 000, rising to 46 000 by 1992. *The Gazette* sold an average of 16 800 copies in 1990 and 17 220 in 1992. Market research conducted by the paper showed that thirty-four per cent of the readers were over sixty while twenty-two per cent of the local population were over this age. The editorial board are now considering the introduction of some 'younger' features in order to attract new readers.

1 What evidence points to the need for changes in the style of *The Gazette*? What arguments might be used to oppose 'younger' features?

2 What new market research methods might be used to assess the type of features most likely to increase circulation?

Summary and comment

- marketing expenditure may be too thinly spread across a mass market or too hazily focused for impact. Targeted marketing makes the marketing mix more cost-effective
- ultimately market research enables the firm to increase consumer satisfaction by more precisely meeting consumer needs. This increases the value of the product relative to its cost, and tends to raise profitability
- market research implicates the whole firm and not just the marketing department. It should be a key ingredient in strategic decision making
- the use and impact of market research depends on the culture and structure of the organization. The more market-orientated the firm, the more responsive it is likely to be towards market research inputs. But there remains the risk of management inertia and resistance to change. Similarly much depends on the quality of communications. Messages from the market may be compromised or lost through bureaucracy or excessively long chains of command
- market research should be proactive in identifying business opportunities and anticipating shifts in demand. By contrast, reactive market research would take place only when prompted by difficulties

- market research must be up-to-date, and the response to its findings must be rapid. Slow decision making using out of date research may well carry a firm in the wrong direction
- the commissioning of market research should be prioritized according to the ratio of its likely value to its likely cost. Expenditure must be accountable and subject to proper budgeting. Each research project should be reviewed to assess its likely value.

7 *The product life cycle*

THE PRODUCT LIFE CYCLE CONCEPT

Every product has a finite life and can only be marketed with any prospect of adequate profitability for a limited period within the market. Each product has a life of its own which passes through certain recognizable stages: **introduction, growth, maturity, and decline**. For some products this cycle is very long (e.g. Lyle's Golden Syrup), while for others it is very short (e.g. most singles in the Top Twenty).

The life of a product may be measured in terms of two critical variables: sales and profit.

►In general, the more closely a product is defined, the shorter its life-cycle. For example the life-cycle for CD players has run since 1983, but for particular models has lasted for only a few years.

► This is the 'classic' profile of a product life cycle. Many other typical patterns have been identified.

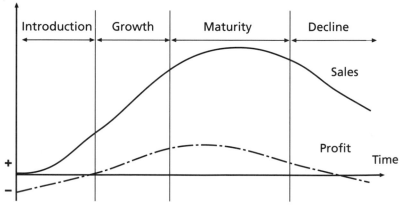

Figure 7.1
The product life cycle

The actual shape of the life cycle will vary widely according to the product and its market. All products have a different length of life cycle, and the time spent in each phase may vary from a few days to many years.

The profile of the product life cycle (PLC) provides an important management tool. By identifying the progress of a product through the successive stages, plans and budgets can be arranged for an optimum marketing mix. In addition, the relationship between products can be better coordinated, while management are assisted in making strategic decisions concerning research and development (R&D) and new product launches.

Stages in the Life Cycle
For a major new product the following pattern would be typical:

1 Introduction stage
This begins with the launch of a new product and its entry into the distribution channels. Competition is usually very limited, and promotion will be **informative**, aiming to create **market awareness**. Customers at this stage tend to be innovators who will take risks and feel a need to seek status. Sales will only increase slowly (especially if the product is a major innovation), and overall losses will be sustained, since marketing costs are high and production on a small scale is costly. The pricing strategy may be geared to 'skimming' with a high price in more specialized markets, or to 'penetration' with a low price in potential mass markets. The product may still be modified according to market intelligence i.e. that which research later reveals about the market.

In practice many products will fail before reaching the growth stage due to inadequate sales, excessive costs, technical problems or a high risk factor.

2 Growth stage
Sales increase at an accelerating rate as losses turn into profits and rise steeply. Competitors are attracted to the market with 'me-too' products that have avoided the major development costs. However the original product is likely to enjoy consumer loyalty and superior distribution. Some smaller firms in the market will be absorbed by larger ones. Promotion will become more persuasive and more strongly brand-orientated. A range of product models may be offered by a firm to reach different market segments. Meanwhile distribution must rapidly widen its coverage and the product may need acceptance by major retail chains.

3 Maturity stage
Sales may still be increasing, but the rate of increase declines until a plateau is reached. Weak or small firms may be eliminated as competition intensifies and successful firms attempt to extract profits from a large and established market. Innovators and originators tend to lose their distinctive qualities as branding, advertising and price discounting reach a climax. In consumer markets retailers are crucial to the sales effort with an emphasis on point-of-sale displays and other sales promotion tactics. In the late maturity stage, falling prices and mounting costs may cause declining profitability, and in a saturated market even the maintenance of market share becomes costly.

► Movements of products along the life cycle may be difficult to detect or predict. The sales curve may follow an unusual or irregular pattern, while external forces such as competition or changes in the economic environment may distort its progress. Constant market research is necessary for the firm to monitor change and to use the PLC effectively.

► Introduction stage.

►Growth stage.

► Maturity stage.

► Decline stage.

4 Decline stage

Products eventually reach the decline stage through the effects of new technologies, or shifts in fashion and taste. The market size begins to contract and, as demand falls, firms may be forced to make deeper price cuts, with profit margins being squeezed. Marketing budgets are cut sharply, and over-capacity becomes widespread. Success may be extended by concentrating on best-selling types and models, or by targeting niche markets. At some point however, managers must decide whether to delete the product, or to attempt its relaunch in an **extension strategy**.

Divide a sheet of A4 paper in five horizontally. Head each segment with a stage of the product life cycle: the last one will be 'extension'.

Go back to the activity at the end of Chapter 1 which deals with Centurian Cycles and Golden Eagle Ltd. Centurian has a traditional ladies' bicycle called 'Madam' which is in its decline stage. Golden Eagle has a new product called 'Wicked' which has just been launched. With reference to both bikes make notes on the stages of the product life cycle.

Extension Strategies

As the product moves into late maturity or decline stage, management may try to extend its life through modifications, repackaging, or repositioning in the market. The goal is to generate a new phase of profitable sales growth without any major capital costs.

Extension strategies may be based on restyling (e.g. new models of mountain bikes); technical advances (e.g. solar power for calculators); product developments for new markets (e.g. Terry's Chocolate

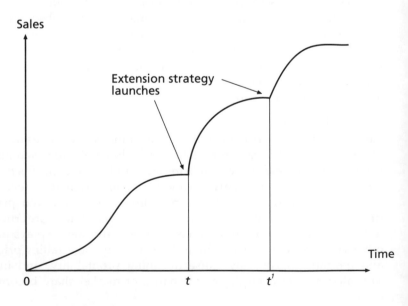

Figure 7.2
Extension strategies

Orange as a moulded bar); wider product range (e.g. new flavours for snack foods); new product uses (e.g. cassettes for computer programmes); more frequent product use (e.g. Cadbury's Creme Eggs throughout the year).

Management will aim to synchronize extension strategies with the PLC pattern, and to avoid unsold stocks of the old product.

 What advice could you give to Centurian Cycles about extension strategies for 'Madam'?

Evaluation of the Product Life Cycle Method

Strengths
- provides a clear model for understanding typical changes in product sales and profits
- by pin-pointing product positions on the PLC, the marketing mix can be adjusted to maximum effect
- assists planning of a coherent and mutually supportive product portfolio (see below)
- encourages management to recognize the market as dynamic, and to adopt a proactive approach.

Weaknesses
- the PLC is often unreliable and misleading in efforts to forecast events. The movement of products along their PLC may be so erratic that effective analysis is not possible
- real sales and profit results are often highly dependent on external factors such as new technologies, tax charges or interest rates
- firms may be tempted into self-fulfilling prophecies, for instance withdrawal of marketing support for a product which then collapses when it could have recovered.

THE PRODUCT PORTFOLIO

At any given time, most firms are marketing a range of different products: these together make up the **product portfolio** (i.e. a 'collection' of products). Each product will have a different life cycle profile, and be positioned at a different relative point on its own curve. Generally firms aim to achieve a balanced pattern of products across the various stages of the PLC. Portfolio management is essential to the firm's stability and long-term growth. It is most important to avoid all major products entering the decline stage at once. Adequate positive cash flow from successful mature products is needed to fund new product research, and for promoting launches through the costly introduction stage.

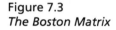 This grid was developed by the Boston Consultancy Group and is often called the 'Boston Matrix'.

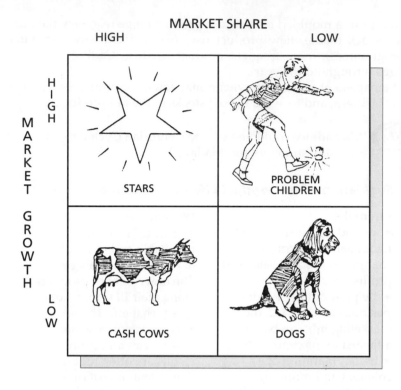

Figure 7.3
The Boston Matrix

To assist analysis of the business portfolio, a grid is often used.

Stars are products with a high market share in a fast-growing market. They can earn large cash inflows, but require high investment levels to sustain a rising market share. Net positive cash flow may be limited, but potential exists for high cash returns in the longer run.

Cash cows are usually ex-stars, where market growth has slowed into maturity. Investment in the product is low, yet it can be 'milked' for large positive cash flows.

Problem children hold only a low market share, but in a fast growing market. If they can be managed towards a higher market share, they may become Stars, but high investment is needed. Equally, problem children with a stagnant or weakening market share may become Dogs.

Dogs have a declining and/or low market share in a static or shrinking market. Usually a firm will dispose of its Dogs, but with low outgoings they can be profitable in specific market segments.

The boxes in the portfolio grid are not secure or self-contained. Markets are dynamic over time, and product positions within the portfolio are subject to constant change. The arrows in the diagram represent the general tendency over time for Stars to become Cash cows, and for Problem children to become Dogs. Management will aim to achieve a balanced range of Stars, Cash cows and Problem children. Funds generated by Cash cows will finance conversion of Stars into Cash cows, and problem children into Stars.

Read the following case study and answer the questions below:

The enterprise was launched in 1981 to exploit a widening market niche for cakes with a 'country' image. Based on a small business park near Oxford, the firm's annual turnover had reached about £400 000 and has benefited from two major supermarket accounts. The cakes were sold in individual boxes with an average ex-factory price of £1. It was estimated that the quality cake market had been growing at around six per cent per annum. Sales data for Country Cakes are shown below:

Product	Numbers sold (000s)			
	1988	1989	1990	1991
Cotswold Fruit	218	205	193	181
Shire Sponge	129	132	135	127
Cider Apple	16	40	57	66
Natural Carrot	–	8	21	20

1 Using the concept of the product life cycle, analyse the sales prospects for each product.

2 Critically examine the company's product portfolio. What advice would you give about its product mix?

Summary and comment

• the concept of product portfolio is very useful in enabling managers to value their product range as an interactive whole. Products can be analysed in terms of their PLC sector positions, and this can then be translated into implications for cash flow and profitability

• the dangers of this approach lie in over-simplifying reality. Product profitability varies widely, and market share and market growth are only two variables in the decision making process. It is difficult to classify products on the grid, and there is no guarantee that the cost of higher market share will yield higher net profits.

8 · The marketing mix: product

Chapter objectives

After working through this chapter, you will:

▌ be able to analyse the product from the point of view of the market

▌ understand the concepts of product value and value analysis

▌ know how firms develop a product mix and position their products in the market

▌ understand how new products are developed, and why some products are deleted

▌ know the meaning of the following key terms: product value (objective, subjective, economic, strategic), value analysis, product mix (width and depth), product position, concept testing, lead time, product deletion.

UNDERSTANDING THE PRODUCT

► Ask yourself, what are the following business enterprises really selling:
a) a country pub
b) a maker of fashion shoes
c) a nightclub?

It is a strange fact that many firms do not know what they are really selling. To list or detail their goods or services is easy. This may define the product in production. But the product in the market, as perceived by the consumer, may be quite different. And since it is the consumer that provides the firm with sales revenue and profit, it is this market perception that must be understood.

The Mini

One of Rover's most famous cars is the Mini. Launched in 1959 it continues to sell today. Rover are producing a car, but what are customers purchasing? The product itself is like a shell. The essential product may be hidden. Transport ... economy ... convenience ... independence ... fashion ... nostalgia for the 1960s ... surprises ... youth ... fun ... optimism? The Mini is all of these and more. As a classic product it confers good taste on its owner, and carries numerous associations from films and advertising. The car has a 'personality', and this is all part of the purchase.

► Think of some famous cars and the kind of person you would expect to drive them.
• VW Golf
• Volvo Estate
• Morris Minor.

Product Value

Only a product with value can be sold. The total satisfaction that the consumer expects to derive from the product – expressed in money terms – must exceed the price, or no sale will take place. This estimation of value by the consumer is critical and at the heart of any marketing strategy. A product is not purchased for its own sake, but for the stream of satisfaction that a consumer expects it to yield.

Objective value refers to the actual qualities of the product that exist independently of the customer. A watch indicates the time to a certain degree of accuracy. It may have other attributes such as being shockproof and waterproof. All this is real value.

Subjective value refers to those sources of pleasure in a product that depend on the customer's personal feelings. For example if the watch is a Swatch it may do far more than tell the time. To the buyer it may make an important statement about their personality and life style.

Economic value means the consumer's estimate of a product's total value expressed in money terms.

From the point of view of the firm a product also has a **strategic market value** in its ability to obtain or advance a share in a particular new market. For instance a maker of professional recording equipment may wish to enter the domestic audio market. Or a small building society may wish to enter the personal loans market. New products act as keys to new markets, and build vital reputations.

The economic value of a product may derive from mainly objective or mainly subjective sources, or a mix of the two. A firm may decide to carry out a formal **value analysis** of a given product or product range. This will involve a thorough investigation into a product's source of practical function and consumer esteem, and the corresponding cost structure in production. Creative thinking will be directed towards widening the gap between producer cost and consumer value. It does not necessarily mean cost cutting. For example, to upgrade a car with real-wood trims and leather seats adds to costs, but might add even more to its value in the market.

 Try making a simple analysis of consumer value for the following products under the headings shown below:

1 A home contents insurance policy.

2 A major brand of training-shoes.

3 A box of soft-centred milk chocolates.

Product	Value features	
	Objective	**Subjective**

► Consumer goods are often divided between:
• **convenience goods**, routine and familiar to the customer
• **shopping goods**, requiring the customer to shop around
• **speciality goods,** where customers are loyal to a brand.

Product Types

Consumer goods are those consumed by private individuals or households. There are **single-use consumer goods** which are for short-term consumption, such as foods, cleaning materials and clothing. By contrast, **consumer durables** provide long-term satisfaction: examples include cars, televisions and furniture.

Consumer services are provided for individuals or households, and include repair work, financial services, insurance, holidays, education and health.

Producer goods are those purchased by firms for use in the production process. They include raw materials and components, industrial equipment and machinery.

Producer services are supplied to firms and include maintenance contracts, accounting, legal and secretarial services.

PRODUCT MIX

► Most building societies offer a wide product mix through a range of savings accounts each with its own brand name, interest rate and conditions.

Many firms sell a wide range of products – some closely related and some very different. Each related group of products is called a **product line**, and it may include a range of models, styles or sizes. The combination of a firm's product lines is called its **product mix**.

Product Mix

Silver Blade Ltd manufactures pen knives, kitchen knives and scissors.

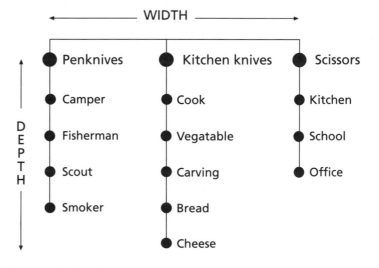

The width of Silver Blade's product mix is clearly three. The average depth in the mix is four $(4 + 5 + 3 = \frac{12}{3})$.

Figure 8.1
Measuring the product mix

A wide mix provides entry to many different markets, while a deep mix allows access to more segments within a market. This analysis assists managers in recognizing the interrelationships between their products, and in building an effective product strategy.

 Note the difference between a wide mix and a deep mix, and decide what kinds of mix are best suited to what kinds of products.

Product Positioning

Using market research it is possible to identify the **position** that consumers consider a firm or product to occupy in the market. **Market position** can be plotted against criteria such as price, quality, status or image. **Competitive positioning** charts a firm in the context of its rivals. **Company positioning** maps the various brands within one firm's product line. This technique helps to define market segments and to place products within market niches.

► Firms may track movements in their product positions through regular surveys of consumers. The relevant marketing mix can then be fine-tuned in response to shifts or deliberately to reposition products.

Figure 8.2
Product positioning

The chart makes it possible to distinguish the quality market (e.g. *The Times*), the mid-market (e.g. the *Daily Mail*), and the popular market (e.g. the *Sun*). Management may aim to reposition a product either because the market has moved away from the product, or because the product has drifted away from its market.

Define 'product position' then try drawing your own map for car manufacturers or clothes retailers. Use price for your vertical axis and a 'youthful' – 'traditional' scale for your horizontal axis.

New Products

► New Products.

New products are needed in a firm:

- as a response to changing consumer demand and competition
- to replace those products reaching the end of their profitable life cycle
- to provide the basis for expansion.

Modified and Variant Products

For example, an electronic sewing machine offers an increased range of pre-set stitching patterns. Brand variants are also common, where a firm offers new sizes, colours or flavours.

Imitative or 'me-too' products

These occur when firms produce their own versions of existing successful products to achieve a market share without heavy development costs. Powerful market support is usually necessary.

Diversification products

Diversification products come about when a firm diversifies its product mix and enters an established market. The new product, though similar to its rivals, offers original features. For example, an electrical goods firm already making fan heaters launches a new style of hairdryer.

Innovative products

Significant innovations open new markets, for example compact discs taking over from vinyl records.

The stakes for firms in product development are high. Both the costs and the potential rewards for new products increase with the degree of innovation involved. A modification may be fairly cheap to introduce. The risks of a failure are low since the product is already established. But the likely rewards are often modest. A new product for an existing market is more costly, with a higher risk of failure. However if a worthwhile market share is taken, then returns may be substantial.

The success rate for new product ideas is remarkably low. Perhaps fifteen to twenty-five viable ideas may be tested to produce one successful idea. Even after launch the failure rate is high, often with around fifty per cent of new products failing within two years of their launch.

Failure by a firm to introduce new products generally leads to a decline in both market share and profitability. No market stands still. A firm with a stagnant product range will find the gap between the market and its own products gradually widening. Competition intensifies, and there is a downward pressure on price. Even a firm whose products are all profitable market leaders must be planning for innovation. In the short term, extension strategies may be needed, while in the long run the next generation of products need developing while time remains.

After the elimination of nonstarters, the firm must **screen** new product ideas, which involves testing for feasibility. This process requires criteria to be set, against which the ideas may be assessed or formally graded. Likely key factors include market research findings, market expertise, production capacity, skills availability and the existing product mix.

Selected products will move forward to **concept testing**, where consumer responses to the proposed product are collected and evaluated. Products that still remain viable will now face business analysis, where detailed estimates of variable and fixed costs are set against projected sales revenue. Profitability can then be analysed, using break even analysis (see Chapter 14) and investment appraisal (see Chapter 26). Finally, product development involves translating the ideas into a saleable product. Prototypes will be made and tested; packaging designs will be selected; branding decisions will determine product positioning; market research will continue in the effort to maximize consumer satisfaction.

▶ The time lapse – or **lead time** – from a product idea to the actual generation of sales in the market, varies widely. A small product modification may only take a few weeks, while a major product innovation in a complex industry (e.g. pharmaceuticals, aerospace) could occupy ten or twenty years. Lead time is important in planning a coordinated marketing mix.

At the end of all these stages, management must decide whether to launch the product into a test market (i.e. not mass national market, but moderately large market, within a limited geographical area) or to abandon (or mothball) the project. Large sums of money are often at risk, and some intuitive decision making is likely. The certainty of success never exists. If a 'go' decision is given, then the product moves into its life cycle, and the sales trajectory will deliver the market's verdict.

 Make notes on the process of new product development by drawing a diagram identifying what should happen at each stage.

Product Deletions

When a product or an extension strategy reaches the decline stage, sales and profit will fall. If the product is **independent** of others in the range, then it certainly should be **deleted** once sales cease to cover variable costs, and no contribution is being made to overheads (see Chapter 14). Usually it should be dropped before this point, when it fails to cover **average total costs**, and perhaps earlier still, when its returns fall below a budgeted minimum based on opportunity costs. Of course managers must be reasonably sure that the decline is not merely caused by temporary circumstances such as a competitor's advertising campaign or a failure in distribution.

▶ Product life cycle, see Chapter 7.

It the product is **interdependent** with others in the range, then the deletion decision is more difficult. A product may be unprofitable in itself, but valuable in encouraging other purchases in the range, in retaining a key customer, or for the prestige of the brand name.

 Use this opportunity to make notes on product deletion bringing together what you learned about the Boston Matrix and extension strategies in Chapter 7.

Summary and comment

• firms tend to understand their products in production terms. Management must grasp the meaning of their product in **market terms** – as experienced by the consumer. It is this analysis that enables market-orientated product development to take place

• although production and marketing are separate departments, their functions are very closely related. The achievement of the best possible product for the market demands detailed knowledge of the technical processes, materials, lead times and costings. The quality of communication between the departments is crucial

• product positioning enables management to be more accurate in their market targeting. All elements in the marketing mix can be sharply focused on precise product positions, or deployed to shift a product into a more favourable position

• models to show product position are plotted according to the perceptions of consumers, **not** management. Targeting a product position is therefore really targeting a picture in the consumer's mind

• the reality of constant change in markets makes new product planning essential. To be effective, there needs to be a culture of innovation within the firm, where product development is urgent and continuous

• assessment of new product ideas is not likely to be objective. Different managers will have different departmental and personal interests that they wish to protect or advance. Caution is needed when a new product idea triggers excessive enthusiasm or opposition

• product deletion is a creative activity. Judged correctly, it releases resources within the firm for more profitable uses. Deletions are necessary for products in irreversible decline, and for new products that fail to meet sales and profit targets.

The marketing mix: promotion

Chapter objectives

After working through this chapter, you will:

▮ understand how all promotional methods are integrated with the marketing mix

▮ know how advertising budgets are set and media chosen

▮ be able to analyse an advertising campaign and its likely impact

▮ recognize the main types of sales promotion and be able to assess their significance

▮ know the meaning of the following key terms: promotion, point-of-sale, advertising elasticity of demand, corporate identity.

Media Watch

The media are saturated with product promotions. Collect examples of different kinds of promotion and try to work out why companies have chosen particular promotion strategies.

PROMOTION

Within the marketing mix promotional activities are intended to increase consumption of the product and so the flow of sales. The consumers arrange the priority of their purchases according to the extent to which their expected benefit (utility) exceeds their expected cost. All promotion aims to increase the consumer's perception of this excess (or consumer surplus).

►Promotion includes:
advertising: all communications designed to increase the priority assigned by the consumer to the purchase of a product

sales promotion: any tactic in the presentation of a product to the market designed to increase the quantity or frequency of purchase

personal selling: the efforts of the sales team to maximize the purchases of the product by specific customers over a given time span.

Figure 9.1   *Maximizing consumer surplus*

The benefit that a product is expected to yield varies with every potential customer. Although the price is usually fixed for consumer products (it may be negotiable in industrial markets), consumers' perception of the price will again vary widely.

Advertising

►Marks and Spencer have a tiny advertising budget relative to their sales. The firm's reputation is its own advertisement.

Meaning and Function

Some products are said to sell themselves. This means that the consumer demand is so intense and the product is so able to meet that demand, that no planned communication between producer and consumer is necessary. For most products this is not the case. The presence of a product needs to be advertised to the population of its target market. Thus advertising is a process of communication designed to stimulate purchase of a given product or brand. This is achieved by influencing consumer behaviour.

For a purchase to occur, the consumer must be aware of the product. The decision to buy then depends on the assessment of expected satisfaction against perceived cost. It follows that advertising will attempt to:

▶ Launching a new brand of shampoo:
'The milk of human kindness' (B)
'Four Seasons Shampoo' (A/B)
'Available now' (A)
and 'ONLY 95p' (C)

- (A) increase awareness of the product and its availability
- (B) increase expectation of satisfaction
- (C) decrease perception of cost.

 Make notes on the functions of advertising (A, B and C) by writing a paragraph for a pamphlet advertising a college course in business studies.

Much research has taken place to gain an understanding of how advertising acts on the consumer. Two well known approaches are:

A – I – D – A	**D – A – G – M – A – R** *
• **A**ttention	• Awareness
• **I**nterest	• Comprehension
• **D**esire	• Conviction
• **A**ction	• Action

* **DAGMAR** stands for
Defining **A**dvertising **G**oals for **M**easuring **A**dvertising **R**esults

Both models stress the need to achieve awareness of the product, to generate a belief in its desirability, and to trigger the action of purchase.

In pursuit of these aims there are two basic advertising functions:

- **to inform** consumers of the product's existence, availability, purpose, features, specifications and price
- **to persuade** consumers by intentionally creating a need or desire to purchase and consume the product.

Advertising Types

Trade advertising is aimed at influencing the managers of distribution channels – those responsible for distribution (e.g. wholesalers and retailers) – to stock and promote a product or brand. It is closely related to personal selling.

Consumer advertising is directed to the end-user of the product, to encourage increased purchasing and usage. This is closely related to sales promotion.

'Information': dominant when the product is innovative and the consumer is unaware of its qualities and availability. It also has a role in convincing consumers that a product is superior to its competitors.

'Persuasion': dominant when a firm fears competition from similar products, or wishes to protect or extend its market share.

Figure 9.2
The information/persuasion ratio

Advertising Media

Each **advertising medium** has its own characteristics:

Television
- high exposure rate
- colour, movement and sound
- can demonstrate the product
- creative: high impact potential

BUT
- expensive
- transient: leaves no record
- difficult to target

Radio
- high exposure rate in target segments
- segmentation of audience possible
- frequent repeat of message
- low cost

BUT
- easily forgotten
- no visual content
- small total audience

Newspapers
- high exposure rate in segment
- strong socioeconomic segmentation
- the advert can be retained
- flexible timing
- gain from paper's reputation

BUT
- mainly no colour
- no movement
- may lack impact

Magazines
- specialist readership
- long life span
- links with features
- good colour reproduction

BUT
- timing less flexible
- no movement

Posters
- very high exposure rate
- colour: can be creative
- situational impact

BUT
- conveys limited content
- only suitable for mass markets.

► Other advertising possibilities include cinema, transport locations, electric and electronic signs, and sponsorship.

The subject of either trade or consumer advertising may be:

- the industry
- the firm or organization (corporate image building)
- the brand
- the product
- a point of view (e.g. political campaigns and pressure groups).

 Make notes, in a table, on the benefits and shortcomings of different advertising media, contrasting them in terms of expense, exposure, and ability to reach closely defined market segments.

Advertising Budgets

There is no simple formula to decide an ideal advertising budget. This is because the exact effect of advertising on sales is not known. In theory a firm should continue to increase advertising expenditure until the profit generated by an extra sale equals the extra cost of achieving that sale. In practice there are some well-known general principles:

- **percentage of past sales method**, which relates spending to funds earned on sales already achieved. No allowance can be made for future expansion or contraction of the market
- **percentage of expected sales method**, which relates more closely to the market, but runs the risk of incorrect sales forecasts
- **competitive parity method**, where the firm aims to match approximately the expenditure of its major rivals. This is common in markets with a few dominant firms, and tends to act as an upward ratchet in spending levels
- **task method**, which rejects the concept of moving from budget to campaign, and instead works from campaign needs to budget decisions. Advertising needs are identified and costed with a final strategic decision on the sums that can be afforded. The method implies the setting of clear priorities.

Advertising expenditure varies widely in its effectiveness, according to the product and the market. A useful concept is the **advertising elasticity of demand**:

> Advertising Elasticity of Demand =
> $$\frac{\text{percentage change in quantity demanded}}{\text{percentage change in advertising expenditure}}$$

High advertising elasticity clearly suggests a market where advertising is worthwhile. However an increase in spending does not guarantee an increase in profit, which depends on the cost structure. Advertising elasticity tends to be high in brand-competitive markets, and at the early stages of the product life cycle.

 Make notes on what advertising elasticity of demand means in terms of making decisions about advertising expenditure.

► Advertising elasticity of demand.

Advertising Campaigns

An advertising campaign or strategy requires careful planning. Management must decide upon its advertising objectives, and relate these to the expenditure, timing, targeting and media mix of a campaign. Timing is important. The firm must decide between a 'drip' and a 'burst' approach:

► The advertiser's dilemma: 'Half of all I spent on advertising was wasted. The trouble is I don't know which half!'

Figure 9.3
Drip and burst advertising

Drip advertising is often related to maintaining brand and product awareness. **Bursts** may depend on competitive pressures and specific events in the product life cycle.

It is also essential to relate the campaign to other elements in the marketing mix. Assuming that target markets for the product are finalized, then the campaign will be assisted by integrated sales promotion. Sales teams will be ready and briefed, with distribution channels well prepared. Pricing policy will have been set, together with sales and profit objectives.

The use of an agency is very common for major campaigns. Agencies can offer a complete range of marketing services, from market research to every part of the marketing mix. Service fees and commission will be charged, but there is the benefit of highly specialized professionalism. Agencies accumulate wide experience and some outstanding talent. The right creative theme for a campaign can be the making of a product (e.g. Levi's 501 jeans advertisements).

► To gain an insight into the world of advertising agencies look at the magazine *Campaign* which you will find in most large public libraries.

SALES PROMOTION

Meaning and Scope

Sales promotion focuses on the **point-of-sale** in the distribution chain. It involves a wide range of techniques designed to increase successful sales outcomes when seller and buyer meet. Included are promotions to the trade, to industrial customers and to domestic consumers. In each case the aim is to accelerate the flow of sales by attracting new customers or by encouraging existing customers to increase their usage rate.

Figure 9.4
The world's top ten brands

Brands and Identities

The use of names and symbols as a recognizable mark of origin has been common for hundreds of years. Modern brands are powerful and valuable. A firm will try to build possible associations for its brand. This may be achieved by the quality or value for money of the product, both reinforced through advertising. Once established, the brand itself leads consumers to expect satisfaction, and therefore increases sales.

A brand name should usually be short, memorable, and far from any undesirable connotation, e.g. Flora Margarine, Penguin books, Sealink Ferries. Once chosen, a brand must be registered together with any distinctive trade mark.

Some firms use a single 'umbrella' brand name for their complete product range (e.g. Bic pens, lighters, razors). This ensures a favourable response from consumers to new products under the same name, while the whole promotional mix can be expressed through a single name. Other firms devise separate brand names for each product (e.g. Distillers' range of Scotch whisky). This tactic increases the sense of product individuality.

There has also been rapid growth in 'own brand' and 'own label' products, sold by national distributors. These are normally manufactured by companies with their own famous brands, which must compete alongside the 'own labels'. A major retailer such as Sainsbury's has a brand identity in its own right, and can ensure high volume sales. The manufacturer selling its product under the 'own label' enjoys large regular orders without any marketing expenses. The original famous brand continues to sell at a higher price in many market segments.

Packaging

Over the twentieth century an increasing proportion of products have become pre-packaged. This reflects the importance of packaging in expressing brand identities in a more affluent and sophisticated market. Packaging has the practical task of protecting the product in distribution and in use. But in a real sense it actually **defines** the product. Packaging determines the quantity in which a product is sold (e.g. a pound of chocolates). It may decide the method of usage (e.g. a squirt of washing-up liquid). It certainly expresses image and identity (e.g. Grolsch lager, After Eight mints). Many firms use packaging that is expensive and impractical because it increases the customer valuation of the product more than it increases the price: e.g. Biarritz Chocolates. Brands and packaging are very closely linked. Styles of lettering and colour choices for product liveries become vital selling points: e.g. the confident bubbly red lettering on a blue background for Cadbury's Wispa. Attractive tins, jars, boxes, and even carrier bags are often valued highly by the consumer. The product benefits from a stronger identity, and brand loyalty is increased.

Colours have significant psychological and social connotations. Firms use colour in products and packaging to create and communicate brand **image**, i.e. use of psycho-social perception of consumers in the target market.

 Make notes on the importance of packaging in the promotional mix taking your own examples from detergents, computer games or compact discs.

Merchandising and Point-of-Sale Display

Other Promotional Methods

Merchandising is the art of attracting customers towards a product, and stimulating their desire to make a purchase. Despite some functional aspects, shopping today is becoming less often a practical chore, and more often a leisure activity. The environment of shops and stores is carefully planned to be interesting yet reassuring, enjoyable yet convenient. Lighting, decor, fittings and display all help to draw the customer towards a purchase. Physical access to goods is very important, and customers are encouraged to inspect and handle the merchandise. Much of the pressure to buy is invisible. Psychological research has been highly influential. Supermarkets, for example, plan the progress of their customers round the store, 'bouncing' their attention and buying patterns from display to display. The store management can plan the behaviour of customers to a surprizingly high degree.

 Make notes on the importance of merchandising and point-of-sale displays with reference to any large high-street store.

Price and Credit

Short-term price cuts are a sales promotion tactic. The chance of a bargain attracts consumer interest, while a lower price will normally raise sales and introduce new consumers to the product. Their effectiveness depends on the relative responsiveness of sales to changes in price (see Chapter 10).

The supply of credit has become an important promotional factor. For costly items such as new houses or cars, special credit facilities at reduced interest rates may be offered. Hire-purchase has lost relative popularity, but many leading retailers issue their own credit cards, backed by major financial institutions. These not only stimulate sales, but also help to solidify consumer loyalty.

Special Offers

The launch of a new product may be assisted by free samples or by special trial packs. More mature products can be promoted with additional 'free' quantities included with the pack (e.g. an extra ten per cent in volume with soft drinks, or an extra tablet of soap). In highly competitive markets, unrelated gifts may be offered, either directly or through the collection of stamps or coupons (e.g. petrol sales promotions). Product packs may carry opportunities to purchase other goods at specially reduced prices, but often require proof

▶ Important colour associations include:

white – purity, cleanness
black – power, mystery
purple – indulgence, extravagance
blue – distinction, coolness
green – natural, calm
red – excitement, heat
orange – warmth, comfort
yellow – sunshine, cheerfulness
brown – utility, practicality
silver – refinement, sophistication
gold – riches, luxury.

▶ **Point-of-sale promotion**: presentation and promotion of products in the place where they are sold.

▶ Charge-card holders' details provide a valuable database for a company's promotional activities.

of purchase. Promotions may also give away tokens for cash refunds or reductions on future purchases. Competitions and prize draws are another popular device to attract customer interest.

 Find examples of companies using price cuts, credit facilities and special offers for promotion. Why do you think these were appropriate for the product?

Exhibitions and Events

They are widely used in industrial markets to sell such goods as vehicles or machinery. A stand at an exhibition can arouse interest and media comment and secure increased orders. Some consumer goods exhibitions, such as the Ideal Home Exhibition, enjoy wide national popularity, and act as a showcase for new products. Special local events can also provide a useful focus.

Direct Mail

Sending promotional literature, direct to trade and private addresses, is increasingly common. It can be targeted efficiently using market research data, and is extremely flexible in its timing and format. Mailshots often carry special offers to increase the response rate.

Sponsorship

A firm may agree to fund an organization or project in return for the promotional use of its name in the related publicity. Sporting, artistic, educational and charitable bodies have all used business sponsorship. The sponsoring firm has the added advantage of associating their brand with a respected person or activity. High fees may be paid to sports or pop stars for being publicly associated with a product.

Corporate Identity

Many firms aim to present a unified and easily recognizable image to their market and to society at large. A logo with the organization's colours and consistent graphic design gives the firm a clear identity to which consumers can respond. In the 1960s and 1970s these tended to be efficiency-related with geometric logos, but modern identities are more organic and people-centred.

▶ BP is estimated to have spent £170m. on the new corporate identity it introduced in 1990.

 Select an appropriate mix of advertising media for each of these products:

1 'Electrochef' is a new easy-to-use inexpensive food processor with a wide range of attachments. 'Fast food that's real food' is the advertising slogan.

2 A travel firm is launching 'Eurostars': coach trips to European cities with cheap hotel accommodation and tickets for major sports events/pop concerts.

Summary and comment

• sales promotion works in the marketplace where sellers and buyers meet. It is a highly flexible part of the marketing mix, and can be adjusted or redirected at management discretion

• all elements in the total mix are intimately related to sales promotion. Its distinction from product development, advertising and distribution is often rightly blurred

• the largest expenditures are reserved for selling into consumer markets. Sales promotion is also important in industrial markets, but tends to be more discretionary and is often activated through personal selling.

(10) *The marketing mix: price*

Chapter objectives

After working through this chapter, you will:

■ appreciate the importance of price in business as a whole, and within the marketing mix

■ understand the market forces of demand and supply, and how they are resolved in price

■ be familiar with the major pricing strategies and their associated pricing methods

■ be able to analyse commonly used pricing tactics

■ know the meaning of the following key terms: price, supply, demand, supply curve, demand curve, price elasticity, cost-based pricing, demand-based pricing, competition-based pricing.

THE MEANING OF PRICE

A **price** is an exchange rate. It states the quantity of one resource that can be exchanged for another. In a modern economy exchange is made more convenient by the use of money, which represents resources. Business is about combining resources to increase their value, and selling them at a price high enough to replenish those resources and leave a surplus or reward.

▶ In a market economy resources are allocated through the price mechanism.

Within the market producers measure costs against price. Consumers weigh price against satisfaction. Provided that the value of customer satisfaction exceeds the value of producers' costs, then a price can exist at which sales take place. Price is at the heart of the market. For the firm, the volume of sales multiplied by price yields sales revenue, a proportion of which is profit. But this profit is earned in a competitive market where the consumer has a choice. If another firm can offer more satisfaction relative to price, their sales – and share of the market – will increase. Thus price is also at the heart of competition.

▶ For the firm the volume of sales multiplied by price yields sales revenue.

Demand and Supply

Demand for a product is the quantity that buyers are prepared to purchase in the market over a given period and at a given price.

Say the farms of a particular area produce a distinctive local cheese. At a price of £2 per lb, total sales for the farmers amount to 600 lbs per week. A series of values for quantity demanded relative to price – called a **demand schedule** – shows:

price per lb (£)	3.50	3.00	2.50	2.00	1.50
quantity demanded per week (lbs)	250	400	600	850	1 200

When plotted on a graph, the schedule forms a **demand curve**:

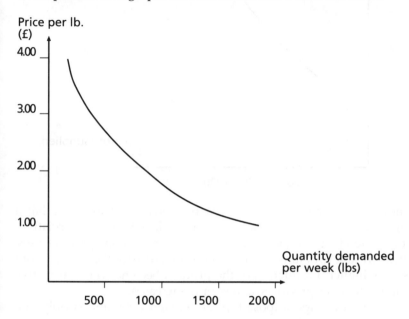

Figure 10.1
The demand curve

The demand curve typically slopes downwards from left to right, meaning that at lower prices a greater quantity is demanded. Why does this relationship hold good? Because as the price of one product falls, consumers are able to obtain greater value (utility) in return for their expenditure. Consumer surplus is now higher. Consumption of the product becomes more attractive relative to other products, and demand increases.

▶ Surpluses of unsold goods puts a downward pressure on price, while a tendency to sell-out exerts an upward pressure.

Now consider **supply** – which means the quantity of a product that firms are prepared to offer in the market over a given period at a given price. The **supply schedule** for the cheese is:

price per lb (£)	3.50	3.00	2.50	2.00	1.50
quantity supplied per week (lbs)	900	750	600	450	275

When plotted on a graph, the schedule forms a **supply curve**:

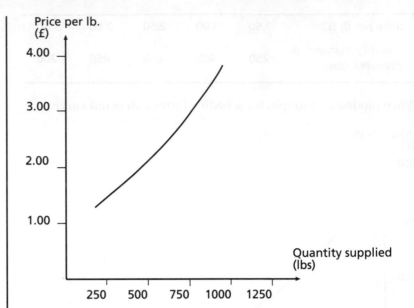

Figure 10.2
The supply curve

► A highly profitable product becomes a 'honey pot' prompting increased output from existing firms and attracting new firms into the market.

The curve typically slopes upwards from left to right, meaning that at higher prices a greater quantity is supplied. Why does this relationship generally hold good? Because as the price of one product rises, firms are able to obtain greater revenue in return for their costs. Profit is now higher. Production of the product becomes more attractive relative to other products, and supply increases.

We can now superimpose typical demand (DD) and supply (SS) curves in a single diagram:

Figure 10.3
Interaction of demand and supply

Only at the **equilibrium price** (E) does the quantity demanded exactly equal the quantity supplied. At this price only the output of firms will correspond with the purchasing intentions of consumers. At a higher price (P1), a surplus of output will remain unsold (Q1, Q2).

But at a lower price (P2) a shortage of output will exist (Q1, Q2). Thus the equilibrium price is also called the **market clearing price**.

Demand Elasticity

The demand for some products is far more sensitive to price changes than others. A cut in the price of potatoes will only slightly increase demand, while a cut in the price of crisps may cause a sharp increase in sales. The responsiveness of demand to price changes is called **price elasticity of demand**. Its value is calculated by the formula:

► Price elasticity of demand.

> Price elasticity of demand =
>
> $$\frac{\text{percentage change in quantity demand}}{\text{percentage change in price}}$$

Price Elasticity

Lyme Lamps Ltd
This is a recently established business making adjustable reading-lights. The firm sells the lights for £20 each, and is currently receiving orders for 200 units per week. The marketing director decides to stimulate sales with a price cut to £18 per light. The result is a rise in weekly demand to 260 lights. What is the price elasticity of demand (PED)?

percentage change in quantity demanded $= \dfrac{60}{200} \times 100\% = 30\%$

percentage change in price $= \dfrac{2}{20} \times 100\% = 10\%$

$\text{PED} = \dfrac{30\%}{10\%} = 3$

A reduction in the price of lamps has led to a three times greater increase in demand.

Demand is said to be **elastic** when the PED value is greater than 1, and **inelastic** when less than 1.

Notice that
• in Figure 10.4 the demand curve is elastic
• since price × quantity demanded = sales revenue, we can identify rectangles of **revenue loss** and **revenue gain**
(check the coordinates P1, Q1, and P2, Q2)
• since revenue loss is smaller than revenue gain, net revenue has increased
• in Figure 10.5 demand is inelastic, and the price cut has caused a net decrease in revenue, a small decrease in price has caused a large increase in demand.

Figure 10.4
Elastic demand

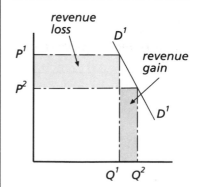

Figure 10.5
Inelastic demand

Look again at Lyme Lamps. The revenue change is simply calculated:

original revenue = 200 lamps @ £20 = £4 000

new revenue = 260 lamps @ £18 = £4 680 (up 17 per cent)

Note that this does not necessarily mean an increase in profit.

If the lamps cost the producer £15 each, then
original profit = 200 × £5 = £1 000.
After the price cut, profit = 260 × £3 = £780!

Elasticity and Net Revenue

► The more exact the definition of a product, the higher is its likely price elasticity. For example, overall demand for lager might be relatively inelastic while demand for Heineken might be relatively elastic.

demand curve	price change	net revenue effect
elastic	increase	decrease
elastic	decrease	increase
inelastic	increase	increase
inelastic	decrease	decrease

Demand curves are not static. Changes in tastes, fashions, or incomes may cause the demand curve to shift position, or change its gradient, and hence elasticity.

For example, at the development stage of the product life cycle, the relevant demand curve might correspond to Dd, Dd, (Figure 10.6 below):

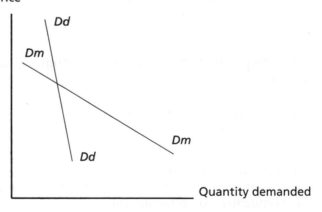

Figure 10.6
Elasticity and the product life cycle

By the maturity stage, the demand has become much greater at most prices, but also much more elastic (Dm, Dm). This may be due to increased choice and competition in the market.

Pricing Objectives and Pricing Policy

Pricing bears directly on a firm's sales revenue and profits. It is therefore the concern not only of the marketing director, but also of the managing director and the whole board. With pricing decisions the success or failure of product ranges and even the survival of the firm may be at stake. Pricing objectives flow from overall business objectives (see Chapter 31). Pricing may be concerned primarily with:

- **profitability** – where the emphasis is on return on capital, or profit goals for a given period
- **sales growth** – where the intention is expansion of the firm and its market share
- **stability or survival** – where the need is either to maintain a position of strength or to ride out a period of difficulty.

These objectives will be translated by marketing management into pricing policies. They will address such issues as price relationships between products, or the use of price reductions and discounts. The policy must be fully integrated with the firm's overall marketing intentions, and the other elements in the marketing mix.

Price Strategies

(a) Cost based

(b) Demand based

(c) Competition based

► A pricing strategy may be:

cost-based: price works forward from cost towards consumer demand;

demand-based: price works backwards from consumer demand towards costs;

competition-based: price is determined in the market place.

Figure 10.7
Pricing strategies

(NM) As you read through the text on various price strategies make notes which (a) briefly define each strategy, and (b) say when its use is appropriate.

Cost-based Strategies

This approach begins with the producer. Prices are derived from analysis of costs combined with allowance for profit. Consumer demand is not directly considered. The following are types of cost-based strategies:

- **cost-plus pricing** involves setting a projected output, calculating total cost per unit, and adding a percentage mark-up for profit.

$$\frac{\text{total cost}}{\text{projected output (units)}} + \text{percentage profit} = \text{price}$$

- **mark-up pricing** is the trade equivalent of cost-plus. The formula is:

cost price + mark-up percentage = selling price

The mark-up percentage is only partly profit, since it must also cover overhead costs. The method is very simple and widely used in the retail and wholesale trades. A trader can achieve some relationship with demand by using different mark-up rates for different products

- **target return pricing** aims to ensure, through sales, a target rate of return on the related investment. The formula is:

$$\text{unit cost} + \frac{\text{target percentage return} \times \text{investment}}{\text{projected sales volume}} = \text{price}$$

This method is used in capital intensive firms, when return on investment is a vital factor.

Demand-based Strategies

These emphasize the consumer, and take as their starting point the strength of demand. Each method, in effect, attempts to evaluate consumer preferences and requires a basis in market research. The following are types of demand-based strategies:

- **perceived value pricing** involves research in asking members of the target audience to estimate the price that they would be willing to pay for the product (or product concept). The results then form the basis of the pricing decision. The concept is extended by using perceived value to drive production and costing decisions. If a product concept has a certain perceived value, then the challenge to the firm is to design and manufacture that product to sell at or below perceived value and still meet the profit target
- **penetration and skimming strategies** aim for different **market depths** in the life of a product. **Penetration** means the attempt to gain rapid competitive advantage through low price, leading to

►Be careful to distinguish mark-up from margin. A chocolate bar costs 16p from the supplier and sells for 20p.

The mark-up is $\frac{4p}{16p} = 25\%$

The margin is $\frac{4p}{20p} = 20\%$

high sales and a high market share. The approach is valuable if major economies of scale exist, or when the hope is to discourage competitors in a new market. **Skimming** the market means the attempt to gain a high margin, by charging a comparatively high price, in order to cream off the profit from a smaller market in which demand is relatively inelastic. This can be effective in targeting luxury market segments, or when launching a risky innovation where the need is early payback on investment (see Chapter 26)

- **variable pricing** involves charging different prices for products that are the same or similar, according to the customer, place or time. For instance customers above or below certain ages are eligible for reduced fares on trains and buses, while others must pay a higher rate. Theatres charge different rates for different blocks of seats. Phone calls are cheapest in the evening, and most costly on weekday mornings. This **price discrimination** is possible when a market can be divided. Each section of the market has its own demand curve with its own shape, which can then be exploited.

Figure 10.8
Demand for rail travel to London

► Demand-based strategies are often closely linked to a product's progress through its life cycle (see Chapter 7).

For example: the rush hour demand curve (D_{RH}) is inelastic and the off-peak demand curve (D_{OP}) is elastic. To fill the trains by selling quantity Q tickets, British Rail can charge a high price (P_1) in the rush hour but only a much lower price (P_2) at off-peak times.

Variable pricing also helps to spread demand across busy and slack periods, and to achieve more even use of facilities

- **marginal cost pricing** uses the same principle in filling unused production capacity. If a sufficient number of customers is paying the full price and covering the overhead costs, then it may be most profitable to attract additional customers at any price greater than variable cost. For example a hotel may generate its main revenue and profit during the summer season. It could then offer bargain winter breaks at much reduced prices. So long as these cover variable costs (e.g. meals and staffing), then a **contribution** is made towards overheads and profit (see Chapter 14).

Competition-based Strategies

Unless it is in a perfect monopoly, the products of every firm are under pressure from competition. In competitive markets, price is almost always a key factor affecting sales.

- **going-rate pricing** means setting a price in line with similar products on the market. When there is little difference between products, the individual demand curves become very elastic. The going rate is held down by competition to the lowest realistic price. Any attempt to price above this level will be very difficult. Pricing at the going rate also avoids retaliation by competitors
- **price leadership** occurs in competitive markets dominated by a few large firms (a situation called **oligopoly**). One firm may emerge as a price leader, whose decisions to change prices are normally rapidly followed by other firms in the industry. In the tea industry Brooke Bond has sometimes appeared to act in this role. Following the price leader is often the most comfortable option for firms. Changes in costs tend to affect every company at the same time. Besides, to break ranks and increase price alone risks losing market share, while undercutting competitors may provoke a **price war** in which all firms lose
- **bid pricing** is used in markets where firms compete to win contracts. **Bids** or **tenders** are made to the customer, who considers the rival offers and then announces a choice of contractor.

Pricing Tactics

▶ Pricing tactics must be carefully integrated with the main pricing strategy.

Having established the best pricing strategy for their products, marketing managers use a variety of tactics to fine-tune pricing in the mix.

- **product-line pricing** means pricing a product in the context of other members of the same product line. For example, a producer of kitchen utensils might price a collander with a high profit margin and a cheese grater with a much lower margin. This responds to market pressures but ensures viability of the product line as a whole
- **complementary goods pricing** occurs when the sale of the main product leads to sales of complementary products (e.g. pens and ink cartridges). A firm may choose to price a major product at a low margin, and rely on a more highly priced complementary product to assist in reaching profit targets
- **product life pricing** involves coordinating relative price with a product's progress through the product life cycle. Penetration pricing might be used at the growth stage, but profit might be obtained from the decline stage by skimming the market
- **loss leadership** means offering one or a few products at or below cost price in order to attract customers, who will then make other purchases which carry normal margins
- **psychological pricing** is the firm's tactical response to consumer perception of prices. Products are frequently priced at just below critical price thresholds. A price of 99p, £19.95, or £9 995 invites

customers to place the product in the price bracket below the relevant threshold. An interesting alternative tactic arises from the price-quality association. Say a firm introduces a new up-market brand of coffee. The consumer may need psychologically to pay extra in order to believe in the quality or exclusivity of the product. For the producer the cost may be no more than a mainstream brand, but a slightly higher price may increase sales!

- **experimental pricing** involves testing prices (i.e. trying different prices with customers to determine equilibrium price) in the market and assessing consumer response. This occurs when firms are uncertain about market value. It is common in markets for second-hand goods and unusual luxuries.

 Read the following paragraph and answer the questions below:

Fruits of the Earth Ltd buys pineapples from the wholesaler for 85p each. The normal selling price is £1.20 with average sales of 200 fruit per week. After the manager decides on a price cut to 99p, sales rise to 270 fruit per week.

1 Calculate price elasticity of demand.

2 Calculate change in revenue.

3 Was the price cut a wise decision? Why?

Summary and comment

- pricing has implications that run to the heart of any business enterprise. It is a key determinant of revenue and profit. Decisions about price will tend to involve the most senior management, although tactical measures may originate lower in the hierarchy, e.g. at branch manager level
- it is essential that price is tightly coordinated with other elements in the mix. The aim is to maximize the positive gap between the consumer's perception of price and value
- distribution channels often account for a large proportion of final price. The selection of distribution channel may vitally influence final price in large sectors of the market
- a price reduction can cause an increase in revenue and a decrease in profits. This applies when the reduction of profit margin outweighs the benefit of extra sales. Equally, a price increase can cause a decrease in revenue and an increase in profit. This occurs when the increase in margin outweighs the negative effect of reduced sales
- price elasticity of demand (PED) is broadly higher for luxuries and lower for necessities. However PED values for individual brands tend to increase with the degree of competition in the market
- for every product, many customers would be willing to pay a higher price. This fact is the basis of variable pricing, which can

only be successful when market segments are easily and securely divided

• marginal cost pricing carries the risk that all customers will come to expect the reduced price, so causing a reduction in sales at the normal full price. Managers must also remember that no profit is made until fixed overheads are covered

• in export markets price will be translated into a foreign currency (see Chapter 42). Since rates of exchange fluctuate, the price payable by overseas customers is liable to move up or down without any change in the UK price quotation

• pricing decisions must be closely integrated with budgets for sales and profit. Changes in price may require flexing of budgets (see Chapter 23).

• price can be so central to corporate objectives that it influences the whole culture of the firm. For instance a business may be based on the principle of price discounting.

11 The marketing mix: place

Chapter objectives

After working through this chapter, you will:

▌ be able to analyse the basic goals of distribution in the mix

▌ be familiar with the main channels of distribution

▌ appreciate the role of middlemen

▌ understand how distribution decisions are made

▌ know the meanings of the following key terms: distribution channel, distribution chain, middlemen (wholesalers, brokers/agents), retailers, direct marketing, producer retail outlet, franchising.

DISTRIBUTION

The pathways of ownership, transport and storage down which products pass, between production and consumption, are called **distribution channels**. The successive stages in the process form the **distribution chain**. These chains form a highly complex web of transactions and deliveries which crisscross physical and financial markets. With large scale production and increasingly international markets, the distribution chains for one product alone may be lengthy and elaborate.

Since direct producer-consumer contract is usually impractical, firms are needed to act as distributors or **middlemen**. Wholesalers and retailers are middlemen who buy and sell as legal owners of the product. Agents also deal in the product, but only on behalf of a seller, and not as its legal owner (e.g. an estate agent). The most common distribution chains are:

▶ The general rule today is that products must find their consumer rather than the other way round.

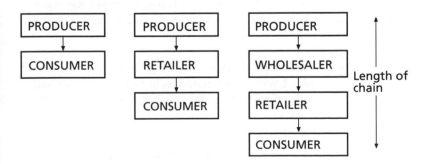

Figure 11.1
Distribution chains

▶ **Wholesaling**: buying in bulk from manufacturers and selling in smaller quantities to retailers.

Wholesalers

The major advantages of wholesaling are:

- **bulk purchasing**
  the manufacturer is able to sell goods in large quantities to the wholesaler, who therefore pays a much lower unit price. Stocks of finished goods can be far lower, releasing finance for the manufacturer and cutting handling and warehousing costs. Delivery costs are also reduced, and the necessary size of the sales force is smaller
- **breaking bulk**
  the wholesaler breaks down large purchases of each product into smaller consignments for each retailer. This greatly reduces transport and delivery costs

Producers ———▶ Retailers
Deliveries/transactions

$3 \times 4 = 12$

Producers →Wholesaler →Retailers
Deliveries/transactions

$3 + 4 = 7$

Figure 11.2
The wholesaler: breaking bulk

In Figure 11.2, without a wholesaler, twelve deliveries/transactions are required between the producers and retailers. By using a wholesaler (W), this figure is reduced to seven.

- **spreading risks**
  by moving output into the wholesaler trade, the producer avoids the risk that stock may fall in value through deterioration or shifts in market demand
- **retailer support**
  the wholesaler assists retailers in enabling them to make small orders of the product, which they would otherwise be unable to do. Often help is also given with technical training and sales promotion. In addition the retailer may obtain vital working capital through the extension of credit.

These benefits carry a cost. Firstly, the wholesaler requires a profit margin, so adding to the final price of the product. Secondly, control over the precise delivery of the marketing mix moves away from the producer. The product may not be handled, merchandised, or promoted in the way that the manufacturer intends.

Retailers

The retailer provides:

- variety and convenience for the customer
- merchandising and promotion
- product information and advice
- final pricing expertise
- credit and delivery services
- after-sales service.

Eighty-two per cent of all shops (283 000 in number) are still small businesses but large multiple stores have now captured sixty per cent of total retail turnover, and the figure is rising.

Key Trends in UK Retailing

- the decline of the small independent retailer, and the growth of large multiples
- the use of cars for shopping with the corresponding advantages of large 'one-stop' out of town stores
- the shift in market power from producers towards large retailers
- an increase in franchising which ties large numbers of small retailers to a single supplier.

The growth of market orientation (see Chapter 5) has fundamentally altered the dynamics of distribution. Instead of channels being producer-pushed, they are now increasingly retailer-pulled. Large retailers are less likely to purchase from what producers have to offer, and more likely to specify what they want to sell. This trend is being accelerated by the progress of information technology. Electronic stock control and accounting systems feed back instant, continuous and highly accurate data concerning demand in the market. The market shares of producers depend on their ability to respond with sufficient sensitivity and speed.

These changes in the relationship between producers, wholesalers and retailers are transmitted through the distribution chains, with the effects of change flowing in both directions.

The changing structure of distribution is causing a decline in the traditional wholesaler. Very large outlets such as superstores and hypermarkets are taking many wholesale functions to retail level. Meanwhile consumers in their cars are in effect carrying out the last stage of distribution themselves. Significantly, less than twenty-five per cent of the grocery trade now passes through wholesalers. Large multiple stores enter into direct contracts with manufacturers and bypass the formal wholesale stage, providing their own central warehouses and distribution system. Shorter distribution chains speed market intelligence, and allow final retail prices to be cut to the minimum. Profitability is still possible, but is likely to require the lower margin high turnover formula (see Chapter 22) of large stores.

► Small local and specialist retailers are, however, likely to flourish. For them, the role of the wholesaler is vital in breaking bulk and in supplying goods from a great variety of producers.

► **Direct selling**: producer sells direct to consumer.

Direct Selling

Direct selling is widespread in industrial markets where the producer's sales force will negotiate orders with the end-user. It is often essential when trading large items of equipment, where technical specifications are paramount.

In consumer markets, direct selling has two main patterns:

1 Direct marketing

A mail order catalogue may be sent to the consumer, who makes their selections and then orders by telephone or post. The method is widely used by firms selling clothing, cosmetics, toys, books and household goods (e.g. Next, Grattans, Littlewoods). **Direct mail**, usually targeted by market segment, yields orders for a specific product or product range. It is particularly popular for the sale of financial services, magazines and home improvements. Direct response advertising urges the customer to order goods directly from the producer or retailer. This method uses television, radio and the press, and is popular for arts and entertainments, music recordings, novelties and gifts.

2 Producer retail outlets

Some producers sell some or all of their output through their own chain of shops. Boots pharmaceutical products, the filling stations of major oil companies, and the tied houses of brewery groups are all examples. Franchising has a similar effect (see Chapter 2).

Direct marketing brings a producer closer to the market, and reduces distribution costs. Postal shopping however loses much of the impact provided by good merchandising, and is impractical for lower value goods.

Agents and Brokers

► Brokers (agents) bring together buyer and seller without themselves owning what is bought and sold.

Firms may employ their own agents, or pay an external (independent) agent to act on their behalf. Agents are normally rewarded for sales on a percentage commission basis. Single company agents will push only that one firm's products, but external agents often have access to a wider network of customers. Raw materials, insurances and housing are all often sold through agents or brokers.

Agents are also widely used in export markets, where their detailed knowledge of local markets, major customers and trading conditions is particularly valuable. However the use of an agent network abroad can make control of the full marketing process problematic. Even so, it is likely to be far cheaper and less risky than establishing an overseas subsidiary, unless export sales have reached a very substantial value.

Distribution Decisions

The most basic objectives of distribution are likely to be maximization of sales and profitability. Increasing sales can raise market share, strengthen competitive position, reduce average costs, and enable the business to grow. The profit margin is critical in determining the level of reward earned by the achievement of sales, and reflected in the return on net assets.

Before setting the distribution mix, the marketing manager should consider:

- **market coverage**
  this must be sufficient to reach sales and market share objectives. It may be intensive where a product is to be available from many outlets (e.g. a soft drink such as 7-Up). Or selective, where outlets are targeted more specifically by market segment (e.g. a luxury hi-fi brand such as Bang & Olufsen)
- **cost of distribution chain**
  distribution chains are essential in achieving sales, but their cost must be carefully related to their net benefit. In a long chain the total distribution cost may exceed the cost of production.

▶ Luxury products tend to have longer distribution chains. For household necessities chains have generally become much shorter.

Example:
A product has a cost at the factory gate of £1 per unit. Mark-ups are:
Producer/wholesaler: 25%
Wholesaler/retailer: 33%
Retailer/consumer: 50%
The effect of successive mark-ups can be represented on a bar chart:

This effect may oblige a producer to accept a lower profit margin in order to keep the price competitive. Notice that a 10p increase in the producer's costs causes a 25p increase in the final price of the product.

Figure 11.3
Mark-ups through the distribution chain

- **distributor services**
  the importance of services offered by the wholesaler and retailer varies widely according to the product and the market. If coverage objectives require product availability in a very large number of outlets, then wholesaling is probably essential. If the market is

concentrated in the hands of a few major retail multiples, then it is their merchandising and promotional skills that are important. In specialist or highly technical markets, middlemen are vital in providing customer information, advice and after-sales service. Equally, a service whose market is highly dispersed (e.g. insurance) can be sold effectively through direct marketing

- **distributor motivation**
  wholesalers and retailers are normally selling the products of many firms, including direct competitors. Means must be found to ensure that sufficiently high priority is given to sales of the product concerned

- **warehousing and transport**
  opting for shorter distribution chains is likely to increase producer stock holding, warehousing, handling and transport costs. The severity of these increases is a significant factor in constructing the distribution network

- **producer control**
  lengthening distribution chains are liable to blur the focus of the producer's intended marketing mix. Control diminishes over the producer's presentation and promotion, while final prices may become unpredictable. Increasing control over the active mix will generally raise distribution costs.

Distribution decisions take account of all the above factors, but it is essential to recognize that the variables are **interactive**. An effort to increase coverage may mean a longer or more complex distribution chain. This will add to costs, and put upward pressure on final price. Similarly, shortening or simplifying distribution chains might reduce costs, and increase sales per outlet. However reduced coverage could lead to a net fall in total sales and market share. In addition, the producer's average cost will also be influenced by length of production runs and total output levels. The aim of management is to find an optimum balance between these conflicting pressures.

► Marketing managers must also integrate distribution decisions with other elements of the marketing mix.

1 Suggest the most appropriate distribution channel(s) for the following products and make notes explaining why you have made these choices:

- specialist books from a small publisher
- a popular brand of biscuits
- a complete business computer system
- up-market delicatessen products.

2 Make notes to show how distribution decisions might interact with:

- pricing decisions (see Chapter 10)
- promotion decisions (see Chapter 9).

Read the following case study and answer the questions below it.

Borders Ltd is marketing a new board game based on international diplomacy. This is being manufactured in a small factory unit near Jedburgh in the Anglo-Scottish border country.

Alison McCrandles, the marketing director, is now seeking an effective national distribution channel for the game. She has already reached agreement in principle with major wholesalers who would ensure wide retail distribution.

At projected output levels, the unit cost will be £4 with a factory gate price of £5.45. The wholesalers require a ten per cent mark-up, while retailers will need to mark the product up by a further forty per cent. Comparable games retail at around £8 and the market is highly competitive.

This morning Ms McCrandles has received a letter from a major UK chain store with branches in all major towns and cities (populations over 50 000) offering to act as sole distributor and working on a mark-up of £2.50 above the factory gate price.

> 1 Compare selling prices and profit margins for the two distribution channels.
>
> 2 What are the possible advantages and disadvantages of accepting the chain store's offer?

Summary and comment

- in consumer goods markets, the balance of power is shifting away from the large-scale producer towards the large multiple retailer. Combined with developments in information technology, this means that the shaping of the marketing mix is increasingly occurring at retail level
- the extent to which producers can directly influence the retail stage depends on their market power and the length of the distribution chain
- it is probably inevitable that distribution chains will become shorter. Rapid changes in demand require producers to move closer to consumer markets. Consumers are increasingly discerning in selecting the producer of their choice, and are using cars for large-scale one-stop shopping
- within firms the production function is extending backwards through closer cooperation with suppliers, while the marketing function is being driven forwards through the closer relationship with retailers
- more accurate segmentation of markets is leading to a more complex fine-tuning of distribution channel structures. One firm may adopt a variety of distribution strategies depending on its target markets

- the growth of very large retailers is exposing smaller producers to the risks of excessive dependence on one buyer. The loss of a particular contract can cause the complete failure of a smaller business
- the quality of relationships between producers and the relevant wholesaler or retailer are vital to marketing success. Effective transmission of the marketing mix depends on communications and cooperation between the links in the distribution chain
- distribution is the least readily flexible element in the marketing mix. However the changing patterns of market segments and the rapid evolution of distribution channels mean that managers must keep their distribution strategy under constant review.

12 Business location

Chapter objectives

After working through this chapter, you will:

■ be able to analyse the major factors influencing location decisions

■ understand the key location trends of the 1990s

■ know the meaning of the following key terms: industrial concentration, industrial inertia, development areas, intermediate areas.

THE LOCATION DECISION

The location decision is fundamental to costs and sales – whether for a new firm finding business premises, or for an established firm deciding to expand or consolidate. There are usually a variety of possible locations for every firm, and a range of criteria for assessing their relative advantages and disadvantages. It is most unlikely that there will be any one perfect location, but rather a choice that is judged to be optimal. This means balancing one factor against another, and may mean some tough choices for senior management: e.g. should a very low cost site be accepted if it isolates the firm from its market?

► Location decisions are strategic and have a long-term impact. They are not based solely on the current balance of factors, but on projections of these factors into the future. A range of locations can provide greater flexibility.

Draw up a table with four columns (one for side headings). As you read about the factors affecting location decisions make notes relating to the following three companies:

1 Manufacturer of products from coconut fibre, imported by sea in bulk.

2 Supplier of in-company training in human-relations skills.

3 High precision engineering company exporting world-wide.

Factors Affecting a Location Decision

1 *Raw Materials and Energy*
Raw material supplies explain the location of extractive industries (e.g. coal mining) by definition. Nearness to supplies of raw materials is also essential for manufacturing firms or industries whose processes involve converting large quantities of raw materials into much smaller (bulk-reduced) quantities of finished products. For example the steel industry requires iron ore and coal, from British or imported sources. The use of electricity and gas from national grids/pipelines has largely freed firms from the location constraints of **energy supplies**.

► Large firms with European markets increasingly view the UK as a 'region' of the European Community, to be judged on its merits. The UK has been described as 'on the rim of Europe' and 'a little out of the way'. This unfamiliar perspective is important: the UK must demonstrate clear business advantages.

► 'Corridors' of business development have grown alongside specific motorway links e.g. the M4 corridor between London and Bristol.

2 *Markets*

In manufacturing, shorter distances between a firm and its market reduces transport costs and better enables the business to understand and service the needs of its customers. Increasing market orientation highlights the sharpened need for market intelligence and research – and the efficient transmission of the marketing mix. Closeness to **markets** allows exploitation of informed communication channels with customers, increases personal contact, and assists after-sales service. Many service industries have to locate very close to their target markets.

3 *Transport*

Transport involves customer and staff as well as supplies and distribution. Firms will aim to minimize the cost of transport in terms of money and time. The transport infrastructure is therefore of great importance. For many firms this means connections to the motorway network. Airports, seaports and rail services may also be highly relevant. Despite strong government incentives, it has proved very difficult to attract firms into remote regions such as Cornwall, west Wales or north-west Scotland. Links into Europe are growing in importance, with corresponding advantages for eastern and south east England. The Channel Tunnel (opening 1993/4) will probably intensify this problem.

4 *Rents and Rates*

Rents and land prices are a major cost factor for many firms. Demand and supply mean that the most preferred locations carry the highest costs. For example, in 1992 industrial rents per square foot were around £12 in London, around £10 in the south-east of England, yet only £2.50 in mid-Wales. The new **business rate** has meant that local authority rates are now standardized across the country. This change caused some sharp increases, especially in the south of England

5 *Labour*

All firms employ **labour**: in many firms this is the most important resource and the largest source of costs. An adequate supply of labour with the necessary skills is essential. For example the motor industry still needs a large engineering-based manual labour force. Local education and training facilities may be important. Salary and wage rates vary widely on a regional basis, tending to be highest in London and lowest in areas of high unemployment. Employers will also be attracted by a harmonious industrial relations record, while a background of union militancy could be discouraging.

6 *Infrastructures*

Firms need electricity, gas and water services, road connections, drainage, waste disposal systems, legal and financial services etc. These elements in the business **infrastructure** vary in availability and cost. City centres with their concentration of professional, financial and office services are attractive to many service industries. For manufacturing and distribution, out of town sites are often preferred.

Here there is better motorway or trunk road access, with industrial estates or business parks where many key services are already provided.

7 *Concentration and Inertia*

Many industries become localized, i.e. concentrated in one locality. For example the ceramics industry is concentrated around Stoke-on-Trent. This **concentration** provides a wide range of external economies of scale (see Chapter 15) as allied industries develop in the same area. These might include specialist transport and trading facilities, training services, suppliers of equipment and users of by-products. Industrial **inertia** occurs when firms remain in an area after the original location factors have ceased to be relevant. This may make good business sense if the costs of relocation exceed the likely benefits.

8 *Government Policy*

From 1945–79 the UK government took a major role in influencing industrial location. It aimed to reduce regional unemployment problems and to prevent excessive urban congestion. Public sector location decisions were directly affected and private sector industrial developments were prohibited in some areas and strongly encouraged in others. Since 1980 the government has placed greater emphasis on market forces. However there are still many governmental influences on business location. Since 1946 governments have pro-Scotland, Wales and the west country, plus the industrial West Midlands.

► There is some evidence that the 'Assisted Areas' policy has not been a cost-effective means of creating new employment. The emphasis now is on selective rather than automatic aid, and the creation of new jobs that would not otherwise have existed.

Figure 12.1

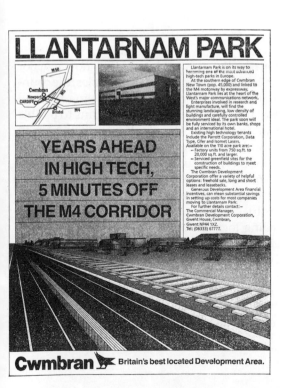

Firms in all assisted areas qualify for **'regional selective assistance'**. This provides project grants made according to costs or jobs created and training grants related to new investment. This aid is now selective, and is supplied at the minimum level necessary for a particular business project to go ahead.

The Department of Trade and Industry also develops industrial estates in assisted areas, which are then let to incoming firms on subsidized terms. Both the UK government and the European Community's 'Regional Fund' direct resources into assisted areas for improvements to the infrastructure: e.g. road or bridge building. Finally, many local councils have active business development policies with their own advertising and advisory services to attract firms.

Since 1945 new and expanded towns have been established by the government, either to accommodate population movements out of the largest cities, or to revitalize assisted areas. Substantial amounts of land and infrastructure for business have been provided as part of each development. The new city of Milton Keynes was the largest project, but the programme is now effectively complete.

9 *Management Factors*

Rarely do firms make a location decision without some prior commitments. A new project may be constrained in location by the firm's existing facilities, e.g. warehouses or depots. The degree of decentralization will affect the willingness of managements to see departments or divisions at a longer distance from headquarters. There are significant indirect costs in relocation which arise in terms of general upheaval, interruption to production, inconvenience to customers etc. Time is also important. A firm may select a site simply because it is available sooner.

10 *The Environment*

A favourable **environment** for the firm, and its staff, is now a major locational factor. Cultural, leisure and educational facilities, the countryside, the housing situation and the quality of shopping have all grown in perceived importance. It is usually vital for firms to be able to retain their key staff in any move. The result has often been to favour the southern half of England and cities with a 'good image', such as Bristol. The university, cathedral and market towns are generally enjoying new popularity (e.g. Cambridge and Exeter). Some cities may also be considered to carry higher prestige (e.g. central London, Edinburgh).

Decision making regarding location carries real costs. The factors are complex, and management may accept an existing or sub-optimal location to avoid excessive expense. Management does not in practice seek to optimize every factor within its control. Often it will be content to maintain a 'reasonable' solution ('satisficing'). Thus its location is not under constant review, but often must be shown to be **unsatisfactory** before any change is likely.

► Many firms are undergoing managerial change as centralized 'organizational cities' break down into 'organizational villages': becoming more federal in organization, with less emphasis on single location decisions, and instead a more plural, diverse picture as different functions are split across a wide range of optimal locations.

Primary Products Ltd uses plastic injection moulding to make a wide range of accessories for young children. These include toys, educational games and playroom furnishings. At present the firm is based in a converted warehouse on a cramped site in south London. The combination of inadequate floor-space, rising rents and local traffic congestion has prompted management to consider a major relocation to a new business unit with an office and manufacturing space at Llantarnam Park in south Wales (see p. 91).

What further information about this proposed location would be required by:

a) the marketing manager
b) the production manager
c) the personnel manager?

Summary and comment

- the decline of the traditional heavy industries (e.g. coal, steel, shipbuilding, textiles, railways) located on coalfields or close to ports has been very significant since 1945. The areas affected are beginning to develop a more diversified industrial base and a larger service economy, but major problems remain
- London continues to act as a hub for the national economy; its reputation as a leading world financial centre is a powerful factor. Although many firms have left London to avoid its congestion and high cost structures, its importance as a market and as a capital city will remain. In addition the development of the 'Docklands' is one of the most dramatic business projects in Europe
- locational forces have become more volatile. The decline of heavy manufacturing, the growth of low bulk and weight industries and the expansion of the tertiary sector have all made business more 'footloose', or unattached to any one area or locational factor
- the growth of electronic communications may reduce the importance of central facilities as firms become more scattered by function and less dependent on any specific location. An increasing number of staff are becoming able to work from home, using electronic media including on-line computer and facsimile machines - a phenomenon called 'tele-commuting' or 'tele-working'
- transport is a vital influence. The motorway corridors reflect this priority, and European links are a growing factor
- the availability of technical expertise and the closeness of universities and research institutions is important to the main 'sunrise' hi-tech industries
- the issue of environmental quality has risen strongly as a priority. This is always stressed in the marketing of a business location

- the 'Business Park' and 'Science Campus' are offering attractive, carefully managed locations for firms in the light manufacturing, hi-tech and service sectors. Emphasis is placed on a high quality environment with a wide range of on-site facilities such as hotels, conference suites, landscaping and security
- local councils and public agencies (e.g. the Welsh Development Agency) have played an important part in attracting firms to their areas. Some towns have marketed themselves aggressively towards UK and foreign firms, often with impressive results
- foreign investment in the UK increased sharply from the 1980s, especially by Japanese, American and German firms. Low land and labour costs and good transport links have been key locational factors.

Production systems

Chapter objectives

After working through this chapter, you will:

■ know the basic types of production

■ understand process and product layout

■ be able to evaluate the forces acting on production management

■ know the meaning of the following key terms: job, batch and flow production.

PRODUCTION TYPES

A firm must decide on the type of production process most suited to its needs. This will affect the types of staff to be employed, the kinds of machinery and equipment required, and the physical layout of the production process in the space available. These decisions do not only affect manufacturing firms. Service industries (e.g. banking, tourism) also have a production process – which may involve paper-work, person-to-person conversation or the use of information technology.

There are three basic production types:

1 Job production
Work is to individual customer order: each product is a one-off.

2 Batch production
Output is in batches, where products pass through each production stage as a group.

3 Flow production
Continuous standardized output is achieved using a specialized production line.

The differences are best illustrated using a simple example:

► The choice of production type depends on the nature of the market.

Cake Making by Job, Batch and Flow Production

Three firms (A, B and C) make cakes in the same town.

Firm A (job production) takes individual orders for wedding cakes and cakes for special occasions. It works from small premises in the town centre with one kitchen and a small office. All the staff are highly skilled, but some are only part-time. Each order is produced separately, with about a dozen orders in progress at one time. The kitchen is crowded with equipment and utensils: these are used as and when required.

Firm B (batch production) is a local bakery which operates from a small modern industrial estate at the edge of the town. They receive regular orders for batches of the different kinds of cakes that they offer. Some staff are skilled, but others are only semi-skilled. Orders are processed in batches of up to 200 cakes at a time. The equipment is arranged by process: food mixers, ovens, icing equipment etc.

Firm C (flow production) is a large factory owned by a public limited company. Its new plant is on a major industrial estate. Cakes are produced to an exact specification on a continuous basis, and output is distributed nation-wide by a fleet of trucks. The workforce are semi-skilled or unskilled, and work on a shift system. Each stage of production has been broken down into simple operations, and there is a separate production line for each type of cake. The costly machinery for each production stage is in constant use.

 Set up a three column table with the columns headed 'Job','Batch' and 'Flow' production. Give a brief description of each. As you read on note down why each of the three cake making firms noted above might have chosen their mode of production.

Job Production

▶ Job production usually relates to highly specific or individual markets.

Job production is found in small-scale services and manufacturing, as well as in major projects such as road and bridge building. Each piece of work is different and to the customer's specification. The firm may be working on a variety of jobs at once, but each one is likely to be at a different stage. Tools and equipment are used irregularly and for a variety of purposes. The layout in the production area is usually fairly informal. Staff need to be skilled and adaptable, often working on their own initiative. Higher pay rates and the use of quality materials may push up costs, but overhead costs such as machinery tend to be lower.

Batch Production

▶ Batch production is often used where a wide product range is necessary or when demand is very variable.

This is typically applied to the manufacture of books and clothes, while production of package holidays has similar characteristics in a service industry. Sufficient demand must exist for output to be in batches or groups of products. The units in each batch pass through each production stage together. Batches are often to varying specifications, and work on a number of batches may be in progress at any one time. Plant and equipment will be more expensive, more specialized, but fairly adaptable. It will be more fully and more productively used through careful management planning. Machinery is likely to be grouped by process: for instance all cutting machines placed together. The workforce will be moderately skilled, their jobs being fairly specialized but still flexible. Overall costs tend to be reduced through more efficient use of resources.

Flow Production

This is essential in the modern production of chemicals, oil, paper, cars, electrical goods, processed foods and many other key industrial and consumer products. Flow production developed in the USA during the 1920s, and has spread all over the world as the basis of cheap mass-produced standard goods. A very large, stable and long-term market for the product is essential. Output is a continuous flow, and includes a narrow range of standardized products. Wherever possible processes are mechanized or automated using costly machines designed for a specific use. These will be arranged according to the planned sequence of processes, forming a production line. The workforce is also highly specialized, using maximum **division of labour**. Tasks are likely to be repetitive, and many workers are semi-skilled or unskilled. Efficiency in flow production demands synchronization and coordination between processes to avoid 'bottlenecks' where queues of semi-finished goods build up. The numbers of machines relative to their speed must be matched, and **work study** is used to predict accurately the time taken by workers for each task. It is vital that all stocks are reliable in their availability, and that breakdowns are minimized by preventative maintenance. Unit costs can be dramatically reduced by bulk materials purchasing and the spreading of overhead costs (e.g. machinery) across very large outputs.

► Flow production is normally best suited to mass markets with constant high levels of demand.

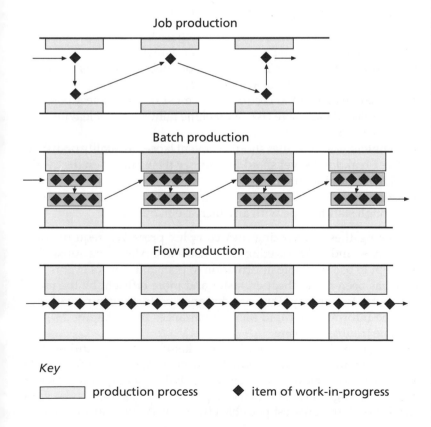

Job production

Batch production

Flow production

Key

production process   ◆ item of work-in-progress

Figure 13.1
Production layouts for job, batch and flow production

Production layout

The physical layout of production facilities must reflect the type of production. The best configuration of machines and equipment in a limited space will achieve the smoothest and fastest movement of work-in-progress between the stages of production.

Process layout means grouping together the equipment for each process. This pattern is usually applied to job and batch production. Products or product batches can move between processes in a variety of sequences, and the workload can be planned for maximum plant utilization.

Product layout means arranging equipment to form a continuous 'line' specially designed for each product type. For flow production this allows the application of division of labour principles and specialized machinery. Work-in-progress forms a continuously moving flow down each product line, giving very high plant utilization.

PRODUCTION MANAGEMENT

The production manager is responsible for organizing that precise transformation of resources that represents the firm's product, and hence its sales. The bulk of a manufacturing firm's costs arise from its production process, as does an even higher proportion of the final consumer satisfaction. This is reflected in the constant weighing of costs and benefits in production decisions:

- production materials should be purchased at the lowest cost, yet the specification must meet customer demands
- sufficient stocks must be held to avoid delivery delays, yet stock holding should always be minimized
- utilization of plant and equipment must be the highest possible, but without excessive risk of machine failure, whilst leaving adequate spare capacity
- maintenance schedules should prevent lapses in quality or disruptive breakdowns, yet should minimize their impact on the availability of production facilities
- labour productivity should be maximized, but there must be enough staff to cope with any increase in output.

Balancing these competing and complex pressures requires clear objectives and a knowledge of constraints. Managers must then attempt to use available information to plan and control events. The task has been made cheaper, faster and more efficient by the use of computer technology. Purpose-designed software can provide full on-line information, rapid alert to variances (see Chapter 23), and flexible trouble shooting.

Production planning should be market-led. The quantities of resources required for each product must be related to capacity and the implications of relevant delivery dates. Flows of output can then be routed through their necessary stages to meet the demands of the market with the greatest possible efficiency. As the starting date for

► Close communication between the production and marketing departments within a firm is essential in matching supply and demand.

each work schedule approaches, instructions regarding materials, manpower and machine usage are issued (this is called dispatching). The progress of each order must be monitored as it passes through successive production stages. Staff called **progress chasers** may be responsible for ensuring that actual events correspond with the schedule.

 Make notes on production planning, using the production and delivery of a training course as an example. Remember that producing leaflets and hand-outs is also a production process.

 Enter ticks in the boxes below to indicate the most appropriate type of production for the business activities listed:

Business activity	Job	Batch	Flow
production of gourmet blue cheese on Dorset farm			
light bulb production for domestic market			
printing books on gardening			
estate agency			
package holiday operation			
shipbuilding			

What are the most critical factors that determine the optimum type of production?

Summary and comment

• in practice firms may combine production types, for instance job/batch, or batch/flow. This can occur in various ways. Two separate processes may operate under one roof. Alternatively a 'basic' product may be manufactured using flow production, and then finished in batches to satisfy particular markets. Or batches may be matched, to use capacity on a flow system

• the boundaries between job, batch and flow are tending to become more blurred. New technology is making machinery far more flexible in its application. The traditional production line is becoming less rigid with its capacity tending to 'soften'. CAD/ CAM (computer aided design and manufacturing) systems and automatic multi-purpose tools combined with faster machine settings are all assisting this trend. Already 'limited editions' and 'customization' are becoming simpler and less costly

- the **mass markets** of the twentieth century are becoming more discerning, less predictable, and less homogeneous (see Chapter 5). They are tending to fragment into many different market segments, so that flow production systems must attempt to meet the different needs of segments and niches in the structure of demand
- in some firms there can be a danger of separate 'production' and 'marketing' cultures developing, with the respective managers seeming to be on opposite sides. Production managers can lose sight of the customer and the market, while marketing managers lack contact with the realities of production. Much depends on effective communications, senior management teamwork, and the quality of strategic leadership.

(14) Cost elements and breakeven analysis

Chapter objectives

After working through this chapter, you will:

▌know the sources of business cost

▌understand the differences between variable, fixed, total and average costs

▌appreciate the concept of opportunity cost and recognize its business relevance

▌know how to draw a breakeven chart

▌be able to manipulate a breakeven chart and solve simple problems

▌understand the arithmetic method of determining breakeven output

▌be able to evaluate the limitations and strengths of breakeven analysis

▌understand the concept of marginal cost

▌know how to draw up a contribution statement

▌be able to apply the concept to business problems and recognize its limitations

▌know the meaning of the following key terms: direct and indirect costs, overheads, fixed, variable and semi-variable costs, total cost, average cost, opportunity cost, breakeven analysis, break- even point, margin of safety, profit-volume analysis, marginal cost, contribution costing.

WHAT ARE BUSINESS COSTS?

A **cost** arises from the consumption of any resource that has a price. The use of a resource that was in unlimited supply with no transport requirement would have no cost. In practice, virtually every ingredient of a business enterprise carries a cost. The task of management is to combine resources in such a way that their cost is exceeded by their market value. The measure of success is profit.

Timber Traditions Ltd operate from a country town industrial estate. Their business is the manufacture of specialist timber window frames and doors for local builders and private customers. The company accounts list the main costs incurred throughout a year's operations:

► Sales revenue minus costs equals profit.

A	B	C

materials
wages
   (for production
   staff)
	power
	maintenance
	marketing
	administration
		salaries
		   (for managers
		   and office staff)
		rent
		rates
		insurance
		depreciation

There are two important observations to be made about these costs:

- only materials and wages (box A) are actually related to physical manufacturing. The other costs (boxes B and C) are all necessary to the business, but are only indirectly related to the actual product
- the costs in box A will vary in proportion to output. The costs in box B will vary to some extent with output, but not on a proportional basis. The costs in box C are fixed, and will not vary in any way with output.

Direct and Indirect Costs

Accounting in a firm shows the resources in use at a given time, and the flow of resources leaving (costs) and entering (revenue) the business (see Chapter 17). The recording and analysis of costs is a crucial part of an accountant's work.

All costs that can be related to a particular product are called **direct costs**. These include:

- **direct materials**: those raw materials and components used in making the product itself
- **direct labour**: all work involved in making the specific product
- **direct expenses**: any other services required exclusively for output of the product, e.g. design fees or equipment hire charges.

All other costs within the firm are called **indirect costs**, because they do not relate directly to the particular physical product. These are the background business costs – or **overheads** – that are not always obvious.

Indirect costs are also split between:

- **indirect materials**: all goods consumed in the firm apart from materials for production, e.g. machine parts, cleaning materials, office stationary
- **indirect labour**: wages and salaries of supervisors, maintenance and security staff, office personnel, sales teams and management
- **indirect expenses**: all other overhead costs including rent, rates, heating, lighting, insurance and depreciation.

The sum of direct and indirect (or prime and overhead) costs is the **total cost**.

This cost breakdown is valuable for accounting purposes in helping to calculate the cost of a particular product, and in reaching pricing decisions. It also corresponds with the logic of the 'profit and loss account' (see Chapter 19).

► The total direct cost is often called the **prime cost**.

► Indirect costs are sometimes called overheads.

► Total Cost: the sum of direct and indirect costs.

Direct and Indirect Costs

Coffee and a cake

A customer sits down in a café with a cup of coffee and a small cake. The bill is £1.50. How can coffee and a cake possibly cost so much? The customer may comment that they could serve the same items at home for less than 30p. But the bill was not literally for coffee and a cake. The cost of direct materials is certainly small. Even the cost of direct labour and direct expenses may be modest. But the customer is surrounded by indirect costs. The wear and tear on the furniture and fittings; lighting and heating; maintenance and repairs; insurances; office expenses; cleaning expenses; rents and rates; publicity: it is these costs, plus a profit margin, that make the bill £1.50. The customer may even be getting good value?

Variable and Fixed Costs

So far we have analysed costs in their relationship to the product itself. We will now look at the behaviour of costs relative to the level of output. To illustrate this we will use the following data:

output (units)	total fixed cost (£k)	total variable cost (£k)	total cost (£k)	average cost (£k)
0	200	0	200	∞
1	200	80	280	280
2	200	160	360	180
3	200	240	440	147
4	200	320	520	130
5	200	400	600	120
6	200	480	680	113
7	200	560	760	109
8	200	640	840	105
9	200	720	920	102
10	200	800	1 000	100

► These values are graphed in Figure 14.1 and Figure 14.2.

Variable costs (VC) are those that vary in an approximately direct relationship to output. Direct materials and labour are the major examples. For instance a twenty-five per cent increase in output by a firm making garden seats will cause a 25% increase in timber usage and a twenty-five per cent increase in direct labour costs. As shown in the data above, every time output is doubled, variable costs are doubled. These costs are represented on a graph as a straight line in relation to output: see VC in Figure 14.1. In the short run, capacity (maximum output) is fixed.

Fixed costs (FC) are those that do not vary with output. They include such items as rent, rates, insurance and depreciation. On a graph they form a line parallel to the output axis – the line FC on Figure 14.1.

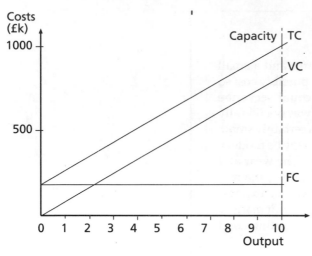

Figure 14.1
Fixed variable and total costs

Notice that the total cost line always starts from the
platform of fixed costs, and not from the origin; at all
points, TC = VC + FC.

Figure 14.2
Average costs: total costs divided by output

Notice that the curve does not touch the cost axis since it
is meaningless to calculate average costs for zero output
– the value would be infinity; the average cost curve is
downward-sloping because the fixed costs are being
spread over a progressively greater output.

Semi-variable costs are those that vary with output on a non-proportional basis. These are likely to embrace maintenance, heating, lighting and administrative costs and marketing expenses. Within a narrow range of output there may well be little change in semi-variable costs. However as certain output levels are reached, increases in these costs will occur. For example an extra maintenance crew will be needed, extra office staff will become necessary, or additional sales representatives must be recruited. In graphical terms, the result will be a roughly stepped pattern.

In practice, most semi-variable costs are composite, including both a fixed and a variable element. For instance electricity carries a standing charge plus a variable rate for usage. In Figure 14.1 the variable parts of semi-variable costs have been included with variable costs, and the fixed parts of semi-variable costs with fixed costs.

Total cost (TC) is the sum of all these three above mentioned cost elements (see TC in Figure 14.1).

Average cost (AC – see Figure 14.2) is simply total cost divided by the level of output. This relationship forms a downward-sloping curve of declining gradient.

 Make notes to define and illustrate variable, fixed, total and average costs in relation to output. Invent your own data for drawing these in graph form.

Business Costs in Practice

Figures 14.1 and 14.2 assume that cost and output relationships are linear. In practice this is highly unlikely. Variable costs will probably be higher at very low output levels due to the expense of small materials orders and inefficient use of labour. Equally, variable costs tend to rise as capacity is approached, when the matching of labour with machinery becomes less efficient, and overtime rates of pay may be necessary. In addition the variable element in the semi-variable costs is likely to follow the same pattern. For example the maintenance costs in a factory may rise sharply when equipment is being used at peak output. The diagram (14.3) below shows a more realistic picture of a firm's cost structure.

This pattern has important implications for the firm's average cost curve (see Figure 14.4).

Partly in view of this last point, many firms choose to operate at around eighty to ninety per cent of capacity. In addition it is often advantageous to hold spare capacity to meet fluctuations in demand, or a sudden but valuable order.

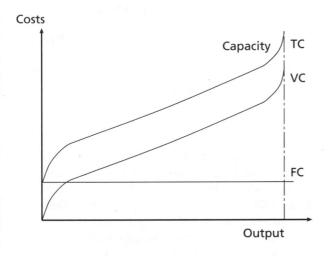

It is important to remember that the above situation relates to the **short run**, i.e. the period over which capacity is fixed. In the **long run**, capacity can be expanded, and a new AC curve may offer a lower minimum average cost. This is caused by economies of scale (see Chapter 15).

 Make a copy of Figure 14.3 to add to the graphs you have already drawn. Annotate it to show that in practice the earlier calculations are unlikely to fit reality. Explain why firms often choose to run below maximum capacity.

Figure 14.3
A more realistic picture of variable and total costs

Notice that the initial fall in AC is steeper due to higher variable cost rates at a low output; the trend is still downwards until around eighty per cent capacity is reached because the fixed costs are spread over a greater output; the gentle rise in average cost towards capacity is caused by the high variable costs across this output range; the lowest average cost (OC) is achieved short of 100 per cent capacity at OQ.

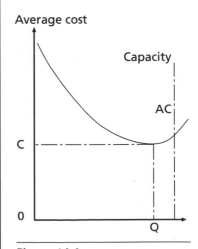

Figure 14.4

Strawberry or vanilla?
You are offered an ice-cream: strawberry or vanilla? You choose strawberry. Since vanilla was your second preference, the satisfaction expected from the vanilla ice-cream is the opportunity cost of choosing strawberry.

Opportunity Cost

Life – and business – are about choice. Choice means having more than one option. The act of choosing means selecting one option and rejecting the others. A rational choice is defined as selecting the option expected to yield the greatest satisfaction. The satisfaction which would be offered by the next best choice is the **opportunity cost** in any decision.

When a choice is difficult, it means that the opportunity cost is relatively high. We can be uncomfortably aware of this when we make a choice by the smallest of margins. The presence of the second-best choice in our imagination can actually spoil our first choice!

The concept of opportunity cost translates into financial terms.

Opportunity Cost of a Car

Two sisters each receive a gift of £10 000 from an elderly relative. The first sister buys a car with the money. The second sister decides to save hers. What is the difference in their assets after one year? The first sister has lost £2 000 in depreciation, as her car is now valued at £8 000. Disregarding running costs, has her choice of a car carried any other cost? The second sister does not still have £10 000: with the interest rate at ten per cent, she now has £11 000. So the first sister has suffered an opportunity cost of £1 000 through rejecting the choice of investing the money. Opportunity cost is very real. In calculating the true cost of running a car, it must be included.

It is the same for a business. A firm may be deciding how to invest £50 000. For this sum they can either replace their old and outdated machinery or build a new office. If they select the office, then the opportunity cost will be experienced in more machine breakdowns, higher labour costs or lower product quality. It follows that management must monitor opportunity costs carefully, and be ready to make a new decision when opportunity cost exceeds the benefits of an existing choice.

 Use the following three headings to classify the costs of running a three year old Ford Escort for one year:

1 Variable costs.
2 Semi-variable costs.
3 Fixed costs.

Costs to Consider:
- repairs, tyres, oil
- depreciation
- AA membership
- insurance
- MOT
- servicing
- road tax
- petrol
- parking
- opportunity costs of capital tied up.

You could then calculate the total cost of running the car over an average 12 000 miles in one year. The result may seem surprizing....

BREAKEVEN ANALYSIS

Constructing a Breakeven Chart

Total revenue = price × volume of sales

Total cost = average cost per unit × volume of output

Thus price/volume and cost/volume are the two key relationships that will determine final profitability. Neither alone is decisive: it is their interaction that managers must analyse.

In order to make this analysis we will make the assumption that all output is sold. As sales increase, so will total revenue. Equally, as output increases, so will total costs. While zero sales means zero revenue, zero output does not mean zero costs. The minimum cost level for any firm is the level of fixed costs. Total costs increase with output from this cost base. Thus no profit can be made by the firm until total revenue 'catches up' with total costs. A simple diagram illustrates the position. Total revenue = TR, total cost = TC, variable costs = VC and fixed costs = FC.

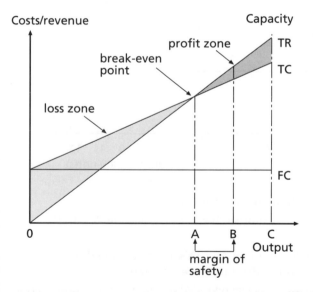

▶The total revenue line starts from the origin, and given a constant price at all levels of output, it must be linear and upward-sloping.

Until output OA is reached, the firm would be making a loss (TC > TR). At output OA, TC exactly equals TR, and the firm is therefore **breaking even**.

Figure 14.5 *Basic breakeven model*

The graphical intersection point on the graph is called the **breakeven point**, and the whole diagram is known as a **breakeven chart**. At output levels beyond OA, a profit is being made, and this increases towards maximum capacity OC, as shown in the profit zone.

Suppose the firm is actually operating at about eighty-five per cent capacity (at OB above). Clearly a profit is being made, but if output were to fall to any level below OA, this would lead to losses. The output range AB is therefore the firm's **margin of safety**.

Breakeven Analysis

Tubular Chairs Ltd

This recently established business produces very modern seating made from moulded plastic and tubular steel. The standardized product sells for £12.50 per unit to wholesalers. The firm's present sales are running at around 9 600 chairs per month (eighty per cent capacity).

Costs per chair are as follows:

	(£)
variable costs: materials	3.50
labour	2.50

fixed costs amount to £52 000 per month.

We can now draw a breakeven chart to see the firm's profitability relative to output and sales. For clarity the variable cost line is dropped.

Figure 14.6
Breakeven chart for Tubular Chairs Ltd

Check carefully how the diagram is constructed:
the x-axis represents output, the y-axis costs and revenue (i.e. money flows).

Since sales are 9 600 units and this represents eighty per cent capacity, maximum output must be 12 000 units.

Fixed costs are given as £52 000, and marked as horizontal to the x-axis.

Total costs:
at zero output = FC which = £52 000.
at capacity output
$$= FC + VC = £52\,000(FC) + £72\,000(VC) = £124\,000(TC).$$

Total revenue:
at zero output and sales   = zero
at 12 000 units capacity output
and sales   = 12 000 × £12.50 (price)
                                  = £150 000.

The breakeven point is identified at the intersection of the TC and TR lines, and breakeven output is found to be 8 000 units.

The profit zone begins at the breakeven point and at the firm's present 9 600 units output and sales, profit is £10 400 (vertical distance ab). This can be simply checked:

TR = £120 000
TC = £52 000 + (9 600 × £6)
    = £109 600
Therefore profit = £10 400

The margin of safety   = present output – breakeven output
                        = 9 600 – 8 000 units
                        = 1 600 units.

Carden Coats Ltd manufacture waxed jackets in a small factory on the outskirts of Manchester. Their sole customer is a major UK chain store, which purchases 1 000 jackets each month. The factory's capacity is 1 250 per month. The company charges the chain store £40 per jacket.

Fixed costs per month are:		The manufacture of each jacket costs:	
rent	2 400	materials	£12.00
rates	800	labour	£13.00
salaries	5 000		
other	800		

Tasks:

1 Construct a breakeven chart from the data given.

2 a) What is the present level of profit per month?
   b) What is the breakeven output?
   c) What is the margin of safety at the present level of sales?

Using the Breakeven Chart

The chart does not merely illustrate the firm's existing position. It can be used to explore changes in any of the three key variables: 1 sales volume, 2 costs, 3 price.

► Computers greatly assist in manipulating a break-even chart.

1 **Sales volume**
   The impact of changes in sales volume is clear from the chart for Tubular Chairs. Any fall in sales below 8 000 units will cause losses. A rise in sales to capacity output would increase profits to £26 000. Notice that a ten per cent fall in volume to 8 640 units causes a sixty per cent fall in profits to £4 160.

2 **Costs**

Suppose that variable costs increased from £6 to £7.50 per unit.

► Output and sales at 9 600 units is now below the new breakeven point (10 400 units). The firm makes a loss of £4 000 (TR = £120 000, TC = £124 000)

Figure 14.7:
Breakeven chart for Tubular Chairs Ltd: 2

Alternatively, with the original variable cost and price, suppose there was a fall in fixed costs to £39 000 per month.

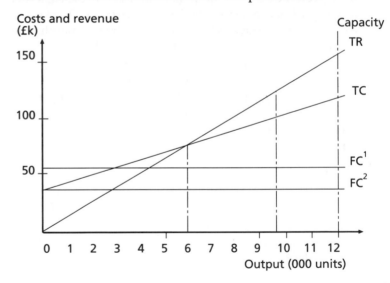

► Output and sales at 9 600 units now yield a profit of £23 400 (up 125%), while the breakeven point has fallen to 6 000 units.

Figure 14.8:
Breakeven chart for Tubular Chairs Ltd: 3

3 **Price**

Finally, with original cost and price data, say there was a fall in price obtainable from £12.50 to £11.

Sales of 9 600 units now yield only £105 600, while TC = £109 600. The loss of £4 000 is the same outcome as that caused by the rise in variable costs (above).

Figure 14.9:
Breakeven chart for Tubular Chairs Ltd: 4

Calculating the Breakeven Point

The breakeven point can be calculated exactly using the formula:

$$\text{breakeven point} = \frac{\text{fixed costs}}{(\text{price} - \text{variable cost per unit})}$$

$$= \frac{\text{fixed costs}}{(\text{contribution per unit})}$$

For Tubular Chairs Ltd:
breakeven point

$$= \frac{£52\,000}{(£12.50 - £6)} = 8\,000 \text{ units.}$$

 Return to your breakeven chart for Carden Coats Ltd.

1 Management is anxious to make use of the excess capacity, which represents unnecessary fixed costs. The board decide to accept the offer of a twenty per cent increase in order size, in return for a reduction in selling price from £40 to £38 per jacket. Evaluate this decision with reference to your breakeven chart.

2 Another major retailer will purchase 600 jackets per month on a regular basis at this new price of £38. The firm has the opportunity to rent additional factory space, and for an increase in fixed costs to £18 000 per month, capacity can be doubled to 2 500 jackets a month. Assess the advantages and disadvantages of this plan, and recommend a decision.

3 If the plan were to be adopted, investigate the effects of:

a) a ten per cent rise in variable material and labour costs

b) a third contract to supply a further 600 jackets at the same price.

Against output is plotted loss and profit as an outcome. This is an alternative presentation of the loss and profit zones shown in the breakeven chart. At zero output the loss is the entire fixed overhead expense (£52 000).

The loss diminishes with output because the sales revenue (SR) yielded by each unit exceeds its variable cost, progressively 'paying off' the fixed costs
(SR £12.50 – VC £6 = £6.50
                                surplus).

Zero profit or loss (i.e. breakeven) is reached at 8 000 units, and thereafter profit increases with output to reach maximum level (£26 000) at capacity.

Figure 14.10:
Profit-volume chart for Tubular Chairs Ltd

Profit-Volume Chart

Tubular Chairs Ltd could also express their costs and revenue relationship on a single profit-volume chart:

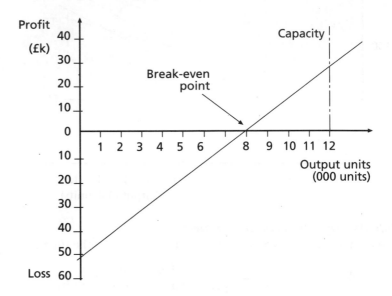

CONTRIBUTION COSTING

Marginal Cost

The cost of producing an item depends on how many are produced. Reducing output means that fixed overheads become a proportionately larger burden and average cost per unit rises. In the most extreme case, if a firm making shoes made only one pair per month then the cost of that pair of shoes would be the cost of the entire rent, rates and other overheads. **Marginal costs** mean the extra cost of producing an extra item.

Marginal Costs

Sprint Footwear Ltd manufactures a single product, running shoes, in one factory. The maximum output (capacity) is 1 000 pairs a month. Costs are as follows:

	£
variable costs per pair of shoes:	
materials	8.50
labour	11.50
	20.00

fixed overheads: £8 000 per month
selling price: £35 per pair

How much does each pair cost the firm to manufacture? In this form the question is unanswerable. Suppose the firm produces at capacity – 1 000 pairs per month:

variable costs £20 × 1 000	=	20 000	
fixed overheads	=	8 000	
total cost	=	28 000	

Therefore each pair costs $\dfrac{£28\ 000}{1\ 000}$ = £28

But suppose the firm is working at fifty per cent of capacity: then

variable costs £20 × 500	=	10 000	
fixed overheads	=	8 000	
total cost	=	18 000	

Therefore each pair costs $\dfrac{£18\ 000}{500}$ = £36

Clearly the 'cost' of each pair depends entirely on the level of output. A reduction in output means that fixed overheads become a proportionally larger burden, and the average cost per unit rises accordingly. Indeed, in the most extreme case, if the firm made only one pair of shoes during the month, the cost would be £8 020!

To tackle this problem, we must bring in the concept of marginal cost (MC). As already mentioned, marginal cost refers to the extra cost incurred by producing one additional unit. So if the shoe factory was producing 800 pairs per month, its marginal cost would be the extra cost of producing an 801st pair. Since it makes no difference to fixed overheads whether the firm produces 800 or 801 pairs, it must follow that MC = £20. Often MC will be constant over a wide range of output, but it may ultimately take the form of a roughly U-shaped curve. In this example MC is always £20. But if the firm was to sell its entire output at £20 per pair, a heavy loss would occur, since the fixed overheads would not be covered. However if it sold one extra pair by special arrangement at £20, then no loss is incurred (all the other pairs sold at a higher price are covering the fixed overheads).

► Marginal cost: the extra cost of producing one extra item.

► On a factory visit, students may be given free samples that might be quite expensive in the shops. The cost to the firm is not the shop price, nor the average cost, but the marginal cost.

 Make notes on marginal cost by using the data for Sprint Footwear.

Contributions to Fixed Overheads

Given that the firm must pay its fixed overheads regardless of production or sales, it may be very useful for costing purposes to split fixed overheads from the variable costs (i.e. materials and wages for those involved in making the product) of production. Take first the sales revenue per unit sold for Sprint Footwear. Then subtract the marginal cost. What remains is called a **contribution** towards fixed overheads:

	(£)
sales revenue	35
marginal cost	20
contribution to FO	15

A breakeven chart shows contributions accumulating through successive sales until the breakeven point is reached, and profits begin to be made.

► Below break-even point, **contribution** is towards fixed overheads. Above break-even point, contribution is towards profit.

Figure 14.11:
Breakeven chart for Sprint Footwear

So if the firm works at eighty per cent of capacity (800 pairs per month), then its contribution costing statement will be:

sales revenue	28 000
marginal costs	16 000
contribution to FO	12 000
less fixed overheads	8 000
profit	4 000

Calculating Marginal Costing

Marginal costing takes the simple **revenue – cost = profit** formula, and by separating variable costs and fixed overheads, distinguishes two steps between sales revenue and profit:

> step 1   **sales revenue – variable costs   = contribution**
>
> step 2   **contribution – variable overheads = profit (or loss).**

Provided that sales revenue exceeds marginal cost, then a positive contribution is achieved (which may or may not yield a final profit). But if marginal cost exceeds sales revenue, then a loss is inevitable, and every unit produced can only add to losses.

Make notes on marginal costing using the data for Sprint Footwear, but assume it is working at seventy-five per cent capacity.

Contribution Costing and Business Decisions

Single Product Problems

Teign Textiles Ltd

A small Devon firm, Teign Textiles Ltd, makes 500 bedspreads each week at an average cost of £10, and with a selling price of £12.50. The factory's maximum output is 600 units per week. One morning the sales manager receives a special request from a new hotel for 100 bedspreads; unfortunately they can only offer £850 for the consignment. Should Teign Textiles accept the order?

At first glance the answer is clearly no. It would mean a price of £8.50 per bedspread, and the loss (selling price – unit cost) would be £1.50 on each one.

Consider now the following costing statement:

	(£)	(£)
variable costs (VC)		
wages	1 750	
materials	750	2 500
semi-variable costs		1 000
		3 500
add: fixed overheads		1 500
total		5 000

With output at 500 bedspreads per week, the unit cost is confirmed at £10.

This can be shown in a unit cost statement:

	(£)	(£)
VCs per bedspread:		
wages	3.50	
materials	1.50	5
semi-variable costs		2
		7
add: fixed overheads		3
total		10

► NB Assume that all semi-variable costs can readily be related to output, and therefore treated as variable.

It is now clear that a selling price of £8.50 will cover the marginal cost, and still leave a contribution of £1.50 towards fixed overheads. In the absence of any better proposition, the firm should accept the order. This is clear from the brief contribution cost statement overpage:

	Without hotel order		With hotel order	
	(£)	(£)	(£)	(£)
sales revenue		6 250		7 100
variable costs	2 500		3 000	
semi-variable costs	1 000	3 500	1 200	4 200
contribution		2 750		2 900
fixed overheads		1 500		1 500
profit		1 250		1 400

This principle of selling spare capacity at any price that yields a positive contribution is very valuable provided that the mainstream market continues to pay the full price.

 Make notes on selling spare capacity. But to make sure you understand the principle re-calculate the data for Teign Texiles as if the offer was for 150 bedspreads at £1 260 for the consignment.

Multiple Product Problems

Most firms produce a range of products that can be related to one set of fixed overheads. This range may refer to different sizes, colours, styles etc., or to a portfolio of distinct products. In order to find the marginal cost of one product, it is necessary to extract its component cost elements from each cost centre. A **cost centre** is any identifiable place or process where costs are incurred. So a machine, an office, a loading bay or a whole department could all be regarded as cost centres. Estimates may be necessary when deciding what proportion of costs at a given cost centre are attached to a particular product (e.g. marketing costs). Once costs have been assigned to each product, then the various contributions can be calculated.

► Small firms may charge all overheads according to a single yardstick, such as output level or direct labour cost.

Larger firms distinguish production overheads from administrative and selling overheads. These must be charged to separate cost centres.

Contribution Costing with Multiple Products

Peak Plastics Ltd makes plastic kitchen products, and its range includes washing-up bowls, plate racks and laundry baskets. Monthly output/sales and prices:

	output/sales (units)	price (£)
washing-up bowls	12 000	3
plate racks	8 000	5
laundry baskets	11 000	4

fixed overheads are £30 000 per month.

The latest month's results on a contribution basis are opposite:

	washing-up bowls (£)	(£)	plate racks (£)	(£)	laundry baskets (£)	(£)
sales revenue		36 000		40 000		44 000
variable costs						
materials	6 000		11 000		7 000	
labour	4 000		9 000		5 000	
semi-variable cost	7 000	17 000	13 000	33 000	9 000	21 000
contribution		19 000		7 000		23 000

	(£)
total contribution	49 000
fixed overheads	30 000
profit/loss	19 000

Notice the weak contribution of the plate racks. Indeed if each product were to share the fixed overheads on a roughly equal basis, then the plate racks become unprofitable:
contribution = £7 000, FO allocation = £10 000, loss = £3 000.

However any positive contribution is valuable in the absence of a better alternative: the plate racks are contributing to the burden of fixed overheads.

► Even a negative contribution does not necessarily mean that a product should be discontinued. The reasons for its losses must first be analysed. The product could be in the development stage of its product life cycle, with high costs and as yet low sales. Alternatively it might be moving beyond maturity and need an extension strategy (see Chapter 7). It could also be subject to a sudden but temporary cost rise or sales slump.

Make notes on contribution costing for multiple products using the data for Peak Plastics. Complete the picture for yourself by working out the effect of deleting plate racks from the product range and relying on the contribution to overheads by other products.

Clare's Café finds that over seventy-five per cent of its turnover arises from meals and snacks sold over an extended lunch-time period. At present the café is open from 10.00 a.m. until 10.00 p.m. However, takings in the evening have been disappointing, and Clare Haddon, the manager, is considering an earlier closing time at 6.00 p.m. As evidence to support this proposal she shows her partner the following information:

customers served after 6.00 p.m. average daily results

		(£)	(£)
sales			68.00
less costs	materials	28.50	
	labour × £5/hr	20.00	
	power	2.50	
	overheads	25.00	
	(apportioned by time)		76.00
profit/loss			(8)

Give your opinion, supported by the information above.

Summary and comment

- the distinction between fixed, semi-variable and variable costs is only meaningful in the short term: i.e. the period in which capacity is fixed. In the long run, fixed costs can be increased (e.g. extend the factory), reduced (e.g. shutdown a production line), or reduced to zero (close down and sell assets)
- although labour is classified as a variable cost, the firm may find that their direct wages bill is fairly constant relative to small variations in output. Harmonious labour relations do not allow for frequent changes in staff levels, and recruitment and training costs are better spent if a long-term permanent labour force is retained. In addition, staff morale and loyalty need to be safe-guarded
- costs are measured for a specific business purpose. Their classification depends on the nature of this purpose. The distinction between direct and indirect costs is the approach of an accountant who is concerned with budgets for costs and profit. The analysis of variable and fixed costs is the approach of a manager or economist who aims to show how costs behave over ranges of output. The different approaches reflect different uses for costing information
- simple linear cost models exist to illustrate a principle that is valid. Across limited output ranges they are often close to reality and very useful. Over wider ranges of output they can be highly unrealistic
- a cost structure is not static. Every cost exists in a dynamic market for resources, the price of which can change without warning. Budgets and cost assumptions must be capable of prompt adjustment as circumstances alter
- collecting cost data can be expensive, and the impression of accuracy can be deceptive. Managers must judge the level of accuracy that is realistic and cost effective. There is also the risk that managers at any level will under or overestimate costs to suit their own purposes: for instance, setting an 'easy' budget
- management accountants use a great variety of technical terms to describe costs. The definition of these terms can vary widely, and must always be checked precisely

Limitations of Breakeven Analysis

- the distinction between variable and fixed costs is in practice neither precise nor clear
- cost assumptions are unrealistic: variable cost will not increase exactly in proportion to output, while fixed costs may change over the range of output represented
- sale of all output at a constant price is unlikely. Higher sales may mean a lower price, and therefore the TR line would probably be curved

- the multi-product firm may not be able to isolate an accurate cost/revenue structure for one product
- the key variables – price, cost and volume – are unlikely to be independent and static, but more likely to be **interdependent and dynamic**
- data for the chart may be based on doubtful estimates, or become outdated

Advantages of Breakeven Analysis
- it clarifies the key relationship between costs and sales
- it focuses management attention on devising strategies for profitability
- it enables managers to explore a wide variety of business scenarios by manipulating elements of the chart
- the smaller the output range, the more realistic the chart becomes. Usually the firm is only concerned with small changes in the variables

Advantages of Contribution Costing
- splits direct costs and fixed overheads, so identifying the product's contribution towards overheads
- enables sales and pricing decisions to maximize final profit through reference to levels of contribution
- avoids any need to use estimates or opinions in allocation of fixed overheads between products. The method keeps to exact data

Dangers of Contribution Costing
- the temptation is to generate increased sales by making deep price cuts. Positive contributions may still be made, but total contributions may be inadequate when set against fixed overheads
- competitive acceptance of cut price business to fill unused capacity may undermine standard price markets, and lead to reduced profitability in the firm or industry
- the distinction between direct and fixed costs is often blurred (semi-variable costs are a problem), making some assumptions unreliable
- marginal cost data can be subject to frequent change. Fixed overheads may also increase abruptly. Thus contribution-based decisions can easily become unrealistic.

(15) *Scale of production*

Chapter objectives

After working through this chapter, you will:

▌ know how and why firms attempt to grow in size

▌ be able to analyse changes in cost structures caused by changes in scale

▌ recognize recent trends in scale economies/diseconomies

▌ understand the practical business context of scale economies

▌ know the meaning of the following key terms: economies and diseconomies of scale, long-run average cost (LRAC), minimum efficient scale (MES).

ECONOMIES OF SCALE AND LONG-RUN AVERAGE COSTS

► Large-scale production often reduces unit cost.

► The Bic Crystal ball-point pen, first launched in 1958, is a classic example of scale economies in action.

Reductions in cost caused by increasing the scale of production are called **economies of scale**. It is important to realize from the outset that reductions in average cost caused by increases in scale are quite distinct from any downward slope in the short-run average cost curve. While capacity is fixed, we are in the short run. Once capacity is expanded with a larger production line or a new and bigger factory, then we have entered the long run.

The size of a firm affects the efficiency of each business function and the organization as a whole. In addition to these **internal changes**, a number of large firms together will also generate an **external** impact on efficiency. The eight major scale economies are summarized below:

1 Production
Plant costs increase with scale more slowly than output. This phenomenon affects factory buildings, machines, and most equipment. **Plant utilization** is likely to be higher as scale increases. Costly specialized equipment becomes economic beyond a certain usage rate.
Raw materials and **components** can be purchased in bulk at lower unit prices. Special cost and delivery deals may be negotiated with suppliers.
Maintenance becomes more efficient with specialist maintenance teams and more accurate data concerning breakdown patterns and their causes.

2 Marketing

Finished goods (i.e. goods that have completed all stages of production) may be bulk-purchased at significant discounts. Expert buyers in larger firms obtain the best contracts.

Product development is costly and time-consuming. 'Research and development' and 'new product' departments become viable with increasing scale.

Promotion economies include cheaper advertising rates, national brands to support a full product range, higher productivity for sales teams, and falling unit costs for packaging.

Distribution becomes more efficient as fleet and bulk transport systems become justified and fully utilized.

3 Personnel

Recruitment of higher calibre staff is easier for the large firm with its wider career structure. Selection is more scientific.

Training and development for staff can be more extensive and sophisticated.

Pay and benefits can often be more generous enabling larger firms to attract and retain good staff.

4 Administration

Administrative overheads increase less than proportionally as output and sales increase. Staff and information technology can be more specialized and better used.

5 Finance

Raising finance is faster and easier for the large firm. Banks more readily grant long-term loans given the greater security. Access is gained to the London and international money markets. A public company can issue and expect to sell large blocks of additional shares. Interest rates on larger loans for major firms are lower, and close to the banks' base rate.

6 Management

Specialist managers can be employed in the larger firm to tackle key business functions and to offer specialized services such as management accounting and operations research (i.e. the analysis of practical problems to achieve optimum utilization of resources available).

Organizational structures can be built for optimum performance. A multi-divisional structure (for different product ranges, for instance) becomes practical, with its own business managers.

7 Entrepreneurial

Reduced risk is experienced through increasing scale. Bad decisions, downturns in the market or simple misfortune can be better absorbed by a larger firm.

Diversification into a range of products and markets also provides greater security and stability.

8 External

Concentration of industry means a clustering of firms in the same industry within a given geographical area. This often leads to the

► Economies of scale help to explain why two major firms – Unilever and Proctor & Gamble – dominate the UK soaps and detergents market.

development of a range of specialized local services e.g. education and training, banking, transport and warehousing. Skilled staff may move more easily between firms.

Suppliers and subcontractors are attracted to the area to provide accessible and compatible services. This is vital for modern integrated production systems and just-in-time stock control (see p 130).

By-products are more readily marketed.

DISECONOMIES OF SCALE

Increasing scale does not only bring greater efficiency. It also causes certain costs to increase disproportionately, and breeds special types of inefficiency. Generally these diseconomies are far outweighed by scale economies, but beyond a certain size they may dominate, and begin to drive up average cost.

The essential nature of scale diseconomies is managerial. The sources of inefficiency affect different organizations to different extents, and in different ways.

- **loss of coordination** can occur as the scale of operations increases. The close-knit structure of a small firm is lost, and departments can take on an independent life disconnected from corporate objectives

- **bureaucracy** means rules, procedures and paperwork to an exact and specified pattern. This ensures that all parts of the organization operate according to formal plans, but can also cause unnecessary delays and excessive administration

- **inflexibility** arises as management becomes increasingly rigid in its effort to maintain control. This is damaging to market orientation, and may prevent exploitation of smaller market segments and niches

- **motivation and morale** can decline with increasing scale, as the individual feels less directly involved in tasks, and less valued personally by the firm. Alienation may develop as staff feel distanced from their work, with a reduced sense of urgency or conviction

- **reduction in initiative and creativity** may occur as employees feel that following rules and instructions is more important than ideas or innovation. 'No one listens' may be the staff perception of management, so that creative thinking withers. Senior managers may become highly conservative, believing that their security depends on maintaining the **status quo**

- **poor communications** easily develop as a firm grows. Managers become remote from subordinates, and misunderstandings occur as messages become distorted through complex communication networks. Excessive delays are likely at bottlenecks in the communication system, while informal communication may degenerate into gossip, or an over-active 'grapevine'

- **slow responses** to change are typical of large ponderous organizations. Shifting markets, new technologies or increased competition

'The specific danger inherent in large scale organization is that its natural bias and tendency favour order at the expense of creative freedom' Fritz Schumacher (1973) in *Small is Beautiful,* Blond and Briggs London.

may prompt a response, but only after elaborate procedures have been followed and the initiative has been lost

- **over-staffing** develops as more supervisory layers of management are installed, and resistance to change prevents staffing levels from being altered to meet changed conditions. Highly graded jobs, that have outlived their usefulness, may remain
- **weak asset turnover ratio** (see Chapter 22) is often the result of investment in plant and equipment that has not been properly appraised. A large firm is liable to carry an excessive value in under-used assets, while a smaller leaner business achieves a higher turnover relative to its capital employed
- **waste** increases when staff feel diminished responsibility and accountability for their actions. Errors may cause major losses of materials or incur heavy charges, while any corrective action is slow and indecisive. Extravagance may increase as employees feel that 'the company can afford it'.

The Long-run Average Cost Curve

Economies and diseconomies of scale can be represented in the **long-run average cost curve (LRAC curve)** for the firm:

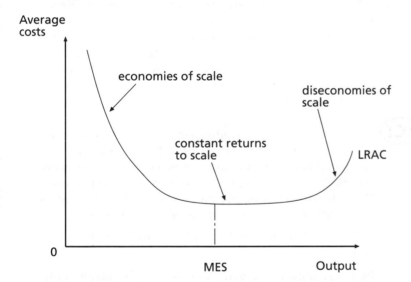

►While economies are greater than diseconomies, the curve is downward-sloping, and vice versa.

Figure 15.1
The long-run average cost curve

The shape of the LRAC curve for a firm is dynamic, and subject to important changes. These may affect new investment decisions and the competitive structure of the industry (see Chapter 27). For example, new technologies in production and information systems have pushed some LRAC curves downward with a steeper initial gradient.

Until the 1960s some firms were tending progressively to increase their scale of production in the pursuit of ever greater scale economies. This led some enterprises to face unexpected diseconomies during the 1970s, and since then the approach to scale economies has been more sophisticated. Different cost centres within the firm may face widely differing LRAC curves. Management must try to structure the

►**Minimum efficient scale (MES)**
is the smallest scale of production at which most or all economies of scale have been achieved; beyond MES no significant cost economies are gained, and diseconomies may set in. Any point on the curve has its own corresponding short-run cost structure covering the output range below that capacity.

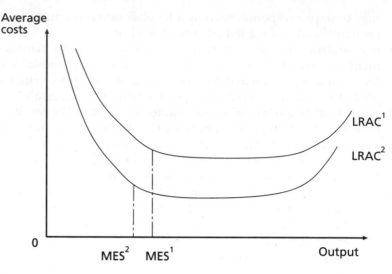

► New technology has made average cost lower at all capacity levels. On LRAC ^{2}, MES is reached before the output required on LRAC ^{1}; MES ^{2} implies that some smaller firms may now be successful in the market.

Figure 15.2
LRAC curve and new technology

organization so that each cost centre achieves maximum efficiency in terms of its scale.

The general fragmentation of markets in recent years has an interesting relationship with economies of scale. The demand for greater choice and individuality among products has combined with a partial shift up-market, and increased sales of luxuries and specialities. These trends have opened many new opportunities for economic smaller scale production. Simultaneously, new technology is making large scale production more flexible and better able to process batches of differing specification within a flow production system (see Chapter 13).

 Pennine Pencils began trading on a rural industrial estate in north Yorkshire at the start of 1984. Their initial capital employed was £120 000. In this first year, output was only 200 000 good quality pencils designed for specialist markets. Variable costs were 6p per unit while fixed costs amounted to £16 000. A profit of 6p per pencil was achieved.

1 What was the average cost and selling price of each pencil?

By 1986 capital employed had risen to £150 000 and output was up to 400 000 units with fixed costs reaching £28 000. Variable costs were constant but the firm cut their price to 18p per unit.

2 How has average cost and profit changed?

The firm then expanded rapidly and entered the mass market with major chain store contracts.

Key Data 1988–92

year	sales (million units)	unit price (pence)	variable cost per unit (pence)	total fixed costs (£k)	capital employed (£k)
1988	1	15	5	60	220
1990	3	12	5	120	400
1992	8	8	4	200	600

3 Sketch a graph to show average cost for the whole period 1984–92.

4 Suggest an explanation for the downward trend in:
   a)   average variable cost
   b)   average fixed cost.

5 Calculate the return on capital over the period.

Summary and comment

• the basic shape of the LRAC curve varies widely according to the industry and the firm. Some curves offer early economies and reach MES at quite low outputs. Others offer continuing net economies up to very high volumes
• net diseconomies of scale and a rising LRAC curve are primarily caused by managerial and human problems in the large organization. Their onset and severity often reflect more on the organization and its management than on scale alone.

▶ Small scale business can achieve valuable scale economies through franchising or joint purchasing and marketing agreements (e.g. an independent hotel within the 'Best Western' group).

(16) *Stock control*

STOCK CONTROL

All goods held by any firm that are **not** part of the permanent fixed assets (i.e. buildings, plant and equipment, fittings) are **stock**. The purpose of stock is to provide an immediate supply of all goods required in the chain of production and distribution. It provides a form of insurance:

- a demand for any item at any stage can be met without undue delay
- a failure in any source of supply will not interrupt the production process.

As part of the **working capital** (i.e. resources that circulate within the business), stock moves through the firm in a continuous cycle. Most stock is only held because it will form part of an eventual sale. As sales are realized, so stock circulates.

There are three main types of **product stock** held by firms:

- **raw materials and components** are the goods waiting to enter the firm's productive process
- **work-in-progress** means the semi-finished goods within the productive process at any given time
- **finished goods** are the completed goods awaiting sale and delivery to the customer.

▶ Most firms also hold **service stocks** which assist the production process: spare parts, lubricants, cleaning materials and office supplies. Their total value is only a small percentage of the value in product stocks.

▶ Stock is the necessary slack in a production system that creates supply to meet demand.

▶ Avoiding overstocking and understocking.

Stocks are resources with a money value. Although they circulate around the firm, their average value is a permanent use of resources. The use of any resource has a cost, which must be set against the corresponding benefit received. The purpose of stock control is to achieve an optimum balance between these costs and benefits.

To make notes on the benefits and costs of stockholding draw up a two column table: one column for benefits; one for costs.

Benefits of Stockholding

- **secure supplies** of raw materials and components are assured. Suppliers may be unreliable, while political or industrial troubles could disrupt deliveries
- **bulk purchase discounts** may be obtained by ordering in large quantities
- **production planning** is simplified if work-in-progress stocks are sufficient to overcome any imbalances between the throughputs of different processes
- **fluctuations in demand** can be absorbed without delays to the customer
- **customer choice** includes the full product range
- **immediate delivery** can follow all sales.

Costs of Stockholding

1 Opportunity costs

Stocks represent idle resources within the firm. These resources could be used for other purposes, and the next best such purpose is the opportunity cost. The minimum opportunity cost must be the current rate of interest, since the firm could always invest any surplus funds. In practice, reinvestment of resources in the business itself will probably earn more than the rate of interest. The true opportunity cost of funds tied up in the stock is often around twenty per cent per annum.

► If real interest rates are high, efficient stock control becomes even more essential.

2 Physical costs

Warehousing and storage, including rent, rates and maintenance of premises.

Documentation and administration, which requires office staff and computer time.

Checking and handling, needing specialist workers and costly equipment.

Insurance and security.

Falling market value, due to changes in demand: for instance fashion-based or seasonal goods.

Stockholding Policy

Striking the right balance between the costs and benefits of stock-holding is rather like walking a tightrope.

A: the cost of holding stock.
B: the cost of not holding stock.

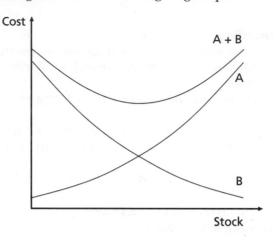

Figure 16.1:
The costs and benefits of stock holding

The aim is to hold the net cost of stockholding at its minimum. This is made more difficult by continuous change in the key variables. Marketing factors are particularly volatile.

Stock Management

Once a policy is set, production management must attempt to implement it. For each type of stock, a range of values must be decided, within which actual stock levels will be allowed to fluctuate. The classic model over-simplifies reality, but it is a useful guide:

Procurement time: average period from placing an order to the arrival of supplies.

Re-order level: is set according to the procurement time, and aims to avoid any entry into buffer stocks.

Buffer stock: the reserve stock which is regarded as a minimum insurance against stockout.

Figure 16.2.
A model of stock control management

Notice that:

- the sawtooth pattern of stock usage will in reality be far less regular
- actual stockholding will occasionally break through the maximum and buffer stock levels
- major changes in the usage rate will show as changes in the down gradients on the graph. Early recognition can prompt corrective action.

In the diagram below the usage rate abruptly accelerates:

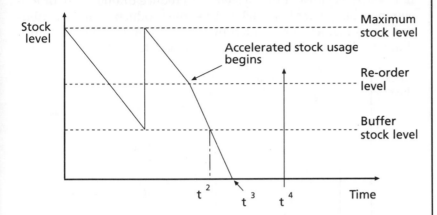

► The increased usage rate suggests breaking into buffer stocks by t^2, and complete stockout by t^3 – but no delivery is scheduled until t^4.

Figure 16.3
Increased production and falling stock levels

Effective operation of such a stock control model depends on a flow of accurate and up-to-date information. Many firms now have computerized on-line stock control, which not only provides the required data, but also automatically triggers the necessary orders as stock is depleted.

The model must take account of seasonal variation and underlying sales trends detected in market research. Even then breakdowns or failures in the production process may occur; demand in the market may change unexpectedly; a competitor may launch a hostile initiative; the wider economy may enter recession or boom. The keynote is flexibility.

A firm may assess its relative stock levels using ratios (see Chapter 22).

Stock value is related to sales:

$$\text{Stock turnover ratio} = \frac{\text{sales}}{\text{stock}}$$

$$\text{Stockholding period in days} = \frac{\text{stocks}}{\text{cost of goods sold}} \times 365$$

The savings from an improvement in stock utilization can be very substantial. Suppose a firm's stock turnover is 2 with sales at £100m., stock at £50m. and profits at £10m. Assume that the interest rate on the value of stock held is ten per cent. Then if stock levels can be halved to £25m. – and the stock turnover ratio increased to 4 – the saving would be about £2.5m. This boosts pre-tax profit to £12.5m. – a rise of twenty-five per cent.

Make notes on stockholding ratios using the example of a firm with sales at £150m., stock valued at £50m. and profits of £8m.

► This was pioneered in Japan under their 'Kanban' system of delivery. Stock control is fully computerized, and orders are made automatically to suppliers, who deliver on a daily or even hourly basis.

Figure 16.4
Just-in-time stock control

Just-In-Time Systems

In essence, the idea of this system is to reduce dramatically or else eliminate altogether key slack links in the production and distribution chain that are represented by stock. Just-in-time stock control dramatically modifies the stock control model.

Typically with this system of stock control:

- the re-order level may be very early in the usage cycle
- the procurement time (t^1) is very short
- buffer stock is non-existent or minimal.

The system depends on a much closer relationship with suppliers, and firms will make reliability a key criterion in awarding supply contracts. Often suppliers will locate physically very close to a major manufacturer (see Chapter 12). The purchasing firm may even provide advisory and training services to its suppliers in order to improve their performance.

The just-in-time principle extends through the whole production chain. Computers are applied in calculating optimal logistics for manufacturing processes. This means that production bottlenecks are avoided, and just the right quantities of components are matched to work-in-progress at the start of each operation. Computerization of customer ordering can connect market demand directly with the production interface. Delivery to the firm's own customers can also adopt a just-in-time approach.

The net effect of these new approaches is to concertina the whole production and distribution sequence. Stock – and therefore working capital – is reduced, and a major competitive advantage is gained in overall costs. A recent study found that firms adopting a just-in-time system could reduce stock by fifty to ninety per cent. This is reflected in the falling stock turnover ratios for manufacturing across the western world.

 Note the advantages and risks of just-in-time stock control. Use Figures 16.3 and 16.4 in your notes.

Forrest Fashions Ltd is a major specialist in printed fashion clothing, founded by a young model, Jane Forrest. The factory holds stocks of undyed fabric in fifty metre rolls. With a usage rate of twenty rolls per week, Sean Fraser, the production manager, aims to ensure that stock levels never fall below forty rolls but also do not exceed 160 rolls. Current practice is to place orders in batches of 120 rolls which take an average of three weeks to arrive.

1 Sketch a stock control chart using this data.

2 The stock level is eighty rolls. A large rush order now arrives which will push the usage rate up to forty rolls per week for the next two months. What action might the production manager take and why?

Summary and comment

• stock control is about striking a balance between the risk of stockout on the one hand, and the cost of stock on the other. Thresholds of acceptable risk vary widely. The chosen solution will depend partly on the culture and traditions of the firm
• there is no simple formula for calculating optimum stock levels. Each firm, product and market is different
• just-in-time increases the stakes in stock control. Without the cushioning of buffer stock, errors translate faster into lost production and late deliveries. The whole decision cycle must increase its speed, and be informed by very accurate and up-to-date data
• computerized stock control systems are only as good as the model with which they are programmed. In dynamic markets the ground rules of stock control must be under constant review.

► The need for adequate liquidity and working capital may affect a firm's stockholding policy. See Chapter 25.

► Many firms have found themselves overstocked during times of recession. Trading with lower stock levels reduces this risk.

⑰ The meaning of accounts

THE ACCOUNTING PROCESS

There are two aspects to the accounting process. The first is the recording of all financial transactions as they occur – purchases, sales, payment of wages, receipt of debts etc. This task is called **bookkeeping**, though with growing computerization it is more properly known as **data processing**. The second aspect is the periodic statements of account that summarize all the detailed financial events taking place from day-to-day.

▶ Bookkeeping and data processing.

▶ Financial accounts.

Who Uses Accounts?

These statements divide into two categories. **Formal financial accounts** are supplied in various forms to meet needs external to the firm's management. These needs arise from:

- **shareholders** who own the firm and wish to monitor the management of their investment
- **employees/unions** who wish to assess the prospects in such matters as wage rises, working conditions and job security
- **lenders/creditors** who need to know if the firm is likely to be a good risk in meeting debt repayments or settling outstanding bills
- **customers** who need assurance that their supplies of particular products are secure
- **local communities/councils** who need to consider such factors as employment changes, environmental planning and housing needs
- **the government** when compiling national economic and business statistics that guide many decisions concerning the economy, tax revenues, assistance to regions etc.

For needs internal to the firm's management, accounting statements are produced in much greater detail and with greater frequency.

These **management accounts** (i.e. accounts to assist management) are normally confidential and relate to particular areas of the firm's operation. They are the vital data used by managers to control the firm and guide it towards agreed objectives. Careful analysis of detailed accounts will also provide warning signals of dangers ahead as well as indicating gateways of possible opportunity.

► Management accounts.

 Coburn Castings PLC manufactures aluminium components, and is a major industrial supplier. The firm is located on an industrial estate on the edge of a medium-sized Midlands town. There is a substantial housing estate nearby, and the firm is one of the largest local employers.

The company had enjoyed buoyant markets during the 1980s, but lately there has been talk of difficulties. No one seems sure how serious these are.

For each of the following four scenarios, state who might wish to see the accounts and why:

1 Management announce that reduced demand means that redundancy notices will be served on 400 of the plant's 1 200 staff.

2 To assist in financing a new labour saving technology, the firm proposes to issue debentures to the value of £8m.

3 The firm accepts the need for pollution filters to be fitted to its two main chimneys. The cost will be £1.5m. However the board can only find sufficient funds for the work to be carried out in three years' time.

4 It is strongly rumoured in the City that a take over bid is about to be announced for Coburn Castings by their main competitor.

The Major Accounting Statements

1 The balance sheet
This is a summary statement that shows a firm's sources of finance and their corresponding uses at a given date.

► The balance sheet is dealt with in detail in Chapter 18.

2 The profit and loss account
This starts by stating the **sales revenue** from trading activity, and then shows a series of deductions for each major type of cost until the trading profit (or loss) remains. After taking into account any costs or revenues arising from non-trading activities, the profit after tax is divided between dividends and **retentions** (funds ploughed back into the business). This figure is then transferred to the balance sheet.

► The profit and loss account is dealt with in detail in Chapter 19.

3 The funds flow statement
This statement (also called 'sources and application of funds statement') shows the means by which balance sheet values have changed over a period. All sources of new funding for the firm are listed, followed by a balancing list showing the uses for those same funds.

► **Company accounts**
The published accounts and reports of companies are interesting documents. They are freely available from the head office of public companies. Addresses can be found in the trade directories in your public library. Make a selection of companies and request their annual report and accounts.

► Disclosure of accounting information is required by the Companies Act 1985. Copies of accounts for all companies – private as well as public – may be inspected at Companies House in Swansea.

► Published accounts are only summary statements. The detailed financial data from which management accounts are prepared remains confidential.

Published Company Annual Reports and Accounts

All public companies issue an Annual Report and Accounts. These contain much interesting information, and are very useful for students.

 The best way to make notes on the following sections is to obtain your own copy of the published accounts of a company, then to look for the following nine features and annotate them.

1 Highlights
Includes a summary of financial results, perhaps with brief reports of newsworthy events in company affairs.

2 Chairman's statement
Features an overview of the company's trading year. It normally adopts an upbeat and optimistic tone.

3 Product and trading information
Often a lengthy and glossy section, indicating the range of the firm's activities. It acts as a kind of showcase.

4 Directors' report
This serves as an introduction to the formal accounts. The material is factual, explaining the nature of the firm's business, its financial structure, its provisions for employees, and any legal or technical notices.

5 The accounts
These include:

- the 'profit and loss account' (see Chapter 19)
- the balance sheet (see Chapter 18)
- the 'sources and application of funds statement'.

6 Accounting policies
A summary of the firm's broad approach to matters of accounting practice, e.g. valuation of stock.

7 Notes to the accounts
Provide detailed explanation of items specified in the main accounting statements.

8 Auditors' report
A legally required statement from an independent external firm of accountants. This confirms that the published accounts have been checked, and represent 'a true and fair view of the state of affairs of the Company'.

9 Notice of meeting
Gives the date and venue for the next annual general meeting, at which all shareholders are entitled to attend and exercise their vote.

Summary and comment

• accounts organize vital financial data relating to firms within a logical and consistent framework. Useful analysis and comparisons can be made by external parties

• in Britain high professional standards are generally maintained. These are required by the law, the Accounting Standards Board and the professional associations

• accounts are expressed in money terms. This is convenient, but cannot express all the variables affecting a firm, e.g. qualities in the staff

• despite appearances, accounts are only ever approximations. Human judgement plays a major part in their formulation

• although firms have major financial objectives, there is a risk of attaching excessive significance to accounting data alone. Non-financial factors can be critical to the firm, yet easily be overlooked, e.g. staff morale, attitudes to change.

(18) The balance sheet

Chapter objectives

After working through this chapter, you will:

▪ be able to make double entry changes in a balance sheet

▪ know precisely the meaning of items typically found on a balance sheet

▪ know how to convert T-form into vertical format

▪ know the meaning of the following key terms: shareholders funds, long-term liabilities, current liabilities, fixed assets, current assets, net assets, goodwill, capital employed, net working capital, accruals, dividends, retained profits, depreciation, authorized share capital, called-up share capital, reserves.

THE SIMPLE T-FORM BALANCE SHEET

A balance sheet is simply a periodic listing of resources in use, with a corresponding list of how those resources were obtained. The two lists are therefore equal by definition (and are said to 'balance'). A balance sheet is always given an exact date, since in any active business the sources and uses of resources are continuously changing (e.g. a bank loan is arranged, a new machine is purchased, more stock arrives, more sales are made etc.). The basic pattern is called `T-form' due to its outline shape.

The Balance Sheet in Horizontal Format

THE BIG BAG CO LTD
Balance Sheet as at 31 March 1992

Sources of funds	(£k)	Uses of funds	(£k)
shareholders funds		fixed assets	
ordinary £1 shares	42	land and buildings	40
retained profits	24	machinery	22
		vehicles	17
long-term liabilities			
bank loans	30	current assets	
		Stock	16
current liabilities		debtors	12
creditors	19	cash	8
	115		115

▶ A balance sheet lists the sources and uses of a firm's funds. The total value of these two lists is automatically equal.

Assets
Fixed assets with which the firm operates the production process and which remain continuously in the firm's possession, e.g. land, buildings, machinery.
Current assets which circulate quickly through the firm, e.g. stocks, money owing (debtors), cash.
Ordinary £1 shares represent the original value of the shares issued to finance the business.
Retained profits belong to the shareholders. This is the part of the profits from previous years not taken as dividends but ploughed back into the business.
Creditors: other firms (e.g. suppliers) whose bills have not yet been paid.
Debtors: customers who have not yet paid Big Bag Co.

Double Entry Changes

A balance sheet is like a financial cross-section through a firm at a particular point in time. Although balance sheets are normally only drawn up at intervals, a new balance sheet could be published every day, or even every hour! Each time it would be slightly different as events involving the firm's resources unfold. Each event requires a **double entry**.

The double entry principle is easy to apply in practice. All examples below relate to the Big Bag Co during the first week in April.

1   Issue extra 8 000 £1 ordinary shares and pay the money into bank

Sources	(£k)	Funds uses	(£k)
shareholders' funds	+8 000	cash	+8 000

2   Withdraw £8 000 from bank and buy a new machine

Sources	(£k)	Funds uses	(£k)
		machinery	+8 000
		cash	−8 000

3   Sell surplus outbuilding for £5 000 and pay the money into bank

Sources	(£k)	Funds uses	(£k)
		land and buildings	−5 000
		cash	+5 000

4   Withdraw £5 000 cash and repay part of the bank loan

Sources	(£k)	Funds uses	(£k)
bank loan	−5 000	cash	−5 000

It is now useful to consider the effect of a trading transaction on the balance sheet. Exactly the same principle applies. Say the firm sells a consignment of bags that cost the firm £4 000, to a fashion retailer for £6 000 cash.

Step 1   reduce stock by £4 000
Step 2   increase cash by £6 000

At this point the balance sheet will not balance! The reason is the £2 000 profit, which must belong to the shareholders and be added to retained profits.

So, **Step 3**   increase retained profits by £2 000.

The result is shown overpage.

► The finance of assets is divided between:
Long-term liabilities: borrowings that need not be repaid for at least twelve months.
Current liabilities: include any amounts owing that must be repaid within twelve months.

► Double entry rules do not exist in order to make the two sides balance but because the two sides balance by definition.

▶ Now suppose that the transaction had not been for cash, but on credit? This does **not** mean that creditors are affected! All entries are exactly the same, except that the £6 000 is entered as debtors (money owing to the firm) instead of cash.

Sources of funds		Uses of funds	
	(£)		(£)
shareholders funds			
retained profits	+2000		
		current assets	
		stock	−4000
		cash	+6000
	+2000		+2000

The result of all these changes is:

THE BIG BAG CO LTD
Balance Sheet as at 7 April 1992

Sources of funds		Uses of funds	
	(£k)		(£k)
shareholders funds		fixed assets	
ordinary £1 shares	50	land and buildings	35
retained profits	26	machinery	30
		vehicles	17
long-term liabilities			
bank loans	25	current assets	
		stock	12
current liabilities		debtors	12
creditors	19	cash	14
	120		120

 Make notes on the changes between the two balance sheets. Check your understanding by changing the second balance sheet to account for a further sale of bags costing £2 000, for a price of £3 000.

Items on the Balance Sheet

It is now necessary to look more closely at each section of the balance sheet.

1 Fixed Assets

Tangible fixed assets refer to all physical assets held by the firm to carry on production on a long-term basis ('tangible' literally means 'touchable'). These typically include land, buildings, machinery, equipment and vehicles. Items are generally recorded at their historic (original) cost. However, some assets can appreciate (rise) or depreciate (fall) in value. Thus property is periodically 'revalued' upwards or downwards while such items as machinery are gradually 'depreciated' (marked down in value) over their useful life. This depreciation is shown as a cumulative total and is subtracted from the historic cost (see Chapter 20).

Intangible fixed assets mean other long-term sources of value that are not physical. When one firm buys another, it may pay a price in excess of the value of the assets concerned. This premium is called **goodwill** and arises from the value of customer loyalty and probable profits to be earned in the future. Goodwill is entered on the balance sheet, but usually written off quite quickly by an accountant. Patents (the legal right to exploit an invention without competition) and 'trademarks' may also have commercial value and appear on the balance sheet. Some firms now value their brands (e.g. Cadbury-Schweppes, United Biscuits) – a subject of much current debate in the accounting profession.

Financial fixed assets represent financial holdings of long-term value outside the company. These can include government and local authority stocks (see Chapter 24), debentures or holdings in other companies.

► In 1988 Rank-Hovis-McDougal became the first company to value its brands (Mother's Pride, Hovis, Mr Kipling, Bisto, Paxo and many more) on the balance sheet. These added £678 m. to the final assets, and to the shareholders' funds.

Holdings in other companies
If company A holds more than fifty per cent of the ordinary shares of company B, then company B is a **subsidiary** of A. If A holds between twenty and fifty per cent of B, B is an **associated company**. If A holds less than twenty per cent of B, this is simply a **trade investment**.

2   *Current Assets*
Stock is usually essential to the process of trading and includes raw materials, work-in-progress and finished goods. All stocks are valued at their cost or, if lower, at their realizable value (value for sale in the market). As stock purchase prices change, so stock value is affected. Firms must choose a consistent method of stock valuation (see Chapter 21).

Debtors refers to amounts owed to the firm by its customers. This is a normal item for most enterprises since the provision of credit is often a competitive necessity in the marketing mix (see Chapter 9).

Cash includes balances at the bank plus any petty cash and cash not yet paid in.

► Fixed assets are called 'fixed' because they remain within the firm. Assets are called 'current' if they are passing through the firm.

3   *Shareholders' Funds*
Also called 'the equity', these resources are the foundation on which the business stands.

Share Capital: all firms have an upper limit on the ordinary or preference share capital that they may use: this is the **authorized capital**. The **issued capital** is that part of the authorized capital that has already been allotted to shareholders. Initially the firm may decide only to 'call up' part of the full value for each share. Hence the value shown on the balance sheet is the **called-up share capital**, i.e. that amount of money already paid to the company at a given time. Note that preference shares only feature in the capital structure of some companies (see Chapter 20); ordinary shares are always the major source of share capital.

Reserves: this is simply the name given to profits and surpluses generated over time and forming part of the company's long-term capital. These resources are not sums of cash being held back to meet

► Reserves in accounting are not cash reserves.

future needs. Indeed, the funds represented by reserves are likely to be invested in buildings, plant and equipment.

There are three important types of reserves:

i **Share premium**

The sale of a company's shares may be at a price above their face value. This surplus is indicated in the share premium reserve.

ii **Revaluation**

Certain fixed assets often appreciate in value (e.g. land, buildings), and when revalued on the balance sheet the corresponding double entry is in the revaluation reserve. This adds to the shareholders' funds, but cannot be distributed as a dividend.

iii **Profit and loss account (retained profits)**

This is normally the major reserve and represents the accumulated profits retained by the firm to finance the business. The retained profit from an accounting period is usually the largest source of new funding (see Chapter 24). This can be found as the last line in the profit and loss account itself (see Chapter 19).

4   *Long-term Liabilities*

A firm frequently wishes to obtain additional long-term finance without it becoming permanent in the form of a new share issue. Indeed, if earnings from loan capital exceed the cost in interest payments, then the shareholders' return can be dramatically increased (see Chapter 24). Loan capital may include:

- **debentures**, which are certificates of indebtedness: the issuing company undertakes to repay the holder the amount specified at a future date, and until then to pay interest at a fixed rate
- **bank loans** (and loans from other financial institutions) are normally available to businesses for periods between one and twenty-five years. Both the availability of loans and the rate of interest depend on the amount requested, the period of the loan, the security available and the firm's business 'track record'. In the past, interest rates were often fixed, but the trend is now towards variable rate loans
- **mortgages** are long-term loans secured on land and buildings and are available from commercial banks.

5   *Current Liabilities*

All amounts that will become payable by the firm within twelve months are called current liabilities. They arise mainly through the process of day-to-day trading.

▶ Current liabilities are sometimes called 'creditors due within the year'.

- **creditors** refers to unpaid bills from other firms (often suppliers). Between one and three months' credit is often allowable between firms and this trade credit can be an important source of finance
- **bank overdraft** means any negative current account bank balance held by the firm. Overdrafts are intended for short-term financial needs and are legally repayable on demand
- **provision for tax** represents the size of any expected tax bill. Tax

liabilities become payable to the Inland Revenue the year after they were incurred
- **dividends payable** are usually announced at six month intervals as an interim and final dividend. A time-lag occurs between declarations of the final dividend and its payment following approval at the company's annual general meeting. It is treated as a liability from the time of declaration in expectation of its later payment
- **accruals** are accumulations of debt for a product or service when charges are not made until after the balance sheet date, e.g. charges for telephones.

Balance Sheet Formats

We will now look at a complete balance sheet, first in the T-form (traditional) format, and then in the widely used vertical format.

Balance sheet: T-form

PREMIER PAINTS LTD
Balance Sheet as at 31st March 1992

Sources of funds	(£k)	(£k)	Uses of funds	(£k)	(£k)
shareholders' funds			fixed assets		
ordinary £1 shares			land and buildings	605	
fully paid		540	plant and equipment	730	
8% preference shares	165		goodwill	80	
share premium reserve	80		investments	120	1 535
revaluation reserve	90				
profit and loss account	475	1 350	current assets		
			stock	420	
			debtors	285	
			cash	110	815
long-term liabilities					
debentures	400				
other loans	210	610			
current liabilities					
creditors	200				
tax provision	115				
dividend payable	75	390			
		2 350			2 350

► The left-hand side answers the question of where did the resources come from, while the right-hand side answers the question of where are the resources now.

In practice, most companies today have dropped the T-form balance sheet in favour of a **vertical format**. Once familiar, this is absolutely straightforward. The data to be entered is unchanged. Only the arrangement of the various sections is different. The two 'sides' must still balance by the same logic. Look briefly through the following vertical format balance sheet. Then read the marginal notes alongside it and check each point for yourself.

Balance sheet: vertical format

PREMIER PAINTS LTD
Balance Sheet as at 31st March 1992

	(£k)	(£k)	(£k)
fixed assets			
land and buildings	605		
plant and equipment	730		
goodwill	80		
investments	120		1 535
current assets			
stock	420		
debtors	285		
cash	110	815	
current liabilities			
creditors	200		
tax provision	115		
dividends payable	75	390	
net working capital			425
net assets			1 960
financed by			
shareholders' funds			
ordinary £1 shares (fully paid)	540		
8% preference shares	165		
share premium reserve	80		
revaluation reserve	90		
profit and loss account	475		1 350
long-term liabilities			
debentures	400		
other loans	210		610
capital employed			1 960

Notes on the vertical format

1 The presentation of fixed and current assets is exactly as the right hand side of the T-form.

2 Now current liabilities are subtracted from current assets. The value remaining is the **net working capital** – the net value of the assets circulating in the process of day-to-day business.

3 Fixed assets plus net working capital = **net assets**. This value amounts to the total assets less current liabilities.

4 Finally add the shareholders' funds to the long-term liabilities to find **capital employed**. This balances with net assets, but at a lower figure than the T-form balance. The difference is the current liabilities: this value has been subtracted from both sides of the T-form balance sheet.

Notice that net working capital is also called **net current assets**. Net assets are also called **total assets less current liabilities**.

 1 Arrange the data below to form a horizontal balance sheet with clear subtotals for shareholders' funds, long-term liabilities, current liabilities, fixed assets and current assets.

2 Convert this balance sheet into a correctly presented vertical format.

The chief accountant has identified the following items for inclusion in the firm's balance sheet as at 31st March 1992.

	£
property	700 000
dividends payable	25 000
stock	290 000
subsidiaries	110 000
reserves	
revaluation	50 000

retained profits	620 000
cash	95 000
goodwill	45 000
debtors	200 000
issued ordinary £1 shares	444 000
provisions for tax	75 000
creditors	220 000
plant and equipment	
cost	500 000
less accumulated depreciation	160 000
loans (over 12 months)	350 000

Summary and comment

• the balance sheet is a key accounting statement required from companies by law
• its format is now far more standardized than in the past, making comparisons easier
• it is the raw material for calculating many key accounting ratios (see Chapter 22), assisting both management and external users. However:
• valuation of many fixed assets at historic cost can be misleading. Replacement costs are often much higher
• inflation more generally remains a major problem. With the abandonment of inflation-adjusted accounting, the changing value of money is a real source of distortion
• the valuation of intangible assets is an increasing problem. While goodwill is hurriedly written off, some firms are introducing brand valuation– while others are not
• firms in the service sector may indicate low tangible fixed asset values, yet have a very high market value. The difference is the value in human assets (e.g. creative designers) – which does not appear in any balance sheet.

19 The profit and loss account

Chapter objectives

After working through this chapter, you will:

▌ understand the construction and logic of a published profit and loss account

▌ know the principles that underlie the recording of revenues and costs

▌ recognize the distinction between profit and cash

▌ know the meaning of the following key terms: trading account, trading/operating profit, non-operating income, profit before/after tax, gross/net profit, retained profit, realization concept, matching principle, exceptional and extraordinary items, liquidity.

A SPECIMEN PROFIT AND LOSS STATEMENT EXPLAINED

 Copy down the profit and loss account for Megasound, leaving a usable space to one side. Then read through the explanation, making notes on what the various items in the accounts mean.

Megasound Ltd is a firm is based in Berkshire where it manufactures high-quality loudspeakers. 1991 was a good year for the firm with sales revenue reaching £2m. for the first time.

► The profit and loss account summarizes a firm's trading results over a period and shows how the resulting profits were used (or how the losses were financed).

► The opening item is always the **sales revenue**. From this all the direct costs relating to production are subtracted. This gives the **gross profit**. Then all overhead costs are subtracted, leaving the **operating profit**. To this non-operating income is added. With subtraction of the interest charges, this becomes the **profit before tax**. Subtraction of tax gives the **profit after tax**. Finally, subtraction of dividends leaves the **retained profits**, which are added to the **reserves**. Remember that all references to profit may also be to loss.

MEGASOUND LTD
Profit and loss account for the year
ending 31 March 1991

	(£k)	(£k)
sales revenue		2 000
less: cost of goods sold		
direct materials	450	
direct labour	630	
manufacturing overheads	150	1 230
gross profit		770
less		
distribution costs	190	
administrative expenses	160	350
operating (trading) profit		420

add	
non-operating income	15
	435
less	
interest payable	35
profit before tax (net profit)	400
tax on profit	140
profit after tax	260
dividends	100
retained profit	160

Together, the items down to gross profit are known as the **trading account**. Its specific contents are not normally disclosed by firms.

The uses of the profit before tax are called **appropriations**. These include taxation, dividends and retentions of profit in the reserves.

Explanation of Terms Used

1 **Sales revenue less costs = profit** is the most basic equation in business. We therefore start with the total revenue generated from ordinary trading activity. This must exclude any VAT element.

Revenue minus costs equals profit.

2 **Cost of goods sold** is the first group of subtractions. This includes all costs related to the product (often called **product costs**) rather than to the operation of the firm as a whole. So we include direct materials, direct labour, plus all overhead costs that can be allocated to the production process.

Revenue minus costs of goods sold only equals gross profit.

3 **Gross profit** is the sum remaining.

4 Next we subtract all other running costs (except the cost of finance). These relate to the firm rather than to the specific product, and are charged for a period (often called **period costs**).
Distribution costs include all outlay on selling and marketing.
Administrative costs feature all remaining overheads including office costs and management salaries.

5 **Operating or trading profit** is the amount remaining after these deductions. It is the surplus achieved through the firm's normal trading activity when all operating costs have been deducted.

6 **Non-operating income** means any earnings arising from outside the firm's normal trading activity. This could be derived from financial fixed assets such as investments in other firms.

7 **Interest payable** on the firm's loan finance is deducted next. This is permitted before profits are subject to any taxation.

8 **Profit before tax** (also called **net profit**) is the profit remaining and is liable to corporation tax. Corporation tax is charged at a standard rate of thirty-three per cent. Small firms (profits less than £250 000) pay tax at a reduced rate of twenty-five per cent, but on a scale of twenty-five to thirty-five per cent if profits fall between £250 000 and £1 250 000.

Revenue minus all costs equals net profit or profit before tax.

9 **Profit after tax** is subject to subtractions/additions arising from extraordinary items (see below page 147), dividends to preference shareholders, and payment of dividends to minority interests (shareholders outside the firm with holdings in its subsidiary companies). Profits remaining are available to the ordinary shareholders.

10 **Dividends** may be recommended by the directors at any rate (e.g. 8p per £1 ordinary share) and must be approved by the shareholders at the annual general meeting. The total distributed profit may be any proportion of profit after tax, although usually more than half is retained.

11 **Retained profit** is that part of the final profit ploughed back into the firm. This will be added to the reserves on the balance sheet.

If a firm makes a loss for a period, then it may pay no dividend, and the reserves will be **reduced**. This would reflect the real loss of resources (assets) from the firm. A dividend can still be paid from the retained profit of previous years. Any loss can be deducted from future profit for the purpose of tax liability.

Principles of Profit and Loss

The principle of prudence is applied by accountants to the calculation of profit and losses. A firm's confident expectation that sales will occur is not sufficient. For sales revenue to be recorded (i.e. **realized**) the product must have been delivered to the customer and either cash received or a debt accepted. This is called the **realization concept**.

To work out a firm's profit over a stated period, it is necessary to decide which revenues and costs to count. The two vital guiding points are:

1 Allow all revenue earned by products sold in the period.

2 Subtract all costs incurred by the firm in achieving those sales.

Suppose a firm starts its financial year on 1 January. At the beginning of February a payment is received from a customer who accepted delivery in December. This sales revenue will be included in the previous year's accounts. Only sales realized during the current year can be counted in that year.

Now suppose the firm buys a large consignment of stock for the Christmas market. By the new year half is still unsold. Only the cost of the stock that was sold before 1 January would be charged to that year's accounts. The cost of unsold stock will be carried forward into the next year. Similarly, a bill for rent to cover the three months November–January would be charged 2/3 to the previous year and 1/3 to the following year.

This insistence on linking or matching the sales of a period with their corresponding costs is called the **matching principle**. It applies equally to the purchase of fixed assets. Suppose that towards the start of their financial year a firm takes delivery of a new and expensive machine. This does **not** mean that their profits are immediately

►To calculate profit and loss, all revenues must be matched to their corresponding costs.

reduced by the cost of the machine. Instead only one year's depreciation (loss of value) will be charged to the profit and loss account. The remainder of the machine's cost will be spread over the future years of its life (see Chapter 20).

The distinction here is between **capital expenditure** and **revenue expenditure**. That part of a firm's expenditure that can be shown as an asset on the next balance sheet is called capital expenditure. This is because it has added to the value of the firm's capital. It does **not** appear as a cost in the current profit and loss account. All other expenditure (e.g. wages, administration) that does not create any future asset is called revenue expenditure. This is because its purpose is to obtain revenue for the firm. It **does** appear as costs in the current profit and loss account.

Exceptional and Extraordinary Items

The goal of all accounts is to convey a 'true and fair' picture of the organization's affairs. Thus any special items that significantly affect the results are highlighted and explained in the **notes to the accounts**.

Exceptional items arise in the course of the firm's ordinary activities, but are unusual in their scale. Example: the bankruptcy of a major customer and the write-off of their debts. Being part of the general process and risks of business, exceptional items are deducted before operating profit along with other costs. They are explained in the 'notes'.

Extraordinary items arise outside the firm's ordinary activities ('extra-ordinary'). They are significant but 'one-off' and not predictable or routine in occurrence. Example: unfavourable political events force a firm to sell an overseas branch and its stock at a loss. Extraordinary items are shown below profit after tax but before the other appropriations.

Profit and Cash

A highly profitable firm may go bankrupt for lack of cash. A firm awash with cash may announce heavy losses. There is no contradiction in either of these statements.

Liquidity means nearness to cash. Cash therefore represents perfect liquidity. All firms need adequate cash to meet their expenses (e.g. wages or rent). Equally, too much cash is wasteful since it earns little or no return (see Chapter 25). An expanding, profitable firm may quickly spend its cash earnings on say stock, wages or new fixed assets. If unexpected bills arrive, it may run short of cash. At the opposite extreme, a declining firm could be trading unprofitably yet accumulate large sums in cash. These may be unused for fear of incurring further losses.

Cash and profit are therefore distinct. Cash is merely a totally liquid form in which to hold resources. Profit is a surplus earned by the use of resources, and may be invested in any form of asset.

►Profit and cash are different.

Draw up a profit and loss account for 1991/2 from the following data:

Portcullis Locks Ltd is a Midlands firm manufacturing locks and mechanical security equipment. During 1991/2 sales revenue was £2 590 000. Stock at the start of the year was worth £430 000 and by the end of the year had fallen in value to £360 000. Materials cost £610 000 whilst direct labour expenses amounted to £805 000. Production overheads have been calculated at £250 000, while total selling expenses reached £195 000. Administration of all kinds cost £300 000. The long-term loans on the firm's balance sheet stood at £420 000 with interest rates at fifteen per cent, while tax on profits was payable at thirty per cent. It was the directors' policy to retain three fifths of the profit after tax and to distribute two fifths in dividends.

Summary and comment

- the profit and loss account is the key operating statement showing how a firm made a profit or a loss with the resources that it controlled
- taken with the balance sheet, it makes an analysis of perform-ance possible
- notes to the accounts may clarify the nature of revenues and costs. However most of the detail is missing from the published accounts
- no rigid rules exist for defining every heading. Much depends on discretion. Caution is needed in comparing data between firms
- the appropriations show how any final profit was divided between tax, dividends and investment in the firm.

Depreciation

Chapter objectives

After working through this chapter, you will:

■ know the meaning and causes of depreciation

■ be able to apply simple numerate methods in accounting for depreciation

■ understand the recording of depreciation on the balance sheet

■ know the meaning of the following key terms: depreciation, straight-line method, reducing balance method, net book value.

WHAT IS DEPRECIATION?

A good quality family car bought new might cost £10 000. One year later its value could have fallen to around £7 000. After three years it might only be worth £4 000, while five years are likely to reduce the value to £2 500. Even after ten years its value will still be falling, and it would be likely to fetch around £1 000. This process of falling value year by year is called **depreciation**. It is a real cost, and a major part of the expense of owning a car.

► Depreciation: fall in the value of a fixed asset over time.

   Although land and buildings often **appreciate** in value, most durable consumer or producer goods suffer from depreciation. Typical fixed assets for a firm – machines, computers, trucks and vans – will all depreciate over time. Just as the private car owner must recognize depreciation as an expense, so the firm must allow for depreciation in its accounts. This allowance has two clear aspects:

► Depreciation is caused by:
• wear and tear
• new technology making an asset obsolete
• changes in fashion or style that reduce an asset's market value.

1 Most fixed assets will be recorded with a falling value over time. This will be shown on the balance sheet.

2 The loss of value in the fixed assets is a cost to the firm, directly reducing the profits. This will be shown in the profit and loss account.

The Depreciation Cycle

The speed at which depreciation occurs may be fairly constant, or it may vary. 'Useful life' may not end until the physical exhaustion of the asset, but it is more likely to end at the firm's discretion, when it is judged to be more efficient to purchase a replacement. The 'useful life' can usually be estimated in advance fairly accurately. When the asset is discarded it generally has some remaining (**residual**) value. When allowing for depreciation in the accounts the sum to be depreciated is the original cost 'less' the residual value.

► Historic cost: the price which the firm originally paid for an asset.

► There is no single correct way of calculating depreciation. But the accountant must ensure that the same methods are used throughout the firm.

Depreciation Methods
The firm must choose a fair and consistent method by which depreciation of its fixed assets can be recognized.

Depreciation
Action Fashion is a newly established company making a distinctive range of leisure and sports clothing. It has decided to purchase a computerized fabric cutting machine at a cost of £16 000. The new machine is expected to have a useful life of four years, and a residual value of £4 000. Two different methods of depreciation are being considered:

Straight-line method
This is a very simple method. It treats the asset as though it will lose value at a constant rate over its useful life. To find the annual depreciation charge, we take the original cost, subtract the residual value, and divide by the useful life in years.

$$\text{i.e. annual depreciation} = \frac{\text{original cost less residual value}}{\text{useful life (years)}}$$

$$= \frac{£16\ 000 \text{ less } £4\ 000}{4 \text{ years}} = £3\ 000$$

The pattern of depreciation can now be shown in a table
('End Of Year 0' means the time of purchase):

END OF YEAR	DEPRECIATION CHARGE (£)	BALANCE SHEET VALUE (£)
0	nil	16 000
1	3 000	13 000
2	3 000	10 000
3	3 000	7 000
4	3 000	4 000

The constant annual depreciation charge would form a straight line on a graph.

 Sketch the graph for the data above (number of years/ balance sheet value). Write your notes on the straight-line method of depreciation alongside.

Reducing Balance Method
This method reduces the balance sheet value each year by a fixed percentage rate. This rate is exactly sufficient to reduce the balance sheet value to equal the residual value by the last year of useful life. Action Fashion will use a rate of twenty-nine per cent:

END OF YEAR	DEPRECIATION CHARGE (£)	BALANCE SHEET VALUE (£)
0	nil	16 000
1	4 640	11 360
2	3 294	8 066
3	2 339	5 727
4	1 661	4 066

►The balance sheet value now falls rapidly at first, but more slowly later.

You will notice that the balance sheet value is still £66 above the residual value at the end of year four. This is because twenty-nine per cent was not quite a high enough depreciation rate. The exact rate can be calculated with the formula below:

if RV =   residual value
   C =   original cost
   n =   number of years useful life

then annual depreciation rate $= 100\left(1 - \sqrt[n]{\dfrac{RV}{C}}\right)$

for Action Fashion the rate $= 100\left(1 - \sqrt[n]{\dfrac{4\ 000}{16\ 000}}\right)$

$= 100(1 - 0.701)$
$= 29.29\%$

  Sketch a graph to show depreciation by the reducing balance method, and write your notes on the method alongside.

Despite the constant percentage rate, the actual annual depreciation charge falls steadily from a high initial level. This contrasts with the constant charge using the straight-line method:

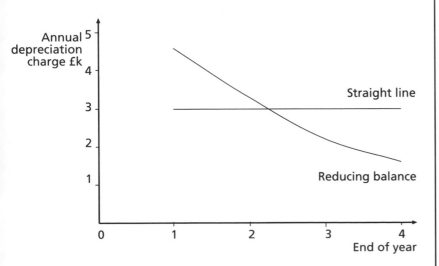

Figure 20.1
The straight-line and the reducing balance methods of depreciation

Depreciation and the Balance Sheet

Fixed assets that depreciate are recorded in the balance sheet after the accumulated depreciation has been subtracted. The resulting figure is called the **net book value**.

FRASER FABRICATION LTD
Balance Sheet as at 31 December 1991

fixed assets	at cost	accumulated depreciation	net book value
	(£)	(£)	(£)
tangible assets			
land and building	220 000	–	220 000
plant and machinery	140 000	55 000	85 000
vehicles	82 000	28 000	54 000

Depreciation and the Profit and Loss Account

Consider a machine costing £50 000, with a four year life and a residual value of £10 000. In each year of its use its value falls by £10 000 on a straight-line basis. '£10 000 worth' of machine is 'used up' in a year's operation. Thus it is a cost that must be entered in the profit and loss account.

Depreciation and Cash

Although depreciation is a very real cost to firms, the profit and loss account entry does not mean that an actual cash outflow has occurred. The literal payment for the asset was made at the time of its purchase. At that point there was a single cash outflow, but no expense was recorded in the profit and loss account. Since then no corresponding cash outflows have taken place, but a series of expenses (i.e. depreciation charges) have been recorded. These depreciation charges in the profit and loss account represent costs like any others. The only difference is that they have been paid for in advance.

So when purchase of a fixed asset occurs, the firm is that amount worse off in cash flow terms than its profits suggest. However each year of depreciation then works in the opposite way. Recorded profits allow for an expense that is not being paid in cash. Therefore the firm is better off in cash flow terms than their profit suggests – to the extent of the depreciation charge.

 Read the following case study and answer the questions below:

Polden Potteries is a small business in Somerset and is drawing up its profit and loss account for 1991/2. Part of this is summarized overpage:

	(£)	(£)
sales revenue		40 000
less: cost of goods sold		
direct materials	9 000	
direct labour	16 000	
production overheads	3 000	28 000
gross profit		12 000

However Hannah Lacey, the owner, had failed to make any allowances for the depreciation of a key asset – a new electric kiln. This had been purchased at the start of the current financial year for £15 000. It was expected to have a useful life of five years when it should have a second hand value of about £5 000.

  Calculate the gross profit of Polden Potteries using

a) the straight-line method of depreciation

b) the declining balance method of depreciation.

Summary and comment

• straight-line is a simple depreciation method widely used in Britain for much industrial and commercial equipment.

• reducing balance has the advantage of writing off the value of the asset quickly while it is fairly new, and slowly as it approaches the end of its life. This matches more closely the real decline in market value over time. Reducing balance is especially suitable for vehicles and electrical equipment

• when considering the net cost of using a fixed asset, the reducing balance method can again be more realistic. In its early years the asset has a high depreciation charge but low maintenance costs. Later, the depreciation charge falls, but the maintenance cost rises. Thus the overall cost recorded might be fairly constant

• however in the long run the firm may receive a fairly constant stream of benefit from a fixed asset – which is periodically replaced. The straight-line method ensures a constant charge, and avoids the risk of deflating and inflating profits merely because of an asset's age

• the accountant must use discretion in choosing the most appropriate method for different assets. The aim is a 'true and fair view'. Consistency is essential

• depreciation is a real process by which a fixed asset loses value over time. The reduction in value must be shown on the balance sheet, and entered as a cost on the profit and loss account

• inflation is a complication. If the cost of an asset rises during its useful life, then the depreciation charges become too small, accounting only for the original cost. This means that profit is overstated, while the balance sheet value is understated.

(21) Stock valuation

Chapter objectives

After working through this chapter, you will:

▌ know how to calculate the cost of goods sold

▌ be able to apply LIFO, FIFO and AVCO as stock valuation methods

▌ understand their relative strengths and weaknesses

▌ know the meaning of the following key terms: goods available, net realizable value.

STOCK VALUATION

► Stocks exist because of a time-lag between receipt of resources by a firm and their onward sale to the customer (or use within the business). See Chapter 16.

As with fixed assets, stock requires valuation. The reasons are the same:

1 A statement of stock value must appear on the balance sheet. As a current asset, stock will normally be turned into cash during the current accounting period. This contrasts with items such as plant and machinery where it is unlikely that their stated value will actually be realized as cash.

2 The value of stock used up is a vital cost in the profit and loss account. Its valuation directly affects reported profits (or loss). This is now explained.

The Cost of Goods Sold

► For wholesalers and retailers, costs of goods sold is the cost of the stock.

For a manufacturing firm costs of goods sold means materials plus direct labour plus production overheads (see Chapter 14).

Gross profit refers to the profit made on the sale of the goods themselves. It is calculated by taking sales revenue and subtracting the cost of goods sold. The principle is the same for both retailing and manufacturing.

THAMES TRADING LTD	(£k)	(£k)	MERSEY MANUFACTURING LTD	(£k)	(£k)
sales revenue		120	sales revenue		220
less cost of goods sold			less cost of goods sold		
opening stock	20		opening stock (all types)	45	
+ purchases	80		+ materials purchases	60	
= goods available	100		+ direct labour	80	
– closing stock	30		+ production overheads	20	
		70	= cost of stock available	205	
gross profit		50	– closing stock (all types)	55	
					150
			gross profit		70

The format for the retailer, Thames Trading Ltd, is very straightforward. To find the cost of goods sold, we start with **opening stock**, and add **purchases** made during the period. The **goods available** means the total stock held by the company during the period, which 'could' have been sold. When closing stock has been subtracted, the value remaining must be the cost of goods sold.

At Mersey Manufacturing Ltd we start with the opening stock of all types – raw materials, work-in-progress and finished goods. We add all new purchases of materials, plus direct labour and production overheads. This now covers all possible inputs to the stock available to the firm over the period. Finally we strip out the value of all types of stock remaining at the end of the period. What does not remain has left the firm, and is therefore the cost of goods sold.

Cost and Net Realizable Value

The cost of goods sold depends on the valuation of stock. How should a firm value its stock? To this problem accountants apply the concept of prudence (i.e. caution). Stock is generally valued at cost. It is never valued at any higher selling price, since a profit is not recognized (realized) until the actual sale takes place. However even a valuation at cost may be too optimistic. Stock can be damaged or go out of date, or its market value may suddenly slump. We are all familiar with signs saying 'Special Offer' or 'Reduced'. Stock may therefore be valued at what-the-firm-can-get-for-it. This is called the **net realizable value (NRV)**. The rule, then, is to value stock at the NRV or at cost, whichever is the lower.

► Net realizable value.

Stock Valuation Methods

In the majority of cases stock is valued at cost. A difficulty now appears. The cost of stock is likely to change over a period. Say that the older stock was cheaper than the newer stock. Then which goods have we sold? The older, cheaper stock? Or the newer, more expensive stock? What does represent a fair valuation of the stock sold? Or the stock remaining? The decision is vital, for it must directly affect both the balance sheet and the profit and loss account.

There are three main methods of stock valuation. They are illustrated in the example below.

 To make your own notes on the three methods of stock valuation change the sales figure for November to fifteen and work out the new values yourself.

Methods of Stock Valuation

SUPERSPORT LTD
The company retails sports clothing and equipment. The manager decides to offer a new style in football shirts. On 1 October, delivery is taken of forty shirts costing £8 each. At the end of the

► Stock valuation methods:

1 **FIFO** (first in, first out) assumes the old stock is sold first. If the old stock was bought at a lower price, recorded profits will be higher.

2 **LIFO** (last in, first out) assumes it is the newest stock that is being used first. If the newer stock was bought at a higher price, recorded profits will be lower.

3 **AVCO** (average cost) a compromise, valuing stock at its average cost. For any period, the cost per item is the average cost of the stock available. This is also the value given to the closing stock. Strictly, the system requires revaluation of the stock after every purchase – as the value of stock held is immediately affected.

► First in first out.

► Last in first out.

► Average cost.

month thirty shirts had been sold at £15 each. On 1 November a further thirty shirts arrive, from a more expensive supplier, costing £10 each. Supersport hold their price at £15, and a further twenty shirts are sold by the end of November.

Here is a summary of the information:

month	purchase	cost	sell	price
		(£)		(£)
October	40	8	30	15
November	30	10	20	15

1 What is the value of the closing stock on 31 November?
2 What is the gross profit on these shirts for the two month period?

The answer to these questions depends entirely on the method of stock valuation. The closing stock level is twenty shirts (total purchases = seventy, less total sales = fifty).

The FIFO (First In, First Out) method means that the oldest stock is sold first. Ten shirts remain in stock at the end of October. During November these 'October' shirts are sold, plus ten shirts from the November delivery. So the closing stock of twenty shirts all cost £10 each.

Closing stock value = 20 × £10 = £200

The LIFO (Last In, First Out) method means that the newest stock is sold first. As with FIFO, ten shirts remain unsold from the October stock. But the sales in November are all from the November stock, so only 10 'November shirts' remain unsold.

Closing stock value = 10 × £8 =   £80
                      10 × £10 = £100
                                  £180

The AVCO (Average Cost) method means that the stock is valued at its average cost. At the end of October, ten shirts costing £8 each remain. In November a further thirty shirts, costing £10 each, arrive. So the value of the stock available in November is:

       10 'October shirts' @ £8   =   £80
    + 30 'November shirts' @ £10 =   £300
       40   £380

The average value of these shirts = $\frac{£380}{40}$ = £9.50 each

Now twenty shirts are sold during November from the stock, so the twenty remaining shirts are valued at: 20 × £9.50 = £190

To find the gross profit, we calculate the sales revenue, and subtract the cost of goods sold.

Sales revenue of fifty shirts, sold at £15 each, is £750. So the correct calculation is:

SUPERSPORT LTD

	FIFO		LIFO		AVCO	
	(£)	(£)	(£)	(£)	(£)	(£)
sales revenue		750		750		750
purchases 40 @ £8	320		320		320	
30 @ £10	300		300		300	
goods available	620		620		620	
less closing stock	200		180		190	
cost of goods sold		420		440		430
gross profit		330		310		320

►No single method of stock valuation is 'correct'. Each method has merits and demerits. But a consistent approach is essential.

Summary and comment

• FIFO is widely used in Britain. It is the most realistic in its assumption of stock 'rotation'. Its balance sheet valuation for closing stock is up-to-date. But its assumed cost of stock issued/sold for the calculation of profit or loss tends to be out of date (oldest stock sold first)

• LIFO is open to firms as a method of stock valuation, but it is not permissible for taxation assessment purposes. It leads to very out of date balance sheet values for closing stock. Usually the cost of stock values for the profit and loss account are up to date, but sudden increases in stock usage could cause 'back-of-the-shelf' stock to be issued at very unrealistic values

• AVCO yields compromise values for both balance sheet valuation and cost of stock values for the profit and loss account. It also tends to smooth out the fluctuations in recorded profit caused by changes in the cost of stock. However it is more complicated to calculate, and its stated cost of stock is one that may never actually have been charged.

22 *Ratio analysis*

Chapter objectives

After working through this chapter, you will:

■ appreciate why ratios are useful

■ understand the meaning of all key accounting ratios

■ be able to investigate a firm's accounts using ratios

■ know how to interpret interfirm comparisons using ratios

■ know the meaning of the following key terms: RONA, profit margin, asset turnover, stock turnover, interest cover, return on equity, earnings per share, dividends per share, dividend yield, dividend cover.

►Applied to the main financial statements ratios are vital in assessing the performance and prospects of a business.

WHY RATIOS ARE USEFUL?

Consider the two major accounting documents. The balance sheet (see Chapter 18) tells us – at a stated date – all the resources held by a firm and how these resources have been financed. The profit and loss account (see Chapter 19) links one balance sheet date to the next. Sales revenue less costs yields a profit or loss. Payments of tax and dividends are indicated, followed by the amount retained within the business. This last sum appears on the new balance sheet as an addition to reserves.

All this data now needs bringing to life. A **ratio** simply relates one quantity or number to another. In a school, the head will want to know the number of GCSE passes. On its own this figure means very little. As a percentage of all entries it becomes more meaningful. However, a thoughtful head might also want to know the proportion of passes at grades A and B relative to all passes. He/she might further explore how this ratio varied between, say, maths and English, and how it had changed over the previous three years. This would be a ratio analysis of exam results.

It is very similar with a firm. 'Sales increased to £10 m. net assets fell to £8 m., and profits rose to £2 m.' This data has very limited meaning when stated in absolute terms. Expressed in relative terms using ratios, it begins to be interesting (e.g. return on net assets = twenty-five per cent). Compared with the ratios of previous years, or with the ratios of competitors, it becomes vital evidence for managers.

►Ratios themselves are easy to calculate. They provide a powerful means of investigating a firm's affairs. But the results are only pointers or clues: decisions, as always, require judgement.

 The best way to store the formulae for ratios is on index cards. However as you work through the following list of ratios keep referring to the data for Quist Electronics (on p. 160) to see how their accounts provide the source figures.

The data in all examples that follow below is taken from the case study that appears in full on page 160.

Efficiency Ratios

Efficiency ratios analyse the efficiency of the firm in its use of resources to generate profit.

►All the ratios below are calculated on data from Quist electronics.

$$\textbf{Return on net assets (RONA)} = \frac{\text{operating profit}}{\text{net assets}} \times 100$$

$$= \frac{18}{75} \times 100 \qquad = 24\%$$

This is the most basic of all ratios, and is sometimes called the **primary efficiency ratio**. It is the task of business management to use resources to create new wealth. RONA measures its success. Typical performance in the UK at present is 18–25%.

The next two ratios are closely related. Each opens a different pathway of investigation into efficiency.

►RONA = return on net assets; also called the primary efficiency ratio.

$$\textbf{Profit margin} = \frac{\text{operating profit}}{\text{sales revenue}} \times 100 \qquad = \frac{18}{225} \times 100$$

►Profit margin.

$$= 8\%$$

This means that for every £1 in sales, 8p is profit.

$$\textbf{Asset turnover} = \frac{\text{sales revenue}}{\text{net assets}}$$

►Asset turnover.

$$= \frac{225}{75} \qquad = 3 \text{ times}$$

This means that total sales are equivalent to three times the value of net assets. In other words, the net assets have been 'turned over' three times.

There is now an important relationship to recognize:

$$\text{profit margin} \times \text{asset turnover} = \text{return on net assets}$$

$$\frac{\text{operating profit}}{\text{sales revenue}} \times \frac{\text{sales revenue}}{\text{net assets}} = \frac{\text{operating profit}}{\text{net assets}}$$

$$8\% \qquad \times \qquad 3 \qquad = 24\%$$

$$\textbf{Stock turnover} = \frac{\text{sales revenue}}{\text{average stocks}}$$

►Stock turnover.

$$= \frac{225}{15}$$

$$= 15 \text{ times}$$

If stocks are too low, then sales may suffer. But stocks are expensive to hold, and the firm wants to minimize costs. So a balance is required. If the ratio gets too low, it suggests excessive stock levels. But the ratio could get too high, with an unacceptable risk of stockout.

► Refer back to this page for each of the examples that follow.

Data for Ratio Analysis

Quist Electronics PLC is based near Cambridge, and has become a leading manufacturer of advanced micro-electronics circuits. It became a public company in 1988, and its 80 million 25p ordinary shares are currently priced at 250p.

Balance Sheet as at 31 March 1992

	(£m.)	(£m.)
fixed assets		
land/buildings	28	
plant and equipment	15	43
current assets		
stock	30	
debtors	36	
cash	6	
	72	
current liabilities		
creditors	33	
tax provision	5	
final dividend provision	2	
	40	
net working capital		<u>32</u>
net assets		<u>75</u>
financed by:		
shareholders' funds		
ordinary 25p shares	20	
reserves	30	50
long-term liabilities		
loans		<u>25</u>
capital employed		<u>75</u>

Profit and Loss Account for the period 1 Apr 1991 to 31 Mar 1992

	(£m.)	(£m.)
sales revenue		225
direct materials	72	
direct labour	56	
production overheads	25	<u>153</u>
gross profit		72
distribution overheads	24	
administration overheads	30	<u>54</u>
operating profit		18
interest payable (@12%)		<u>3</u>
profit before tax		15
tax on profits (33%)		<u>5</u>
profit after tax		10
dividends		<u>4</u>
retained profit		6

$$\text{Days' sales in debtors} = \frac{\text{debtors}}{\text{sales}} \times 365$$

$$= \frac{36}{225} \times 365$$

$$= 56.8 \text{ days}$$

► Days' sales in debtors.

This value measures the debtors in terms of the number of average days' sales that they represent. Most firms specify the length of the credit period allowed to customers. If the actual credit period is much longer, then it suggests a need to tighten credit control.

Liquidity Ratios

Remember that liquidity means 'nearness to cash'. The firm's current liabilities are really pending demands for cash. The creditors must be paid, tax bills settled, dividends distributed. Even an overdraft can be recalled at short notice. The value of the current assets is therefore vital. These assets are 'current', precisely because they are short term and designed to be turned into cash. **Liquidity ratios** measure the firm's **safety** through the balance between current assets and current liabilities.

► Liquidity ratios measure the firm's safety from risk of cash flow problems.

$$\text{Current ratio} = \frac{\text{current assets}}{\text{current liabilities}}$$

$$= \frac{72}{40}$$

$$= 1.8$$

► Current ratio.

Traditionally this ratio should be between 1.5 and 2, but it can vary widely depending on the type of business.

$$\text{Acid test ratio} = \frac{\text{cash} + \text{debtors}}{\text{current liabilities}}$$

$$= \frac{(6 + 36)}{40}$$

$$= 1.05$$

► Acid test ratio.

This is a more severe test of liquidity. Stock is the least liquid current asset. A firm cannot be sure how quickly or how easily cash can be raised from stock. The acid test is the current ratio with 'stock stripped out'. Its typical value is 1, but again what is considered satisfactory will depend on the particular business.

Debt Ratios

Essentially there are only two sources of funds for a firm: the shareholders' money and borrowed money. These are very different. The shareholders' money is not repayable, and although a dividend is desirable, it is not obligatory. Borrowed money is repayable, and the payment of interest is obligatory. The risk involved in a firm's level of debt can be measured by ratios.

► Debt ratios measure the risk involved in the firm's level of debt.

►Gearing ratio (see chapter 24).

$$\text{Gearing ratio} = \frac{\text{long - term liabilities}}{\left(\text{shareholders funds} + \text{long - term liabilities}\right)}$$

$$= \frac{25}{\left(50 + 25\right)}$$

$$= 33.3\%$$

This ratio shows the proportion of long-term funding that is debt and interest bearing. While RONA is greater than the rate of interest, the highly-geared firm will enjoy greater than proportional returns to the shareholders' funds. But if RONA falls below the interest rate, then the profit available to the shareholders falls sharply. The risk is that profits will be insufficient even to pay the interest charge, with insolvency as the final threat.

►Interest cover ratio.

$$\text{Interest cover} = \frac{\text{operating profit}}{\text{interest charges}}$$

$$= \frac{18}{3}$$

$$= 6$$

This value measures the number of times the profit would pay or 'cover' the current interest charges. The higher the value, the safer the firm. Interest cover is often regarded as a clearer indication than gearing of a firm's exposure to the risks of indebtedness. It has the advantage of relating the actual profits to the actual interest payable.

►**Investors' ratios** measure the attractiveness of a firm to investors.

Investors' Ratios

The ultimate owners of a company are the shareholders. Their reward takes the form of dividends, and the increase in value of their investment (i.e. a rising share price).

►Return on equity ratio.

$$\text{Return on equity} = \frac{\text{profit after tax}}{\text{shareholders' funds}} \times 100$$

$$= \frac{10}{50} \times 100$$

$$= 20\%$$

This percentage uses the profit remaining after interest and tax payments to show the return on shareholders' funds alone.

►Earnings per share.

$$\text{Earnings per share} = \frac{\text{profit after tax}}{\text{number of shares}}$$

$$= \frac{£10m.}{80m.}$$

$$= 12.5p$$

Since the crude number of shares is not significant, this value only has meaning when compared over time.

$$\text{Price earnings ratio} \quad = \frac{\text{market price of share}}{\text{earnings per share}}$$

$$= \frac{250p}{12.5p}$$

$$= 20p$$

►Price earnings ratio – P/E ratio.

This ratio relates the market value of a share to its level of return as a unit of investment. The ratio is widely used in City analysis. A high ratio shows confidence in the share, while a low ratio suggests doubt about future prospects. The ratio can be distorted by short-term market abnormalities, e.g. a take over bid.

The next measurements all relate to the payment of dividends.

$$\text{Dividends per share} \quad = \frac{\text{dividends}}{\text{number of shares}}$$

$$= \frac{£4m.}{8m.}$$

$$= 5p$$

►Dividends per share.

As with earnings per share, this value only has meaning when measured over a period.

$$\text{Dividend yield} \quad = \frac{\text{dividends per share}}{\text{market price of share}} \times 100$$

$$= \frac{5p}{250p} \times 100$$

$$= 2\%$$

►Dividend yield.

This value relates the return on a share – expressed as a dividend – to the value of the investment (share value).

$$\text{Dividend cover} \quad = \frac{\text{profit after tax}}{\text{dividends}}$$

$$= \frac{£10m.}{£4m.}$$

$$= 2.5 \text{ times}$$

►Dividend cover.

This multiple shows the number of times the directors 'could' have paid the dividend.

RATIOS IN ACTION

Imagine a town centre where a large imposing shop is in the process of closing down. Notices announce 'Final Reductions', 'Everything Must Go!'. Perhaps it was a traditional firm, a landmark in the town. What has gone wrong? Where are the directors now? Was there no warning? Did they study their accounts a year ago? And what action did they take? Were their prices too high, or too low? Was the product mix right? Did they borrow too much, did they invest enough?

This is what accounts for management – or **management accounting**

– is all about. We can analyse accounts rather as a doctor would examine a patient. For temperature, blood pressure and pulse-rate we may substitute profitability, efficiency and liquidity. The aim is **diagnostic**: what is going wrong – and right?

The 'readings' are simple to make. But skill is required in spotting the vital connections. For example Lucifer Lighting Ltd, a firm manufacturing table lamps, has a low 'acid test' ratio at 0.6. However their current ratio is an overweight 2.4. The accountant finds that the stock turnover ratio is falling at 3.1. There is now a strong suspicion that the firm is carrying excessive stock.

As a means of analysis, ratios are most powerful when compared over time. Gloucester Glass Ltd find that their RONA has fallen from 28% to 21% over 3 years. 'Asset turnover' has been fairly constant at around 3, but the profit margin has fallen from 9% to 7%. Closer analysis of the internal accounts shows that the gross profit margin is steady, but the value for expenses: sales revenue is rising sharply. Distribution and marketing expenses relative to sales have not changed significantly, but administrative expenses: sales revenue has nearly doubled. The accountant decides to explore further. Suppose each administrative expense is related to sales? Is the culprit paperwork in the office, or could it be management expense accounts? It is a management accountant's job to find out.

Interfirm Comparisons

Managers may also find it revealing to make ratio comparisons with other firms, or with industry averages. These could provide a valuable means for assessing the firm's own performance.

> ### Interfirm Comparisons
>
> Wigtown Woollens Ltd
> Mr Crane, the company accountant, is examining his firm's ratios at the end of the financial year. The following data is included:
>
> | | |
> |---|---|
> | RONA | = 18.8% |
> | profit margin | = 8.2% |
> | asset turnover | = 2.3 |
> | stock turnover | = 4.9 |
> | days' sales in debtors | = 68 days |
>
> Considering a year of difficult trading conditions, results seem reasonable.
>
> Now look on the page opposite at a comparison with three other firms in the woollens industry.
>
> It can readily be seen that Wigtown's performance is **relatively** weak, although it does not have the worst ratios on every criterion.

►Firms should watch key ratios continuously. Computerized accounts make this possible and **target ratios** can be set for the period ahead. Actual performance can be compared with targets (see Chapter 23).

	Wigtown	Cheviot	Kielder	Swaledale
RONA	18.8%	20.6%	36.2%	27.8%
profit margin	8.2%	7.9%	11.3%	9.9%
asset turnover	2.3	2.6	3.2	2.8
stock turnover	4.9	8.8	6.0	5.6
days' sales in debtors	68	55	48	72

 How would **you** assess Wigtown's performance in the light of this information? Check each ratio with the earlier part of this chapter to make sure you know what each implies for Wigtown's performance.

Even more valuable are interfirm comparisons over a number of years. These enable management to analyse their own firm's progress relative to that of others, and to spot both encouraging and worrying trends.

In practice most of the data needed for useful interfirm comparison is confidential, and published accounts are limited in their scope and comparability.

 Read the following case study and answer the questions below.

In 1991 total sales at Carlton Carpets Ltd amounted to £800 000 with a profit before interest and tax of £32 000. The summarized balance sheet as at December 31 1991 is shown below:

►The 'Centre for Interfirm Comparisons' in London enables firms to submit their accounts anonymously, and then to receive a detailed comparison with the data for other firms in their industry.

	(£k)	(£k)	(£k)
fixed assets			
land and buildings		205	
plant and equipment		83	
investments		<u>40</u>	328
current assets			
stock	36		
debtors	210		
cash	<u>6</u>	252	
current liabilities			
bank overdraft	69		
creditors	<u>111</u>	180	<u>72</u>
			400
financed by:			
shareholders' funds			
ordinary £1 shares		100	
reserves		<u>120</u>	220
long-term liabilities			
mortgage		95	
other loans		<u>85</u>	<u>180</u>
			400

Now calculate the ratios of your choice to answer the following questions:

1 Does the firm appear to be efficient?
2 Assess the firm's liquidity.
3 How stable is the firm's financial structure?

Summary and comment

- ratios should be understood as financial signals. They provide **indications**, not answers. Ratio analysis highlights areas for investigation
- ratios on their own have very limited meaning. They are valuable when compared with those of previous years, internal targets, or competitors
- interfirm comparisons must be treated with caution. Each company has different assets, products and markets. There is no single 'correct' or 'standard' pattern
- the most valuable use for ratios is the analysis of trends over time, both within and between companies
- ratios relate by definition to results from the past. They do not predict the future, which is always liable to be different
- different firms use different accounting definitions. Great care must be taken to ensure that ratios are calculated on a common basis
- for some ratios, such as RONA, the higher the value the better. For most ratios, there is no single 'ideal' value. Often a range of values is considered satisfactory, and only movement outside the range boundaries is cause for concern
- abnormal or worrying ratios may be a **quantitative** signal indicating a **qualitative** problem. For example, falling turnover ratios might be traced to a troubled relationship between the sales manager and sales team
- all business activity is subject to external forces. Changes in the law, the national economy, or world conditions may radically affect ratios.

(23) *Budgeting*

Chapter objectives

After working through this chapter, you will:

▋ recognize the nature and purpose of a budget

▋ know how budgets are drawn up in a company

▋ understand the master budget and its links with sub-budgets

▋ be able to analyse budget variances as a technique of management control

▋ know how a pyramid of ratios may be constructed and applied

▋ know the meaning of the following key terms: standard costing, budget variance.

BUDGETS IN BUSINESS

Well ahead of the start to the relevant financial year, a budget committee is formed from directors and senior staff representing the key functions (in small firms the accountant alone may be the budget coordinator). This committee sends broad outline plans to the departmental heads who then settle their objectives for the year. The committee has the vital role in coordinating the operating aims of the firm. These are set by senior management and will reflect longer-term corporate objectives.

From the outset it is essential to isolate the key factor which will be the primary constraint on the firm's operations during the year. This is often sales. But it could be machine capacity, staff skills, or available finance. All plans and budgets must reflect this constraint. A failure here could typically lead to a huge output of products that the marketing department could not possibly sell. There follows a series of negotiations between departments and the committee in which plans are hardened into detailed budgets. Departments must involve their staffs in the planning, while the committee must maintain coordination and ensure conformity with overall goals.

Budget Structure

What is called the firm's budget is actually a whole series of sub-budgets covering all areas of operation. The essential pattern is easy to understand. The simple profit and loss account format indicates the basic sequence of budgets. Each element is planned through the months ahead to create a satisfactory overall outcome.

The starting point is sales, pricing and corresponding sales revenue. The marketing department will project sales levels by product,

▶A budget is simply a financial plan.

▶Budgets are usually for one year ahead, which is short time horizon. However budgets have to be consistent with longer-term corporate objectives.

▶All budget plans must be realistic. A budget is not a target but a **commitment**. The level of performance required by the budget should be neither 'ideal' nor 'soft', but a real intended standard.

customer, and outlet types, on a month-by-month basis. The estimates depend on market research, analysis of trends and the detailed opinions of sales staff.

As a likely 'key factor', the **sales budget** usually has special importance. Clearly it must be tightly interlocked with the **production budget**, which must be based on budgeted sales levels plus or minus any planned changes in stock levels. It will be necessary to plan the scale and timing of output around available capacity. A **plant utilization budget** will allow machine time and identify any peaks or troughs around the normal utilization level. The **materials budget** will indicate the flows of raw materials, components and finished goods needed to meet the production schedule. Similarly the **staffing budget** must specify the direct and indirect staff required, by department and grade. The personnel manager can then plan necessary recruitment, training and deployment. The **production overhead budget** attempts to allocate the fixed overheads (e.g. rent, rates, insurance) that can be directly related to production. Finally these various production budgets can be expressed in financial terms through the **production cost budget**. In profit and loss terms, this is the vital total that, subtracted from sales revenue, gives gross profit.

The **administrative expenses budget** embraces a wide range of items including management salaries, office expenses and non-production overheads. The **selling expenses budget** is drawn up by the marketing department and represents the cost of the marketing mix. It will include costs of advertising, sales promotion, distribution and the sales office.

The cost elements that give rise to operating profits have now been budgeted, and the vital step then is to draw up the **master budget**. This includes a projected profit and loss account and balance sheet, and so commits the firm to an overall level of performance that should be in accord with corporate objectives.

There are two other financial budgets that relate specifically to the balance sheet. Firstly, the **cash budget** or the **cash flow forecast** is a month-by-month estimate of all cash flows and the aggregate cash balance. This is essential to ensure solvency (see Chapter 25). Secondly the **capital expenditure budget** will depend on the level of funding provided by senior management. This will then be distributed between rival projects seeking financial backing (see Chapter 26). **Investment budgets** normally extend over a number of years, and planning in any one year must take account of costs incurred by projects in progress.

Functions of Budgets

The functions of the budget are:

- to create a coordinated strategy to reach corporate objectives
- to generate communication and interaction among managers in setting budgets
- to identify costs, question their necessity, and sharpen efficiency

►The importance of budgeting can hardly be overstated. It is the resource control system for the firm and a basis for managerial responsibility.

- to assign responsibility for financial decisions and commitments
- to assist delegation of responsibility while retaining effective means for monitoring performance
- to represent a system of control over operations and cost centres
- to provide yardsticks against which actual outcomes can be compared, so pin-pointing where management action is required
- to motivate the organization in meeting budgetary demands.

Variances and Control

As soon as the budgetary period starts, managers can begin to monitor actual outcomes for **variance**. Favourable variances are shown as positive, and unfavourable variances as negative. The relative size of a variance is shown by its expression in percentage terms.

►Variance is the difference between what is budgeted for and what actually happens.

Example of Budget Variance
BOURNEMOUTH BAKERIES LTD

Sales budget report

White loaves to external outlets

April (month 4) budget actual		variance		Cumulative (4 months) budget actual		variance	
(£k)	(£k)	(£k)	%	(£k)	(£k)	(£k)	%
16	17.1	+1.1	+6.9	65.4	68.2	+2.8	+4.3

The accountant or budget officer in a firm should supply senior management with full monthly budget reports. These will include all the major budget statements, with variances shown for monthly and cumulative data. Modified reports may be prepared for specific managers. It is essential that the information is clearly presented, speedily distributed and promptly analysed. Consequent action should be triggered by the variances.

Standard Costing takes a given production process and calculates the exact value of its materials, labour and allocated overheads per unit of output. Budgets can then be built up using the standard cost.

Example of Sales Budget Report
BOURNEMOUTH BAKERIES LTD

Sales budget report: April (month 4)

	BUDGET			ACTUAL			VARIANCE					
	own shops	other outlets	total	own shops	other outlets	total	own shops		other outlets		total	
	(£k)	(£k)	(£k)	(£k)	(£k)	(£k)	(£k)	%	(£k)	%	(£k)	%
white	22	16	38	22.4	17.1	39.5	+0.4	+1.8	+1.1	+6.9	+1.5	+3.9
brown	10.5	12.5	23	9.9	8.8	18.7	−0.6	−5.7	−4.3	−29.6	−4.3	−18.7
cakes	28	13	41	27.3	13.3	40.6	−0.7	−2.5	+0.3	+2.3	−0.4	−1

It is clear from Bournemouth Bakeries sales budget report that sales are proceeding broadly to budget, with one major exception. Sales of brown bread to other outlets are nearly thirty per cent below budget. This problem requires urgent investigation. What was the January variance? What action was taken? What is the real trouble? Was the budget unrealistic? Has a supermarket account been lost? Is competition greater than predicted? Have deliveries failed?

It would be impossible for manufacturers to explore the background to every result with which they are presented. The general rule is to focus investigation only on sources of significant variance. Since budgets are by definition estimates, small variances are usually acceptable. Management attention should be attracted once a variance moves outside a reasonable margin above or below budget.

Management by Exception

►Management by exception.

The concentration by managers on abnormal features of a firm's operation is called 'management by exception'. The principle is based on the assumption that there is no purpose, or time, for managers to examine systems that are functioning normally.

Note that it is not only negative variances that matter. A positive variance may indicate a rich new opportunity: a chance to reduce costs or a sudden gap in the market. Managers will aim to increase such a variance and learn from its implications.

Variances are not only caused by unexpected changes in **volume** (e.g. increased sales), but also arise from changes in **price**. An accountant investigating a positive sales variance would wish to know what proportion was due to increased volume, and what proportion to increased price.

Analysis of Variance – Volume or Price?

A firm is selling a single product.
Budgeted sales: 100 items at £10 each = £1 000
Actual sales: 110 items at £11 each = £1 210

Of the +£210 variance, how much is due to higher volume, and how much to higher price?

The rule for analysis is:
  volume variance x budget price
  price variance x actual volume

So
  volume variance = 10 x £10   = £100
  price variance = £1 x 110   = £110
                                  £210

The same principles are used to analyse a cost variance.

Analysis of Cost Variance

Firm B is selling a single product.
Budgeted cost: 1 000 items at £5 each = £5 000
Actual cost: 950 items at £4.80 each = £4 560

Of the –£440 variance, how much is due to lower volume, and how much to lower unit costs?

The same rule for analysis as above is used:
volume variance = 50 x £5   = £250
cost variance = £0.20 x 950   = £190
                                 £440

► Information technology has made variance analysis faster and cheaper to undertake.

 The manager of Ace School of Motoring Ltd is examining the company's results for April. The sales budget had projected 2 700 one hour lessons at £15 each. In reality a disappointing March had prompted a cut in fees to £13.75. Even so, the number of one hour lessons taken was only 2 400.

Calculate (a) the volume variance and (b) the price variance from budget targets.

Flexible Budgets

Variance may arise from controllable or non-controllable factors. For example a positive production cost variance may be due to increased efficiency, or a reduction in sales/output. If the firm uses standard costing then the exact sources of the variance can be analysed. In some cases **fixed budgets** with rigid sales assumptions are inadequate, and a **flexible budget** is needed. This means that a budget is produced in a range of versions for different levels of potential output, for example 80%, 90%, 100%. Thus if sales are 10% below budget, the '90% version' can be used to check on controllable variances.

Pyramid of Ratios

We know that a budget specifies certain levels of sales and costs. It is therefore also a plan for a range of accounting ratios – which in turn often express key management objectives. The analysis of variances can also be applied to accounting ratios. Because ratios express financial relationships, the investigation of ratio variances may lead an accountant to the heart of a business problem. The analysis becomes even more penetrating when we recognize that ratios form a logical pattern or hierarchy. This can be represented as a 'pyramid of ratios':

► The apex of the pyramid is the return on net assets or capital employed. This breaks down into:

1 Profit/sales – and analysis of the profit and loss account.

2 Sales/net assets – an analysis of the balance sheet.

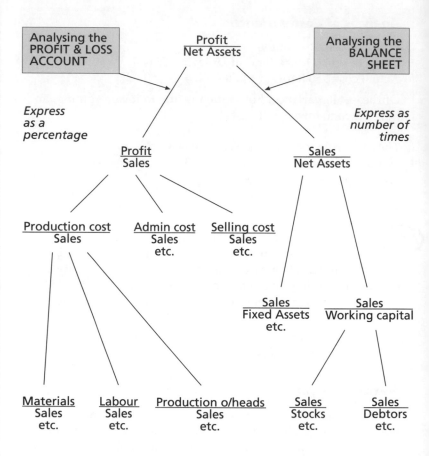

Figure 23.1
The pyramid of ratios

Remember that:

$$\frac{\text{profit}}{\text{sales}} \times \frac{\text{sales}}{\text{net assets}} = \frac{\text{profit}}{\text{net assets}}$$

Each arm of the pyramid can be broken down further through the various items on the profit and loss account and balance sheet. Using the master budget it is simple to produce budgeted ratios. Actual results and actual ratios then allow detailed variance analysis to proceed.

Summary and comment

• budgeting is essentially a planning and control system. It enables managers to translate goals into detailed commitments at every operational level

• often the process of setting budgets is as valuable as the budget itself. How does this cost arise? How great is the benefit derived? How much could we sell to this customer? Such questions can lead to reduced costs and increased sales

• budgets must be realistic. They are only effective in human terms if genuinely negotiated and not simply imposed. In this way staff feel a sense of ownership for their particular budget, and respond to it with commitment

- variances should work as a management alert system. Progressively higher levels of percentage variances trigger correspondingly more urgent management action
- information technology has made the operation of budgetary systems cheaper and more effective. Managers can depend on rapid and frequent access to data
- a budgetary system must not incur costs greater than its benefits. Budgeting itself works within a budget – for time and money.

(24) *Raising finance*

> ►Every business has to make its resources work at least as efficiently as its rivals. Any prolonged failure to do so will mean falling dividends and ultimately the failure to pay interest on debt. The result will be at best decline, and at worst take over or liquidation.

> ►It is also possible for a firm to reallocate resources inside the business. For example surplus land might be sold to finance some new vehicles.

> ►Funding of fixed assets and expansion.

> ►Provision of working capital.

Chapter objectives

After working through this chapter, you will:

■ appreciate the meaning of finance

■ recognize the different types of finance needed by a firm

■ know the main sources of finance for fixed assets and working capital

■ understand how firms select their sources of finance

■ be clear about the principles of financial gearing

■ know the meaning of the following key terms: equity, debt (long term, medium term, short term), working capital, retained profits, share issues, prospectus, under-writing share issues, offers for sale, tendering, placement of shares, rights issue, debentures, Eurobonds, sale and leaseback, venture capital, gearing, trade credits, overdrafts, bill financing, debt factoring.

TYPES AND USES OF FINANCE

Types of Finance

You will find it useful to look again at the format of a simple T-form balance sheet as shown in Chapter 18.

There are two basic types of finance available to any business:

1 **Equity**, which is share capital put up at risk by the shareholders. The money is not repayable, but, if profits permit, the shareholders receive a dividend. Equity also includes profits that have been retained within the business.

2 **Debt**, which includes all forms of borrowing from sources external to the firm. These funds are repayable, and usually carry an interest charge.

The Uses of Finance

There are two essential types of use for all business finance:

1 **Funding of fixed assets and expansion**, including the purchase of property, plant and equipment, and the take over of other firms

2 **Provision of working capital**, covering stocks, debtors and cash.

These will now be analysed more fully.

Fixed Assets and Expansion

Every business has assets that represent its physical and trading existence over the longer term. For most firms these include land, buildings, plant, equipment, holdings in other companies and general investments, plus any valuation of goodwill and brand names. Methods of funding include:

- retained profits
- share issues
- debentures
- Eurobonds
- medium and long-term loans
- short-term loans
- mortgage loans
- sale and leaseback
- hire-purchase
- venture capital.

1 Retained profits

Part of after-tax profits – often about one third – are used to pay dividends to the shareholders. The remaining two thirds are retained within the company, providing the major source of funding (often over sixty per cent of the total) for asset purchases and investment. Being an internal source of finance, this **ploughed back profit** can be used at the directors' discretion with no lenders to satisfy. However retained profits are not a 'free' source of finance. The opportunity cost of each investment project is the value of the next best option available. The minimum opportunity cost is the interest rate obtainable at the bank. New funds in a business add to the net assets on which management must make an adequate return. For public companies this point is underlined by the market price of their shares and the need to maintain confidence among investors.

2 Share issues

A company might decide to invite investors to purchase a new issue of shares. A private company will have to arrange this with existing shareholders and business associates. For a public company there is a wider range of options:

- a **public issue** means that the shares are sold by the company direct to business investors and the general public. The procedure will normally be carried out for the firm by an issuing house – a City institution with the necessary expertise. A **prospectus** will be supplied (and published in the national press), giving full details of the company's business activities and financial performance to date, together with plans and prospects for the future. Investors are invited to apply for an allocation of shares, which may be scaled down if the issue if over-subscribed. An issue is usually **underwritten** (insured), so that any shares unsold through the issue are automatically purchased by the underwriters. The whole process is expensive for the issuing company, and often costs around ten per cent of the issue value.

►Share issues.

Media Watch

Look at the financial pages of a quality newspaper for news about share issues. Collect news cuttings to illustrate the topic.

- an **offer for sale** is also a public issue, with the difference that all the shares are first sold to an issuing house, which then resells them at a higher price. This method may be suitable for a private company that is going public
- **issues by tender** set a minimum price for the shares, and investors are then invited to make bids for their required allocation. The final price set is the highest consistent with sale of the complete issue
- a **placing** occurs when most or all of the new shares are sold ('placed') direct to institutional investors such as insurance companies or pension funds. This method can be useful for small and less well known companies, but a discounted share price will be needed to attract support
- a **rights issue** involves offering existing shareholders the right to buy additional shares in proportion to their current holding at a reduced price. This does not give the shareholder a profit, since the share price falls to cancel out the gain. However if the shareholder does not want to increase his stake, the rights can be sold at a price that will prevent any loss. Rights issues are a cheap method of raising share capital for well established public companies.

All shareholders require a return on their investment. A new share issue, therefore, adds to the resources available to management, but also adds to the capital on which a competitive return must be made.

It is important to appreciate that, although the proportion of the adult population who own shares has greatly increased (up to twenty-two per cent by 1992), these privately-owned holdings only represent about twenty-five per cent of the total value of issued shares, a proportion which has fallen from around fifty per cent in the 1960s. The reason for this reduction is that much business expansion has been financed through **indirect investment** by households, i.e. –

► Large financial institutions are the dominant investors in British industry. Their fund managers make many of the key decisions in purchasing new issues, and holding or selling existing stocks.

- placing funds with investment and unit trusts
- making contributions to pension funds
- paying premiums to insurance companies.

3 Debentures

► Debentures (loan stocks/bonds).

A firm with sufficient financial standing may issue and sell promises to pay a given sum at a future date (called the **maturity date**), plus a fixed annual interest payment. These debentures are usually secured on assets of the company (repayment of the loan can be enforced in the last resort by selling these assets). If debentures are quoted on the stock exchange, they can be bought and sold with eventual repayment to the holder at the maturity date. Debentures are **not** shares, and carry no voting rights. There is a legal obligation on the issuing company to make interest and final payments to debenture holders before any dividends are distributed. Some loan stocks are convertible, which means that at a future date the holder is entitled to convert the loan into ordinary shares at an agreed rate.

4 Eurobonds

► Eurobonds.

Deposits of a foreign currency in a European bank (e.g. pounds sterling in a German bank, or dollars in a French bank) are called

Eurocurrencies. These deposits arise from investors seeking higher rates of interest than are available in their home country. They also provide a major source of funds for large companies, which can negotiate long-term loans in Eurocurrencies called Eurobonds.

5 Medium and long-term loans

Many firms obtain loans for an agreed period (term) from the banking system. Bank finance used to be primarily short term, but loans are now available for periods of up to twenty-five years. Long-term loans are for a period exceeding ten years, and are used to purchase a major asset such as land or buildings. Medium-term loans extend for a period of one to ten years, and are used to fund assets with a shorter life span such as machinery, vehicles and office equipment. The conditions of the loan are often specially designed to meet the business need. Repayment patterns can be related to the projected earnings of the investment project concerned. This may mean an initial period without repayment, or even the delay of repayment until the end of the term. Interest rates can be fixed or variable, or negotiated at agreed intervals. The longer the term and the higher the business risk, the greater the bank's requirement for security. This involves committing a specific fixed asset (e.g. property) to cover repayment in the event of default. Small business owners may be obliged to pledge their private property as security.

6 Short-term loans

These are bank loans for up to one year granted for a stated purpose, such as the purchase of vehicles or office equipment. The loan is repaid with interest, usually on a monthly basis.

7 Mortgage loans

If a firm wishes to purchase a major marketable asset such as land or buildings, then a mortgage loan may be obtained, using the asset as security. This is exactly the same principle as applies to house purchase. Banks, insurance companies and pension funds all offer business mortgages that may have terms of up to thirty-five years.

8 Sale and leaseback

This means that a major fixed asset is purchased and then sold to a financial institution (often an insurance company) which **leases** it back to the business. Therefore the firm is renting the asset over an agreed period. The rental charge will relate to interest rates, and the asset acts as security.

9 Hire-purchase

A firm purchasing an asset makes one initial payment, while the bulk of the cost is met by a **finance house** (e.g. Mercantile Credit). The remaining balance plus interest and service charges is then settled in a series of instalments over an agreed period.

10 Venture capital

The term means the provision of equity finance (share capital) to support smaller businesses, often in their start up stages. Many merchant banks have a venture capital subsidiary, while 3i (Investors

►Loans.

►Finance managers must ensure that a firm has sufficient liquid assets to make debt repayments as they fall due.

►Sale and leaseback.

►Hire-purchase.

►Venture capital.

in Industry) Ventures is Britain's largest source of venture capital. A wide range of business ventures may be supported, including innovative technologies, medical products and professional services. Often the sums provided are relatively small, and in the £5 000 to £100 000 range. However the venture capitalist will expect a real influence in the firm's management.

Working Capital

Within every business there are resources – called working capital – that continuously circulate, entering and leaving the business in a cycle. **Cash** is needed to buy materials and pay labour. Materials, semi-finished and finished goods are held as **stock**. Sales take place but payments may remain outstanding as **debtors**. The value of resources tied up in these ways fluctuates, but its average value is considerable in most firms (see Chapter 25).

1 Trade credit

Firms do not normally pay for their supplies at the time of receipt, but benefit from thirty to ninety days (or even longer) as a period of credit. This becomes a long-term source of working capital, although it may involve the loss of discounts for prompt payment. It is especially important for small firms, but large retailers often sell goods at a profit before they have paid the supplier.

2 Overdrafts

The firm is allowed by its bank to have negative balances ('in the red') up to a maximum sum outstanding for a limited period. Both the period and the overdraft limit can be re-negotiated. As a method of borrowing it is very flexible and convenient. Interest (at about three per cent above base rate) is only payable on the amount overdrawn, and formalities are kept to a minimum. However an overdraft is only intended to meet short-term needs (e.g. a seasonal lull in sales), and is repayable on demand. In practice though, many firms continue to renew overdrafts on a semi-permanent basis.

3 Bill finance

A **bill of exchange** is a legal document that amounts to a special cheque, usually payable three months after it is signed. A firm supplying goods to another company in the UK or overseas draws up a bill which is signed by the customer. This may then be 'accepted' (guaranteed for payment) by a merchant bank, which will charge a commission. However the bill can then be 'discounted' (sold at a discount) on the London discount market. The net effect of this is to bring forward the date at which cash is received by the supplier firm.

►The largest UK debt factor is International Factors owned by Lloyds Bank.

4 Debt factoring

Debt factoring means receiving money in advance on the sums owed to a business. A typical business may have the equivalent of two months' sales owing at any given time (i.e. up to around twenty per cent of the value of annual sales). A **factor** will advance around eighty to eighty-five per cent on debts outstanding, and pay the remaining balance (less charges) as payment is received. In addition the factor will take over the administration of invoicing and credit control, as well as providing protection against bad debts. Such a service strengthens cash flow by releasing large amounts of working capital. This in turn allows the firm to settle its own bills faster, gaining early-payment discounts and a good credit rating.

5 Reducing stock

A major item on most balance sheets is stock (see Chapter 16). This again represents resources tied up, which **might** be released to work more profitably in the business. Stock levels may be run down by temporarily reducing output, reducing prices or intensifying the marketing effort. However the firm must be careful that the value of lost sales or a dented reputation through the greater likelihood of running out of stock does not exceed the savings.

6 Asset sales

Any asset held by the company carries an opportunity cost: i.e. the loss of benefits arising from the next best use of those resources. A firm can therefore examine its asset stock to find items whose value could be turned into cash and more valuably used elsewhere in the business. This might involve sale of a car-park or a surplus warehouse, a piece of under-utilized machinery, or even the boardroom! There may also be the possibility of rental income from letting under-used assets.

Gearing

The **financial gearing** of a firm means the proportion of capital employed held as debt, or the ratio between debt and equity (share capital). Taken together, debt and equity act as the driving force of the firm. Their combined action provides the dynamic for production. Their relative sizes represent a gearing relationship (see Chapter 22).

►Even if the firm does not use a factor, attention to credit control can release valuable cash by ensuring prompt payment by customers.

►Gearing.

Gearing

A firm is financed by £400 000 in ordinary share capital, and £100 000 in long-term loans.

$$\text{gearing ratio} = \frac{\text{debt}}{\text{equity} + \text{debt}} = \frac{\text{£100 000}}{\text{£500 000}} = 20\%$$

The gearing ratio has critical implications. Equity yields no fixed rate of return: dividend levels can be determined by the directors. Debt carries an interest rate and interest is an obligatory payment beyond the directors' control. Thus the level of dividends can be related to the firm's performance, but interest must be paid regardless of performance.

For a fuller understanding of gearing consider this analogy: on a bicycle in a high gear you go very fast downhill. Stay in high gear going up hill and you will go slower and slower. Follow the same route in a low gear and you will break no speed records on the downhill section, but equally you will continue to make reasonable

►As profitability falls, a high-geared firm risks reaching the point at which total profits fail to cover interest payable. If no other sources of ready cash exist, the business may be forced into liquidation.

progress uphill. Business enterprises have 'uphill' and 'downhill' stretches and their gearing has parallel implications.

 Work carefully through the following example to make notes on gearing.

Effects of Different Gearing Ratios

Blue Ltd and Red Ltd are identical companies, except in one respect: they differ in gearing.

	Blue (£k)	**Red** (£k)
total equity	800	400
total debt (interest 10%)	200	600
capital employed	1 000	1 000
gearing	20%	60%

The rate of interest on debt is 10%.

Consider the following results (all amounts in £k):

Year 1: return on capital of 24%:

	Blue (£k)	**Red** (£k)
operating profit	240	240
interest payment	20	60
profit before tax	220	180
tax @25%	55	45
profit after tax	165	135
return on equity	20.62%	33.75%
interest cover	12	4

It is essential to understand each of the steps above:

- a 24% return on £1m. capital employed means an operating profit of £240 000

- the next stages are simple arithmetic

- the return on equity = $\dfrac{\text{profit after tax}}{\text{total equity}} \times 100$

- the interest cover is the number of times that operating profit will 'cover' the interest payable

Now examine the results for years 2 and 3 overpage:

When return on capital is **above** the interest rate, shareholders will do best from high-geared Red. Its return on equity will be better than low-geared Blue, which means
a) there is more available per share for dividends;
b) the market price of the shares will rise.

Year 2: return on capital of 12%:

	Blue *(£k)*	**Red** *(£k)*
operating profit	120	120
interest payment	20	60
profit before tax	100	60
tax @25%	25	15
profit after tax	75	45
return on equity	9.37%	11.25%
interest cover	6	2

Year 3: return on capital of 6%:

	Blue *(£k)*	**Red** *(£k)*
operating profit	60	60
interest payment	20	60
profit before tax	40	0
tax @25%	10	0
profit after tax	30	0
return on equity	3.75%	0%
interest cover	3	1

► High gearing can be a particular temptation to firms when rapid expansion seems possible.

Parity occurs when return on capital **exactly matches** the interest rate (10%). Low-geared Blue has twice as much profit to distribute to shareholders, but twice as many shareholders to distribute it to.

When return on capital falls **below** the interest rate, high-geared Red's return on equity falls below Blue's. Red has fewer shareholders to distribute to, but has spent almost all its profits on interest.

The lowest return on capital at which Red can meet its interest payments from earnings is 6%. Blue has a safer rating: it need only achieve 2%.

The situation can be shown graphically:

Figure 24.1
Return on equity and return on capital

Once interest cover sinks below 1, the firm can only meet its fixed interest obligations by using some part of its assets to fill the gap. In short, it is living on borrowed time.

Read case studies A and B and answer the questions below each.

A   Derby Designs Ltd produces original designs and full-scale prototypes for the engineering industry. Rising costs and flat sales led to a depressed profit of £30 000 in 1991. This was in relation to £300 000 in owners' equity and £180 000 in long-term liabilities. Now Nick Woodthorpe, the managing director, has decided that a £120 000 investment in new computer equipment is the only way to improve performance. Jim Hance, the finance director, has arranged funding through a long-term loan with interest on this and all other borrowings at fifteen per cent.

1   Comment carefully on this decision.

2   The actual profit for 1992 showed a disappointing advance to £40 000. Explore the implications of this.

B   Fresco Fabrics Ltd have been producing original curtain fabrics on a small scale for five years. The managing director, Liz Bateman, has now obtained the offer of a breakthrough contract to supply the John Lewis Partnership. An expansion of capital is essential, and Mr Kimber, the company accountant, estimates that £30 000 in new finance is required for additional machinery. At present the firm is funded by £50 000 in shareholders' equity and £20 000 in long-term loans. Being a small private company, none of the directors/shareholders are able to put forward any further finance of their own.

1   Make a check-list of all the sources of funds mentioned in this chapter.

2   From this list select three possible fund-raising strategies for Mr Kimber to investigate.

3   Assess the advantages and disadvantages of these options.

Summary and comment

• the range of options in obtaining finance depends very much on the size and status of the firm and the nature of the intended investment. Large firms have major advantages in their access to public share subscription, institutional backing and international capital markets. They are regarded as a lower risk and can borrow at reduced rates of interest

• in general, high risk projects normally require equity finance, while investments with more predictable earnings may be funded by term loans. A need for additional working capital can be met by short-term bank loans, by retained profits or from other internal sources. However each industry, each firm and each financial need is different, and funding approaches vary widely

- the relative cost of finance from different sources must be carefully assessed. Debt finance is loaded with an interest rate which may be variable. Equity finance requires a reward to shareholders in dividends, and should generate retained profits. Internal finance carries an opportunity cost which may be difficult to isolate
- as the term, risk and relative size of a loan increase, so the conditions imposed by the lender are likely to become more demanding. Accordingly, indebtedness may cause management to sacrifice some part of its independence in decision making
- high-gearing is a high risk strategy. It is advantageous while the rate of return on capital significantly exceeds the rate of interest. A reversal of this relationship will sharply depress profits available for distribution, and may pose a potential threat to the solvency of the firm.

Cash flow and working capital

Chapter objectives

After working through this chapter, you will:

▌ understand the concept of liquidity

▌ be able to construct a cash flow forecast

▌ appreciate the distinction between profit and cash flow

▌ recognize the working capital cycle in a typical firm

▌ be able critically to analyse working capital requirements

▌ know the meaning of the following key terms: petty cash, liquidity, spectrum of liquidity, insolvency, net cash flow, cash flow forecast, cash flow crisis, cash mountain.

WHAT IS CASH?

►Money is an official token, representing a claim on resources. To a business, a £10 note represents, perhaps, a small sheet of steel, a pane of glass, a bag of screws, or an hour of labour. It is the general acceptability of money – or cash – to settle almost any kind of debt, that makes it so useful.

All firms hold various amounts of cash during their trading year. The balance sheet shows the cash balance on one particular date. A small amount of **petty cash** will be kept in the office for minor day-to-day expenditures. It will be kept to a minimum since it is a security risk and carries no interest. Most of the cash total will be held in the firm's bank accounts: in a current account for short-term needs, and in a deposit account for longer-term requirements. Large firms may have substantial deposits with merchant banks and other city institutions, which can be released given appropriate notice.

►Liquidity.

Liquidity

Liquidity simply means closeness to cash. Pure liquidity is cash. Turn to Chapter 18 and look at the typical headings down the right hand side of a T-form balance sheet. The value of the assets is recorded after each heading. But value is not the same as cash. The land and buildings may be very valuable, but it would be difficult and time consuming to turn them into cash. Vehicles would be easier to convert into cash, stock easier still, while debts can usually be factored for ready cash. Thus the assets represent a **spectrum of liquidity**, the structure of which should be planned and monitored by the firm. A large need for cash and a low level of liquidity would cause serious problems.

Why is Cash Important?

Any active firm receives a continuous flow of demands for cash. These are to meet many different expenses. Unless the firm is able to meet these demands, it will become **insolvent**, and could potentially

ASSETS

LOW

Land and buildings
Plant and equipment
Vehicles
Stock
Debtors
Cash

LIQUIDITY SPECTRUM

HIGH

Figure 25.1
The liquidity spectrum

face liquidation. The frequency and pattern of cash demands varies widely. Some expenses recur every week or month – for example wages and materials. Others such as rents or rates or insurance premiums are regular, but occur at longer intervals. Yet others are irregular needs, but may involve large sums when they do occur – for instance, new buildings or machinery.

Because cash is so important, managers could be tempted to ensure an excess of cash over projected requirements. A safety margin is wise planning, but a significant excess is wasteful. Cash holdings earn little interest, and therefore carry an opportunity cost relative to funds being used profitably in the business. For example, a firm could use its surplus cash to invest in labour-saving machinery.

Sometimes a firm may hold large sums of cash for a special reason. This may be to finance a major project, or even to make an offer for another firm. A **cash mountain** within a firm should only occur as part of a calculated management strategy.

CASH FLOW FORECASTING

The **cash flow forecast** is a month-by-month statement of expected inflows and outflows of cash.

► The cash flow forecast is an important part of the firm's budget: see Chapter 23.

The Cash Flow Forecast

New Flame Ltd
Annabel and Chris Pugh decide to start in business – making and selling candles. They hope to begin trading on 1 April 1992. With savings of £3 000 as starting capital, they approach their local bank for an overdraft agreement. The manager asks for various business projections, including a cash flow forecast. Annabel first draws up a statement of key financial estimates:

1 The average selling price of the candles will be £2. Half the customers are likely to pay in cash, the other half with a month's credit.

2 Sales are expected to be 500 candles in the first month, 1 000 in the second month, and 2 000 in each month thereafter.

3 2 000 candles will be made each month, at a cost of £1 000 in materials. Their labour costs will be £1 500 per month.

4 Rent for some small premises will be £600 per quarter, payable in advance.

5 Other overhead expenses are likely to amount to £300 per month.

6 At the beginning of the first month it will be necessary to spend £1 000 on fixtures and fittings.

This information enables her to construct a projected cash flow statement for the first six months' trading.

Look briefly at the items below, and the columns of data. Then check carefully through the explanatory notes, and verify the reasoning for each column.

EXPLANATORY NOTES

1 The cash inflows are listed first. When originally received, the owner's capital represents an inflow.

2 Notice that for each month's sales, half the value is received in cash immediately, and the other half, on credit, is received one month later.

3 Materials, labour and overhead payments are straightforward. The rent appears at the start of trading, and again three months later (in July). Payment for the equipment is a single outflow, in April.

4 Subtract the total outflows from the total inflows to find the **net cash flow**.

5 Add the **balance brought forward** to give the **balance carried forward** to the next period.

Item	Apr	May	Jun	Jul	Aug	Sep
cash inflows						
owners' capital	3 000	–	–	–	–	–
cash sales	500	1 000	2 000	2 000	2 000	2 000
credit sales	–	500	1 000	2 000	2 000	2 000
total inflows	3 500	1 500	3 000	4 000	4 000	4 000
cash outflows						
materials	1 000	1 000	1 000	1 000	1 000	1 000
labour	1 500	1 500	1 500	1 500	1 500	1 500
rent	600	–	–	600	–	–
overheads	300	300	300	300	300	300
equipment	1 000	–	–	–	–	–
total outflows	4 400	2 800	2 800	3 400	2,800	2 800
Net Cash Flow	(900)	(1 300)	200	600	1 200	1 200
Balance Brought Forward	–	(900)	(2 200)	(2 000)	(1 400)	(200)
Balance carried forward		(900)	(2 200)	(2 000)	(1 400)	(200) 1 000

It is clear that New Flame Ltd will need an overdraft in order to begin trading. This will peak at £2 200 by the end of May, followed by a steady return to credit. Annabel will need to negotiate overdraft facilities for more than £2 200 (£3 000 could be ideal), so that any adverse variances in the budget can be financed.

 Make your own notes to explain the cash flow forecast, but raise the labour costs to £2 000 per month, and the rent to £800 per quarter.

The Cash Flow Crisis

Inaccuracy in a cash flow forecast may arise through lower-than-expected cash inflows, or higher-than-expected cash outflows. Some possible reasons are shown below:

Cash inflows down	Cash outflows up
depressed sales	increased wage settlement
reduced prices	rise in material cost
increased debtors	higher overheads
bad debts	intensified marketing
failure of an asset sale	unexpected repairs
	unforeseen events, e.g. legal action

►If cash reserves are about to be exhausted the firm will need some source of short-term finance, such as a bank overdraft. If no immediate credit can be negotiated a **cash flow crisis** exists. It may be possible to sell some stock cheaply, to factor some debts, or to dispose of a surplus fixed asset quickly. If even these measures prove inadequate, then the firm is insolvent and could be forced into receivership.

PROFIT AND CASH FLOW

Some of the most acute cash flow crises occur in profitable firms. Consider a firm that has discovered a really successful business formula. Projected sales – as reflected in the cash flow forecast – are expected to be highly profitable. Naturally the management wish to expand and exploit the market more fully. To do this requires an increase in output. More property, increased investment in plant and equipment and higher levels of working capital are all necessary. Perhaps bids for other less successful firms will speed expansion. **More cash is needed**. Every decision to commit more cash could be justified in the long run. But the profits are in the future, and cash is needed now. This phenomenon is called **overtrading**. This is extremely tempting when a firm has a winning product, especially if this coincides with a time of economic expansion. The flaw – and it can be fatal – is the mismatch between cash flow and profit.

Cash and profit are not the same. Cash is simply the holding of assets in a perfectly liquid form: it is no more than a statement at the bank. Profit is a trading outcome, a surplus of revenues over costs for a given period. The surplus itself is most unlikely to be stagnant in the form of cash. Probably it will have been invested in new fixed assets and distributed to the shareholders as dividends.

It follows that a **cash rich** firm could be unprofitable. Plentiful cash could exist for many reasons, including an inability to use it in the business profitably. Cash alone no more implies profit than, say, stock alone. For profit to occur, there must be a recorded surplus of revenue over costs.

► Cash and profit are not the same. Very profitable companies can have cash flow crises. Cash rich companies can be unprofitable.

 Read the following case study and answer the questions below.

Julie and Elizabeth Thorlby make reproduction nineteenth-century porcelain dolls, dressed in period costume. The business is about to expand and will enter a proper workshop on 1 July at a quarterly rental of £750 (payable in advance). Each doll costs £1.50 in materials.

Labour costs are £2 000 per month. Monthly overheads amount to £500. Output will be a constant 50 dolls per week, while sales are projected as follows:

JULY	80	OCTOBER	180
AUGUST	100	NOVEMBER	320
SEPTEMBER	120	DECEMBER	400

Dolls are sold for cash at £20 each.

1 If the cash held at the end of June is £1 000, draw up a cash flow forecast for July-December.

2 Comment briefly on the situation of the business.

WORKING CAPITAL

Working capital is simply the amount of resources that a business needs to operate on a day-to-day basis. Business involves the purchase of resources which are then transformed into a product that is sold to customers. No firm can achieve this process instantaneously. There will always be a gap between obtaining the resources for production, and the sale of the eventual product. In financial terms, we are concerned with the gap between payment for resources and the receipt of sales revenue for the corresponding product. However, the burden of this gap is cushioned by the firm's current liabilities. These provide short-term (less than twelve months) credit for the finance of current assets. For example, trade creditors are effectively financing part of the firm's stock. Therefore:

> Net working capital = current assets – current liabilities

The cash that is finally realized as a sale is recycled to provide the cash necessary to purchase more materials, and to pay the other costs of production. Provided that unit price exceeds unit cost, then a profit is also generated.

 Make notes on net working capital showing each item involved in its calculation.

► Profit as a percentage of the resource flow is the **profit margin**.

Working Capital Management

Working capital requirements must be carefully budgeted, and actual levels closely monitored. Working capital is essential for two major reasons:

1 **Trading**: stocks to meet consumer demand; debtors to provide customer credit; cash to meet expenses.

2 **Liquidity**: taken together, current assets provide the potential cash to meet all current liabilities that require payment.

► A firm cannot afford to run short of working capital. It is the 'life-blood' of the business.

Stock is necessary for any business to function (see Chapter 16). Manufacturers need raw materials, work in progress and finished goods; wholesalers and retailers trade in finished goods; even service

► Stock is necessary for production and for the satisfaction of consumer demand (marketing), but carries a high opportunity cost.

► Working capital circulates through the fixed assets.

Figure 25.2
The circulation of working capital

industries carry consumables (such as stationary). Stock has two critical interfaces. The first is with **production** in ensuring sufficient raw material to meet schedules and to allow flexibility in speeding or advancing output or in adjusting the product mix. The second is with **marketing** in keeping distribution channels filled, and in responding rapidly to changes in demand. However stock carries a high opportunity cost. It often represents as much as forty per cent of the net assets and keeps resources tied up that could be used profitably elsewhere in the business.

Debtors are unavoidable in many lines of business, since customers expect a period of credit. This may vary from one week to two months or more. Competition is a key factor in determining the 'going' credit period.

► Debtors are expensive. Waiting for customers to pay for goods/ services involves a minimum opportunity cost of interest earnings foregone.

Credit control is a vital operation, and effective pressure must be put on customers who exceed the agreed credit terms. Initially this will take the form of polite reminders, but progressively firmer measures may be necessary, culminating in legal action. In extreme cases, where the amount involved is very large, and a trade customer is probably unable to settle, an application may be made for their compulsory liquidation. Management must balance the gains from pressurizing late payers against administrative costs and the negative effects on customer relations.

Many firms try to build a trustworthy credit relationship with customers, and to assess carefully their credit risks. Sometimes a discount is offered for immediate or prompt payment, e.g. two per cent discount if the invoice is settled within twenty-eight days. This, though, can be a costly tactic which slices back the firm's profit margin.

Cash is essential in running any business and we have already explored the need for careful budgeting using a cash flow forecast.

► Cash flow control.

Creditors refers to all sums of money owed by a business and falling due for repayment within twelve months. **Trade creditors** is usually the most important item, and means payments owing to suppliers. When one firm supplies goods to another, there is usually an allowable time lag before payment. The period of trade credit extended by suppliers is usually between thirty and ninety days. This period of

► Creditor control.

▶ The value of debtors will normally exceed the value of creditors because the goods and services received are only one element in the final selling price – which includes labour, overheads and a profit margin.

▶ Current liabilities may include bank overdrafts and provisions for taxation and dividends (see Chapter 18).

credit helps to compensate a business for the time lags in payments represented by their own debtors. For most firms, the credit periods applying to suppliers and customers are similar.

Trade creditors can be a major source of finance, especially in retailing, where debtors are small, and goods received may be sold for cash before the corresponding payment is due. Managers will attempt to obtain favourable credit terms from their suppliers. Firms that are large-scale purchasers have market power, and may drive a hard bargain with smaller companies. However reliable long-term relationships with suppliers are also important.

Liquidity is crucial to a firm's financial health. Although current liabilities represent a valuable source of finance, they remain liabilities, i.e. subject to early payment. Generally the firm must ensure that the liquidity constituted by its current assets exceeds by a safe margin the level of its current liabilities. This is measured by the current and acid test ratios which show the number of times the firm could settle its current liabilities using its current assets.

$$\text{Current ratio} = \frac{\text{current assets}}{\text{current liabilities}}$$

$$\text{Acid test ratio} = \frac{\text{current assets} - \text{stock}}{\text{current liabilities}}$$

The acid test is a more severe assessment of liquidity, and strips out stock, since this is the least liquid current asset (it may be hard to sell, and its market value may have fallen).

A wider picture of liquidity can be obtained by using:

$$\frac{\text{net working capital}}{\text{sales}}$$

The actual value may vary widely between firms and industries. These ratios are most meaningful when compared over a period of time.

 Read the following case study and answer the questions below.

Midland Models supplies good quality plastic models in kit form to the UK and overseas markets. Sales in the last financial year reached £1.2m., while profit before interest and tax was £120 000. Net assets at the end of the same period were valued at £1.4m.

The firm's audited accounts are being considered. The managing director believes that the present level of working capital is excessive.

Raw materials are valued at £160 000, while work in progress is worth £120 000. The company holds finished goods to the value of £210 000. Debtors are shown at £310 000 on the balance sheet, with £110 000 in the bank. Meanwhile creditors total £350 000 and there is a provision for tax of £30 000. There are no other current liabilities.

The finance director feels that the criticism is unfair. The production department needs ample stocks to meet an unpredictable order pattern, while export customers are always slow to pay. The balance in the bank is needed to avoid a repeat of the cash flow crisis experienced three years ago.

The managing director is unconvinced, and proposes a fifty per cent reduction in all types of current assets to be achieved without delay.

1   Does Midland Models appear to have an excessive level of working capital?

2   How could the managing director's proposal be carried out? How would it affect financial ratios in the firm?

3   Could the finance director's arguments be justified?

Summary and comment

• managers must always ensure that sufficient cash is available to meet labour costs and regular bills. Forward planning is needed to ensure that enough cash can be obtained to pay for major investments, and to cope with unexpected events

• adherence to the cash flow forecast must be carefully monitored. The forecast depends on accuracy in predicting sales and costs. Internal changes (e.g. increased waste) and external changes (e.g. increased energy prices) can seriously affect actual against forecast data. Managers must be ready to adjust or revise the forecast as events unfold

• an adequate supply of cash is essential, but it carries a real opportunity cost. The firm's purpose is not to hold funds, but to use them in business to generate profit

• the faster the expansion of a firm, the greater the likely pressure on cash flow. The costs of acquiring, equipping and operating new business units usually outpaces the corresponding increase in sales revenue. A cash flow crisis may develop even though the business is trading profitably

• apparently excessive cash holdings – a cash mountain – may be held for a strategic purpose (e.g. a bid for a rival firm), or for tactical flexibility (e.g. in wage negotiations)

• the value of cash held by a firm does not necessarily represent the cash available. Other assets, such as debtors, stock or surplus fixed assets, are **relatively** liquid, and can be converted to cash if necessary. However this liquidation of assets may be time-consuming, involving significant losses through selling at a discount, and disrupt those areas of the firm affected

• the allowance in the firm's accounts for the depreciation of fixed assets (see Chapter 20) represents a real cost but not a cash outflow

- working capital means the net assets within a firm that are continuously circulating or being 'turned over'. A business aims to operate with as little working capital as possible
- managers must plan their working capital requirements for the trading period ahead. This is formalized in the master budget, which shows a projected balance sheet and profit and loss account. Variances from budgets should be investigated for their working capital implications
- all elements in the working capital cycle need to be constantly monitored. For any given profit margin, the faster the working capital can be driven round the cycle, the greater the return on net assets
- the ratios used to measure working capital need re-calculation on a regular basis. In practice, they may vary considerably over a year. This will reflect the fluctuating requirements for working capital according to season, sales trends, competition etc.
- one of the commonest causes of business insolvency is over-trading, where the rate of sales expansion is excessive relative to the working capital available.

(26) Investment

Chapter objectives

After working through this chapter, you will:

▮ understand the meaning and importance of business investment

▮ be able to use the simple methods of investment appraisal

▮ know how to use discounted cash flow techniques

▮ recognize the non-numerate influences on investment decisions

▮ know the meanings of the following key terms: average rate of return (ARR), payback method, discounted cash flow (DCF), present/net present value, internal rate of return (IRR), required rate of return (criterion rate).

THE MEANING OF INVESTMENT

Every business has fixed assets. These remain in the firm from one trading period to another, and represent the capacity of the firm to produce goods and services.

Fixed Assets as Investments

Bridgewater Biscuits Ltd is a small specialist producer of high quality traditional biscuits. Its fixed assets include:

land	computers	buildings
office equipment	processing machines	vehicles
ovens	fixtures and fittings	packing machines
loading equipment		

Unlike the working capital that circulates within the firm, the fixed assets are 'static'. This is the 'hard' structure of the firm, as opposed to the 'soft', more liquid assets that flow through it (see Chapter 25).

The balance sheet values each type of fixed asset, and shows their progressive **depreciation** in value. Clearly a point is reached when an item needs replacement. Equally the business may be expanding, and need an extra machine, vehicle or computer. Then again, a new technology may tempt management to purchase equipment on the grounds of increased efficiency. In each case the firm is considering an **investment**.

Any investment will be expected to yield a stream of financial benefits over its life. The extent to which the value of these benefits exceeds their cost will determine the relevant level of profit – or **return on investment**.

► Return on investment.

Most firms have a large number of different ideas for investment that they would like to undertake. However finance is limited, and only those projects with the best returns can be selected. In order to identify these the first step is to relate all the likely returns (cash inflows) to the likely costs (cash outflows).

Returns	Costs
Cash inflows	**Cash outflows**
profits on goods/services produced by investment	initial outlay
costs saved	opportunity costs of internal finance
government grants (if applicable)	interest on external finance
residual value	

Investment Appraisal

Analysis of the various costs and returns to show the overall gain or loss to a firm is called **investment appraisal**.

Average Rate of Return and Payback Methods

Average rate of return (ARR) is a simple calculation of the average annual percentage return on the investment. Suppose Bridgewater Biscuits is considering the purchase of a new automated food processing machine (machine A). Its purchase price is £10 000, and it is expected to produce returns over four years (we will ignore any scrap value in these examples).

Look at the table below. Do not be confused by the terms or layout. 'EOY' stands for 'end-of-year'. Year 0 means now – so EOY 1 means 'one year from now'. Remember that 'cash inflows' may represent **reduced costs** as well as additional revenues.

Investment Appraisal by Average Rate of Return

Machine A: ARR analysis

EOY	inflows/outflows	
	(£)	
0	–10 000	
1	+3 000	
2	+4 000	
3	+5 000	
4	+6 000	(total inflows = £18 000)
net return	+8,000	(total outflows = £10 000)

$$\text{Average annual return} = \frac{£8\,000}{4} = £2\,000 \text{ per year}$$

Investment appraisal methods:
- average rate of return
- payback method
- discounted cash flow method
- net present value method.

► Average rate of return (ARR).

$$\text{average annual rate of return} = \frac{\text{average annual return}}{\text{original investment}}$$

$$= \frac{£2\ 000}{£10\ 000} \times 100 \qquad = 20\%$$

This means that for each year of its life the machine should make a twenty per cent average return on the original investment.

Now suppose a different machine (B) was also offered to the management. This has identical costs to machine A, and will serve the purpose equally well, but its projected returns follow a different pattern.

Machine B: ARR analysis

EOY	inflows/outflows
	(£)
0	−10 000
1	+6 000
2	+5 000
3	+4 000
4	+3 000
net return	+8 000

► **ARR advantages**:
• a simple concept, familiar to all business managers
• easy to calculate

disadvantage:
• ignores the timing of cash flows.

The ARR equals twenty per cent, exactly as before. Apparently the two machines leave nothing to choose between them. But is this true? Machine B brings maximum returns much sooner than machine A. If the returns were invested each year in a bank account, then it is clear that machine B would be preferable. Larger sums would be earning interest for a longer period. This raises a very important issue: **a sum of money to be received at a given date is always more valuable than that same sum received at a later date.**

The **payback method** means calculating the length of time taken by an investment to recover its original outlay.

► Payback method.

Consider again machines A and B each requiring an initial outflow of £10 000.

EOY	inflows/outflows (£)	
	machine A	machine B
0	−10 000	−10 000
1	+3 000	+6 000
2	+4 000	+5 000
3	+5 000	+4 000
4	+6 000	+3 000
	+8 000	+8 000

Look first at machine A. At EOY 2, total inflows are £7 000; at EOY 3, the total is £12 000. The payback point – when total inflows are equal to the original investment – must occur during year 3. Assuming the

► **Payback advantages**:
• very simple and quick to use
• whole focus is on timing of cash flows
• reflects the risk factor by selecting projects with earliest payback

disadvantages:
• disregards all cash flows beyond the payback period, so fails to measure overall profitability
• fails to recognize that money received early in the payback period is more valuable than money received later.

► **Discounted cash flow (DCF)**.

inflows are evenly spread over each year, the exact payback point is calculated by interpolation as follows:

Inflows at EOY 2 = £7 000. We need a further £3 000 to reach the original outlay (£10 000). The period EOY 2–3 yields an inflow of £5 000. So £3 000 out of £5 000 should be received after three fifths of one year

i.e. $\dfrac{3}{5} \times 12$ months $= 7.2$ months

Therefore the payback period equals 2 years 7 months. The same calculation for machine B shows a payback period of 1 year 10 months. Clearly there is now a preference for machine B.

Discounted Cash Flow (DCF)

This concept is essential to understanding the other two methods of investment appraisal.

We start with an apparently simple question. If the interest rate was ten per cent, which would you prefer to receive:

a) £1 now
or b) £1.15 in a year's time?

If you took the £1 now and invested it at ten per cent, then after one year you would have £1.10. So choice (b) at £1.15 is more valuable than (a). Now consider £1 today, or £1.10 in a year's time? It is clear that these two options have the same value: it does not matter which you choose. This establishes an important principle:

1 £1 today is worth £1.10 in a year's time
or 2 £1.10 in a year's time is worth £1 today.

In statement 2, we are saying that £1.10 in a year's time has a **present value** of £1. It is worth looking closely at the simple arithmetic involved.

To increase £1 to £1.10, we multiply by 110/100, or 1.1
To decrease £1.10 to £1, we multiply by 100/110, or 0.909

These multiplication factors are useful. Given a ten per cent interest rate, we can make two further statements:

1 To find the value of any sum in 1 year, we multiply by 1.1
2 To find the present value of any sum payable in 1 year's time, we multiply by 0.909.

We will focus on statement 2. When a sum of money is reduced, we refer to a discount. Thus when we multiply a sum payable in 1 year by 0.909, we are using a **discount factor**.

Exactly the same principle applies to sums payable in 2, 3 or any number of years' time. We continue to assume a 10% interest rate.

To find the future value of a sum invested for 2 years, we simply multiply by 110/100 **twice**.

$$\left(\frac{110}{100}\right)^2 \; = (1.1)^2 \quad = 1.21$$

So to find the present value of a sum payable in 2 years time, we multiply by 100/110 **twice**.

$$\left(\frac{110}{100}\right)^2 = (0.909)^2 = 0.826$$

We can now calculate a series of discount factors:
Interest rate = 10%

Number of years until sum is received	multiply by	=	discount factor
1	100/110		0.909
2	(100/110)²		0.826
3	(100/110)³		0.751
4	(100/110)⁴		0.683
5	(100/110)⁵		0.621

Given a ten per cent interest rate, it is now easy to calculate any present value.

Examples
What is the present value of (a) £100 payable in 3 years time; (b) £1 500 payable in 5 years time?

  a) £100 x 0.751 = £75.10
  b) £1 500 x 0.621 = £931.50

These discounts reflect the time value of money: the further payment is moved into the future, the lower its present value becomes.

Notice that the discount factors become more severe as the cash flows are placed further into the future. This is natural, since the amount needed to yield £1 in five years' time will clearly be far smaller than that required to yield £1 in one year.

What would happen if the interest rate increased to 12%? A new table could easily be constructed. To increase a sum by 12% we multiply it by 112/100. So to discount a sum by 12%, the factor is 100/112, or 0.893. The rest of the arithmetic follows the identical pattern. Fortunately these discount factors are readily available in a grid without any further calculation (see Appendix 1).

Now consider the significance of discount factors. Any sum of money to be received at any time in the future can be given a present value. So a firm that has estimated the future cash flows arising from an investment project can convert them to their **true** present value at any relevant rate of interest. This concept is known as **discounted cash flow (DCF)**.

▶ The **present value table** is an appendix at the end of the book.

Required Rate of Return:

These examples derived the discount factors from a ten per cent interest rate. In practice, a firm is concerned with the opportunity cost of capital. A project is only advantageous if it can earn more than the next best alternative. The 'next best' might be represented by the overall average rate of return the firm expects from its investments. When this discount rate (in this instance the opportunity cost) is applied to the cash flows, it is called the required rate of return or **criterion rate**.

► **NPV**
advantages:
• fully reflects time value of money
• allows the application of different discount rates according to circumstances, expectations etc.

disadvantages:
• the net present value of a project lacks the clarity of, say, a ten per cent return on capital. NPV has meaning, but it is not money in the normal sense
• NPV values are not directly comparable when the size of projects differs.

Discounted Cash Flow

Suppose Bridgewater Biscuits is considering two more costly but more highly automated machines, each using improved technology, and each costing £15 000. Again we will assume no residual values. The cash flow projections are as follows:

EOY	inflows/outflows (£)	
	machine C	machine D
0	−15 000	−15 000
1	+3 000	+11 000
2	+5 000	+8 000
3	+7 000	+4 000
4	+12 000	+2 000
	+12 000	+10 000

Machine C appears to be the best choice, since it earns an extra £2 000 over the four year period (ARR for machine C = twenty per cent, machine D = sixteen point six per cent).

But we now know that simply to add up the cash flows is unsatisfactory. The sooner each £1 is received, the greater its present value is. DCF provides a more realistic valuation of projects through the calculation for a series of cash flows (arising from a project) of their **net present values (NPV)**. The arithmetic is simple:

Machine C: NPV calculation (@10% interest rate)

EOY	cash flow (£)	discount factor	present value (£)
0	−15 000	1.000	−15 000
1	+3 000	0.909	+2 727
2	+5 000	0.826	+4 130
3	+7 000	0.751	+5 257
4	+12 000	0.683	+8 196
	+12 000	net present value =	+5 310

Machine D: NPV calculation (@10% interest rate)

EOY	cash flow (£)	discount factor	present value (£)
0	−15 000	1.000	−15 000
1	+11 000	0.909	+9 999
2	+8 000	0.826	+ 6 608
3	+4 000	0.751	+3 004
4	+2 000	0.683	+1 366
	+10 000	net present value =	+5 977

It is now clear that contrary to appearances, machine D is the better choice (NPV is greater by £667).

Internal Rate of Return (IRR)

The internal rate of return (IRR) method uses the concept of discounting to give an exact percentage yield for an investment project. It is defined as the rate of discount that will reduce the net present value of a project's cash flows to be exactly equal to zero. This discount rate is called the **internal rate of return (IRR)**. To decide whether a project should go ahead, the IRR can be compared with the firm's required rate of return.

Internal Rate of Return Appraisal

Bridgegwater Biscuits is now considering the purchase of a packaging machine (machine E). The estimated cash flows over a three year life are:

Machine E: IRR calculation (@10% discount rate)

EOY	cash flow (£)	discount factor (10%)	present value (£)
0	−5 000	1.000	−5 000
1	+3 000	0.909	+2 727
2	+2 000	0.826	+1 652
4	+1 000	0.751	751
	+1 000	net present value =	130

At a ten per cent discount rate, the investment rate is profitable. What rate is needed to make NPV zero? A trial and error method is necessary. We will try twelve per cent:

Machine E: IRR calculation (@12% discount rate)

EOY	cash flow (£)	discount factor (12%)	present value (£)
0	−5 000	1.000	−5 000
1	+3 000	0.893	+2 679
2	+2 000	0.797	+1 594
4	+1 000	0.712	712
	+1 000	net present value =	−15

A twelve per cent rate has led to a slight 'overshoot', and NPV = −£15. This error is small enough to disregard, though the true IRR is around eleven point eight per cent (i.e. the discount rate at which NPV is exactly equal to £0).

► **IRR**:
advantages:
- provides a clearly understood percentage rate of return
- takes into account the timing of cash flows
- makes projects of different sizes comparable

disadvantage:
- more complex in calculation.

A graph helps to clarify the process:

Figure 26.1
Investment appraisal by IRR

Explanation

The horizontal axis shows a range of discount rates. At 0% no discounting occurs, and cash flows are 'worth' their full value. So NPV = £1 000 (see total of cash flow column, table above). As the discount rate increases, so the NPV must fall – until it reaches zero. This is by definition the IRR – in this case 11.8%. Up to this discount rate, the project is profitable, since its NPV is positive. At any discount rate higher than IRR the project becomes unprofitable, since its NPV is negative. For the packaging machine to be purchased, the company's required rate of return must not be higher than 11.8%.

 Look at the marginal notes on the advantages and disadvantages of different methods of investment appraisal. List the criteria by which these methods are judged. Use the criteria to construct a table – one column one criterion. Write the methods down the side of the table, and use ticks or crosses to show how they compare.

 Invicta Investments is considering project P which carries an immediate cost of £50 000 and which is expected to yield a stream of returns as follows:

End of year	1	2	3
(£k)	75	15	5

The alternative is project Q with the same initial cost and a single return of £110 000 at the end of three years. The firm's normal discount rate for investment appraisal is ten per cent.

1 What are the ARR values of the projects?

2 Project Q does not yield 'payback' for three years. What is the payback period for project P?

3 For each project, calculate:
   a) the net present value
   b) the internal rate of return

4 What conclusions would you draw about the two investment proposals?

Summary and comment

• the stream of future cash flows used in the appraisal methods may be highly inaccurate. It is derived from **expected** sales or cost savings, which may not actually occur. The relevant market research may have been flawed; the equipment or the product may develop faults; hidden expenses may emerge

• unexpected levels of competition may develop. Other firms may be about to make the same investment, and may be more effective in their marketing

• new technology always carries risks. 'Teething' problems are common, but major failures are always possible

• in the first selection of a project, personalities in the management team may be important. Concealed rivalries and personal ambitions can play a large part in selecting investment projects

• the human implications of an investment must be considered. Savings through job losses may be rational, but any resulting loss of motivation and morale among staff could outweigh the gains. Trade unions may exercise significant power in accepting or rejecting the impact of change

• interest rates are always important as the ultimate opportunity cost, or as the price of borrowed funds. Sharp changes in the interest rate are always possible

• a major underlying factor is the **economic outlook**. The prospect of recession, where demand for the firm's products may fall steeply, is very discouraging to investment. Managers may prefer to protect their liquid assets, and to avoid any new risky exposure to interest rates and problems with interest cover

• some investments are in intangible assets, whose benefit to the firm cannot be quantified. For example the launch of a new logo and house colours may be highly beneficial, but no precise cash returns can be attached to the scheme

• instability in an industry, a country or in the world raises business risk. All future cash flows carry risk factors, and their increase reduces the attraction of investment

• with the growth of knowledge-based industries, many firms make their biggest investments in **people**, through recruitment, training and benefits packages. The financial advantages to the firm depend on the complex process of personnel development, and cannot be tabulated in a cash flow statement.

27 *Monopolies and mergers*

Chapter objectives

After working through this chapter, you will:

▌appreciate how monopolies and mergers may threaten the operation of competitive markets

▌know how the government attempts to control this problem

▌be able to evaluate the arguments for and against large dominant firms

▌understand the phenomenon of concentration in industry

▌know the meaning of the following key terms: monopoly, merger, demerger, disinvestment, asset stripping, concentration ratio, Monopolies and Mergers Commission, Office of Fair Trading.

MONOPOLIES, MERGERS AND MARKETS

What is to prevent any firm from raising its prices and profits, lowering its product quality and offering a reduced level of customer service? Always, and everywhere, the answer is **competition**. The more competitive the market, the less the opportunity exists for any firm to exploit the consumer through excessive prices or inferior quality. Indeed, competition generally leads to the lowest possible prices and the most efficient possible production.

► If competition in a market is so effective that every firm must be equally and completely efficient and must offer the same, lowest possible price to consumers THEN **perfect competition** exists.

 Collect news stories on monopolies and mergers from the financial pages and annotate them to show what they illustrate.

The Problem of Monopoly

Where one firm is literally the sole supplier of a product, then a **pure monopoly** exists. In the real world however, there is generally some competition, and it is only a degree of monopoly power that occurs. This situation may work against the consumer by:

► In reality market firms are spread on a spectrum between perfect competition and pure monopoly.

- keeping prices artificially high to yield excessive profits
- protecting inefficiency and lack of quality
- removing the incentive for research and innovation.

In Britain a monopoly is not illegal. But the force of law is available to break up an existing monopoly or to prevent a monopoly being formed if it is thought to be against the **public interest**. The term public interest is rather vague. Essentially the law is hostile to monopoly unless special circumstances suggest that its drawbacks are outweighed by some wider benefit. For example, a monopoly might be necessary to achieve vital economies of scale, or to compete effectively in export markets, or to maintain employment in a development area.

Monopoly Power

The essence of monopoly power lies in the exclusion of competition from a given market. This can occur in the following ways:

- **resource concentration** in one geographical area may allow one firm to gain control over the major supply of a key product. This can occur with certain minerals and agricultural goods (e.g. diamonds from South Africa or certain wines from localities of France)
- **minimum efficient scale (MES)** for an industry may be so high that there is only room in the market for one firm to harness the full economies of scale. Would-be competitors producing on a smaller scale face impossibly high unit costs
- **marketing barriers** occur when one or more dominant brands are heavily advertised and very widely distributed. Competitors may find it prohibitively expensive to launch a new brand and gain trade acceptance
- **transport costs** in supplying certain distant markets may prevent any competitive challenge to a local firm without such costs
- **small and captive markets** allow monopoly when the market is too small to support more than one firm (e.g. a taxi rank in a small town), or when the market is 'captive' in a particular circumstance (e.g. a theatre bar)
- **restrictive practices** create artificial monopolies through firms making agreements to restrict competition (see below)
- **legal monopolies** exist where one firm is granted sole rights of supply. This occurs in nationalized industries (e.g. British Coal), in issue of official licenses (e.g. broadcasting franchises), and in patent protection.

What are Anti-Competitive Practices?

Monopoly in itself is not necessarily a serious problem. The threat to the public interest arises from one or more firms using market power to prevent fair competition in the market.

Typical anti-competitive practices include:

- **price agreements**, where firms deliberately maintain prices at an artificially high level (see Chapter 11)
- **cartels**, where a group of firms agree on output or price, or collaborate to share out the market between them
- **control of distribution or retail outlets**, where powerful firms threaten their customers with a block on supplies if competitor products are stocked
- **excessive advertising or sales promotion**, when dominant firms allow battles between competing brands to add a major layer to their cost structures.

► Where governments wish to ensure the fair and efficient operation of a free market economy, they must set the rules for business competition. The government acts in the market as a kind of 'referee'.

► MES: see Chapter 15.

► Anti-competitive practices 'jam' the price mechanism and prevent the efficient allocation of resources.

► The household detergent market is dominated by Unilever and Procter & Gamble. High fixed capital and marketing costs combine to form a barrier against competitors.

> **Monopoly Legislation**
>
> The major laws relating to monopoly and competition are:
>
> - **Monopolies and Restrictive Practices Act 1948**
> This set up the Monopolies and Mergers Commission (MMC) to investigate actual or potential monopolies, and to advise the government on necessary action
> - **Fair Trading Act 1973**
> This established the Office of Fair Trading – headed by the Director-General of Fair Trading – to refer cases to the MMC and generally to protect consumer interests
> - **Restrictive Trade Practices Act 1976** (original act 1956)
> This requires registration of any agreement between firms to restrict competition (e.g. charging common prices or supplying only approved dealers), and provides for legal judgement on agreements by a Restrictive Practices Court
> - **Resale Prices Act 1976**
> This prohibits any agreements between suppliers and retailers to enforce a minimum price at which goods may be sold (books and medicines are exempted). **Recommending** a resale price is not illegal
> - **Competition Act 1980**
> This made any anti-competitive practices by firms subject to investigation and ultimate prohibition, while making nationalized industries also liable to MMC enquiry.

Mergers

It is inevitable that successful companies will grow. Their very success will attract resources. Growth may occur through:

- internal resources: e.g. ploughed back profits or new share issues
- obtaining loans
- merging with other companies.

▶ Mergers and take overs are likely to bring a direct and immediate increase in market share.

A merger is the combination of two or more separate companies into a single business entity. The process can be by mutual agreement, where most of the owners exchange their shares for equity in the newly enlarged company. In many cases, however, one firm is clearly dominant, and the merger becomes a take over or acquisition. This involves one company making a bid for the other in order to gain a controlling interest (more than fifty per cent of the equity), often against the wishes of directors in the company acquired.

Many of Britain's largest firms were formed through mergers. This is evident in such names as Thorn-EMI or Rank-Hovis-McDougall. In other cases one name embraces many formerly independent companies: e.g. Hanson, BTR, Trafalgar House. The record shows that mergers tend to occur in short periods of intense activity. The last two 'merger booms' occurred in 1967–72 and 1984–9.

Why Do Mergers Take Place?

In each case there are usually several reasons, and the importance of each depends on business circumstances. The main motives are:

- **economies of scale**
  merger brings an immediate increase in the scale of business, often causing a fall in the average cost of production, marketing, administration and other functions (see Chapter 15 for details). The greatest economies are likely in capital-intensive flow production, where the high fixed cost of specialized plant can be spread over a larger output

► Economies of scale, see Chapter 15.

- **market strength**
  a merger usually increases market share, and can reduce the pressure of competition. This may enable the firm to trade at higher margins, or support a higher cost structure

- **risk reduction**
  a larger firm may be better able to survive downturns in the market, or a more general recession. Mergers are also often a route to **diversification**, where a widened product and market range is expected to increase security or growth

- **defensive strategies**
  mergers may themselves be defensive. A firm that is relatively small and weak may recognize that merger is inevitable. The aim is then to secure the most favourable partner and the best terms for shareholders

- **complementary products and markets**
  the products of two firms may be thought likely to make an effective match, so reducing costs and increasing strength in the market. Equally, firms may have complementary markets with strengths in different geographical areas or distribution networks

- **acquisition targets**
  mergers may be driven by a firm's desire to obtain the markets, customers, brands, patents, technologies or staff of another competitor company

- **asset valuation**
  one firm may bid for another on the basis that its market value (share price x issued shares) is below the true value of its assets. If successful in this strategy, the new owners may sell off unwanted divisions or subsidiaries of the firm taken over, so recouping part of the purchase price. There may also be opportunities for **asset stripping**, where the new owners sell certain items of property and plant, so yielding positive cash flow and a proportional capital gain

- **managerial motives**
  managers may be encouraged in merger plans by the prospect of increased status and rewards. Expansion can become an end in itself as the ambitions of senior staff are fuelled by a succession of acquisitions.

The Merger Process

When one firm is bidding for another, it may offer the shareholders of the target firm one or a combination of the following:

- a cash price per share
- its own shares
- fixed interest loan stock (i.e. IOUs or certificates of indebtedness bearing a fixed rate of interest).

The method of payment may have important consequences for the successful bidder's gearing ratio once the merger is complete.

An outright bid is often preceded by the predator building up a significant stake in the equity of the target firm. This might be purchased by a public company in a **dawn raid** – a surprise burst of buying activity on the stock exchange at the start of the trading day. Once an intention to bid is announced, the firm has twenty-eight days to make a formal offer.

The procedure for bids by public companies is regulated by the independent City Takeover Panel. This lays down an exact timetable through which bids may progress, and is designed to protect the shareholders of all parties concerned. Time is allowed for the target company to make its case for rejecting the bid and for the bidder to revise its terms. The bid must either succeed or fail within sixty days of the original offer.

Control of Mergers

The main types of merger are:

- **horizontal**, when the firms have similar products (e.g. one brewery buying another)
- **vertical**, when the firms are in the same industry but at different stages in the production chain (e.g. a brewery buys a chain of pubs)
- **lateral**, when the firms are in a related area of business (e.g. a brewery buys a mineral water producer)
- **conglomerate**, when the firms produce unrelated products (e.g. a brewery buys a chain of newsagents).

Mergers are liable for referral to the MMC when they would create a market share of twenty-five per cent or higher, or when they involve the acquisition of assets worth £30m. or more. The DGFT assesses merger proposals and makes recommendations to the Trade and Industry Secretary, who then may make a formal referral to the MMC. In practice the possibility of a referral often deters a planned merger.

Mergers in Practice

In some cases mergers may fulfil their declared (and undeclared) aims. But do mergers really improve business efficiency? Do they benefit the shareholders? A recent report (Peacock and Bannock 1991) finds no evidence that mergers have any positive effect on **overall** business performance. But behind this judgement lie many successful mergers and many that fail.

► Gearing ratio, see Chapter 22.

► A famous dawn raid occurred on 13 April 1988 when Suchard – the Swiss chocolate makers – took thirty-five minutes to build a thirty-five per cent stake in Rowntrees. This raised the curtain on a take over battle in which Nestle´ won the final victory.

► Monopolies and Mergers Commission (MMC).

► Since 1990 the European Community has had the power to investigate and control merger proposals when the companies involved have large scale sales both worldwide and within the Community.

All too often the high hopes raised by managers at the time of the merger are never fulfilled. The reasons include:

- **compatibility**

  every firm has a unique 'culture': a style of action, an outlook, a complex web of loyalties (see Chapter 36). These cultures can be very difficult to merge, and the effort may cause resentment, rivalry, and general dislocation. Technically too, different systems of management, accounting, research, sales and marketing may prove hard to combine. Often the expected synergy fails to occur

- **cost**

  after the merger occurs, all aspects of the combined firm's policy, organization, products, operations and finance must be assessed, restructured and integrated. This carries real costs, and may cause conflict and upheaval. In addition, the management time and energy expended has a heavy opportunity cost

- **industrial relations**

  mergers are likely to cause redeployment and redundancy. Among employees a mood of uncertainty prevails. New teams of managers may wish to change established methods of negotiation and communication. Morale and motivation may fall, disputes may increase and key staff may leave

- **diseconomies of scale**

  gains in efficiency are often less than planned, while the firm's increased complexity and scale can cause unexpected problems. Proportional administrative expenses may rise, the arteries of decision making may become clogged, and responsiveness to change may diminish. Sometimes these factors lead to a demerger, when a previous merger is broken up. For example, Dunlop and Pirelli, the tyre makers, demerged in 1982.

Smaller scale demergers may take place when sectors of a merged business are sold off (this is called **disinvestment**). It often involves a management buy-out (see Chapter 3).

Business Concentration

An industry whose output is dominated by a few very large firms is said to be highly **concentrated**. The degree of concentration is usually measured by a **five-firm concentration ratio**. This is calculated as follows:

$$\frac{\text{sales of 5 largest firms}}{\text{total industry sales}} \times 100$$

▶ Contested take overs normally increase the value of the target company's shares, and this represents a premium to be paid by the bidders. The record suggests a likely fall in post-merger profitability, and this premium cost may not be recovered.

Five-firm Concentration Ratio

An industry includes ten firms with total UK sales of £550m. in 1992:

Firm	Sales (£m.)	Firm	Sales (£m.)
1	126	6	33
2	121	7	24
3	80	8	19
4	64	9	15
5	60	10	8

Five-firm concentration ratio

$$= \frac{126 + 121 + 80 + 64 + 60}{550} = \frac{451}{550} \times 100 = 82\%$$

It is clear that this industry is dominated by a few large firms – a situation that is called **oligopoly**. Suppose that firm 2 makes a takeover bid for firm 6. If successful, the result would be a rise in the concentration ratio to 88% and an increase in firm 2's market share from 22% to 28%. Thus the bid would be liable for referral to the MMC.

▶ United Biscuits owns many major brands such as McVities biscuits, KP crisps and Terry's Chocolates.

The extent of actual concentration varies widely in British business.

UK five-firm concentration ratios	
	%
leather goods	13.1
toys and sports goods	18.0
footwear	38.8
industrial chemicals	47.8
ice-cream and confectionery	65.3
soap and toiletries	54.3
man-made fibres	93.2
motor vehicles and engines	84.1
tobacco	98.8

Source: CSO Business Monitor PA1002, 1991 (published 1991)

▶ In 1990 Unilever bought 56 companies which formed half the company's total growth that year.

These ratios give only a general indication of an industry's competitive structure. Much depends on how we define the industry and on how many other firms exist apart from the five largest. The real issue is power in a particular market. The size of a firm alone does not necessarily correspond with market power. A conglomerate may be a very large firm, yet lack a dominant share of any one market.

A common defence by firms in highly concentrated industries is to argue that the consumer benefits from producers large enough to benefit fully from the technical economies of scale. Much depends on the Minimum Efficient Scale (MES) for the industry concerned. The

MES for industrial diesel engines is very high and represents over fifty per cent of the UK market. To split the market between say five firms would lead to inefficiency. In the case of washing powder the MES is only equivalent to about ten per cent of the UK market. This implies that ten firms could share the market without any necessary loss of efficiency.

 Annual sales in a major consumer goods industry are as follows:

Firm	Sales	Firm	Sales
	(£m.)		(£m.)
A	280	E	126
B	244	F	73
C	205	G	48
D	189	others	37

Firm A now announces a hostile takeover bid for Firm F.

1 On what grounds might the Monopolies and Mergers Commission object to this bid?

2 How might Firm A claim that the take over was in the public interest?

3 Calculate the industry's five-firm concentration ratio, before and after the proposed take over.

Summary and comment

• few MMC reports lead to any legal action by the government. Equally, even the threat of an MMC referral causes many firms to end anti-competitive activities. MMC recommendations are usually accepted on a voluntary basis

• investigations by the MMC are very slow and often take two years or more. However their thoroughness and attention to detail are valuable in combating monopolistic practices

• the emphasis of UK monopoly and merger policy is on assessment of the public interest. But the balance has shifted towards **competition** as the key criterion. Referral of a merger proposal to the MMC is only likely if it threatens the consumer with higher prices or restricted choice

• UK monopoly and merger policy has tended to make judgements in the context of the British market alone. Arguably a merger giving market dominance in Britain may be in the wider national interest of competing effectively with large firms in Europe and the rest of the world

• the most basic argument for mergers is that they can result in more efficient use of the resources involved. A bid by one firm for another is effectively a claim by the bidder that it could bring better management to bear on the other firm's resources

- it is difficult to assess the performance of individual firms after a merger since published accounts do not yet demand any break-down of results
- there is widespread evidence that a **threat** to firms of being taken over can in itself act as a spur to greater efficiency. However this can lead to short-termism among managers, who may for example cut the research budget in order to keep up apparent profits
- mergers carry both costs (e.g. reduced competition) and bene-fits (e.g. economies of scale) to firms and to society. A cost-benefit assessment would attempt to balance the positive and negative effects on the public interest
- only one to two per cent of all proposed mergers are actually prevented through the mechanisms of UK merger control. How-ever the major effect may be preventative, with many potential mergers never being proposed. It should be remembered that today's high standard of living in the industrial world is under-pinned by a relatively small number of very large firms operating in world markets. Low unit costs achieved through their vast scale of production are supported by huge research budgets and an ethos of constant innovation.

Personnel management: recruitment, selection and training

Chapter objectives

After working through this chapter, you will:

▌ know the meaning and scope of personnel management

▌ be able to analyse the role of personnel management within the business organization

▌ understand the 'human resources' approach

▌ be aware of current trends in personnel management

▌ understand the principles of human resources planning

▌ appreciate why and how jobs can be analysed

▌ know how firms recruit potential employees

▌ be able to evaluate methods for selecting staff

▌ know the meaning of the following key terms: labour turnover rate, internal recruitment, external recruitment, head-hunting, Catell's 16PF (Personality Factor) Test, performance appraisal.

THE FUNCTIONS OF PERSONNEL MANAGEMENT

Personnel departments vary widely in prestige, size and functions. In some firms they are merely providers of staff and problem solvers when personnel matters go wrong. In other firms the personnel department is at the centre of all people-related decisions, and comes even to represent the essential ethos of the company.

Typical major functions fulfilled by the personnel department are:

- **human resources planning**, which analyses all labour grades and skills in terms of projected demand and supply
- **recruitment and selection**, which involves attracting and identifying the best candidates for posts available
- **training and management development**, which includes assessing and fulfilling training needs in accordance with the manpower plan
- **terms of employment**, which is a wide area of concern including the observance of business laws; disciplinary matters; implementation of redeployment, redundancies and dismissals; maintenance of health and safety at work, plus welfare and social functions
- **pay and benefits**, which must be assessed and structured to attract, retain and motivate staff of the necessary calibre; there must also be efficient administration

► Personnel management: making and implementing decisions that will provide the firm with the human resources necessary for its optimum performance.

► see Chapter 30.

► see Chapter 29.

- **industrial relations** which means ensuring effective communications between representatives of management and the workforce, not only to resolve grievances and disputes, but also to benefit from employee ideas and suggestions.

Depending on its status and importance, the personnel department may also address some broader corporate goals, such as employee motivation (see Chapter 34), communications within the firm (see Chapter 35), the reputation of the firm, the management of change (see Chapter 36) and the development of the corporate culture of the company (see Chapter 36).

Personnel Management Within the Firm.

Once a business has grown in size to 150 to 200 employees, a personnel manager becomes necessary, at least to ensure fair and legal practice, but also to recruit staff of the required quality, to organize proper training programmes, and generally to bring expertise to 'people problems' throughout the firm.

The basic **policies** of the personnel department are decided by the personnel manager or director in conjunction with the other directors or senior management. Policy statements set the direction and priorities of the department: for instance, 'levels of pay and rewards will be above the industry average to attract and retain a high quality of staff'. Policies must then be reflected in **strategies** for action. These will have a fairly long time horizon, be broad in scope, and be subject to revision as events unfold: for instance to adopt pay systems that better reflect individual performance. Such strategies are translated into detailed **tactics** and **operating plans**. These will be much more specific, with a short time frame and expressed as measurable targets: e.g. introduction of a new staff grading system.

The Human Resources Approach

▶ Some firms have renamed their personnel function with the title 'human resources'.

The **human resources** approach means regarding people as an economic resource that requires combination with other resources to achieve organizational goals. Many personnel departments grew in size and importance during the 1960s and 1970s, but faced sharp retraction in the 1980s. The rise in unemployment reduced the traditional need for recruitment, while the rapid decline in trade union power made industrial relations less prominent in management thinking. Since then many firms have reduced the size of their head offices, decentralized many functions, and adopted the concept of all resources – human included – being focused on profit-led objectives with closely measured results. Human resource managers are not independent professionals or specialists, but 'people strategists' and facilitators who are tightly integrated members of the management team. This fits in with the growing idea of more flexible, proactive organizations that are less hierarchical and bureaucratic.

▶ The human resources approach regards people management as a mainstream profit driven activity rather than a specialist service.

Explain briefly how a personnel manager might contribute to tackling the following problems:

1 The managing director at Steel Box PLC is considering relocation of the firm's main steel-cutting and fabrication plant from Birmingham to south Wales.

2 The marketing manager at Tryfan Tents Ltd is alarmed by a sharp rise in returned goods from retailers. Apparently the stitching in the lightweight hiking range is failing and causing the tents to leak.

3 The sales teams at MicroEngineering PLC must combine all the usual marketing skills with advanced technical knowledge of the firm's hi-tech product range. Salaries and conditions are excellent with most staff in their mid to late twenties. Why then, do sales teams keep losing their best personnel to rival companies?

HUMAN RESOURCES PLANNING

The essence of human resource planning is to match and synchronize the firm's demand for and supply of labour. The demand for labour depends on:

* staff being promoted, leaving, retiring etc.
* projected expansion, reorganization etc.
* changing skill requirements
* technological change.

► Human resources or personnel planning is often called 'manpower planning' even when the majority of staff are female!

► Labour demand.

These are all complex variables and the firm must attempt to estimate demand as accurately as possible. Often management will make these estimates using their own judgement and experience. Decisions may be taken by senior management alone or based on reports from the line managers of each department, division, branch etc. Greater accuracy may be obtained by using statistical techniques for forecasting requirements or by using work study to assess the staff-hours for the projected level of activity.

The supply of labour likely to be available depends on:

► Labour supply.

* the current workforce: its size, skills, qualifications, productivity and potential
* the external labour market: its size, age structure, availability and mobility, skills and qualifications.

In analysing the current workforce, management should be able to use staff records. It is helpful to calculate the **labour turnover rate**, which is defined as:

► Labour turnover rate.

$$\frac{\text{number of employees leaving in one year}}{\text{average number of employees during year}} \times 100$$

A moderate staff turnover rate is desirable as it brings 'new blood' into the organization and opens promotion prospects. But a high turnover rate would be adverse, suggesting staff dissatisfaction and causing instability, dislocation and high costs in recruitment and training.

 1 Make a list of all the factors you can think of which might lead to a high labour turnover.

a) Regard the items on your list as possible causes and work out a plan for researching the situation to decide which are the most important causes for a particular firm.

b) Choose two of the items on your list and write down what the firm might do to reduce labour turnover caused in these two ways. Try to think through the wider implications, for the company, of your suggestions. For example if you decide to put up wages, then this cost will have to be paid for.

The external labour market is chiefly influenced by:

- **demographic factors** such as the age structure of the population, which determines the number of school and college leavers
- **macroeconomic factors**, especially the overall level of demand which is a key determinant of the employment level
- **competition** from other employers, which may cause shortages of particular skills
- **education and training**, which affects the availability of younger age groups and the skills and qualifications offered.

From all the data collected regarding the projected levels of labour demand and supply, the human resource plan will be constructed. Although always subject to amendment, it is an important guide in both recruitment and training.

Job Analysis

People are only employed by firms for the tasks which they undertake to complete. These sets of tasks – or jobs – each form interrelated parts of a firm's total productive process. Jobs are the building blocks of business activity. Sound construction of jobs is vital to operating efficiency.

► Job analysis is essential to maintaining efficient deployment of staff – often the firm's greatest source of cost.

Job Analysis

'Chief Dogsbody' was how Lucy Barrett described her job at Farnham Foods. In theory she was employed as assistant sales manager, but Chris, her boss, was usually out meeting supermarket buyers, or chasing contracts in Germany. She was left answering the phone, showing round customers, tackling the post and sorting out distribution failures. She'd given up on 'small UK accounts' - which was meant to be her 'special responsibility'. The real irony was that Liz, the new export accounts clerk in the other office, was bored with not enough to do.

In the case in the box opposite, the lack of job analysis is causing serious inefficiency as well as dissatisfaction among staff. Effective job analysis enables management to construct and define jobs, and to place them for greatest efficiency in the organizational structure. A **job description** provides detailed factual information about the position, under such headings as:

- title
- grading
- location
- immediate superior
- purpose
- duties

- responsibilities
- special features
- skills and qualifications
- promotion prospects
- pay and benefits
- conditions of employment

 If you are employed yourself, write a job description for the job you do. If you are not employed, interview someone who is, and compile a job description using the headings above.

A **job specification**, states the requirements made by a job on its holder. The component tasks of the job are listed and matched with necessary knowledge, skills and attitudes.

Job Specification

A company seeks a clerk in the accounts department who will be chasing small debts by telephone. This job may require **knowledge** of elementary accounts, **skills** in the use of both telephone and information technology, and the personal qualities of confidence and courtesy towards others.

It is important that job analysis should provide for regular revision and re-analysis, since jobs are constantly changing. Particular skills diminish and increase in importance, while departments and sections shrink and expand in their workload.

 In the previous activity you drew up a job description. Write a corresponding job specification by listing the characteristics and the skills a suitable applicant for the job should have.

The Task of Recruitment

The most basic task is to establish the vacancies which the firm wishes to fill, and then to confirm or construct the job description. Most vacancies exist through staff leaving or retiring, but expansion and reorganization may also demand recruitment. When vacancies occur they are not always filled, or the opportunity may be taken to make major alterations in the job description.

► Recruitment means attracting the most suitable applicants for job vacancies in an organization.

Recruitment Methods

The methods used must try to achieve the best balance between cost and time against choice and suitability of applicants. The first possibility is **internal recruitment**, where the post is advertised within the firm or a particular person is invited to apply (or even appointed directly). This saves expense, while the performance of the applicant is already well known. They are also likely to be familiar with the organization's style and culture. Internal recruitment keeps open career pathways for existing staff, and is a source of motivation. However it will trigger a chain reaction of vacancies within the firm, and loses the advantage of new ideas and new perspectives brought in by outsiders.

In most cases **external recruitment** will be necessary, and there is a range of ways by which the vacancies may be advertised:

- **local press**, which is widely used for clerical and manual positions
- **national press**, which is used for managerial and professional positions
- **specialist magazines and journals** which reach particular groups of professional and technical staff
- **job centres** which are run by the Department of Employment, and provide a free service mostly used for manual and junior positions
- **local careers service, schools, colleges and universities**
- **private employment agencies**, which may be general, covering lower grades of staff, or specialist in supplying managerial, professional and higher grades.

The use of private employment agencies has sharply increased in recent years. Firms are relieved of the need to advertise, and the agency may have a wide range of candidates on their register. Agencies will also carry out all or part of the selection process. But these services are expensive, and although agency selection is often expert and impartial, it cannot take account of the firm's working culture or networks of human relationships.

Recruitment adverts are usually abbreviated interpretations of the job description and job specification. It is essential that they provide candidates with the main details of the job and the qualifications, experience and personal qualities required.

► To fill some senior posts, a firm may use **head-hunting**. This means that a potential candidate who works for another employer is asked to apply for or is offered a post. The process may be through informal channels, but agencies also offer a head-hunting service.

 Recruitment advertising is of course marketing of jobs. Look back to Chapter 9 and write notes to show the parallels between promoting products and services and recruitment advertising. You may well find it helpful to take cuttings of job adverts from the newspapers to illustrate your notes.

Application Procedures

 Look at the job advertisements in the newspapers and select a few. Ring up and ask them to send you application forms and further details. When they arrive evaluate them:

a) do the further details give the applicant the necessary information about the job?

b) is the application form well-designed to collect the information the employer will need to short list applicants?

c) do both together serve to make sure that only suitable people apply, and that the employer can judge that those who have applied are suitable?

Interviews

The interview is still the most widely used selection procedure. The evidence suggests that it is not a very good predictor of candidate suitability, but the importance of meeting a potential employee face to face remains. The main purposes of an interview are to assess:

* candidate's likely competence in the job
* any personal qualities that are an additional advantage or disadvantage
* general character and personality.

The firm may adopt a one-to-one, two-to-one or panel approach to the interview (a panel is a group of people who take turns to ask questions). Panel interviews tend to be highly formal and are used most in the public sector and for some senior positions. One-to-one interviews allow for an informal approach. To gain the advantage of several opinions, a sequence of short one-to-one interviews may be arranged. It is important that interviewers have familiarized themselves in advance with candidate details, and have agreed any special strategy or allocation for questions.

Candidate Testing

Some firms set tests to complement the interview process. The main types are:

* **knowledge/skills tests** aim to establish the candidate's competence in specific tasks, e.g. keyboarding speeds or proficiency in a foreign language
* **aptitude tests** are intended to indicate the candidate's potential to gain skills or pursue a particular career. These would include general intelligence tests. More specific tests – say for an engineering apprenticeship – might assess manual dexterity and spacial reasoning. Generally aptitude tests are most important when the costs of training are particularly high
* **personality tests** may be used if a particular personality type is thought necessary for the job, or found to be particularly unsuitable. Such psychometric tests aim to detect introversion or extroversion, convergent or divergent thinking, creative potential, likely behaviour under stress etc. For example **Catell's 16PF (Personality factor) Test** works through responses to a series of questions, and allows a 'personality profile' to be constructed for comparison with the profile thought most appropriate in the job concerned.

► Many managers are amateurs when it comes to interviewing. A personnel department can offer useful advice and assistance.

► Most personality tests are easy to administer. The skilled task is to interpret the results.

► Because most employees work as members of teams, performance in a group situation can be an important indicator of suitability.

More complex projective tests need the expertise of psychologists to be effective. Even a simple list of the candidate's leisure interests may be revealing of personality type

• **group situation tests** bring groups of candidates together, whose performance is closely observed in a variety of challenging tasks and situations.

All tests are subject to serious limitations. They are difficult to apply objectively, and results are frequently distorted by candidates either feeling over-stressed or attempting to supply 'favourable' responses. Tests may allow valid inferences about candidates' skills or aptitude when the tests are taken, but they have a poor record for predicting actual candidate performance in the job.

 1 How might the personnel department of an international construction company recruit:

    a) experienced surveyors

    b) crane operators?

2 What might be the most suitable selection methods for an airline wishing to appoint:

    a) trainee pilots

    b) cabin crew?

TRAINING

For the great majority of major business enterprises, training is not an optional extra. It is a key means by which firms can gain competitive advantage and sustain or expand their market share. Specific benefits of training include:

• increased labour productivity (output per man-hour)
• ability to use new technology
• greater flexibility from a wider skills base
• improved product quality and customer service
• greater motivation and commitment.

However many firms still perceive training as an expensive investment where the returns are unknown and unmeasurable. By its nature training brings long-term rewards, and managers tend to be driven by their immediate problems. When a business needs to reduce its costs, training can be an obvious choice for cutbacks. Firms may also fear the loss of expensively trained staff to rivals who have not made any comparable investment.

Large firms will have a formal training policy, and this will determine whether the training function is regarded as a short-term supplier of needs or a longer-term investment. The practical forms of training will depend on the nature of the business and its distinctive quality. In a hotel chain it would be customer based, while in an engineering firm it would be technically based.

Before any training plan can be constructed, the firm must identify its **training needs**. These exist wherever the value of an improvement

► Britain arguably suffers from too sharp a divide between academic and vocational study. Many commentators suggest that we need to give much greater status to vocational and technical achievements.

in employee performance is greater than the cost of its achievement through training. Training needs arise both through the demands of the job itself, and through changes in the structure and activities of the enterprise. They can be analysed for:

- the company: its labour requirement projections, its introduction of new technology, its changing structure and product base
- the department: its changing workload and demand for skills
- the team and the individual: any gaps between existing knowledge and skills and those needed for optimum performance.

 In two previous activities you drew up a job description and then a job specification. Take the same job and consider what training needs the job holder has in order to improve performance and adjust to changing circumstances. How could these training needs be satisfied?

> ► **Performance appraisal**: regular, individual interviews with employees to assess their performance in the job, to set targets for improvement and to discuss the means for reaching those targets. It helps to discover and clarify training needs.

Summary and comment

- personnel excellence is essential for achieving the levels of quality required in modern business. Recruiting and nurturing this excellence makes personnel management indispensable
- personnel management has tended to operate with a 'caring culture', at a distance from the main business functions. There is a trend towards its re-integration with mainstream business decision making
- the nature of the personnel department is shifting from being 'product led' - concerned with employing people - towards being 'market led' concerned with supplying staffing requirements
- the human resources approach blurs the old distinction between shop floor and management staff and binds personnel management into the main productive activity of the firm
- the personnel department has to justify its expenditure like any other cost centre. Its total performance is becoming more strictly accountable
- personnel management is finding an increasingly important role in communicating the firm's objectives and values to employees
- macroeconomic pressures are a key influence on personnel management. The business cycle impacts directly on recruitment, rewards and employee relations
- human resources planning provides a good opportunity to assess critically the real value of jobs performed. Often posts continue to exist after their justification has largely disappeared
- the danger of job descriptions is that rather than being definitions, they become **limitations**. Staff can be led by them to adopt a static and inflexible approach to their role. People grow into jobs and may be carried by their enthusiasm and imagination far beyond their job's original boundaries. Some firms are scrapping formal job descriptions and offering statements of

► (see Chapter 32).

broader objectives instead

• selection decisions should meet the long-term interests of the firm as well as immediate staffing needs. Some candidates represent an investment whose value will not be fully realized until long after their appointment

• organizations should be wary of breeding inward looking or convergent cultures where appointments only confirm the corporate self-image. Injections of unfamiliar assumptions and ideas may be essential to growth and innovation

• the continuous process of restructuring and filling jobs is a vital means by which an enterprise can respond to change. Often resignations and appointments are a key source of adaptation and renewal

• if the quality of a firm is represented by the quality of its staff, then recruitment and selection is not a routine task. Major firms are increasingly recognizing that employment is not merely a matter of exchanging money for time or tasks completed. It is a deeper relationship between a human organization with its own culture and values, and a human being with their own needs, abilities and aspirations

• skill shortages are a serious threat to expansion in British industry. Such shortages may discourage use of the most advanced technology, and while weakening competitiveness, encourage some firms to locate elsewhere in Europe

• low levels of skill among the workforce mean lower levels of value added to the product and lower real wages. This may attract 'screwdriver factories' where only assembly is taking place, but fail to secure 'sunrise industries' and hi-tech manufacturing

• employers have a direct economic motive in providing their employees with training for job-related skills. They do not have the same incentive to give training for **transferable skills** - skills that have a wider application across a number of different jobs. Yet these skills are essential to achieve a more flexible and sophisticated workforce

• some large firms provide all levels of training, but smaller employers too often regard training, for more than their immediate needs, as too costly and likely to encourage good staff to leave

• offering high quality training with effective career planning is more likely to retain key staff and to attract outstanding recruits. People who are well-qualified and ambitious look critically at a firm's training opportunities

• during and after training, it is important for staff to be given the opportunity to use their new knowledge and skills. It is very discouraging if these are ignored or even rejected by line managers

• training should not be regarded as an occasional or specialized activity. It must be a continuous function that is integral to the firm's life and growth.

29 *Personnel management: terms of employment*

Chapter objectives

After working through this chapter, you will:

■ know how pay structures and pay rates are decided

■ understand redundancy and dismissal procedures

■ be aware of employment law and its impact on staffing decisions

■ know how the health and safety and the welfare of employees are promoted

■ know the meaning of the following key terms: time rates, payment by results, measured day work, salaries, Health and Safety Executive.

PAY STRUCTURES

Pay and benefits are key factors in recruitment, a prime source of motivation, and the greatest source of cost in business. Consequently most firms develop a policy for pay and benefits at the highest management level. This is likely to address:

- the balance of pay against other benefits
- the mix of fixed rates against piece rates or commission
- the variation of rewards between different jobs
- the extent to which rewards-related decisions will be decentralized
- the relative level of rewards the firm will offer (e.g. a high-pay, high-expectation policy).

It is usually the task of the personnel department to devise a formal pay structure. This often roughly corresponds to the levels of the hierarchy for each department or branch. Any such system raises questions of fairness, which larger firms may try to resolve through **job evaluation**. A common method is to use a form of grading system which ranks jobs by some interpretation of the skills, responsibilities and qualifications required. For example a simplified structure for an administrative office might be:

grade 1: simple clerical duties
2: dealing with public enquiries
3: junior supervisory
4: section manager.

It is traditional to operate separate structures for manual and non-manual work. In addition, some firms also maintain different grading structures for technical and managerial positions.

Analytical job evaluation is a more precise approach, and involves breaking certain jobs down into their component parts, and allocating 'points' according to such factors as effort required, skill, responsibility and working conditions. These jobs, which have been broken down, become 'bench-marks' for all others, which are then slotted into the resulting scale. Such a method is costly, but may be more widely acceptable in a large organization.

Rates of Pay and Rewards

Pay for a job may be at a fixed or 'flat' rate, or it may be incremental according to length of service or merit.

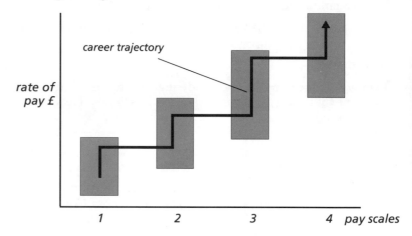

► Job evaluation.

Grading structures often include sub-grades which act as the rungs in the pay and promotion ladders which staff climb. The pay scales within grades often overlap to allow for differences in experience or age.

Figure 29.1
A grading structure

Traditional payment systems distinguish between wages for manual jobs which are paid on an hourly or weekly basis, and salaries for non-manual jobs that are paid monthly. The main methods of payment are:

1 *Wages*

Time rates are fixed and paid on an hourly or weekly basis regardless of the worker's output (e.g. £5.75 per hour for a thirty-eight hour week = £218.50 per week).

Payment by results is often called piecework. Its simplest form

---

Time Versus Piece Rates

Time rates are widely used where the nature of the output makes measurement difficult or impossible (e.g. most services). Their drawback lies in failure to make a clear result/payment connection allowing employees to 'time-serve' or 'coast'. Staff who work to a high standard may resent being paid at the same rate as those who are less efficient or less conscientious. Payment by results (piece rates) provides employees with a direct incentive to maximize output. In practice workers may adopt restrictive 'norms' for production to protect easily attainable targets. In addition new work practices may be resisted.

involves payment directly related to output or the time taken to achieve a certain level of output.

Some systems combine time and piecework rates by paying a basic rate up to a standard level of output, beyond which payment is by results.

Measured day work involves setting a level of performance (the 'incentive level') for the worker which is agreed in advance and paid at a fixed rate. The employee has the responsibility to reach this level, and may progress to higher levels at higher rates.

2 *Salaries*

Salaries can be paid on a fixed rate for all staff doing the same job, with individual increases only available through promotion to a different job. Usually however there is scope for personal progression through the salary grade according to age, length of service or merit.

Single Status

Some firms have abolished the distinction between their manual and white collar (non-manual) staff, to adopt **single status**. All staff then enjoy the same payment systems and benefits (e.g. pensions and holiday rights), often bringing a much improved package for manual workers. Apart from simpler administration, the aim is to dissolve the barriers between management and manual workers, to give all staff a unified sense of responsibility and commitment in the organization.

Bonus and Share Option Schemes

Some firms use bonus schemes to supplement earnings. Bonus payments may be made according to:

* time of year (usually Christmas)
* personal merit
* productivity on plant-wide basis
* profitability.

A more recent development has been employee share option plans (ESOPS), where staff receive their bonus in the form of ordinary shares in the company, sometimes at a preferential rate. Such schemes have certain rules concerning the sale of shares and tax liability. The aim is to encourage greater employee identification with the firm and its need for profitability.

Overtime

Many companies provide opportunities for employees to work overtime at higher rates of pay (e.g. 'time and a half', or one and a half times the normal rate), especially for manual staff. This normally arises because of a short-term need for increased output. In some firms it becomes a regular occurrence and a substitute for additional full-time staff. Although this can be cheaper and more flexible than recruiting new staff, there are dangers in relying on the arrangement. Then a withdrawal from overtime by either side can cause serious

► **Commission:** a form of piece rate payment. Sales staff often receive a basic salary plus a percentage rate of commission on sales achieved.

► **Flexitime** : an employee must attend work for some stated 'core time', but can complete their working hours when they choose.

problems: resentment among employees or short-staffing for the employer.

Setting the Rate of Pay

Labour exists in a competitive market like any other resource. The firm has a demand for labour while its value to the firm is greater than its cost (pay and benefits). The worker will supply labour while his/her valuation of the rewards is greater than the opportunity cost – no one will take overtime indefinitely: sleep becomes more valuable! These forces of demand and supply are reconciled in the real labour markets through recruitment, pay bargaining and redundancy. The actual level of pay and benefits offered depends mainly on the following factors:

- **demand for the product**: affects output, and hence the need for staff
- **elasticity of product demand curve**: rewards for staff are the major cost affecting price, in turn bearing on the level of sales
- **demand for particular skill or qualification**: some types of staff are more sought after than others
- **supply of labour type**: there are always shortages and surpluses of different skills
- **nature of the job**: the attractiveness of the job, the training necessary, the occupational hazards etc.
- **trade unions and professional organizations**: the greater their power relative to the employer, the higher the likely level of rewards (see Chapter 30)
- **benefits**: pay depends partly on the value of the benefits package that is offered.

Benefits

Most jobs carry some benefits in addition to wages or a salary. These are variously called 'fringe benefits' or 'perks', or are included in the concept of a 'rewards package'. Some range of benefits is now widely expected by employees, and can be important factors in retaining their loyalty and in increasing motivation. There are also tax advantages making benefits cheap relative to their value for employees. The most common benefits are:

- **pensions**: all employees contribute to the basic state pension scheme, but firms can opt out of the earnings-related element and provide their own more generous scheme
- **holidays, hours and leave**: the amount of paid holiday granted by firms is tending to increase (4-6 weeks is common). Flexible working hours are valued by employees, especially if they need to fit work around domestic commitments. Paid or unpaid leave of absence may also be available
- **loans, grants**: these are provided by some firms to assist with season tickets, buying a car, house purchase or relocation. Loans may be at reduced interest or interest-free.
- **expenses**: more senior positions often include entitlement to refund

of expenses (or a company credit card) for travel, meals, hotels etc.
- subsidized **canteen and social facilities**, company cars, health insurance, discounts on the firm's products.

 Look through the employment advertisements in the local or national newspapers to discover modes of payment and other benefits of employment. What kinds of jobs seem to be associated with what kinds of benefits?

Redundancy and Dismissal

There are many reasons why a firm may need to eliminate jobs and reduce certain inputs of labour:

- new technology replaces manpower
- the cost of labour increases
- a merger leads to rationalization (see Chapter 27)
- the firm relocates.

Efforts are usually made to avoid compulsory **redundancy** by using natural wastage (non-replacement of staff leaving), redeployment and re-training, early retirement and voluntary redundancy. If compulsory redundancies are unavoidable, then management must take great care in handling the procedure in order to minimize ill-effects on all concerned. To be made redundant is a great personal blow to many people, and the event may create a deep sense of insecurity in them and other staff. If trade unions are recognized, then proper consultation must take place. A fair basis for selecting staff to be made redundant must be chosen – often the 'last in, first out' principle. Notification of the individual concerned should be sensitive and prompt after the decision is made, in order to avoid destabilizing rumours.

A firm may wish to **dismiss** an employee who is incapable of reaching an acceptable standard in the job, or whose conduct is unsatisfactory. Both these grounds for dismissal are legally considered to be 'fair'. However the relevant manager will usually make efforts to assist the employee to become competent or to improve their conduct before resorting to formal dismissal. If dismissal does become necessary, the firm must be careful to check the terms of the employee's contract, and to follow the formal disciplinary procedure that they have agreed. Under the Employment Protection Act there are various grounds for dismissal that are automatically 'unfair', such as joining or refusing to join a trade union, or becoming pregnant. Any dismissed employee is entitled to claim unfair dismissal and to take their case to an **industrial tribunal**. Efforts will then be made to settle the matter through the Advisory, Conciliation and Arbitration Service (ACAS). If this fails, and if the tribunal finds in favour of the employee, then reinstatement or compensation may be ordered.

► Unemployment see Chapter 39.

► **The Employment Protection Act 1978** specifies the minimum periods of notice and scale of redundancy payments. In practice, many employers offer more generous terms, which may be embodied in agreements with unions.

Sex and Race Discrimination

It is illegal for employers to discriminate on grounds of sex or race. The key legislation is as follows:

- **Equal Pay Act 1970** requires employers to offer equal pay and conditions of service to men and women for equal or broadly equal work, or for work of 'equal value'. An employee with a grievance under the act will take the case to an industrial tribunal for judgement
- **Sex Discrimination Acts 1975 and 1986** prohibit discrimination in such matters as recruitment and selection, promotion and retirement ages. Two kinds of discrimination are banned. **Direct discrimination** occurs when a person is treated unfavourably because of their sex (e.g. a man taking precedence in promotion). **Indirect discrimination** means setting conditions which are applied equally, but favour one sex (e.g. unnecessary regulations regarding physique). Again, discrimination claims are taken to an industrial tribunal. The 1975 act created the **Equal Opportunities Commission** which promotes equal opportunities, and can instruct an employer to end a form of discrimination
- **Race Relations Act 1976** prohibits discrimination on grounds of race, with the same pattern of application as the sex discrimination laws. Complaints can be brought to a tribunal which has the right to award compensation. **The Commission for Racial Equality** promotes fair and harmonious race relations. It can bring a complaint to a tribunal on its own initiative.

► Many major firms have active equal opportunities programmes.

► With few exceptions job advertisements must not specify race or gender as necessary for the job.

Health and Safety

Many jobs involve activities where failure to follow the correct procedure can cause death or serious injury. Almost every work place has the potential to endanger health and safety.

Health and safety can be put at risk through a work environment that is badly designed, ill equipped or poorly maintained. Work practices – official or unofficial – may be inherently dangerous. Training may be inadequate. The attitude among employees may be casual or dismissive towards safety, while the final responsibility for all safety factors must rest decisively with management.

The **Health and Safety at Work Act 1974** states that every employer has a duty to ensure, as far as is reasonably practicable, the health and safety at work of all employees. This means making the work place physically safe, and then ensuring its safe use through the design of work practices and by proper training, supervision and leadership.

For employees, a recognized trade union has a legal right to appoint **safety representatives**, and require the formation by the employer of a safety committee. The safety representatives will carry out checks and investigations into safety, and liaise with both the employer and the safety inspectorate. The safety committee will study safety reports, make proposals for improvements, and promote safety awareness. The terms of the 1974 act are enforced by the **Health and Safety**

► In Britain about 500 people are killed in accidents at work each year, and around 250 000 people are injured badly enough to need three or more days off work. Many other people – some retired – suffer from long-term industrial disease.

► Accidental deaths at work have halved since 1974.

Executive (HSE), which maintains a range of specialist inspectorates. HSE inspectors can examine business premises at any time and order improvement – or if necessary launch prosecutions.

 Hartlepool Hydraulics was close to liquidation in early 1990 due to an excessive cost structure and the impact of foreign competition. A major restructuring followed with investment in new technology and concentration on specialist hi-tech markets. A single status agreement was accepted by all staff in 1992.

Year	Total employees	Labour turnover
1990	4 000	28%
1991	2 800	36%
1992	2 000	15%

Classification by skill	1990	1992
unskilled	52%	20%
semi-skilled	20%	14%
skilled	15%	40%
administrative and professional	13%	26%

Questions:

1 What would be the likely changes in the pattern of rewards offered by the company?

2 How might the firm have achieved the personnel changes indicated?

Summary and comment

• firms with the best results and reputations tend to offer above average rewards and have above average expectations of above average staff
• the choice of payment system must depend on the nature of the work. Where commitment to the organization is important, time rates are appropriate. If the firm is merely purchasing a discrete labour process, then piece rates may be suitable
• payment-by-result schemes, with their direct link to output, can be inappropriate during a recession
• although pay is important, employers can gain a good reputation and a highly motivated staff through the quality of their benefit schemes, their training, and their concern for individuals
• flexible benefit systems allow staff to choose up to a certain value from a 'menu' of different benefits. This increases the value of benefits to the individual employee at no extra cost to the firm
• firms are tending to develop a smaller core of well rewarded permanent full-time staff. Part-timers and contract staff will receive payment at the market rate and without the full rewards package

- enforcement of employment law in Britain tends to be by advice and warning, with formal prosecution used only as a last resort. Large firms are highly sensitive to criticism that might become public
- like quality, safety needs to be 'in-built' rather than 'added on'. It needs to be an automatic factor in every decision.

Personnel management: employee relations

WHY TRADE UNIONS ?

Employees generally have many common interests such as fair treatment, proper training, secure employment and improved pay and benefits. Inevitably these aspirations will not always be fulfilled by employers in pursuit of objectives such as profitability. It is to assist employees in defending or advancing their shared interests that trade unions exist. Quite literally, they are a 'union' of employees in one or more 'trades'.

Unions vary widely in their character and in the nature of the services they provide. However six main subjects of trade union negotiation or activity are:

1 Pay rates and productivity agreements.

2 Working hours, staffing levels, training, redundancy.

3 Conditions of work, health and safety.

4 Grievance procedures; suspensions and dismissals.

5 Communications with management, the media and the government.

6 Employee services e.g. insurances and mortgages, clubs and social facilities.

► The modern trade union movement has its origins in the industrial revolution when terms of employment were extremely harsh and no 'welfare state' existed.

 Contact a local branch official of a trade union and interview him or her to discover what he/she does in this capacity. Use the points one to six above as a check-list for your interview.

Types of Trade Union

Craft unions: skilled workers in a particular trade, e.g. printers in the National Graphical Association (NGA).

General unions: workers across a wide range of industries; mass membership of semi-skilled or unskilled staff, e.g. Transport and General Workers Union (TGWU).

Industrial unions: workers of all skill levels in one particular industry, e.g. National Union of Railwaymen (NUR).

White collar unions: administrative, clerical and technical staff, e.g. Manufacturing, Science and Finance (MSF).

Trade Union Structure

The number of trade unions in Britain has fallen from 453 in 1979 to 309 in 1991. This has been due to a series of mergers designed to increase both bargaining strength and efficiency. Each union is entirely independent and self-governing, but most unions belong to the **Trades Union Congress (TUC)**, which provides coordination and national representation for the trade union movement.

The internal structure of unions varies widely, but there is a typical pattern. Each union has a **president or general secretary** and a national headquarters with full-time officials, who carry out the policies decided at the national conference. Larger unions have a regional or district structure, also with full-time officials whose task is to assist the local branches. The foundation of a union is its branches, which may cover a particular place of work or all members in a wider locality. Each branch elects a secretary and holds regular meetings, but these are often poorly attended. They also elect delegates to the national conference. To conduct day-to-day union business in the work place, **shop stewards** are elected. The duties of stewards have tended to expand, and include representing the views of members to management, and negotiating many aspects of pay, conditions, hours and manning levels. In addition there is the duty to ensure constant feedback to the shop floor, and to recruit new members.

Within a place of work the various shop stewards may form a committee and elect a **convenor** to negotiate on their joint behalf with management. The committee might be limited to one union, but often it is a joint committee including stewards from all the unions involved. It is important to realize that management is often actively supportive towards all of these arrangements. Industrial relations need a proper structure with well-developed channels of communication.

The Closed Shop

Also called a 'union membership agreement', this means that all the workers within a given industry or work place must be members of a stated union. This tends to increase union bargaining strength, and enables agreements with the employer to be enforced without giving benefits to any non-union members. It is also supported by some employers, as creating a more stable environment for negotiation, and avoiding conflict between unions. The closed shop has also aroused strong opposition. Staff may have genuine objections to joining the union, and if expelled may lose their jobs. Under the **Employment Act 1982** at least eighty per cent of the workforce, in a ballot, must support a new closed shop agreement, or eighty-five per cent be in favour of one continuing. Exceptions to the principle of dismissal for non-union membership were introduced, including personal conscience, non-membership of the union before the agreement and unreasonable expulsion from the union.

Decline in Union Membership and the 'New Unionism'

In recent years there has been a very significant decline in the total membership of trade unions, from twelve point two million in 1979 to eight point two million in 1991. This has been caused by:

- large scale closures in manufacturing industry where unions were traditionally strongest
- new technology eliminating unionized jobs
- employment growth occurring fastest in service industry where unions are weaker
- the more restrictive legal framework
- a tendency for firms to negotiate directly with individuals and smaller work groups
- some shift in public attitudes away from trade union values.

With long periods of high unemployment and a shift in the balance of power towards greater management authority, a 'new unionism' has emerged. This involves a clearer belief that the success of the business will further the interests of union members (more jobs, more security, higher wages, better conditions), and can lead to a stronger sense of partnership. Some firms (e.g. Nissan in Tyne and Wear) have negotiated **single union agreements** where only one union is recognized and allowed to represent the workforce. This can be associated with a **no-strike agreement**, where the union undertakes not to withdraw labour during disputes, which are settled by pendulum arbitration (see p.235). Such agreements often also involve single status and labour flexibility (no restrictions on tasks that members will accept).

Employers' Associations

These are organizations representing the interests of employers for a particular industry. There are about 1 300 associations in Britain, but many are very small. Local associations may form a national federation (e.g. the Engineering Employers' Federation) with a national committee and a range of specialist sub-committees. A major function is to negotiate on a national basis with trade unions, but they also provide an important range of commercial and other advisory services.

Employers' associations and individual employers can join the **Confederation of British Industry (CBI)**, which represents employer interests at a national level. It has a director general and its own specialist committees, and as well as providing advice to members, it communicates employer interests to the media and government.

Collective Bargaining

To negotiate separate agreements between each employer and each employee would be impossibly inefficient and very unfair in its outcome. A system where agreements are made on a collective basis is usually to be preferred. In Britain **collective bargaining** is 'free', in that agreements reached are not normally subject to any state control.

► Research shows that strike activity is highly concentrated in a few plants in a few industries. Even during the years of highest strike activity ninety-eight per cent of work places remain strike free. The vast majority of trade union members never experience a strike during their working lives.

This allows for market forces to operate, but risks polarized confrontations where the monopoly power of one side in the labour market may unjustly prevail.

There are many subjects for collective bargaining, but the question of pay and other rewards is the most central and will serve best to illustrate the process. The outline of a bargaining situation is clear. While the firm will seek to minimize the cost of its labour inputs, the workforce will aim to maximize the value of its rewards.

► When you take your car to a garage for repairs, the mechanic is paid significantly less per hour than you are charged for labour. The difference is a source of profit to the company.

Figure 30.1
Basis for wage bargaining

Collective Bargaining Scenario

£ per hour   1   2   3   4   5   6   7   8

wage rate of labour per hour   *value added by labour per hour*

There is clearly a zone between £5 and £7 per hour which represents a surplus for the employer. Employees will wish to narrow this zone with a higher wage, while the employer will wish to widen the zone with a higher rate of value added by labour.

Bargaining can be of two types:

1 **Distributive**, where the employer's loss is the employee's gain, or vice versa (e.g. the wage rate rises to £6 per hour with no change in the value added by labour).

2 **Integrative**, where the goal is an outcome that benefits both sides. In pay bargaining this would involve a **productivity deal**, where the workforce gain a pay increase and the firm gains from increased output per man-hour: e.g. the wage rate rises to £6 per hour and the value added by labour rises to £8.50 per hour.

Before the actual bargaining begins, both sides will need to prepare their case and ensure that their negotiators are armed with all the necessary information and arguments to support their case. A vital factor will be the relative bargaining power of the union in making its claim. This depends on:

- **supply of labour**
  employers will be influenced by skill shortages or surpluses, while the union will need to consider the rate of unemployment
- **demand for the product**
  the firm's need for labour is derived from demand for the product; employers are influenced by short and long-term prospects

- **capital substitution potential**
  if pay rates rise, the firm is more likely to invest in labour-saving machinery
- **relative labour cost**
  the ratio of labour cost to total cost will determine the effect of pay rises on final price and hence sales
- **structure, funding and solidarity of unions**
  the strongest position will be enjoyed when bargaining is by a single union that is well-funded and solidly backed by members
- **negotiation skills**
  the skills of either side in framing demands and in conducting negotiations can be decisive
- **macro-economic trends**
  union power is weakened by recession and strengthened by a boom. The general level of demand for labour is related to the current level of output and the economic prospects ahead
- **the state, media and public opinion**
  public sector claims may be constrained by government pay 'norms' or cash limits. In high public profile industries (e.g. transport), media and public opinion can be significant.

The Bargaining Cycle

Negotiations between the two sides will follow an agreed agenda. Usually both sides make an opening statement setting out their position and emphasizing their expectations and demands. This stage is sometimes called the 'battle cry', as both management and unions stake out their ideal terms, on which they know a compromise is likely. The differences between the two sides are now clarified. The main negotiations follow where issues are explored in detail and some element of compromise begins. Bargaining techniques and inter-personal skills become very significant. A careful balance must be struck between concessions and demands, between objective and subjective argument, between speeding and slowing the negotiations. A crucial point will come – normally during an adjournment – when decisions must be made and the management team will emerge with an offer. In pay negotiations both sides will have a private scale of responses and expectations.

► Research has shown that strike-activity is highly concentrated in certain areas, industries and plants. Significantly, even during the worst years, 98% of manufacturing plants remained strike-free.

Employers
negotiating position

| ideal | realistic | fall back |

2   4   6   8   10   12   % increase in pay scales

fall back   realistic   ideal
negotiating position
Unions

Figure 30.2
A wage bargaining model

The situation shown here offers good prospects for reaching agreement: a settlement in the range six and eight per cent looks likely.

It is clearly important that there is at least some overlap between the two scales. If not, non-pay factors may bridge the gap, or else – under pressure – a fall back position may begin to slide. Eventually either a settlement will be reached or deadlock will prevail and a dispute begins.

 Look for news cuttings of employer/employee negotiations to illustrate your notes on collective bargaining.

Industrial Disputes

When negotiations fail, a state of dispute may smoulder for a time with further meetings, restatements of position and drawing up of deadlines. If industrial action follows, there are various sanctions that the union may take:

- **withdrawal of cooperation**, e.g. ceasing to attend joint meetings
- **work to rule** or **go-slow** will both reduce output
- **overtime ban** may disrupt production
- **token strike** has short duration and serves as a warning to management
- **strike**, which may be partial or total, for a fixed, repeated or indefinite period.

A strike becomes official when it has trade union backing. Under the **Trade Union Act 1984** this can only be given when a ballot among members has shown majority support. In practice, about ninety-five per cent of all strikes are unofficial, but these tend to be less serious and shorter in length.

A strike clearly places immediate and strong pressure on employers, who are normally unable to continue their main operations. Orders will be lost and relationships with important customers may be endangered. Meanwhile the union members will suffer from loss of earnings, and the union's funds will be depleted by strike pay or other campaigning action. Solidarity among strikers is practically and psychologically important. **Picketing** (persuading other workers to join the strike) often takes place outside the place of work, and **blacklegs** may expect hostility.

A union may seek support from other workers. If this is successful, **secondary action** might typically involve persuading truck drivers employed by other firms not to make deliveries at a strike-bound factory. If the employer in dispute tries to evade the strike by, for example, shifting work to another plant or another company, then the goods may be 'blacked' by other workers. However secondary picketing (i.e. picketing an employer who is not a party to the dispute) is illegal.

As the strike continues, the employer may re-enter negotiations or make an improved offer. Alternatively, he/she may be more resolved, and maintain or even withdraw the previous or final offer. In extreme cases the employer may dismiss striking employees for breach of contract, or decide to close down the work place, making the staff redundant.

▶ The code of practice associated with the Employment Act of 1980 suggests six pickets as a maximum for the entrance to a work place. Pickets may not use threatening or violent tactics.

▶ It is popularly believed that Britain is subject to frequent strikes and industrial disruption. In fact, most unions rarely organize industrial action, and in many large firms strikes are virtually or wholly unknown. Even in Britain's period of greatest unrest (the 1970s) the record was better than in the USA, Canada or Italy.

The underlying trend of the 1980s and 1990s has been a steady decline in the frequency of strikes. Working days lost through stoppages averaged twelve point nine million per year during the 1970s, and seven point two million in the 1980s. In 1990 there were one point nine million days lost - and there were 630 strikes, the lowest figure for fifty years.

Conciliation and Arbitration

If all efforts to resolve a dispute through collective bargaining fail, then **arbitration** may be requested from an independent third party. Some industries have their own built-in arbitration procedures. Particularly important are the services of ACAS (Advisory, Conciliation and Arbitration Service), which is government financed but strictly independent. If requested, ACAS officials will conciliate and mediate in a dispute, bringing the two sides together and helping them to find sufficient common ground for a settlement. Where a dispute has reached deadlock, and with the consent of both sides, the arbitration service will give a judgement that must then be accepted by all concerned. In recent years the device of **pendulum arbitration** has been used, especially as part of single union agreements. This means that the arbitrator is presented with the final positions of the two sides and must make a straight choice between them, with no further compromise. The effect is to encourage a 'pendulum effect' on the two sides as they compete to occupy the most 'reasonable' position in the centre ground.

► Arbitration: the settlement of a dispute by an independent third party (person or organization).

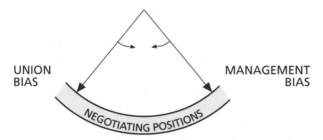

Figure 30.3
Pendulum arbitration

Often the final arbitration is unnecessary as the pendulum effect brings an earlier settlement.

Conflict in Business Organizations

Strikes and major disputes are only the high profile part of conflict in organizations. Conflict has many other less obvious but still very damaging symptoms. For example, high or rising rates of labour turnover, absenteeism, accidents or customer complaints can all be signs of excessive conflict. Ultimately, an organization can become paralysed by conflict, and thus highly inefficient - and fatally unable to respond to change. Formal grievance and dispute procedures are important, but do not touch the real sources from which conflict springs. Examples of these might include:

• rigid and authoritarian management with a lack of bottom-up communication, causing a build-up of frustration
• rapid or poorly planned change, causing dislocation and a decline in the status and prospects of some employees
• decline in the firm's markets or market share, causing the threat of redundancy
• lack of involvement, boredom and alienation (see Chapter 34) among staff

- badly designed organizational structure (see Chapter 32) that divides the workforce, distorts communication and overloads some staff.

The really vital task for management is to **create rather than assume** a unity of purpose. This is not the same as requiring everyone to act in the same way. The firm may get the best from its staff by tolerating many different methods of moving in the same direction. Broad strategies include:

- **worker participation** means involving staff in the machinery of decision making. This might be through a **Joint Consultative Committee** which brings together managers and worker representatives on a regular basis, with a formal constitution. Meetings may tackle many subjects of mutual importance (e.g. job security, working conditions), so improving the flow of communication and tending to build understanding and trust. A danger lies in crossing wires with the process of collective bargaining. Some firms have set up a **company council** with representatives of all grades, that is free to address major planning issues. A very few firms have introduced employee directors with seats on the main board
- **profit sharing** is designed to encourage a unitary view of the firm and to motivate employees in such areas as quality, sales or customer service (see Chapter 30)
- **open styles of management** involve cultivating a more unified and less conflict-prone culture in the organization. Single status often brings all-staff social facilities, common eating and relaxation areas and less hierarchical privileges. An 'open door' policy (literally keeping all office doors open where possible), and a stronger information flow to employees can also be helpful.

 Industrial disputes are only one, rather rare, symptom of conflict in a business. List all the other symptoms of conflict you can think of, and make notes on how worker participation, profit sharing, and more open styles of management might alleviate conflict.

 Read the data below and answer the questions.

Transport and General Workers' Union

membership: main industries
    transport: air/roads/docks
    manufacturing: cars; engineering; chemicals; food
        processing; textiles
    energy
    hotels/catering/cleaning
    water, health and public services
    agriculture.

► In 1981 the Japanese firm Toshiba took over from Rank a loss-making television plant in Plymouth. A single-union no-strike agreement was reached with the EETPU and single status was introduced throughout the factory. Ten years later employment had trebled, output was up eightfold to 600 000 sets per year – and not one day had been lost through strikes.

Membership numbers

1979	2.1m.	1987	1.3m.
1981	1.7m.	1989	1.3m.
1983	1.5m.	1991	1.2m.
1985	1.4m.		

Unions amalgamating with TGWU
National union of Agricultural and Allied Workers
National union of Dyers and Bleachers.

Questions:

1 How would you account for the TGWU's membership data?

2 Why might other smaller unions wish to amalgamate with the TGWU?

3 How might a decision by a company's workforce to join TGWU – in a single union agreement – benefit the employer?

Summary and comment

• the geographical, occupational and social mobility of the labour force is increasing, with wider educational and training opportunities and accelerating technological change

• in the past fifteen years there has been a major decline in male-dominated blue collar manual employment, due to de-industrialization and new technology. This has greatly weakened some sectors of the trade union movement

• to retain members and to attract new recruits, unions are tending to stress the specialist services they can offer, while placing greater emphasis on partnership with management

• the emphasis on productivity in collective bargaining is likely to remain. There is increasing recognition that improvements in real rewards – and job security – depend on a competitive level of value added by labour

• the need for legal restraints in industrial relations is now widely accepted: the issue is the balance of advantage provided by the law

• the concept of involving the labour force in decision making is gaining ground both through joint committees and in more autonomous work groups, project teams and 'cells', where all members participate in problem-solving

• as hierarchical pyramid structures become flatter and even begin to dissolve into open 'networks', so the traditional opposition between 'management' and 'workers' loses force. The emerging trend for the future suggests an organic kind of unity in which common purpose is achieved less by confrontational bargaining and more by mutual consent.

(31) *Decision making*

Chapter objectives

After working through this chapter, you will:

▌ know the meaning and nature of decision making

▌ understand the use of a simple decision model

▌ appreciate the role of intuition and creativity in the decision process

▌ recognize the problems and realities of decision making in organizations

▌ know the meaning of the following key terms: objectives, mission statements, environmental constraints, decision trees, scenario planning.

DECISIONS AND MANAGEMENT

Management is the art of making the best use of available resources to fulfil agreed objectives. This means:

- recognizing problems and opportunities
- responding by making decisions
- ensuring that decisions are efficiently implemented.

Objectives

▶ Objectives: a statement of what an organization wants to achieve.

Objectives are a statement of what an organization wants to achieve through its operation. A firm's formal objective is given in its memorandum of association (see Chapter 3), and larger firms may publicly state their general philosophy and values in a list of objectives. For most PLCs profit is only one goal among others.

Objectives provide criteria for decision making. Most firms harden these general objectives into more dynamic **aims** which are intended to drive the organization forwards in the chosen direction. **Mission statements** are focused declarations of intent, designed to energize staff at all levels to work in a common cause.

▶ The objectives of most public companies do not merely express the narrow financial interests of the shareholders. Employees, customers, the community and the environment are all often quoted as interests to be satisfied.

In practice the overall objectives of a large firm need translating into terms that have meaning for each operation or function. This may mean that one objective is particularly highlighted.

Constraints and Opportunities

Business operates in a real world and decisions are not taken in a vacuum. Before making any decisions a manager must always assess the limitations of a situation. These exist both inside and outside the firm and affect every function. Some examples are in the box opposite.

DECISION MAKING CONSTRAINTS

Human

staff numbers	labour availability
skills and experience	national pay awards
training programmes	education and training provision
attitudes	employment laws
trades unions	

Production

installed machinery	suppliers
capacity	environmental controls
technological base	planning laws
warehousing	

Marketing

market research data	distribution networks
new product research	competition
product portfolio	aggregate demand
sales team	advertising codes/laws
trade barriers	

Finance

cash flow	credit-worthiness
liquidity	availability of loans
gearing	interest rates

The decision maker is also confronted by internal and external opportunities. Inside the firm there may be staff with hidden skills, machinery with an interesting alternative use, or a potential source of new funding. Outside the firm a sudden gap in the market may emerge, or a significant new technology. The window of opportunity can open suddenly, and profitability may depend on being able to respond before it closes.

Decision Models

In business, managers make decisions that involve large sums of money and other people's jobs. To achieve the optimum (best possible) outcome usually requires a systematic approach. For this purpose a **decision model** is useful.

► A **model** is a representation of reality that assists understanding of structure, operation and meaning.

- **problem awareness**: detecting the existence of a problem before its details become clear
- **define objective**: clarifying the objectives or desired impact of the decision to be made
- **collect information**: researching quantitative data and qualitative evidence; investigating possible causes and effects; identifying constraints
- **develop options**: generating ideas; selecting list of credible options
- **evaluate and decide**: assessing the plus and minus factors; projecting outcomes; testing and trialing against objective; deciding on

► Notice the logical order for decision making.

optimum solution

- **implement**: planning necessary action; ensuring the decision is carried out; checking actual events; taking corrective measures
- **monitor consequences**: reviewing outcomes relative to objectives; learning from experience.

Monitoring consequences returns the manager to the problem awareness stage so that all the stages together make up a continuous cyclical process.

Decision making

Kennards Ltd

Richard Hopkins has recently been appointed managing director of Kennards, a traditional department store. Kennards has a loyal customer base and an excellent position in a university town. However there are signs of under-performance. The objective for the first year is to increase return on capital to twenty per cent. An early target of Richard's attention is the in-store restaurant.

Problem awareness:
the restaurant on the third floor is running at a slowly increasing loss; both menu and decor seem dreary and dated.

Define objective:
make restaurant a key attraction for the store and profitable in its own right, otherwise find the best alternative use for the space.

Collect information:
investigate restaurant accounts; interview manageress and staff; devise questionnaire for a survey of all customers; check building regulations for possible alterations.

Develop options:
collect numerous ideas from management and staff. Final options include:
1 Straight refurbishment.
2 Shifting company accounts from the top floor and opening a new café/restaurant with a roof garden.
3 Closure and replacement with a new outdoor leisure depart ment.

Evaluate and decide:
Obtain estimates for building, refurbishment and refitting work; draw up projected revenue and cost statements; test market for outdoor goods and new menus; make optimum choice: 'option 2'.

Implement:
Plan move of office space to basement; place fitting contracts; draw up timetable for all works; check progress; recruit and select new restaurant manager.

Monitor consequences:
Analyse any variance between budgeted and actual results for costs and revenues; assess impact on staff.

▶ Every decision carries an opportunity cost.

A slightly more graphic picture of the decision process is shown below:

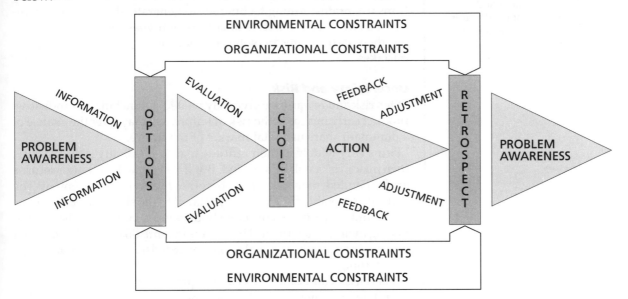

This model offers an open-ended sequence, with a recurrent cycle. Notice that feedback begins to be received once the decision has been put into action, and this is likely to prompt adjustments to the original plan. **Environmental constraints** refers to all limitations existing outside the organization.

Figure 31.1
A decision-making model

 Use the diagram above to illustrate the decision making process at Kennards Ltd.

Reason Versus Intuition

No one fully understands the concept of **intuition**. Traditionally it has been considered a stronger feature in women than in men. In any event, there are some weaknesses in the step-by-step rational approach, which tends:

- to over-value quantities at the expense of qualities
- to value predictability and rigid programmes of behaviour while discouraging imagination
- to imprison managers in the **parts** of a decision while intuition can absorb the **whole** situation and reach to its heart.

Of course reason remains essential to managing any organization. For many problems there is most unlikely to be an effective decision without thorough research, careful analysis of alternatives and vigilant control in practice.

Creativity

Creativity is the capacity to use an input of resources or ideas to produce an output of greater value. The process of **creative thinking** is of great significance but remains a partial mystery. The quality of any decision depends on the quality of the ideas originally conceived.

▶Abraham Zaleznik at Harvard Business School is highly critical of scientific management and believes that one of its effects is the suppression of imagination and creativity.

The importance of creative thinking increases with the seniority of management. Executive courses exist for its cultivation, and many firms use brainstorming techniques to generate ideas. Some organizations have a creative style or culture of management, often allowing their staff greater personal freedom to explore – and to make mistakes.

Uncertainty and Risk

Often risk and reward are inversely related. Launching an innovative product early increases the risk of failure, yet may offer the chance of a dominant share in a vital market of the future.

Firms vary widely in their attitude to risk. If stability is the priority, then major risks will be avoided. But if fast growth and high returns are demanded, then risk taking becomes the art of management. The scale of acceptable risks is clearly related to the size of the enterprise. Some ambitious firms consciously develop a culture of risk-taking among their management. This means that mistakes – within defined limits – are not only acceptable but regarded as evidence of managerial learning.

Where risks and outcomes can be quantified, **decision trees** are a useful device. They relate the outcome of an event to the probability that it will occur.

Suppose a friend owes you 50p. He offers to toss a coin: tails he owes you nothing, heads he pays you £1. Is this fair? For one toss of the coin you either receive nothing or £1. But over a series of tosses you would lose your money and receive £1 on an equal number of occasions. Thus the average value of one toss must be 50p. Put another way, you have a fifty per cent (written as 0.5) chance of receiving nothing, and a 0.5 chance of receiving £1.

$$0.5 \times 0p = 0p$$
$$0.5 \times £1 = \underline{50p}$$
$$50p$$

So your friend's proposal was fair!

The same principle can be applied to business.

A Decision Tree

Indie Records Ltd
An independent record company believes it has a recording with great potential and an artist who could be a future star. Already they have received a cash offer of £300 000 for the rights. Alternatively they could market the record in the UK, spending £200 000. There would then be an estimated forty per cent chance of achieving higher sales projections yielding £600 000 profit. But there would also be a sixty per cent chance of lower sales yielding only £400 000. Finally they could make a video and additionally release the record in America, for a total cost of £600 000. On the twenty per cent chance of a major hit, returns would then be £1 200 000, while there was a seventy per cent likelihood that a minor hit

would generate £900 000. There would also be a ten per cent risk of a flop in America, with total returns of only £500 000.

This information can be shown as a decision tree:

Figure 31.2
A decision tree

The tree is drawn from left to right, but interpreted from right to left. Start on the **right hand side** and **work backwards**. The 'sell copyright' option is simple with its £300 000 yield. The 'market record' option has two possible outcomes, and their combined expected value is shown projecting from the outcome node. The 0.4 (40%) probability of receiving £600 000 is worth 0.4 × £600 000 = £240 000. This figure is called an expected value. Similarly the 0.6 probability of receiving £400 000 is also worth £240 000. Hence the total expected value is £480 000. We must then subtract the marketing costs of £200 000 to show a final expected value of £280 000 for the option. This is lower than the value of the 'sell copyright' option, and thus can now be rejected. Notice the symbol used indicating a branch of the tree that may be 'cut off'. We now apply the same calculation process to the 'make video and release in America' option. Its final expected value turns out to be £320 000, implying rejection of the 'sell copyright' option, and a decision to make the video and release in America.

Note that all the figures (except the copyright sale) would be estimates only. The expected values are not literally expected, but are statements of average worth. The firm would actually choose the 'make video etc.' option only if it could afford the risk of the worst outcome – a 10% chance of receiving £500 000 and so losing £100 000 on the venture.

The decision tree would only be one element in the actual decision process. Other factors would vary from the implications of a £600 000 negative cash flow in making the video and financing the US release, to the degree of uncertainty of the cash estimates themselves.

Make your own notes on decision trees by drawing one for a company choosing between two options. Option one costs £420K with a sixty per cent possibility of sales of £500K and a forty per cent possibility of sales of £700K. Option two will cost £700K with a ten per cent possibility of yielding £2000K, a thirty per cent chance of yielding £800K and a sixty per cent chance of yielding £700K.

The Impact of Change

When making a short-term tactical decision, a manager can often assume that any unforeseen change of circumstances will be small. How many meals should a hotel restaurant prepare to serve next Saturday? Circumstances could change, but next Saturday will probably be similar to last Saturday. Now consider the directors of the hotel deciding on a proposed building project to add fifty new bedrooms. It will be three years before any profit is expected. But how will the town's reputation change? Will demand for business conferences increase? Will the government authorize a link road to the motorway?

Business is a kaleidoscope of risk and opportunity. The pattern changes continuously. To ignore or discount change is to invite disaster. In the 1970s Swiss watch manufacturers decided to continue using mechanical technology. The result? Electronic watches from Japan destroyed nearly half of Switzerland's watch industry.

Often change is a continuous process, with its effects building steadily over time: for instance the growth of supermarkets and the decline of small grocers. But change can be **discontinuous** when a whole business context changes quite abruptly.

► Management that anticipates change is said to be pro-active. Management that responds to change only when it has already occurred is called reactive.

Discontinuous Change

In 1974 the world price of oil quadrupled in a few months. Fuel economy was suddenly important. New oilfields became worth developing, and the first serious post-war recession began.

Many large firms found all their projections and plans thrown into confusion. Led by Shell, a new approach called **scenario planning** developed. This involves planning for a whole range of 'what if' situations, where in each case one or more of the basic assumptions are changed. When the Gulf War broke out in 1991, Shell already had thorough plans to cope with any major crisis in the Middle East. In some markets, a company's ability to manage change successfully may be its greatest competitive advantage.

Decision Making in Practice

There is always a gap between theories in textbooks and action in the real world. Decision models tend to assume that all managers are impartial and open minded. In practice, managers have all kinds of personal reasons for favouring particular decisions. For instance few marketing managers will favour cuts in the advertising budget. People become attached to particular causes or projects, which they may obstinately support long after any rational case has disappeared. Similarly people find security in familiar patterns of behaviour, and may oppose change in a defensive spirit.

Different people may perceive the same evidence differently. Often people's values and beliefs harden into prejudices that place a distorting filter between themselves and reality. Even experience can be a liability when it leads to automatic assumptions.

Personalities and internal politics are a crucial internal constraint in many organizations. 'Not upsetting Mr Jones' can easily become a major preoccupation. 'Pleasing Mrs Smith in personnel' may seem wise if one is hoping for early promotion. In other cases whole departments may conduct private battles between one another, and the abandonment of a new product may be seen in production as a victory over the marketing department.

There is often a great distance between the strategic decisions reached by a firm and the actual business of tactical management, which may be messy, compromised and inconclusive. Many middle and junior managers pay lip service to formal decisions while actually concerning themselves with day-to-day survival. Lack of time and pressure of work may mean that short cuts and second-best options are necessary. Managers may adopt an approach that the US economist H A Simon calls 'satisficing'. This means making decisions to produce adequate or 'satisfactory' outcomes in terms of a few key criteria. A sales manager might wish to avoid any conflict with staff, and yet achieve just enough sales to satisfy the board.

(**ACT**) Krackle Krisps Ltd was launched in 1984 to enter the highly competitive snacks market. The firm gradually introduced a range of six flavours in ordinary potato crisps, and a further three flavours in a 'crinkle cut' style. They also produced a snack for the adult market called 'Potato Pearls', and a novelty line for children called 'Tiger Tails'. Emphasis generally was on quality and freshness, with shorter distribution chains than the major manufacturers.

Strong sales in 1991 and optimistic sales forecasts for 1992 led the company to expand its production facilities. However, in practice it was not long before sales began to falter, and only intense marketing efforts averted an actual decline. By the beginning of 1992 it was clear that significant over-capacity existed (about twenty-five per cent of a maximum of 2.5 million packets/year output). Simon Smith, the managing director, was anxious to consider a new product that might bridge the gap until some more general sales growth was resumed. When a special meeting took place in early March, two rival alternatives were proposed.

Sara Bassett, the marketing director, supported a new product called 'Shuttles' based on a 'space' theme. The target market would be children under sixteen with sales in schools as well as in shops

▶ The gap between the theory and reality of decision-making is often very wide.

and supermarkets. Latest market research seemed most encouraging:

'Shuttles': Sales Forecast for First Year

Original	Burger flavour	Total
400 000	200 000	600 000

The factory cost was projected at 10p per packet with a selling price to wholesalers of 12p per packet. After distribution and mark-ups the product would retail at an average price of 20p per packet. Unfortunately the production process would require machine modification costing £5 000.

On the other side of the table, Graham Martin, the sales manager favoured another product called 'Bangles'. This would be a hoop-shaped snack in plain and pizza flavours. Its image would be young and fashionable, with marketing aimed at the 15–30 age group. The cost price structure would be identical to that of 'Shuttles', but with a simpler machine process, the extra capital cost would be only £2 000. It was estimated that total sales in the first year would be 300 000 of the plain version and 150 000 for the pizza flavour.

1 Work through the decision-making process carefully, making careful notes under the headings below. Remember to make use of the numerical evidence.

   a) Problem diagnosis
   b) objectives
   c) constraint
   d) information
   e) choice
   f) review

2 What further information would you consider obtaining before making your final decision?

Summary and comment

- objectives are the guidance system for decisions in matters of policy, strategy and tactics. Their effective communication to all staff is therefore essential
- most decisions do not exist on their own as discrete problems. They are vitally inter-connected with many other decisions at different levels. Decisions are usually also interactive: tackling one problem may alter the optimum solution for another
- in practice many decisions are **informal**, and remain **implicit** (not openly announced). In small firms or closely knit management teams decision-making may be more a matter of mutual discussion and tacit understanding
- the scientific approach to decision-making is a powerful tool. However many decisions have vital dimensions that are only accessible through intuition and creative thinking

- well-defined problems benefit most from tightly-organized, rational decision processes. The most long range and least clearly structured problems may benefit from speculative, unconventional and even 'crazy' thinking
- the rigidity of some decision structures breeds a subculture of subversive or 'illegal' decision-making. This occurs when some managers know that their proposals will not be accepted, and so secretly pursue their own ideas regardless of official approval. Senior managers may even turn a blind eye in the hope of positive outcomes
- when a group of people (e.g. a committee) address a decision, support may build too rapidly around a solution that appears to please the majority. A kind of 'group-think' sets in, and people uncritically support a decision that they would reject if thinking alone
- in some firms decision-making tends to be concentrated at the top of the management hierarchy. Such centralized firms face the problem of gaining staff identification with decisions passed down the organizational pyramid (see Chapter 32)
- many firms are tending to push more decisions closer to their point of impact. This means increased **delegation** and greater personal responsibility for all managers
- decisions must often be made under pressure. Firms need increasingly rapid reactions in response to problems and opportunities.

(32) *Organizational structures*

> ► An organizational structure is the agreed network of responsibilities that makes possible the coordinated use of resources.

Chapter objectives

After working through this chapter, you will:

▌ know the main theories of how organizations work

▌ be able to interpret organization charts and recognize different structure types

▌ understand the significance of a firm's span of control and its use of delegation

▌ grasp the concept of centralization and decentralization

▌ know the meaning of the following key terms: scientific management, human relations approaches, systems theory, contingency theory, formal and informal organization, management hierarchy, span of control, line management, chain of command, delegation, functional structures, divisional structures, matrix structures, federal structures.

THEORIES OF ORGANIZATION

Business activity is the organization of human and material resources to achieve an agreed objective. Its efficiency and success depend on the effectiveness of that organization. This will almost certainly require:

- **leadership** to provide direction and coordination
- **specialization** which is the acceptance by people of defined tasks and duties for which they are responsible
- **hierarchy** which is the arrangement of people in layers of authority
- **communication and coordination** to ensure that the work of specialist staff in the hierarchy combines to achieve objectives
- **motivation** which means the will among people to fulfil their agreed tasks.

In a small enterprise these features are often fairly informal. A small bakers, for example, will have an owner or manager who provides leadership. There will be some kind of hierarchy or 'pecking order' among staff, who will specialize in, say, food preparation or counter sales. Communication will be verbal and direct, while motivation will depend on a team spirit and the 'atmosphere' of the shop.

As an enterprise grows, these features need more precision and planning. The alternative would be confusion, inefficiency and waste.

Large business organizations first appeared in the nineteenth century as the industrial revolution made possible mass production and distribution. Theories have evolved about how organizations work have developed in the twentieth century. There have been four broad approaches.

1 Classical

Early theories tended to regard human organization rather as if it were a machine. These **mechanistic** views emerged in the work of F. W. Taylor (1856–1917), who developed the principles of **scientific management**. This meant defining a task and then carrying out a scientific style of research to find the most efficient methods of operation. The worker was trained to follow precise instructions, and paid according to the results achieved. Soon after, Henri Fayol (1841–1925) described the operation of a **formal organization**. This included:

- clear direction or objectives for all activities in the organization
- a chain of authority running down the organization where each employee has a superior to whom he is responsible
- specialization in responsibilities of staff and functional departments.

Formal organizations also construct systems of rules and procedures. Called **bureaucracy**, this phenomenon was first analysed by Max Weber (1864–1920), who stressed the importance of officials behaving in accordance with known rules, rather than personal preference.

► Bureaucracy doesn't mean inefficiency and 'red tape'. It means operating according to rules rather than in a whimsical and idiosyncratic way.

2 Human relations

Elton Mayo (see Chapter 34) and his Hawthorne experiments (1924–36) showed the importance of human relationships at work as a key factor in the efficiency and motivation of staff. He also revealed the influence of hidden informal structures of power and influence at work. It was clear that regarding organizations as machines did not achieve the best results, and that management should respond to human needs. This analysis was developed further by Maslow in the 1940s, and Herzberg in the 1950s (see Chapter 34).

3 Systems theory

A system is an arrangement of parts that work together to form a whole. An organization is a complex social system containing a range of sub-components such as social systems, technical systems and internal structures. Each of these sub-components has a separate existence, but they are also interdependent. Greater than the sum of its component systems is the organization itself, which interacts with the wider economic, technological, social and political environment.

A famous application of systems theory was in the study by Trist and Bamforth (1951) of the coal industry in Durham. Underground coal cutting had just been mechanized, yet the expected productivity gains had not occurred. The research found that the miners had previously worked as small, closely-knit social groups. The new mechanized 'long wall' method placed the men in large anonymous shifts, each completing only one stage in production. It was proposed that the **socio-technical systems** had been unbalanced. The answer was a 'composite long wall method' which retained the new technology, but enabled shifts to tackle different tasks with stronger group identities. The key measures of performance all improved.

4 Contingency theories

The 'contingency approach' to organizations comes from research by Lawrence and Lorsch (1967) into a range of American firms. They found that different firms, and different departments within firms, adopt widely differing structures to suit their particular needs. The most successful firms had the best methods of resolving the tensions created by their own (necessary) diversity of inner structures.

In Britain, Burns and Stalker (1961) studied the structure of firms in the electronics industry. They found two major types of management system:

- **mechanistic systems** were machine-like in their emphasis on rigid hierarchies, specialized work roles and the obedience of subordinates
- **organic systems** were more like a living organism, where control and communication work in a network with emphasis on mutual assistance and achievement of goals.

The Formal Organization

The best way to understand the structure of an organization is to draw a map or model. This is called an organization chart, and we will look first at its basic principles. A highly simplified example is shown below:

ABC Ltd has a traditional pyramid structure, spread out like a family

► An organization chart shows the **formal** pattern of authority and responsibility.

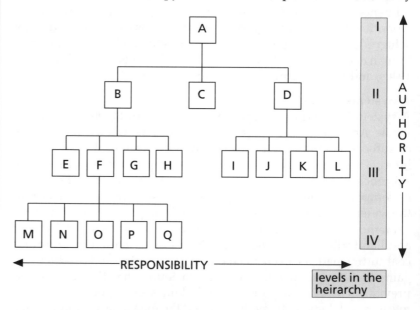

Figure 32.1
Organization chart for ABC Ltd

tree from the top towards the bottom. This top-bottom dimension represents **authority** and **responsibility**. The highest position of authority is held by A, to whom B, C and D are responsible. Below this point only part of the structure is shown, but B for example controls the work of E, F, G and H. Similarly, E has authority over staff M–Q.

The pyramid structure of authority in an organization is called a **hierarchy**. The layers in the structure are called **levels in the hierarchy**. The number of subordinates for whom each manager is responsible is called the **span of control**. For example, the span of control for A is three, for B four, and for E is five. The top-down pathways of authority are called **line management**. Say B is the production manager. Then B to E (supervisor) to P (foreman) is a pathway of line management authority. Such a pathway is called a **chain of command**. Production and marketing are typical **line functions** within a company, which means that they are primary to the purpose of the organization. By contrast, accounting and personnel are called **staff functions**, meaning that they are secondary in purpose (the primary purpose of a firm is not to draw up accounts). Often there are direct links between staff functions and line managers: for instance personnel may advise on health and safety requirements. Notice that communication generally can take three directions:

- top-down: e.g. instructions down line A to D to K
- bottom-up: e.g. request on route Q to E to B
- lateral: e.g. discussions between F and J.

So far we have been discussing the formal structure of ABC Ltd. This assumes that the authority and communication between people in an organization follow the official pattern. In reality most organizations also experience an invisible and informal structure. Suppose E is regarded as a weak supervisor. Then N may find it more effective to bypass his authority and deal directly with B. However H may have some lingering grudge against B, but happen to know C socially. And since C has specially favoured relationships with A, H feels able to disregard B, taking pride at having hidden influence within the firm. Some lightly drawn hidden pathways are probably inevitable in any organization, but managers must treat them with great caution. Too easily they lead to an inbreeding of mistrust, speculation and rumour, which in turn cause misunderstanding, inefficiency and weakening of team effort. Informal structures can be symptoms of faulty staff selection or weaknesses in the formal structure.

Delegation

Delegation means a manager passing part of his or her authority to a subordinate, while retaining full responsibility for the consequences. Most managers know that they could not possibly fulfil the whole of their jobs without delegating some tasks to those for whom they are responsible. The ability to delegate the right tasks to the right staff is a key quality in a good manager. Certain core parts of their job require the particular expertise, skills and status of the manager. These tasks must not be delegated. But to ensure concentration on these core elements, delegation of other tasks is essential.

Other advantages of delegation are:

- the development of specialized skills is encouraged
- subordinate staff gain valuable experience and a track record on which to base their future promotion

► Effective delegation requires the right balance between **trust** and **control**.

- motivation is increased as staff feel more important and more trusted
- the subordinate can make immediate decisions in the light of circumstances at the time.

Delegation always carries a risk. If a task delegated is not properly performed, then the manager is still to blame. Typical problems in delegation include:

- the subordinate proving to have inadequate expertise or training
- abuse of the manager's trust through carelessness or incomplete work
- the subordinate exceeds the boundaries of delegated authority
- insecurity in the manager who fears the implications of holding ultimate responsibility.

The extent of delegation in an organization varies widely. It particularly depends on:

- the consequences of errors (the higher the risk factor, the more difficult is delegation)
- the experience and quality of staff
- the confidence of management
- the leadership style and traditions of the organization.

Span of Control

The span of control – or number of subordinates reporting to a superior – is closely related to the extent of delegation. As a superior's span of control increases, so the demands on him or her by subordinates will increase. For this reason, the larger the span of control, the greater the extent of delegation likely. There is no perfect span size, but studies suggest that for general management a range of five to eight is typical. In very complex work the span may be under three, while for routine work, lower in the hierarchy, spans often rise to twenty or thirty or higher. The optimal span depends on the complexity of the work, the experience and calibre of management and staff, and the potential seriousness of errors.

   Narrow spans of control require more levels in the hierarchy and a taller pyramid structure. Wider spans allow fewer levels and a flatter pyramid.

   Tall pyramids allow a high degree of supervision, but have a tendency to be rigid and bureaucratic in their behaviour. The trend in the 1990s is towards 'de-layering': that is, cutting out layers of middle management and creating a flatter structure with wider spans of control. This reflects:

- the need to be more responsive to change, with shorter chains of command and more sensitive bottom-up communication
- the advance of market orientation and the need for all managers to be closer to the market interface
- the pressure to cut administrative overheads and achieve a leaner organization.

► BP recently announced a new 'flat' organization, cutting at a stroke its layers of management from eleven to only five.

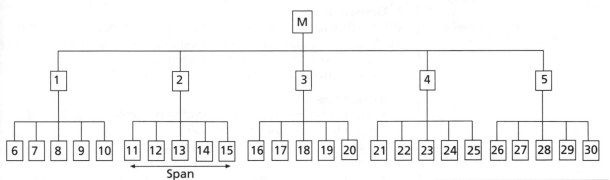

Span

Five levels in the hierarchy are necessary when using a span of two, while only three levels are needed when the span is increased to five.

Figure 32.2
ABC reconstructed

 Read the data and follow the instructions.

Zoe Ashby was managing director of Papyrus Ltd, an expanding company in the specialist paper business. Her production director was Ian Thompson who had four works supervisors each responsible for a team of eight skilled operatives. The marketing director, Matthew Collis had two strands of responsibility. His promotions manager was Toby McNeill with six regional representatives. Rachel Smithers was export sales manager with representatives in Frankfurt, Paris, Milan and Madrid. As finance director, Shahid Kahn had two section heads, each of whom was assisted by five office staff.

1 Draw up an organization chart for Papyrus Ltd.
2 State the span of control for each of the four directors.

Structure Types

The actual structures chosen by organizations vary enormously in pattern and style. However four broad types can be distinguished:

1 Functional

Each major business function (e.g. production, marketing, personnel) has its own department and hierarchy of management authority.

► Functional models are based on management responsibilities.

Advantages:
- specialized departments can offer higher levels of expertise
- clear vertical chains of command assist control
- coherent career pathways exist for staff.

Disadvantages:
- functional departments tend to pursue their own sectional interests
- lateral communication and coordination may be difficult
- the model is not suitable for diversified products or multiple locations.

► Divisional models are based on products, locations or models.

2 Divisional

When a firm has several product types, physical locations or distinct markets, then it may create corresponding divisions: in effect mini-companies, coordinated by top management. Often functions such as strategic planning and finance remain at the head office level.

Advantages:
- increased flexibility to respond to particular conditions of product type, location, market
- greater motivation for managers in running a semi-autonomous division
- distinct profit centres assist closer monitoring of performance
- enables policy and major strategic decisions to be freed from day-to-day management.

Disadvantages:
- the danger that divisions operate without regard to the interests of the whole organization
- divisions may resent central management, causing a sense of 'distance' between the divisions and head office.

► Matrix models are based on both management responsibilities and project goals.

3 Matrix

This is a newer type of structure that combines both vertical and horizontal lines of responsibility. Typically, the vertically structured specialist functions remain, but across them is superimposed horizontal lines of **project responsibility**, forming **project teams**. This means that an accountant for example might have conventional line responsibility, while also belonging to a project team and answering to a project manager. The aim is to align the specialist functions into an integrated system for the fulfilment of specific goals: for instance a special order for a key customer.

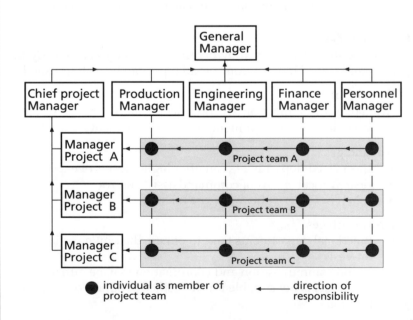

Figure 32.3
Matrix structure

Advantages:
- overcomes isolation of departmental hierarchies
- focuses resources on meeting the project in hand
- project management is market orientated, in giving large customers direct management access.

Disadvantages:
- the risk of conflicting line and project responsibilities
- the more complex structure may lead to confused and wasteful use of resources.

4 Federal

Some firms consist of virtually freestanding businesses, with headquarters providing only coordination and some element of control.

The balance of power between headquarters and the federation members varies, but headquarters usually maintains some key financial controls. Federal structures may arise from takeover bids that form conglomerates (see Chapter 27).

► Federal structures are based on a range of separate business entities.

Advantages:
- an entrepreneurial spirit can flourish in each business
- bureaucracy is minimized
- layers of middle management are avoided
- access remains to the financial resources of headquarters.

Disadvantages:
- the authority of the headquarters may be resisted
- only possible to achieve limited economies of scale
- risk of 'organizational sprawl', with loss of direction and focus.

 Draw up a table to summarize the advantages and disadvantages of the different structures described above.

Centralization and Decentralization

Many firms centralize some functions while decentralizing others. For example, finance and accounts may be controlled from head office, while personnel and production may be managed locally. Similarly within a single location decision making may be centralized at the top or dispersed down the hierarchy.

Centralize or Decentralize?

Centralization may encourage efficiency as the managerial overview enables all resources to be put to their optimum use. Scale economies are fully harnessed, planning is easier, and administration is streamlined.

But mistakes become magnified. Branches or small departments may lose their incentive to work through a lack of independence, with orders being sent from head office. Decisions may be slow and poorly suited to local circumstances.

Decentralization allows faster and more flexible decision making that can respond readily to circumstances. Red tape is reduced, while

► Centralization: the concentration of decision making among the most senior management at the 'centre' of the organization.

► Decentralization: dispersion of decision making throughout the organization, with greater independence in the firm's operational units – e.g. factories, departments, branches.

LOW   HIGH

DECENTRALIZE ←———— ECONOMIES OF SCALE ————→ CENTRALIZE

←———— SIMILARITY OF MARKETS ————→

←———— NEED FOR UNIFORMITY ————→

←———— GEOGRAPHICAL CONCENTRATION ————→

←———— SAFETY HAZARDS ————→

Figure 32.4
Centralize or decentralize?

► There is no perfect degree of centralization. The approach varies by industry, by firm, and by period.

Centralization was popular in the 1960s, as very large firms began to use mainframe computers and to present a corporate identity. Since the 1980s the trend has been to decentralize, aiming for flatter structures and increased delegation.

creative thinking and initiative are increased. Motivation among management and staff should improve with greater personal commitment to work.

But it risks a loss of coordination, as the operating units of the firm pull in different directions – wasting resources and undermining top management's goals. Work may be duplicated at lower levels and managers may busy themselves 're-inventing the wheel'.

 Use Figure 32.4 to decide which of the following enterprises should have a centralized structure, and which should have a decentralized structure:

a) a mass-production manufacturer of injection moulded plastic products for the consumer market, with a single large factory

b) a chain of health centres

c) a major engineering company.

Summary and comment

- organizational structures are maps of resource mobilization. They should reflect clearly the firm's objectives. For example, a divisional structure might reflect selling as the firm's central activity, or a matrix structure could suit a construction firm with complex projects
- the wrong structure can cause many problems, such as over or undermanning, slow decision making, poor communications or conflicting loyalties
- tall, rigid hierarchies are often product driven. Flatter, more flexible systems are often market orientated
- the traditional manufacturing organization with a mass work-force (often called **Fordist**) tended to be hierarchical, with high supervision levels. With the growth of new technology and customer-related services, the shift is towards smaller, flatter 'core' organizations that are networks rather than pyramids (**post-Fordist**)
- flatter structures imply wider spans of control, more delegation, increased trust and greater staff autonomy. The corresponding trend in the 1990s is towards decentralization
- the management's role is changing from supervision of subordinates towards the leadership of teams. Teams tend to be project or goal-focused
- effective structures are in a state of constant change. Small firms must be particularly careful to update their structure as they grow. Adjustment to change is easier for organic than for mechanistic structures
- the first emergence of the firm as a networked system is being made possible by information technology. Skill and judgement is replacing much physical labour, while electronic transmission and memory replaces many physical events.

(33) Leadership

Styles of Leadership:

autocratic: decisions imposed by the leader

democratic: the group shares the decision making

laissez-faire: members of group are left to make their own decisions.

Chapter objectives

After working through this chapter, you will:

▍ understand the qualities and functions of leaders

▍ be able to evaluate the major leadership styles

▍ know the key theories that analyse leadership in organizations

▍ know the meaning of the following key terms: autocratic leadership, democratic leadership, laissez-faire leadership.

LEADERSHIP QUALITIES AND STYLES

Leadership is a key management quality. All tasks are ultimately achieved through people. Without leadership, the talents of people as well as physical resources are wasted, and an organization will rapidly lose ground to its competitors.

Many studies have attempted to identify the vital qualities of a good leader. This has proved very difficult, since different leaders in different situations seem to have different qualities. Today it is more common to try to identify the appropriate management style for different management situations. The idea that styles rather than personal qualities should be analysed was influenced by a famous study of leaders in a boys' camp described by Lewin, Lippitt and White in 1939.

Styles of Leadership

1 Autocratic leadership

The leader aims for personal control. He/she is clearly separated from the group, who must obey orders. Virtually all decisions are made by the leader, who only releases a minimum of information to subordinates. Communications are 'top-down', with little chance for feedback. Working methods are strictly specified, and little allowance is made for individual preferences. Praise and promotion are difficult to anticipate or understand: the leader's motives remain unknown.

2 Democratic leadership

The leader involves the group in decision making, and aims to work by **consent**. Argument and discussion are normal, and although the leader makes final decisions, members of the group are all able to contribute freely to debate. Formal communications have open pathways, with a variety of routes both 'down' and 'up' the hierarchy. Subordinates decide their own methods of work, often checking output and quality themselves. Individual needs are actively considered, and the distribution of rewards is according to clear criteria.

3 Laissez-faire leadership

'Laissez-faire' means literally 'leave to do'. The leader is present and may make known some broad objectives, but otherwise has a very limited role. The group members are allowed to make their own decisions and follow their own individual wishes. Communications are confused, often conflicting and largely informal. Powerful informal groups may develop, with their own widely differing 'norms'. Rewards will be unpredictable.

 Decide on the optimum leadership style relative to the situations below and tick the columns accordingly.

Situation	Autocratic	Democratic	Laissez-faire
Senior fire officer tackling warehouse blaze.			
Leader of team at advertising agency generating new themes for a client.			
Experienced social worker responsible for inner-city team.			
Office manager organizing company social outing.			

Fred Fiedler

Fred Fiedler (professor of psychology and management at the University of Washington) published *A Theory of Leadership Effectiveness* in 1967. He wanted to discover the leadership factors likely to achieve maximum performance in a group. He describes two styles of leader:

1 relationship-motivated leaders who gain most job satisfaction in relationship with people.

2 task-motivated leaders who get most job satisfaction through successful completion of the task in hand.

Fiedler argues that either style can be the 'right' style depending on the situation. This in turn depends on the extent to which the circumstances are favourable to the leader.

The key factors are:

- leader-member relations – quality of leader/group and leader/individual relations
- task structure – the degree to which the task is clearly described and structured
- leader's position–power – the rights and powers of the leader for instance to reward or discipline staff.

Fiedler then related leadership styles to the extent to which the situation was favourable or unfavourable. This analysis showed that the task-motivated leader was more effective if the situation was very favourable or very unfavourable. In the intermediate situations a relationship-motivated leader was more effective.

Blake and Mouton

Robert Blake and Jane Mouton are psychologists who have led an American behavioural science consultancy. They assume that the

Figure 33.1
The management grid

from R. Blake and J. Mouton (1962) *The Managerial Grid: advanced management office executive*

goal of management is both to generate efficiency in the task and to create a creative innovative climate. Their managerial grid (1962) relates a manager's concern for production and concern for people:

A large range of possible managerial patterns can now be examined. The five key combinations are:

1,1 **impoverished management**: responsibility is avoided both for tasks and for people.

1,9 **The 'country-club' management style**: the emphasis is on people and a sense of cosy 'togetherness'. The task is very secondary.

5,5 **The 'dampened pendulum' style**: this is the compromise position. Extremes of the pendulum (1,9 or 9,1) are avoided, and adequacy is the goal.

9,1 **Task management**: authoritarian leadership focuses on the task and treats people as mere tools.

9,9 **Team management**: demands high concern for both production and people. Human needs are satisfied within a team that is motivated by excellence in the task.

Charles Handy

In his *Age of Unreason* (1989) Charles Handy looks again at leadership, given the trend towards greater delegation and federalism. Leadership should be a quality that exists throughout the organization. Each leader must help to shape and transmit a clear vision which gives purpose to work and stretches staff towards their potential. Correspondingly the model of the leader as a teacher, counsellor or friend is more appropriate than the model of the leader as guardian, inspector or judge.

In a modern organization the leader should support a learning culture within the firm where staff are colleagues and co-learners. Learning will only occur if staff can make mistakes and know that they will be forgiven. In this supportive atmosphere risks can be taken and creative ideas proliferate.

Summary and comment

- the team under autocratic leadership is likely to depend heavily on the leader for any success, and to lack development in self-discipline or self-motivation. Efficiency may be high when objectives are clear and supervision level high. Pro and anti-leader factions are likely to divide the team
- democratic leadership leads to a strong group that is more self-reliant, with multiple communication pathways between members. Individuals are more likely to be self-disciplined, and efficiency is probably good without being exceptional. The leader has a lower profile, and his/her authority causes little resentment
- the laissez-faire leader has very limited importance to the group, whose members participate vigorously in all decision making. Efficiency is very variable, and self-discipline is essential. Conflict between group members is a constant problem
- it is debatable to what extent effective leadership depends on the person or the task/situation
- some theorists such as Fiedler stress the importance of the right leadership style for the right situation. The effectiveness of the various leadership styles depends on the situation in terms of the task and the people involved
- by contrast, Blake and Mouton insist that maximum concern for people and production is **always** the best management style
- Handy's more radical idea of leadership as a basic human quality exercised by everyone is gaining ground. Firms are moving away from a 'culture of command' towards a 'culture of consent'. Decision making 'ripples' through 'flatter' federal organizations that show intelligence at every level.

(34) Motivation

THE MEANING AND IMPORTANCE OF MOTIVATION

► Everyone is motivated by private needs of some kind. These may be tangible, such as money, or intangible, such as a sense of pride or self-respect. It is a vital task of management to understand these needs and attempt to harness their power through the rewards offered by jobs in the organization.

Motivation means a human being's strength of desire to act in a particular way. A person who is highly motivated is keen to start an activity, and works at it with a sense of urgency and personal commitment. A poorly motivated person is relatively unconcerned about the activity, and approaches it with a lack of energy or direction. You will know from your own experience the importance of motivation in getting things done.

The productivity of every person in the firm depends centrally on their level of motivation. Even more than this, motivation determines the vitality of the organization and its ability to anticipate and respond to the forces of change. It is a kind of electricity in the air. There is no substitute for it.

 As you read through this chapter note down how each theory highlights a source of motivation, and how each theory could be applied to improve employee motivation.

F. W. Taylor

Frederick Taylor worked at the Midvale Steel Company, Philadelphia during the 1880s, where he rose from shop floor labourer to chief engineer. Here he evolved the concept of 'scientific management', which simply means the application of scientific principles to the process of management. From 1889 he worked at the Bethlehem Steel Company, where he conducted famous experiments into labour productivity. His ideas were formalized in the *Principles of Scientific Management* published in 1911. His work focused on the concept of **cost effectiveness** in the labour force. Taylor assumed that all individuals are motivated by personal economic gain, and that in their behaviour they closely resemble machines. His approach was therefore mechanical in maximizing cost effectiveness. This involved a scientific analysis of the task to find the most efficient methods. Workers could then be trained accordingly, and motivated through 'scientific' payment according to effort and results.

Taylor's ideas have been very influential. Indeed, 'Taylorism' has become a philosophy of management, active across the industrialized world. The very real productivity gains it brought to the Bethlehem Steel Co. went on to occur in most major industries, and fitted well with increased mechanization and the development of assembly line methods. But Taylorism also has serious limitations, because it is an **inadequate view of human beings**. The motivational power of money is limited.

Elton Mayo

Elton Mayo was professor of industrial research at Harvard University, and over the period 1924–32 carried out what became a world famous research project at the Hawthorne plant of the Western Electric Co. in Chicago. The results were published in *The Human Problems of an Industrial Civilization* in 1933. Before he arrived at Western Electric, the company had conducted the 'optimum illumination investigation', which used control and test groups of workers to determine the effects of changes in lighting intensity on efficiency. The mysterious outcome was a sharp rise in output by all groups regardless of lighting. Mayo started with similar assumptions to Taylor, and further explored this phenomenon in the 'relay assembly test room' experiments. These involved altering rest breaks, lunch times and working hours for one group of women workers. Again, output increased whether conditions were made better or worse. The explanation has become known as the **Hawthorne effect**. Western Electric was a dreary anonymous place to work, and the tasks were repetitive and boring. Output in experimental groups was rising for **human**, not physical reasons. It was the personal attention and recognition of research teams that was the source of the Hawthorne effect.

Later the 'bank wiring room' investigation closely analysed how fourteen male workers behaved as a group. The men quickly established their own sub-groups with social and working 'norms' that cut across the company's rules and incentive systems. These **informal groups** with their own leaders were very powerful in determining productivity.

Mayo's work established the 'human relations' approach to management and motivation. It revealed that human needs were far more complex than the simple desire for money, and that human relationships vitally affect how hard and how well people work.

Abraham Maslow

Abraham Maslow was an American psychologist who studied human motivation. In 1954 he published Motivation and Personality, and this proposed a hierarchy of needs.

▶ 'What the workers want from their employers beyond anything else is high wages and what employers want from their workmen most of all is low labour cost......' F W Taylor.

▶ Mayo founded the 'Human Relations' approach to management.

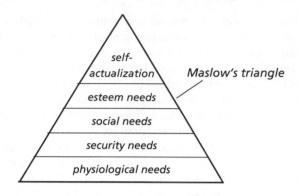

Figure 34.1
Maslow's hierarchy of needs

► Maslow suggested that each level of need in the hierarchy must be satisfied before the next level becomes a motivational force. For example, a worker will not be concerned about the quality of work relationships while fearful of the ability to earn a basic living. Once a need is fulfilled however, it loses its power to motivate, and only the next unfulfilled need is significant. If correct, this has an important message for management. Once the workforce feel secure in earning an adequate standard of living, their aspirations cannot be met by pay rises alone. Jobs must offer the potential to satisfy deeper and higher human needs.

- **physiological needs**: the basic physical requirements of food, shelter, warmth and sleep
- **security needs**: the need to know that physical safety is assured
- **social needs**: the need for rewarding relationships with other people
- **esteem needs**: the need for self-respect and the respect of others
- **self-actualization needs**: the need for fulfilment of inner potential.

Frederick Herzberg

Frederick Herzberg was professor of management at the University of Utah, he carried out a survey of engineers and accountants in Pittsburg during the late 1950s. The respondents were asked to describe sequences of events that had made them feel very dissatisfied and very satisfied in their jobs. The results were published in *The Motivation to Work* (1959). Two distinct sets of factors emerged: **maintenance or hygiene factors** that were the dissatisfiers, and **motivation factors** that were the source of satisfaction.

It can be concluded that the presence of motivation factors is a key source of job satisfaction, but their absence is a very minor source of job dissatisfaction. Conversely, the absence of hygiene factors is a key source of job dissatisfaction, but their presence is a very minor source of job satisfaction. The conclusion for management is that while it is important to get the hygiene factors right, they are only a base line from which the motivators can operate.

Douglas McGregor

Douglas McGregor was professor of management at the Massachusetts Institute of Technology, and is best known for his celebrated **Theory X and Theory Y** analysis described in *The Human Side of Enterprise* (1960). Two sharply opposed interpretations of people at work are offered. (See Figure 34.3 at bottom of p.265)

McGregor argued that the Theory X pattern is indeed widespread, not as a natural condition, but as a **consequence of management**. The Theory Y scenario will not always be attainable, but the task of good management is to create the conditions where it can prevail. Enormous reserves of hidden potential in the workforce can be released in this way. Theory Y is not 'soft' management: it is a highly exacting vision of what people at work might become.

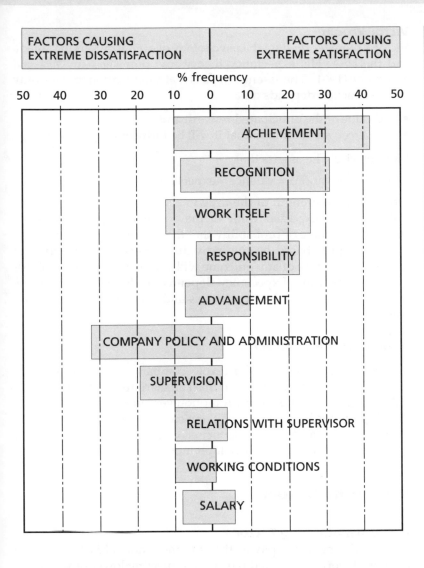

Figure 34.2
*Dissatisfiers and satisfiers:
Herzberg's theory*

Theory X	Theory Y
• the average person dislikes work and will avoid it	• work is natural to man and is not fundamentally disliked
• most people must be pushed, controlled and threatened by punishment if they are to work adequately hard	• people can use self-direction and self-control towards objectives to which they are committed
• the average human being wants to avoid responsibility	• the average person grows first to accept and then to seek responsibility
• such people are unambitious and have security as their greatest need.	• the greatest human need is self-actualization, for which most people have large funds of creative potential – mostly unused at present.

Figure 34.3
*McGregor's Theory X and
Theory Y*

Victor Vroom

Victor Vroom worked on the psychology of organizations in Canada and the USA. His expectancy theory was published in *Work and Motivation* (1964). The essential idea is that a motivation towards any course of action depends on:

- the value of the anticipated reward, **and**
- the perceived likelihood that it will be forthcoming

More precisely he asserts that:

force (motivation) = valence × expectancy,

where **force** is strength of the urge to act, or degree of motivation. **Valence** is the expected value of the outcome. **Expectancy** is the subjective estimate of probability that the outcome will occur.

The concept is based on the individual's personal perception of reality. The valence of any outcome will vary both between individuals and over time. Expectancy depends on the behaviour of the organization, and on the experiences and prejudices of the person concerned.

► Notice the parallel between Vroom's theory and the concept of expected value in decision trees (see Chapter 31).

The Expectancy Effect

A marketing manager of a textile company is told to expect promotion if she can increase market share for a key product. Although she would value promotion very much, she has heard such promises before and seen them come to nothing. She therefore opts for a quiet life. Conclusion: high valence and low expectancy does not produce high motivation.

Motivating Factors

Pay as a Motivating Factor

F. W. Taylor regarded pay as the only motivational factor. Human relations theorists regarded pay as only meeting lower order needs, and therefore limited in its value as a source of motivation. Herzberg's research confirmed pay as a weaker motivator or source of job satisfaction. Yet most people in most jobs would undoubtedly name pay as their major reason for going to work. In this they are no doubt telling the truth, but as a fact it fails to explain the springs of motivation while actually at work. An important distinction must be made between the motivation to **hold a job** – where pay is a key factor – and motivation **within a job**, where money is far less important. This explains the apparent contradiction between Herzberg's findings and the attitudes of most people towards their job. Indeed, for most people with permanent employment on time rates, the motivation force of pay applies primarily to the maintenance of their livelihood. However a rate of pay that is perceived to be unfairly low for the demands of the job would be de-motivating. The prospect of a higher pay rate is often associated with promotion and increased

► Pay may be the main reason for holding a job yet not the major source of motivation when working within that job.

responsibility. Where pay becomes a badge of status and a factor in this sense of recognition and self-esteem, then it is a significant motivator.

For workers paid by piece rates or commission, or who are dependent on bonus schemes, pay is much more directly motivational. It is noticeable that such jobs tend to offer less scope for meeting higher order human needs, and the simple incentive of money becomes a general substitute.

Job Satisfaction

Research into the sources of human motivation has produced a powerful case for making job satisfaction much more widely attainable. The work of Herzberg in particular points to the importance of enabling employees to experience achievement, recognition, responsibility and satisfaction in the work itself. It is a popular observation that many jobs are inevitably dull and unrewarding. This is a view that modern personnel managers would reject. Using the logic of McGregor's attack on Theory X, it can be argued that jobs are not inevitably dull, but are made dull by the way in which they are constructed. There are several important methods by which firms have attempted to increase job satisfaction:

► It is often possible to re-design jobs in order to meet a fuller range of human motivational needs.

1 Job rotation
A group of workers may all be performing relatively simple but different specialized tasks. The tasks and the group are formed into a carousel system, where each individual performs each task for a limited period before moving on to a period at the next task, in a continuous rotation. The method does not make the work itself more satisfying, but it gives the worker greater variety, with a wider range of competencies. From a managerial viewpoint, labour flexibility is also increased.

2 Job enlargement
This simply involves increasing the range of tasks included within a worker's job description. The additional tasks do not in themselves increase responsibility, and are on a similar level to the existing job. The aim is not to increase the **amount of work** for the individual, but its **variety**.

3 Job enrichment
This is a more radical approach that means the vertical extension of a job to allow the worker access to greater responsibility and the satisfaction of higher level motivational needs. With the support of training, more demanding tasks are specified, and the worker is granted greater independence in decision making. Where possible staff are enabled to take charge of a complete process, section or area in the organization of work. Jobs can be deliberately designed to provide scope for fulfilling the higher human needs that are most strongly motivational. For some types of job this is obviously difficult to achieve, but once a commitment to enrichment exists, there is usually some potential. However managers may find that job

enrichment schemes can carry demands for higher pay, and that resentment can be caused if skill boundaries are too freely crossed.

4 Autonomous work groups

The principles of job enrichment can be applied to a number of related workers whose responsibilities are combined to form an autonomous work group. This means that the group take responsibility for a particular department, process or product, often only with broad supervision from a superior manager. The planning and allocation of work with such functions as maintenance, quality and safety may all be brought within the authority of the group. The concept has been refined, and has spread to many firms, some of whom organize production on a cellular model. This involves reconfiguring the traditional production line to form areas or discrete stages, responsibility for each of which is taken by a 'cell' of workers. There is often job rotation within the cell, but also greatly increased potential for job enrichment. Participation in a complete stage of production enables each employee to see the **meaning of their work**, which in itself encourages a sense of involvement and responsibility. The informal group dynamics first analysed by Mayo can then be orchestrated to coincide more fully with organizational objectives. Similar strategies have been developed in service industries, where 'family groups' of staff take responsibility for complete units of work.

► Famous experiments of this type began at Volvo and Philips in the 1970s.

 Take any job with which you are familiar. Either analyse it for the job satisfaction it creates, and/or suggest how it could be restructured to be more satisfying.

Organizational Culture

If an organization is serious about moving its relationship with staff beyond a simple exchange of work for money, then a real shift in its values will be necessary. Efforts to meet a wider range of employees' needs are only likely to succeed if management assumptions are reasonably close to McGregor's Theory Y. Otherwise staff may be understandably suspicious of enrichment schemes that only seem a

---

Motivation

Alpha Automotive Parts Ltd had been suffering from problems with industrial relations and quality control. The firm was then nearly bankrupted by the early 1990s recession during which nearly half the management and workforce were made redundant. To survive, major changes were needed. A single status agreement was reached with unions where routine assembly work was broken up into semi-autonomous cells where employees shared all jobs and controlled quality themselves. Continuous training was built into every job. Intermediate levels of management were stripped out, making the organization structure flatter and communications more direct. Managers began to mix freely with shop floor staff and a Company Council was established where representatives of all levels could discuss any agenda.

technical ploy to improve short-term productivity. In some firms new ways of organizing work to increase motivation have been part of a wider transformation in attitudes throughout the enterprise.

 Read the following case study and answer the questions below.

Southern Office Supplies (SOS) Ltd

'Roll on Friday'. Paul Scobie had arrived for work. This was his favourite remark.

'Another week. And forty more till Christmas.' Vickie Reader was an invoice clerk. She looked at her watch. 'Never mind, five minutes of today have gone already.' The phone rang. She groaned. 'Here we go...'.

SOS Ltd was a large regional office supplies wholesaler, also dealing with major corporate customers. Andy Fraser was manager of the main warehouse. His thirty-five strong staff had been attracting critical attention from senior management. How did Mr Fraser account for so many dissatisfied customers? Unexplained delays and omissions in orders? Incorrectly addressed packages? He spoke frankly to Christina Mardle the senior despatch clerk.
'Why can't staff follow simple instructions to do a simple job?' he enquired. They all know the procedure back to front. It should be a well-oiled machine. What's going wrong?'

'It's not lack of instructions. And it's not lack of common sense' she paused, 'it's sheer boredom. Order after order. Package after package. Hour after hour. Day after day. The customers are just names off the computer. They could be anyone.'

Fraser interrupted.
'But the staff are well paid. They've got good working conditions. A subsidized canteen. What more do they want?

1 Answer Mr Fraser's last question making specific reference to Maslow and Herzberg.

2 Look through the various theories of motivation in this chapter and then make two suggestions for improving motivation in this warehouse, showing how the particular theories relate to your suggestions.

Summary and comment

- the real value of employees in terms both of the quantity and quality of their output depends on the level of their motivation. This is therefore a central concern of any effective manager
- a century ago motivation was assumed to depend on little more than the receipt of wages in exchange for labour. Research in the social sciences has revealed the wider range of human needs that demand satisfaction at work. Instead of paying people to fit jobs, the emphasis has shifted to designing jobs that fit people
- where work fails to meet the full range of human emotional needs, the result is boredom, frustration, alienation and waste
- the development of Taylorism and scientific management runs parallel to the rise of Fordism – mechanical mass production for uniform mass markets. The shift towards people-centred management and the recognition of the needs of employees has an interesting echo in the phenomenon of Post-Fordism: new flexible technology making diverse products for complex, fragmented markets
- pay is likely to remain the key motivator for the growing numbers of part-time, contract and temporary staff. For those with a career in the organization, meeting more complex inner needs becomes the most powerful source of motivation
- by adding new vertical scope to the responsibilities of employees, job enrichment schemes tend to cut through the lines of traditional hierarchies. This may imply a flatter and more flexible organizational structure
- the importance of making staff feel that their views are taken seriously can hardly be overstated. Personal consultation and recognition are essential to any strategy for motivation
- proper training demonstrates to employees that their jobs are important. It encourages higher standards and makes the individual feel more involved with the organization
- motivation to improve performance is much strengthened by continuous high profile feedback on progress to date. This may even be most effective if made public and competitive
- the careful extension of increased trust to employees breeds motivation. Most people are keen to accept responsibility and justify the trust shown in them
- the growing use of autonomous work groups to improve motivation represents a kind of micro-decentralization. The equivalent trend in organizational structures (see Chapter 32) is to decentralize authority to the lowest management level at which it can still be effectively exercised. This principle is also called **subsidiarity**.

(35) *Communication*

Chapter objectives

After working through this chapter, you will:

∎ understand the theoretical basis of communications in an organization

∎ know the main methods of communication and why they are used

∎ be able to assess the typical barriers to communication

∎ appreciate the role of informal communications

∎ know the meaning of the following key terms: conception, encoding, transmission, filters, reception, feedback.

THE IMPORTANCE OF COMMUNICATIONS

A business is a social organization embedded in the human world. Its dependence on **communications** is both

* internal, for information, motivation and coordination
* external, with the shareholders, bankers, suppliers, customers, markets, the community and the government.

Any firm is a maze of communication pathways along which messages are travelling. Imagine the endless conversations and meetings, the filing baskets filled with memos and letters, the flicker of computers and VDUs, the receipt and transmission of faxes, the coloured lights that flash on and off across the telephone switchboard. A business is only 'live' when communicating.

► Communication: the transmission and receipt of messages between people.

The Communication Model

Communication means the transmission and receipt of messages between people. The word transmission suggests the world of tele-communications which is the basis for the best known and most useful communications model:

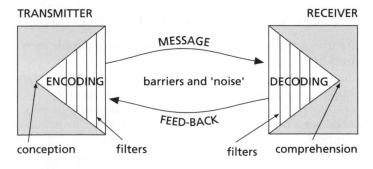

Figure 35.1
A model of communication

1 Conception

The person becomes aware that they have a message to communicate, and establishes the outline of its content. For example the sales manager recognizes that the sales team need further briefing on the selling points of a new product.

2 Encoding

The message is translated into words, symbols, diagrams or images. For example a text is prepared regarding the product.

3 Transmission

A medium is selected, and the encoded message is directed towards the receiver. Distortion is liable to arise from two sources: failings in the act of transmission and external barriers between the transmitter and the receiver. For instance the sales manager addresses the sales team in a soft monotone after a lingering pub lunch.

4 Filters

The human brain acts as a filter on incoming messages, many of which are rejected or highly coloured by beliefs or emotional needs. For instance the salesman for the west Midlands has just been criticized for under-performance, and whispers to the London Rep. that the whole talk is time-wasting propaganda.

5 Reception

To prompt any response, the message must be understood and processed by the receiver. For instance the salesman for Yorkshire understands the message and relates it to recent customer enquiries.

6 Feedback

Communication is made two-way when a response to the message is sent back to the transmitter. For instance the west of England salesman asks if the product can be delivered in smaller quantities and at more frequent intervals.

 Draw your own version of the communication model and annotate it with an example drawn from your own experience.

▶ The same message is interpreted slightly differently by every individual. Differing personalities, beliefs and experiences all combine to add to and subtract from the intended meaning of the message.

Selecting Communication Methods

The object of communication is to achieve understanding in the receiver and an appropriate response. Much depends on the choice of media and the route by which the message travels.

The choice of communication method will be influenced by:

- the nature of the message: e.g. complex ideas or simple facts
- the importance of feedback
- the degree of formality: i.e. a chat in the canteen or a formal memo
- the importance of speed in transmission and response
- the relative cost, including the opportunity cost of time used
- the need for a permanent record (mainly lacking in spoken communication)

- the corporate culture, which may be bureaucratic (favouring paperwork), or organic (favouring a personal approach).

The organization chart of a firm (see Chapter 32) indicates the basic structure of formal communication. In any pyramid type model the emphasis will tend to be on vertical communication, i.e. messages that move down or up the hierarchy. Downward communication is the basic structure for command and control, while upward communication is the vital feedback channel. Lateral communication is designed to provide coordination for different objectives and activities within the firm. Mechanistic systems (see Chapter 33) with tall pyramids have long communication lines which may be very slow or become blocked. Feedback is likely to be limited and late. More organic systems, often using 'flat' or matrix models, sacrifice some unity of command for shorter faster links and more use of lateral connections.

Communication Channels

Alex Bevalas (1948) carried out research into the properties of five well-known models of communication network. Notice the condition that communication can only occur where a line directly connects two members of the group.

▶ The use of five person networks is purely illustrative. Groups may be larger or smaller, and the networks may interlock with others of the same or a different type.

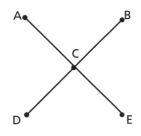

WHEEL
Dominated by leader C; centralized; fast performance; low creativity; low interactivity.

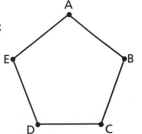

CIRCLE
No necessary leader; slower perfomance; non organic; higher interactivity.

CHAIN
Led by A or C; heirarchical; moderate performance speed; low creativity; low interactivity.

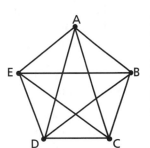

ALL-CHANNEL
No necessary leader; slow perfomance; organic; net-work based; decentralized; high interactivity and creativity.

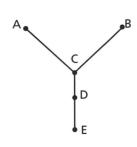

'Y'
Led by C; moderate performance speed; fairly centralized; low creativity; low interactivity.

Figure 35.2
Communication channels and networks

Look at each kind of communication network. From your own experience identify a situation which had that kind of network. Did it aid or hinder communication?

Barriers to Communication

The perception of human beings is too complex for any communication to be received exactly as intended (even 'yes' or 'no' can convey hidden meanings).

► The structure of an organization can become encrusted with barriers to communication. This leads to reduced motivation and trust, weaker coordination and slower responses to change.

> Anna Jenks wanted to do an art foundation course, and felt she had been virtually forced to join Shield Insurance by her father. The company's north western claims bureau was in Manchester, and her uncle had helped her to get a job in the motor department. It was very boring, but she was supposed to be grateful. Mr Hammond (the section leader) was conducting her first appraisal interview. He was a dull middle-aged man who spoke very quickly in a fussy voice, and ended each sentence with a suggestion of mirthless laughter.
>
> 'So are you enjoying your new job?' he asked with a short official-sounding laugh.
>
> 'Er, yes.' Anna gazed at the poppy in his lapel.
>
> 'Only "er, yes"?' He smiled.
>
> 'No, er, I mean ... yes.' Somewhere she could see a whole field of poppies.

Barriers to communication exist:

in the transmitter
- poor presentation fails to hold attention
- lack of credibility in the eyes of the receiver
- badly structured or unfocused message
- wrong timing
- complexity of message pitched too high or too low
- excessive use of jargon
- lack of empathy with the audience

between transmitter and receiver
- wrong route of message
- poor choice of media
- excessive bureaucracy
- uncongenial environment
- 'noise' from distracters
- 'Chinese whispers' effect as message is re-transmitted
- deliberate manipulation of message in re-transmission

in the receiver
- attitudes or bias filter the message
- hostility towards the transmitter or the message

- low motivation
- personality differences
- inadequate background knowledge
- overload of information
- limited concentration span.

Other Problems in Communication

Many other more complex difficulties can reduce or distort a flow of communication:

- social or educational differences between the two sides can cause misinterpretation of messages, while stereotyping of 'workers' or 'management' can be a problem
- emotional energies such as fear, anger or insecurity can grossly distort communication and lead to the message being given interpretations entirely unintended
- 'group-think' occurs when an individual becomes submerged in a group identity, and loses the capacity to think independently
- 'halo/horns' effects occur through people tending to swing in their response to extremes of acceptance or rejection of what they hear, and then projecting this judgement onto all else they hear from the same source
- previous experience of life and at work creates a 'picture' of the world that makes sense to the individual. Messages that do not fit into this picture are often simply rejected (this is called cognitive dissonance)
- organizational pressures may lead to management or staff feeding only information that they think would be found acceptable
- lack of confidence prevents many people from communicating their views or feelings. This is a particular problem in large groups.

Informal Communications

Formal organization structures do not reveal the complex invisible networks of informal contacts and alliances. Many staff obtain advice from anyone but their supervisor, and know good 'sources' for all kinds of information. A network of gossip, rumour and intrigue can easily develop, in which more is to be learned in the canteen or the cloakroom than from senior staff. Some informal off the record communication is inevitable, and can be a catalyst to the achievement of official goals. But a busy grapevine is usually a symptom of communication failure, and can deeply undermine morale and motivation.

 From your experience of any organization, identify the kinds of messages which travel through the formal communication channels, and those which travel through informal channels. How would it affect the organization if messages now travelling only in informal channels were transmitted through formal ones?

▶ 'One look was enough'
'His eyes went straight through me'
'I could see she was nervous'
'He patted me on the shoulder'
'I didn't like the way you came in'
'We've still heard nothing'.

Non-Verbal Communication

There is a complete sub-text to much communication in a non-verbal form.

The main types of non-verbal communication are as follows:

- **gestures**, e.g. wagging of the forefinger
- **body contact**, e.g. handshakes
- **posture**, e.g. refusing to sit down
- **eye contact**
- **critical space**, e.g. standing over a person
- **silences**, adding impact, creating uncertainty
- **dress and accessories**, e.g. a dark suit and a large fountain pen suggest power.

 Read the following case study and answer the questions below.

Klockwise was a young firm in the novelty gift business. The original product remained a particular success: ceramic-faced clocks customized with the buyer's name and logo. The original team of owner-managers were all aged around twenty-one when they started the company and had worked closely together. Even today decisions were often reached through informal chats and general agreement.

Desperately Deborah looked through her diary. Holding the receiver, she stared hard at November 24th.
'We agreed to deliver yesterday? Sixty clocks?' she faltered. 'Yes of course I'll check that right away.'
The following morning a letter arrived from the personnel manager of the life assurance company in question. Since gifts to clients had to be posted in good time for Christmas, they would not now require any clocks. The specimen clock was accordingly returned.

Nicholas, the marketing director, was aghast and furious.
'Our largest single order. And with huge potential. I made three visits to clinch the deal. I thought we had a production team?
'We did'. Deborah spoke in a flat voice. 'Tim says he's leaving. And David says that if Tim goes, he goes too.'

'But why didn't you tell me?' Tim later appealed angrily to Deborah. 'You must have known it was an exceptional order. How could you even think we would deliver by November 24th? I could have told you that was impossible. Nicholas doesn't even know how the clocks are made. He takes orders and seems to think the products will appear by magic' Deborah felt unfairly criticized.
'I simply did my job,' she countered. 'To me it was just another order. I put it through like any other. No one said anything. It wasn't my responsibility.'

Questions:

1 What went wrong at Klockwise ? Where does the responsibility rest?

2 What changes would you recommend to prevent such a failure occurring again?

Summary and comment

• the pattern and style of communication in a firm accurately mirrors the values and culture of the whole organization. For example a secretive and formal system would reflect a rigid mechanical organization. Open and informal communications are typical of more organic systems

• firms need a balance between vertical and lateral communication. Lateral communication is the least emphasized in conventional management models, yet it is essential to flexibility and proactivity in an organization

• communications with employees are gradually becoming less confrontational and more participative: i.e. managers and staff are tending to work more in a partnership and less in opposition

• failures in communication are a classic diseconomy of scale. Too often a 'brontosaurus' principle operates: the organizational brain is remote from the muscles of an ungainly body (and there may always be a Tyrannosaurus Rex in the form of a rival firm...!)

• in too many firms only lip service is paid to the concept of bottom-up communication. Not only is motivation vitally affected by the sense of being heard and taken seriously, but staff at lower levels are the best source of ground floor 'intelligence'

• no one pattern or system of communication is inherently superior to another. Different objectives and different situations call for different styles of communication. For instance management of a traditional, stable market, as against management of a radically new and expanding market.

Corporate culture and change management

Corporate culture and change management

Chapter objectives

After working through this chapter, you will:

▪ understand the meaning of corporate culture

▪ be able to analyse a firm's culture

▪ recognize the pressures for change on business organizations

▪ know how change is resisted and achieved

▪ know the meaning of the following key terms: power cultures, role cultures, task cultures, person culture, atomistic, holistic, management by exception.

CORPORATE CULTURE?

► Corporate culture: a system of beliefs held by an organization or 'body'.

When a group of people work together, it is inevitable that some distinctive patterns develop. The word 'culture' means beliefs about value and meaning, and their expressions in a way of life. Cultures exist in families, neighbourhoods, regions, countries – and firms. A **corporate culture** is a system of beliefs held by an organization or 'body', about its objectives, its products, its customers, its staff and itself – and how these are expressed through its decision making and operations. An understanding of corporate culture provides a deep insight into the behaviour of a firm and its likely response to the **process of change**.

► The capacity to respond effectively to change is a key to business success.

Some organizations have a culture that is highly responsive to change, and seem eager to embrace its possibilities. Others feel their identity and security threatened by change, and attempt to resist or slow down its impact.

Cultural Types

► Techniques of market segmentation (see Chapter 5) classify consumers according to their lifestyle. Firms can similarly be analysed by cultural type.

There are many criteria under which corporate culture can be classified. A useful model is provided by Roger Harrison (1972) and Charles Handy (1985). They distinguish four broad cultural types, on a spectrum of discretion for the individual employee.

Power cultures are centralized and authoritarian. Senior managers keep a firm grip on power and employees must submit to organizational demands. The best service is given to the best customers.

Role cultures are usually hierarchies where each person's job is tightly defined and highly specialized. The aim is to produce a uniformly high standard of service.

Task cultures are less hierarchical, looser organizations where

Figure 36.1
Types of corporate culture

Adapted from *How to Describe Your Organization* by Roger Harrison 1972 and *The Gods of Management* by Charles Handy 1985.

individuals and teams are relatively autonomous and are achievement-driven.

Person cultures allow complete discretion for the individual on a basis of equality and mutual cooperation.

In recent years there has been much discussion of an 'enterprise culture' (see Chapter 1). Firms can be classified according to the strength of their entrepreneurial characteristics.

► The entrepreneurial quality tends to be strong when a business is new or small, and weaker as it ages or grows. Although this is not necessarily true. Some large and long established firms are strongly entrepreneurial, while a small family firm can have a low entrepreneurial propensity.

TYPE A	TYPE B
flexible	*inflexible*
market-led	*product-led*
change-oriented	*change-resistant*
fast reflexes	*slow reflexes*
outward-focused	*inward-focused*
risk-taking	*risk-avoiding*

HIGH ◄ ENTREPRENEURIAL CHARACTERISTICS ► LOW

Figure 36.2
Type A and Type B: entrepreneurial characteristics

Another approach is to plot the ethos or culture of firms on a two-dimensional grid. The x-axis grades firms from being **atomistic** to being **holistic**. An atomistic firm emphasizes the diversity of individuals, and has only a weak identity, with little sense of 'belonging'. A holistic firm is more than the sum of its parts, with a powerful ethos,

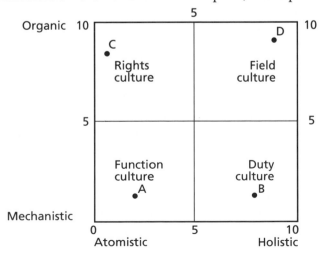

► Firm A has a 'function culture' with well defined roles and all its actions geared for practical results. The 'duty culture' of Firm B stresses the organization rather than the individual, with a strong sense of hierarchy. Firm C's 'rights culture' arises from the belief that each individual has a contract to fulfil, with a corresponding set of rights. A 'field culture' means that Firm D is cohesive yet non-hierarchical, with its staff interacting as though within a corporate 'magnetic field'.

Figure 36.3
Classifying corporate cultures

a distinctive style and a strong sense of 'belonging'. The y-axis grades organizations between being mechanistic and organic models. Mechanistic firms are rigid and hierarchical, while organic firms are flexible and non-hierarchical.

It is important to stress that no one type of corporate culture is either right or wrong. Different cultural types perform best in different business environments. However all environments are subject to change.

 Three ways of classifying corporate cultures have been given. Use one of them to classify the culture of any organization you know.

The Importance of Change

Business conditions change with every day that passes. Some firms remain unaware of change or delay their response, with fatal results. As with the principle of natural selection, it is only the fittest that survive.

The ability to detect a need for change is a prime skill of management. Sometimes the need makes newspaper headlines (e.g. new safety laws after a major accident), but often it is virtually invisible. Forces for change may arise inside or outside the organization.

1 **Internal pressures**
- objectives may change in content or emphasis
- appointments and resignations may introduce new energies or remove old barriers
- staff skills, backgrounds and needs change
- research and development brings new products and processes
- financial disciplines may demand economies or changes in direction.

2 **External pressures**
- markets change with new customers and new demands
- society changes in its attitudes and values
- competition may challenge products as well as markets
- new technology moves from laboratory to commercial applications
- new management techniques are publicized
- the government makes political changes (e.g. privatization), or introduces new laws (e.g. pollution regulations)
- economic trends change direction (e.g. from recession to expansion).

Managers should aim to be aware of change before it makes any unplanned impact on the organization. In practice this is not always possible, and like doctors they must become expert at using symptoms to make an early diagnosis.

Events that are unfolding according to plan do not require management attention. Management by exception means being constantly vigilant to those events that diverge from expectations, and so may indicate unplanned change.

► The proactive firm searches the time horizon and deliberately initiates change, while the reactive firm tends to wait for evidence that change has become unavoidable.

► Symptoms of change:
- budget variances (see Chapter 23)
- changing sales and market share
- employee relations problems
- rising labour turnover
- increased management conflict
- critical feedback from customers
- messages on the 'grapevine'.

Resistance to Change

Any period of stability creates a sense of familiarity and security. This causes a kind of solidifying process in attitudes, methods and patterns of behaviour. Loyalties develop towards systems and places as well as other people. Human beings are nest builders! Even reorganizing the desks in an office can cause staff a painful sense of dislocation. The phrase 'the end of an era' can become applied to very trivial matters. The main reasons for resistance to change are:

- the possible threat of redundancy
- expected loss of earnings or status in absolute terms or simply relative to others
- de-skilling, where a previously valued skill is no longer required
- adverse effects on friendships, social patterns or domestic commitments
- underlying suspicion towards management intentions
- fear of the unknown, e.g. using new technology.

In resistance to change, motivation theory may swing sharply into reverse gear. The stronger the perceived threat to the security and other vital interests of employees, the stronger their likely resistance.

► The key to acceptance of change is the involvement of staff at all stages in its planning.

Achieving Change

Firms need systems of forward planning to avoid being overtaken by events. Statistical techniques, simulations and computer models can assist forecasting. Scenario planning (see Chapter 31) makes managers answer 'what if ...?' questions.

Key Factors in Effecting Change

- **planning** by phases or stages to a clear timetable that can be reviewed and revised as events and outcomes unfold
- **training** for staff, providing new skills and better prospects, combined with greater flexibility in accepting different work roles
- **awakening to benefits** for those employees who may have a negative bias in their perception of change: e.g. new career opportunities
- **communications** that are open and thorough: the appearance of secretive manoeuvring should be avoided; negotiations with staff or their representatives should be honest and opened early; counselling can be offered to individuals most affected
- **participation** where possible of all staff in the change process: delegation enables staff to design their own parts of the change process – which are far more likely to be accepted than those imposed by management
- **compromise** where essential strategy is not endangered: symbolic compromise over details of working life (e.g. breaks) can help win agreement on the major issues.

The speed of change is partly driven by events and partly decided by management. Much depends on the build up of change pressure. If events move very fast and the organization very slowly, then the likelihood of sudden and rapid change increases. If the structure of the organization is inflexible, then chaotic or revolutionary change may result.

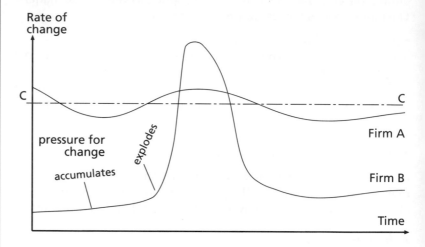

▶ The line CC is the average rate of change acting on the two organizations. Firm A maintains a consistently high pace of change, and is therefore unlikely to require sudden upheavals. Firm B is change-resistant and allows pressure to build until bursts of intense change are unavoidable.

Figure 36.4
Organizational change

A Culture for Change

The capacity of any organization to recognize change pressures and to adapt effectively arises directly from its collective or corporate culture. Particularly important features of the organization are:

- the quality of its internal and external feedback systems
- the flexibility of its structure.

This may explain why there is a trend in the 1990s away from tall, rigid and hierarchical structures (type A), towards flat, flexible and open structures (type B). In type A firms, feedback is subject to delay, blockage and distortion as it climbs backwards up long chains of command. Type B organizations relay pressure for internal change rapidly through few layers of management. With responsibility diffused into virtually all work roles, the firm's perception of change is much increased. Such firms have an outward-focused culture that is vigorously interactive with, for example, customers and suppliers. The rigid hierarchies of type A firms cannot adapt to change until they receive a command to do so. By contrast, type B structures adapt continuously to change, and staff begin to initiate their own training and to adjust their own roles.

Some major companies are now consciously developing a learning culture that thrives on change. This means a high level of motivation, initiative and experimentation among staff, where mistakes are treated as valuable opportunities to learn. A learning culture depends on people feeling secure. This means mutual support within teams and – within defined limits – real acceptance when mistakes are made. To cope with change is not enough: it needs to be embraced – and even celebrated.

 Read the following case study and answer the questions below.

'A wonderful shop' said everyone in the town. Pledgers was a real ironmongers. It seemed to sell almost everything: from mouse-traps to six inch nails, from wheelbarrows to garden seats. Occupying a busy corner of the market square, the shop was cluttered and cramped. Staircases and narrow passages enabled customers to explore the rather dark interior. No one seemed to mind the slow service and some customers had been regulars since the 1950s.

Old Mr Pledger did not even bother to oppose the planning application from Texas Homecare to build a large out-of-town store. Even his son, who ran the garden department, seemed uninterested. As for the other staff, they didn't want to upset Mr Pledger: they knew about his sudden rages. Besides there was a question of loyalty. Pledgers was a landmark for the town. People would arrange to meet 'opposite Pledgers'.

The planning application was successful. By the following spring a large branch of Texas saw its first customers arrive in the immense car-park outside. There were no mousetraps and few staff. Meanwhile life at Pledgers continued – and ended – without change. Old Mr Pledger was said to have retired. No one knew where his son had gone. The shop was empty. The posters on the whitewashed windows announced 'Final Sale'.

1   How would you describe the culture at Pledgers?

2   Why did such a well-established business fail?

3   What advice could you have given to enable the business to survive?

Summary and comment

• leadership style normally corresponds closely with corporate culture. Often however the values of the leaders stake out the direction in which they intend the culture to shift

• senior appointments are a good guide to a firm's true cultural direction. It is usually only senior managers who are able to bring about real cultural change

• firms may acquire or develop splits in their corporate culture, causing serious conflict. There may be lateral, between divisions in the organization, or vertical, between the divisions and head office. Once cultural enclaves develop, they can be difficult to bring back into the mainstream culture

• a firm's corporate culture determines the character of its employee relations. All organizations exert pressure on members to conform to their cultural norms. A spectrum exists between cultures of partnership and cultures of conflict

- a major obstacle to the success of mergers is the difficulty of combining two different business cultures. In practice many managers and staff leave a firm rather than submit to an alien culture
- some major companies are now consciously developing a 'culture of excellence' often called 'Total Quality Management' (TQM). Every person is expected to carry out every task with excellence, which culminates in providing the customer with an ultimate standard of product quality and service. Notice that excellence can exist simultaneously with any other cultural type
- in planning for change, firms need always to allow for unexpected events. Contingency plans are a reserve support system to cope with change that would otherwise be overwhelming
- resistance to change can be valuable in forcing management to examine their assumptions and in highlighting likely problems for adjustment
- conservative elements in an organization prevent excessively rapid change, while encouraging stability and continuity.

National income, output and expenditure

► No understanding of business is complete without an understanding of the economy and the key principles by which it operates.

NATIONAL INCOME

Economists identify four **factors of production**. These are:

Factor	Reward
land	rent
labour	wages
capital	interest
enterprise	profit.

The chief factor input of many households is labour, rewarded by wages (or salaries). However it is quite common to let a room or a garage for rent, to hold deposits in a bank or building society for interest, and by owning some shares, to receive dividends (profits). Now imagine making a list of these income sources for every person in the UK to cover one year. The grand total is called the **national income**. It is calculated in exactly this way by the government in the **national income accounts**.

Consider the total value of all the goods and services produced in the UK over one year: i.e. the **national output**. By definition this has been yielded by combining the factors of production. It follows that the cost of these factor inputs – wages, rents, interest and profits – must equal the value of total output. In fact national income and national output are just opposite sides of the same coin:

► UK national income in 1990 = £478 billion
wages and salaries: 73.6%
profits: 19.5%
rent: 6.9%.

The profits shown here are a gross value, which means that they include interest payments.

UK national output for 1990 = £477.7 billion

	(£bn)	%
agriculture, forestry, fishing	7.1	1.5
energy and water	24.3	4.8
manufacturing	107.0	21.2
construction	36.1	7.2
transport and communication	34.0	6.7
distribution, hotels, catering	70.1	13.9
banking, finance, insurance etc.	87.3	17.3
public services	76.6	15.2
other services	31.0	6.1
home ownership	30.7	6.1

Source: CSO *Blue Book*

► Note the sum of the items does not add up to the stated national output because of adjustments and residual error in official statistics.

► No reference has been made so far to taxation or foreign trade. They qualify but do not alter the identities, and will be explained on p.288.

The next step is simple. All output must either be purchased or added to stocks. It follows, therefore, that total expenditure in the economy must equal total output after allowing for net changes in stocks. We now have the identity:

national income ≡ national output ≡ national expenditure.

We can see that the value of national expenditure is also equivalent in value to national income. Of course households save as well as spend, but their savings are used by firms and the government for investment – i.e. expenditure on capital goods (long-lasting durable goods e.g. machine tools). Thus the identity holds good.

The Standard of Living

This term is much used – and abused. It is generally taken to mean the rate at which goods and services are consumed by the average household or individual. The population of the UK in 1990 was 57.7m., so the average income per person was:

$$\frac{£478bn}{57.4m.} = £8\ 327$$

Ten years earlier, in 1980, the value of national income was only £201 billion. But before making any comparisons we must:

- allow for the change in population size
- adjust money values to take account of inflation (see Chapter 23).

Inflation from 1979 to 1990 amounts to 89%. In 1980 national income is therefore worth £179bn × 1.89 = £380bn in 1990 terms. The population in 1980 was 56.3m. Thus income – per head is:

$$\frac{£380bn}{56.3m.} = £6\ 750$$

► GDP = Gross Domestic Product – the total money value of all final goods and services produced in an economy over a one-year period.

The true increase over ten years is therefore from £6 750 to £8 327 per person or about 23.4%. In terms of living standards, GDP statistics must always be treated with caution. Significant factors to consider are:

- the proportion that is investment rather than current consumption
- the nature of expenditure: e.g. defence costs
- the distribution of income among the population
- the social and environmental costs of production.

The Circular Flow of Income

Figure 37.1
The circular flow of income: a simple model

Begin by imagining a simple economy where households and firms are in a direct relationship: all incomes are spent without savings, there is no government or public sector, and no foreign trade. Households express demand for goods and services. Firms meet this demand by employing the factors of production: land, labour, capital and enterprise. For these services they make payments that form their costs and the factor incomes that reach households. These households (or consumers) now spend their incomes, receiving goods and services in return, and supplying revenue to firms. This revenue can then be used to employ further factor services, and the cycle begins again. Notice that in terms of money there is a circular flow between households and firms.

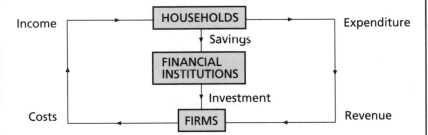

Figure 37.2
The circular flow of income: showing money flows

This is a model of the same simple economy, except that only **money-flows** are now shown, and the assumption that all income is spent has been dropped. Clearly households do not spend the whole of their incomes: part is saved and deposited in a range of financial institutions (commercial banks, finance houses, pension funds etc.). These savings represent a diversion or **leakage** from the circular flow, and mean that the spending by households is correspondingly less than the factor incomes paid by firms. However firms do not rely solely on demand from consumer spending. They also obtain an additional **injection of demand** through the financial institutions that lend for investment in industry. In this sense the banking system acts as a kind of 'clearing house' between the savings intentions of households and the investment intentions of firms (see Chapter 41). The relationship between the resulting leakages and injections is of crucial importance.

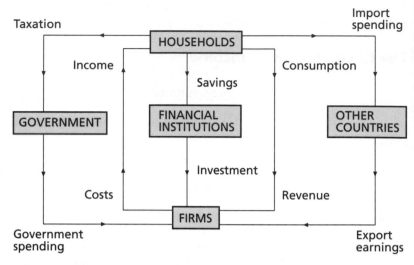

Figure 37.3
The circular flow of income: financial institutions, government and overseas trade

In the real economic world there is a government sector, and there is overseas trade: both exert an important influence on the circular flow. To finance the goods and services that it provides, the government levies taxes on incomes (and on spending), which means that the **disposable incomes** of households are considerably less than their gross earnings. As this is more money diverted from the circular flow, it is another leakage. However when government spending takes place, it represents another injection of demand for firms.

The sale of imported goods diverts a part of households' spending to other countries, and is therefore a leakage. But exports also yield extra revenue from overseas, and represent an injection into the UK circular flow. Therefore:

total leakages = savings (S) + taxation (T) + imports (M)

AND

total injections = investment (I) + government spending (G) + exports (X)

Economic equilibrium always exists when total demand equals total supply. In our model, this means that total planned leakages must equal total planned injections. If leakages exceed injections, the revenue received by firms is less than the value of total output (or factor incomes). The result is increasing stocks of unsold goods, causing firms to reduce output, which in turn reduces incomes. If injections exceed leakages the reverse process occurs: effective demand is greater than the value of current output. Firms expand production and incomes increase. It is clear that the relationship between leakages and injections is vital in determining the size of national income.

 To make notes on the circular flow of income draw your own diagram and annotate it.

The Multiplier

This is one of those concepts that can look very difficult, but is actually quite simple. You should now have a clear picture of injections and leakages. Consider an economy in equilibrium. There is no net force to cause expansion or contraction. Then suppose that a large firm decides to increase its investment by £1m. What will be the consequences? In the first place, other firms will enjoy extra orders for their capital goods worth £1m. But that is not all. Where does the extra £1m. actually go? To produce the extra capital goods the other firms will need to employ additional factors of production, and pay out additional factor rewards which take the form of increased incomes for households. This extra money will then be spent again, creating another rise in demand for the output of firms. This second round of spending will not increase demand by a full £1m., since it will be reduced by our three sources of leakage. Suppose that for every extra £1 that households receive:

> 30p is paid in taxes
> 10p is saved
> <u>10p is spent on imports</u>
> = 50p in total leakages.

It follows that the extra demand on the second round of spending will be £500 000. When this spending creates a yet further increase in output and incomes, the same leakages will occur again, and demand will rise by £250 000. The cycle continues like a fading echo through the economy. The final increase in demand will be:

£1m. + £500 000 + £250 000 + £125 000 + ...n = £2m.

You can see that an initial £1m. increase in injections has had an end value of £2m. in terms of extra demand and extra output. In other words it has been subject to a **multiplier effect** of 2. The value of the multiplier is easily calculated for any data. In the above example the total rate of leakages was 50p in the £, or 0.5. This is called the **marginal rate of leakage** since it refers to any extra £1 spent

$$\text{The multiplier} = \frac{1}{\text{the marginal rate of leakage}}$$

Or in the example:

$$\text{The multiplier} = \frac{1}{0.5} = 2$$

It is clear that the smaller the rate of leakage, the more powerful the multiplier effect. However the multiplier can also operate in the reverse direction. A decrease in any source of expenditure (e.g. a cut in investment or government spending) will be subject to the same multiplier effect in reducing demand and output.

Annotate your diagram of the circular flow of income to show the multiplier effect. Work out for yourself the decrease in demand created by a reduction in investment of £2m. with a multiplier value of 1.5.

Aggregate Demand and Aggregate Supply

We have already explored basic demand and supply curves for individual products (see Chapter 9). It is also possible to extend the principle to the whole economy.

► The diagram relates the overall level of prices (on the y-axis) to the real level of national income or output (on the x-axis). 'Real income' means that the value is measured at constant prices, undistorted by inflation.

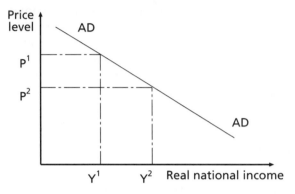

Figure 37.4
The aggregate demand curve

The aggregate demand curve is downward-sloping since a reduction in the price level increases the purchasing power of incomes and wealth, so enabling consumption to increase. Thus a fall in the price level (P1 – P2) causes a rise in national income/output (Y1 – Y2).

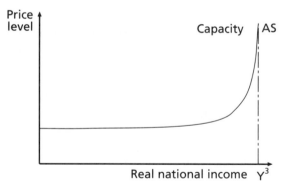

Figure 37.5
Aggregate supply curve

Just as firms have a limit to their productive capacity, so does the economy as a whole. At first the curve is virtually flat (i.e. perfectly elastic) since there is spare capacity in all the firms, and an increase in output will not cause costs to rise. However as capacity is approached the curve sharply steepens, due to an increasing number of firms running short of factor inputs (especially skilled labour), and being forced to offer progressively higher rewards (e.g. higher wages). These higher costs are passed on to the consumer in a higher level of prices. When capacity is reached, it follows that output cannot rise, and so any attempt to expand output can only cause a corresponding rise in prices.

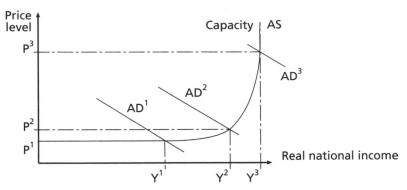

► National income level Y1 can be achieved at price level P1. A higher level of demand (AD2) pushes up prices to P2, while AD3 hits capacity and causes a sharp rise in prices to P3. This problem is explored in Chapter 40.

Figure 37.6
Demand, capacity and price

 Draw your own versions of the graphs illustrating aggregate demand and aggregate supply and annotate them.

Economic Growth

This means an increase in the level of real national income. Important ways by which this can be achieved include:

1 Increased factor inputs

- net investment in capital goods, e.g. building new factories
- a rise in the working population
- the discovery of new natural resources, e.g. North Sea oil.

2 Increased factor productivity

- new and more efficient technologies, e.g. computer-aided manufacturing systems
- increased education and training, improving skill levels in the workforce
- economies of scale (see Chapter 15)
- improved management in combining factor inputs.

Such changes have the effect of shifting the aggregate supply curve to the right, enabling real national income to increase without any sharp rise in the level of prices.

(ACT) It is found that for every pound earned:
    8p is saved
    20p is paid in taxes
    12p is spent on imports.

1 What is the value of the multiplier?

2 If an extra £100m. is spent on investment, by how much will national income be expected to increase?

What would you expect to be the business effects of the following events?

1 A rise in the rate of VAT to 22%.

2 A reduction in business rates.

3 An environmental tax placed on all industrial goods liable to cause pollution.

4 A surge in economic growth in countries that are major trading partners.

5 A cut in the rate of income tax to 20p in the £ with unemployment at a record low level.

Summary and comment

• the performance of all firms is affected by changes in the economy as a whole. Even a highly profitable and well-managed enterprise may fail due to adverse economic conditions, such as a combination of falling demand, higher interest rates, increased taxation or greater competition from imports

• it is essential for managers to pay close attention to economic trends and forecasts. These may provide some advance indication of dangers or opportunities ahead. For instance, many investment decisions are heavily dependent on longer-term economic prospects

• there is no necessary equality between the planned savings of households and the planned investment by firms. Their actual values must balance, since the resources saved by a society become resources available for use in a future period – the economic definition of investment. But these resources are not necessarily devoted to spending on capital goods. They may simply become increasing stocks of unsold goods, so causing firms to cut output, with downward multiplier pressures on national income. Eventually equilibrium will be reached, with planned savings equal to planned investment, but at a reduced national income level. The sequence works in reverse if planned investment exceeds planned savings, and the eventual equilibrium will be at a higher level of national income

• the actual marginal rates of leakage in the UK are approximately 32p in the £ for direct taxation, 10p in the £ for savings, 18p in the £ for indirect taxation, and 32p in the £ for imports. This gives a rough multiplier value of 1.33

• in the short run, economic growth tends to depend on increased factor inputs. In the longer run it is increased investment and factor productivity that are significant

• an interesting feature of economic growth is its tendency to push the largest source of income and employment from the primary to the secondary to the tertiary sector over the long term. These stages are sometimes described as pre-industrial, industrial and post-industrial.

38 *The business cycle*

THE BUSINESS CYCLE AND ITS STAGES

Over the past hundred years in Britain, economic growth has averaged around one point five per cent per annum. The figure for the past ten years has been higher, at about two point five per cent. These values represent the trend path of output. But the actual level of business activity weaves above and below the trend path in a cycle of booms and slumps. Although irregular in its intensity and in the duration of its phases, the cycle has a distinct pattern.

Stages of the Business Cycle

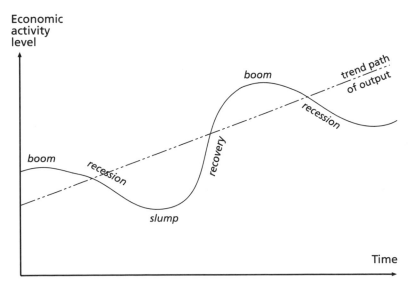

► The only years of negative growth between 1960 and 1991 in Britain have been 1975, 1980, 1990 and 1991.

Stages of the Business Cycle
Boom: business expectations high; sales high; stocks low; output near capacity; profits and investment high; unemployment low with labour shortages; prices rising.
Recession: optimism fades; sales start downwards; stocks begin to build; profits are lower; investment cut; unemployment begins to rise; prices usually rise more slowly.
Slump: pessimism dominates; sales low; de-stocking is widespread; output is low with extensive spare capacity; profits and investment are depressed; unemployment high; prices often tend to stabilize.
Recovery: expectations rising; sales increase; re-stocking begins; output increases and spare capacity is brought back into use; profits and investment rise; unemployment starts to fall; prices begin to accelerate.

Figure 38.1
The business cycle

The average length of the modern cycle is about four to five years (the peaks and troughs are called the **upper** and **lower turning points**).

The Cycle in Practice

Reality is more complex than the classic four-phase pattern suggests. Not only can the boom–to–boom length of the cycle vary widely, but the exact profile of each phase is unique. Booms and slumps can be prolonged, while recoveries and recessions can be shallow or steep. Deceptive upturns or downturns can occur, which fail to lead to the next boom or slump. The cycle is also influenced by government policies and by wider world economic and political events.

With the Wall Street crash in 1929 the booming US economy moved into a steep recession which then spread rapidly all over the world. Britain was already in a long slump, which worsened to become the great depression of the 1930s. It appeared as if the cycle could become stuck in an indefinite slump. After 1945 the cycle was far milder and faster moving, with a strong underlying growth trend. But in 1973–74 the quadrupling of world oil prices pushed the economy into a sharp recession and unprecedented inflation. Unemployment began a long climb which continued through the next recovery. In 1979 a second oil crisis ushered in the deepest recession since the 1930s: unemployment soared and inflation surged again. Large numbers of manufacturing firms were forced out of business. A slow recovery from 1981–84 led to a long boom, with abundant new business start ups and the rapid growth of the service industry. The new pattern of high growth was broken by a serious trade deficit and renewed inflation. Another severe recession began in 1989.

 Draw a timeline 1929–93 and on it mark the periods of boom and slump.

Causes of the Cycle

Many theories have been advanced to explain the business cycle. The most important ones will be briefly explained.

1 The multiplier-accelerator theory

We have seen how the multiplier (see Chapter 37) amplifies the upward or downward effect of any change in the level of aggregate demand. In practice the theoretical state of equilibrium never actually occurs and the economy is always in the process of expansion or contraction. Suppose demand and output are rising due to increased investment. This involves not just one investment project with multiplier effects, but a continuous flow of additional investment spending, with continuous multiplier effects. This might represent a recovery phase turning into a boom. We now meet the **accelerator**.

► On 24 October 1929 – 'Black Thursday' – Wall Street experienced its greatest ever crash. Within one week, American investors had lost 40 000 m. dollars.

The Accelerator

A truck operator, delivering consumer goods to retail outlets, owns ten trucks, each costing £50 000, and needs to replace one vehicle each year. However, demand for his services then expands by twenty per cent in one year, making necessary the purchase of two extra vehicles. His order to the manufacturers is thus for three vehicles – one for replacement and two for expansion – costing £150 000 in all. Next year the economic climate is still good, and demand increases by around another ten per cent. The firm therefore orders two vehicles costing £100 000. In the following year the boom flattens out and demand is steady. No extra trucks are needed, and one replacement vehicle is ordered at £50 000. A slight downturn begins in the succeeding year and demand falls by ten per cent. No extra vehicles are needed, and no replacement is needed either. No vehicle order is placed.

Year	Change in demand	Vehicles ordered	Value (£k)	Change in order value
1	+ 20%	3	150	+ 200%
2	+ 10%	2	100	– 33%
3	0	1	50	– 50%
4	– 10%	0	0	– 100%

This simple example has serious implications for the producers of capital goods. Compare changes in demand for consumer goods to the resulting changes in demand for capital goods. A 20% rise in demand for consumer goods causes a 200% rise in demand for capital goods. Just a **slowing in the rate of expansion** in consumer goods industries then causes a major contraction in capital goods industries. **Stable** demand for consumer goods inflicts a further 50% **fall** in orders for capital goods. A 10% fall in demand goes on to cause a collapse in demand to zero for capital goods. These changes in demand all carry multiplier effects, and when repeated across the country help swing the economy into booms and slumps.

2 The inventory cycle

In America stock is called 'inventory', and the concept of a cycle is based on the pattern of orders placed by retailers. If a fall in demand – and hence retail sales – occurs, then stock starts to build up, with a mounting opportunity cost. Retailers (and wholesalers) respond by targeting lower stock levels. This means that orders to manufacturers for new stock are severely reduced or even stopped altogether. Output and incomes fall as a phase of de-stocking takes place. Once stocks are sufficiently low it is necessary to start ordering again at a moderate rate even to meet depressed demand. This is often experienced by manufacturers as an increase in demand, so starting a modest expansion in output and incomes. This continues to grow as re-stocking keeps ahead of sales. But the relationship is volatile. Any

► Retailers may resort to frequent 'sales' during periods of recession.

decline in sales – or even a slowing of sales growth – may cause a sharp fall in orders.

3 Government intervention

During the great depression of the 1930s the government claimed that there was little it could properly do to initiate recovery. At exactly the same time, Keynes was writing his *General Theory* that led later governments to become actively involved in trying to influence the business cycle. In recent times government policies have included:

- changes in public spending which increase or reduce aggregate demand
- changes in direct and indirect taxation designed to affect consumer demand and factor supply
- changes in the rate of interest which affect business investment, consumer borrowing and the rate of saving
- exchange rate policy which affects the demand for imports and exports.

These 'levers' of economic policy are often used in combination, but their accuracy is doubtful and there can be unintended effects. There is also a significant political cycle at work. Governments face elections every four to five years, and often aim for a recovery or boom to be in progress at the end of their term of office. Tax and interest rate cuts are possible tactics in the pre-election period.

 1 Take your previous notes on the multiplier effect and add notes on the accelerator.

2 Make notes to show the effect of, the inventory cycle and government intervention on the circular flow of income.

Impact of the Cycle on Business

The business cycle is beyond the control of any one firm. For some firms the cycle provides only a gentle ebb and flow in the underlying pathway of growth. Such firms are called 'recession proof', and tend to trade in necessities (e.g. supermarkets). At the opposite extreme, the business cycle can create new business opportunities, which may then be seriously undermined only a few years later. As so often, risks and rewards are very finely balanced.

Decision areas where the business cycle makes a particular impact include:

- **investment decisions** which are based on expectations of future sales. When forecasting the cash flows arising from an investment project, it is essential to allow for cyclical changes in the economic climate. Basing decisions on performance during a boom can lead to grossly over-optimistic business expansion
- **capital structure** which needs to be appropriate and sustainable over the course of a complete cycle. A particular danger is allowing a boom to prompt excessive borrowing and the development of very high gearing. During a recession sales fall and interest rates

► The retail chain Next crashed from a before tax profit of £62 m. in 1988 to a £41 m. loss in 1990. Its share price touched 6p in December 1990.

may rise (as over 1988–90), leaving the firm very vulnerable to falling interest cover and difficulties with repayments

- **market exposure**, which means the structure and nature of markets on which the firm is reliant. Some markets are low risk where sales and profit margins may be unspectacular, but can safely withstand any economic downturn. Other markets are far more volatile and prone to dramatic expansion and contraction as the economy shifts from phase to phase. A useful guide is **income elasticity of demand**. This measures the change in quantity of a product demanded relative to a change in incomes:

$$\text{income elaticity of demand} = \frac{\%\text{ change in quantity demanded}}{\%\text{ change in outcome}}$$

► Income elasticity of demand: change in demand for a product in relation to changes in incomes.

Broadly, income elasticity below 1 indicates a necessity, and values above 1 indicate a luxury. During a boom, demand for luxuries can increase very quickly, causing fast growth in 'frothy' business opportunities, which can then subside suddenly with the onset of recession. Many service industries are prone to this effect. For example a product with an income elasticity of 4 may find that a ten per cent rise in disposable incomes within its target market leads to a forty per cent rise in sales. Hasty expansion can then be very dangerous if two years later the same arithmetic moves into reverse

- **labour flexibility** in terms of employee skills, numbers and hours which vitally affect the firm's ability to adapt in a changing economic climate. Flexible skills enable management to vary their product mix at short notice. The use of part-time temporary and contract staff enables the total labour input – and costs – to be varied without the disruption and expense of redundancies.

 Make notes to show which kinds of firms are most and which are least vulnerable to the business cycle. What implications does this have for the marketing mix?

Large firms make use of **business forecasting** which takes careful account of economic trends. In this task managers can use their internal sales and market research data together with macroeconomic forecasts issued by the government and a range of external organizations. Various statistical series provide indicators of movement through the business cycle:

- **leading indicators** point to changes in economic activity around six to twelve months in advance. Examples include the CBI survey of business optimism and the FT-SE share index
- **coincident indicators** directly represent the cycle itself. They include real GDP, the volume of retail sales and the CBI index of firms working below capacity
- **lagging indicators** reflect the state of business activity about a year earlier. The key examples are investment and unemployment.

Economic Indicators are frequently quoted and commented on in the financial news. Collect examples and make your own notes on the way in which commentators use indicators as evidence of the state of the economy.

 Look at the diagram and answer the questions below.

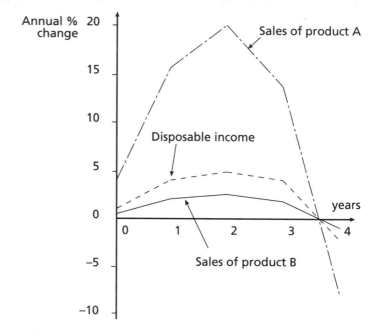

Figure 38.2
Sales and incomes changes

1 Suggest possible identities for Products A and B, giving your reasons.

2 Indicate ways in which a firm selling only Product A might be affected by the information given.

3 What is the probable income elasticity of demand for Products A and B?

Summary and comment

• the effect of the retail inventory cycle can be dampened by manufacturers' stocks. As retailers cut their orders in a recession, so manufacturers tend to increase stocks. When orders begin to increase, manufacturers can initially supply from stock without increasing output

• however, the development of just-in-time delivery systems is tending to connect demand and production more directly and to reduce the effect of stock levels on the business cycle

• the growing integration of European economies is tending to mean that movements in the business cycle are no longer so dependent on economic events in one country – or on the policies of one government

- the business cycle can be very uneven in its impact on the regions within a larger economy. In the 1980–1 slump, the manufacturing parts of the Midlands and northern Britain were far more severely affected than the south. But in the sharp downturn of 1990–1, construction and service industries were worst affected with disproportionate impact in the South East
- sudden changes in the output of one particular firm or industry can cause local business cycles that strongly exaggerate or counteract national patterns. Contrasting examples in the early 1990s include pit closures in the South Wales valleys and the oil industry-led expansion in the Aberdeen area of Scotland
- economic forecasting is still liable to be inaccurate and misleading despite the use of increasingly sophisticated computer models. Not only are there many internal and external variables involved, but their interactivity can be very complex.

(39) *Unemployment*

Chapter objectives

After working through this chapter, you will:

▊ understand the meaning of employment and unemployment

▊ be able to distinguish the causes and types of unemployment

▊ understand the strategies and problems of governments in their efforts to reduce unemployment

▊ know how the level of unemployment affects a firm's personnel department

▊ know the meaning of the following key terms: cyclical unemployment, frictional unemployment, structural unemployment, regional unemployment, technological unemployment, seasonal unemployment, residual unemployment.

WHAT IS UNEMPLOYMENT?

► In common usage unemployment refers to labour but it can also apply to idle land or capital.

Unemployment is a subject about which feelings run high, and it has always been a major political issue. The non-use of land and capital carries what seems a wasteful opportunity cost, but the non-use of labour – or people – increases the social security burden and carries additional human costs in poverty, social decline and psychological damage. Work is a fundamental human need and for many people it is an important source of their identity and self-respect.

The Great Depression

As the British economy followed the USA into a dramatic downward spiral, so unemployment soared. By 1932 twenty-three per cent of the working population were without a job. In the regions of heavy industry the rate was thirty eight per cent and locally up to seventy-five per cent. Factories closed and stood empty, ships rusted in estuaries and farmers left crops to rot in the fields. National income fell and social hardship became acute. This is the paradox of a slump. People are in great need, and wish to work. Natural and man-made resources are ready and available. And yet nothing happens. The wheels of business simply fail to turn.

The reason is lack of demand. Resources will not be employed unless there is a demand for their output at a price that sufficiently exceeds their costs. When this condition is not met, unemployment is the result.

An increasing level of demand from the circular flow of income draws resources into employment. The higher the level of aggregate demand, the higher the proportion of the labour force that will be employed. **Thus demand is the motor of employment**.

However there is an important qualification. In the 1960s when the economy was working at or near capacity, about 300 000 people remained unemployed. It is now clear that the current equivalent figure is around 1.6 m. If demand were to be increased further(e.g., in 1988 at the peak of a boom) then inflation (and the trade deficit) would rise very sharply indeed, with unacceptable consequences (see Chapter 40). The reasons for this change are complex, but possible factors include:

• employers tending to reward their permanent 'core' staff above the market rate to ensure loyalty and motivation. Workers outside the 'core' are employed casually or not at all
• the effective 'dismissal' of the long-term unemployed from the labour market, so that the active labour market only operates above a certain base level of unemployment
• bottlenecks in the economy, meaning that as demand increases, some industries reach full employment long before others. Rising inflation then quickly forces the government to curb demand
• lack of training leads to inadequate skills among the workforce, so discouraging investment and preventing workers from filling the vacancies that exist.

1 Add the historical facts to the timeline you started in Chapter 38.

2 Make notes to explain why unemployment sometimes remains high when demand is high.

Although we speak of the labour force as a whole, every worker in the market is unique. People vary in qualifications, skills, experience, motivation, where they live, age and sex. For some groups of workers there is always a very high level of demand, and virtually no unemployment. For other groups the reverse is true.

Unemployment statistics are usually presented both as a national average and on a regional basis. Regional unemployment rates are affected by:

• level of demand in specific industries
• local levels of aggregate demand
• technological developments affecting particular jobs or processes
• trade union influences
• 'going rate' for local wages.

▶ In 1988, at the peak of a boom, the unemployment rate in parts of Northern Ireland was still 30%. Yet in the more prosperous towns of the South East, the rate was under 3%.

UK Unemployment Rates (%)

	1966	1978	1989	1991	1992
North	2.5	8.2	10.0	10.6	11.0
Yorkshire	1.1	5.5	7.7	9.1	9.6
East Midlands	1.0	4.7	5.6	7.8	8.5
East Anglia	1.4	4.7	3.6	6.2	7.1
South East	0.9	4.0	3.9	7.4	8.7
South West	1.7	6.1	4.5	7.5	8.6
West Midlands	0.8	5.1	6.6	9.0	10.3
North West	1.4	6.9	8.4	9.9	10.3
Wales	2.8	7.6	7.4	9.2	9.5
Scotland	2.7	7.6	9.3	9.2	9.2
Northern Ireland	5.3	10.5	15.1	14.1	14.2
UNITED KINGDOM	1.4	5.7	6.3	8.5	9.4

Economists classify unemployment in a range of types:

- **cyclical unemployment** is caused by the general lack of demand during a recession and slump (e.g. early 1990s)
- **frictional unemployment** is caused by the short-term pattern of workers changing jobs due to the contraction and expansion of labour demand in different firms and industries
- **structural unemployment** is a severe frictional type, as a whole industry faces long-term decline (e.g. coal mining or ship building)
- **regional unemployment** is often the result of structural change since industries tend to be geographically concentrated (e.g. textiles in west Yorkshire)
- **technological unemployment** occurs when new technology makes a certain type of worker unnecessary – or uncompetitive with machinery (e.g. computerization of printing in the 1980s)
- **seasonal unemployment** exists when demand fluctuates sharply between seasons and workers become jobless during slack periods (e.g. winter in seaside resorts)
- **residual unemployment** refers to those workers who lack the personal skills to retain any paid job.

Government Policies

Governments aim for 'full employment' but this does not mean zero unemployment. A certain base level of unemployment appears to be necessary to allow structural change to take place in the economy and to avoid the risk of inflation caused by the 'bidding up' of wage rates.

Measures to prevent or reduce unemployment can include:

- **increased public spending**
  higher spending on schools, hospitals, housing, defence, transport and other projects increases demand in the economy and creates jobs
- **reduce tax and interest rates**
  lower taxes leave consumers with a larger net income to spend, so

► Post-war levels of unemployment were extremely low. In 1950 the national rate was 1.6% and in the West Midlands only 0.5%. Even by 1970 the overall rate was still only 2.6%. Yet since 1980 the rate has never been below 7%.

raising demand. Cutting interest rates helps mortgage borrowers, encourages consumer credit spending and makes it cheaper for firms to invest

- **improve training**
  more and better training tends to make workers more productive and therefore more valuable to firms (see Chapter 28). It also helps workers to adapt to technological and structural change, equipping them with skills to find new jobs
- **regional policy**
  in areas of high unemployment, a range of government incentives are available to attract business enterprise and so to create more jobs (see Chapter 12)
- **assist labour market efficiency**
  job centres, careers services and a variety of job awareness initiatives help people to fill the vacancies that exist.

 Make notes to show the possible effects of the different kinds of government intervention on the various types of unemployment listed earlier.

To put government policies in perspective, it is necessary to consider briefly the past. The 1930s had demonstrated the evils of mass unemployment. Governments after the Second World War used Keynesian demand management to maintain full employment. This involves the government in using public spending and interest rates deliberately to hold aggregate demand at a level yielding full employment. The approach was successful for about twenty years, but eventually broke down as increases in demand brought rising inflation and increased imports without any lasting impact on unemployment. Meanwhile the oil crises of the 1970s, the recession of the early 1980s and widespread deindustrialization brought the unemployment rate to fourteen per cent (or 3.2 million jobless) by 1983. The problem was largely left to market forces as the Conservative government made the defeat of inflation its priority. However with declining union power, wage rates tended to become more flexible, while a significant expansion of youth training took place. After the upswing/boom of 1984–1988 the unemployment rate had fallen to eight point one per cent, but rose again with the recession of the early 1990s.

▶ Since the 1980s government policy has shifted away from stimulating the demand for labour towards the **supply side**. The emphasis has been on better training, increased mobility and reduced trade union power.

 Add the historical facts above to your timeline.

Effects on the Firm

The level of employment directly affects all firms and has particular importance for the personnel function:

- labour turnover normally falls with increasing unemployment. Staff are less able to find alternative jobs, and tend to value their existing employment more highly. This can cause a rising average age and increasing conservatism among staff

- recruitment of staff becomes easier with higher unemployment, and the selection process is likely to become more exacting. When labour shortages occur the reverse pattern applies and firms need to market themselves as attractive employers
- pay and benefits are strongly influenced in their movement by the tightness of the labour market. As the supply of labour in the market increases, so firms feel under less pressure in negotiating pay and benefits. But labour shortages are usually quick to bring improved rewards, especially if in the context of a general business upturn
- industrial relations depend partly on relative bargaining strengths which in turn depend on the prevailing demand for labour. Generally unions tend to moderate their claims as unemployment rises, with less chance of disputes leading to industrial action
- the personnel department can find that its apparent importance and actual influence is much increased during periods of labour shortage. Conversely, as a provider of manpower, its role may be diminished by unemployment. Recruitment, in-house training, rewards and employee relations all move up the agenda when the labour market is tight.

 Draw up a two column table. Head one column 'high unemployment' and the other 'low unemployment'.Use the table to summarize the situation of firms under the different circumstances.

 Read the following statistics and answer the questions below.

Unemployment rate (% of working population)			
	1989	*1990*	*1991*	*1992*
North West	8.6	7.4	9.9	10.3
South East	3.9	3.7	7.4	8.7
UK	6.4	5.7	8.5	9.4

1 Why has unemployment been persistently higher in the north west than in the South East?

2 Why might the unemployment rate in the South East have risen relatively faster than in other regions?

3 How would you account for the trend in the UK unemployment rate over the period shown?

Summary and comment

- before 1980 governments attempted to maintain 'full employment' by influencing the level of demand. As this proved increasingly to cause inflation, policy shifted to the 'supply side', with more emphasis on freer labour markets, increased training and reduced trade union power
- the rapid shrinkage of the public sector has tended to make market forces more widespread in setting employment levels
- the greatest source of new jobs is in the small firms sector, but this can be vulnerable to recession
- high regional rates of unemployment have been essentially structural as traditional heavy industries have declined. This problem may be less acute in the future, as much adjustment has now taken place
- a balanced and diversified local economy has been most effective in resisting recent rises in unemployment. An area is vulnerable when it depends heavily on one industry or one employer
- the rapid expansion of service industry in the 1980s created much new employment, but it is clear that many jobs in consumer services can disappear during an economic downturn
- a personnel department will only enjoy long-term status and influence in a firm if involved with human resources at every level. Its management need to establish an importance that is independent of short-term changes in the labour market.

40 Inflation

THE MEANING OF INFLATION

► Inflation means a fall in the purchasing power of money.

Inflation means a persistent rise in the general level of prices – or, put another way, a steady fall in the purchasing power of money. It is important to remember that £1 has no fixed value: indeed, its value changes every day. As the level of prices rises, so the value of money falls. £1 in 1914 – the outbreak of the First World War – had the equivalent buying power of £44.25 by 1991: or, put another way, 2.3 pence then was equivalent to £1 now.

From 1920 to 1935, prices in Britain were actually 'falling' in a **deflation** that amounted to about seventy per cent over the period. Since 1935 the price level has risen in every year. Almost all western industrial countries have experienced rising prices, mostly in the form of a 'creeping inflation' at an annual rate of below ten per cent. Low inflation rates are often seen as a sign of steady economic growth, as aggregate demand keeps slightly ahead of aggregate supply. Britain's inflation rate averaged just over three per cent during the 1950s and 1960s. A rapid acceleration into **strato-inflation** then occurred as rates soared to peaks of twenty-five per cent in 1975 and eighteen per cent in 1980. The rate since 1982 has been fluctuating in a band between two and a half per cent and ten per cent.

► With **hyper-inflation** the annual rate becomes first hundreds, then thousands per cent. The value of money collapses, savings are wiped out and all business confidence is lost. The most famous hyper-inflation was in Germany in 1923–5, when the inflation rate reached millions per cent, and thick wads of million-mark notes were needed to buy even a loaf of bread.

 Add the historical facts above to your timeline.

Measuring Inflation

The government measures movements in the rate of inflation through the retail price index (RPI). A representative sample of household goods is used to establish a typical spending pattern. This provides 'weighting' factors to reflect the relative importance of the selected items (clearly a five per cent rise in the price of gas has a far bigger impact than a five per cent rise in the price of matches). Price levels for the chosen products are then checked across the country, and combined according to their weights at a 'base' date. This value is given the index number of 100. Prices of the same products are then researched each month and expressed as a percentage of the base prices. Their weighted average forms the monthly index. The last base date was January 1987, and the value in February 1992 was 136.3. This means that the price level over the period had risen by 36.3 per cent.

Real and Nominal Values

Nominal prices are those actually quoted by firms. **Real prices** measure the purchasing power represented by a nominal price.

▶ The £1 coin was introduced in 1983. In the terms of that year its value has already slumped to 61p (1992).

Real and Nominal Values: Prices

A retail price index was as follows:

year	index
1	100
2	106
3	112

Suppose that product X sold for £10 in year 1, and for £11 in year 3. The nominal price has risen by 10%. But has the price really risen? Prices generally have risen by 12% over the same period. Now convert the year 1 price into year 3 terms:

$$£10 \times \frac{112}{100} = £11.20$$

We can now see that product X is actually **cheaper** today in real terms, i.e. after allowing for inflation.

This concept is very useful. With an index of inflation it is simple to convert the prices of any year into the terms of another year. Consider the price of a pint of milk and a gallon of petrol:

	1971	1981	1991
pint of milk	$5\frac{1}{2}$p	$18\frac{1}{2}$p	32p
gallon of milk	34p	£1.61	£2.20

the prices for milk and petrol can now be converted into 1991 terms. The method involves:
using the price index (right)

multiply 1971 prices by $\dfrac{661.2}{100}$ multiply 1981 prices by $\dfrac{661.2}{368.7}$

In constant 1991 prices, the table now reads:

	1971	1981	1991
pint of milk	$36\frac{1}{2}$p	33p	32p
gallon of petrol	£2.25	£2.89	£2.20

▶ A retail price index for these years is:
   1971 = 100
   1981 = 368.7
   1991 = 661.2

► Interestingly, when the 50p coin was introduced in 1969, its value in today's terms was £4!

 Make notes on calculating constant prices. For your own example, use the fact that green peppers were selling for 32p a lb in 1971, and 69p in 1991

Exactly the same principle can be applied to the published results of companies, or any other financial data spread over time.

Real and Nominal Values: Company Accounts

Morley Motors PLC
The firm's annual report and accounts for 1991 included the following bar chart:

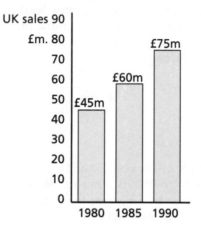

Figure 40.1
A decade of progress

At first glance a shareholder might indeed perceive 'a decade of progress'. However a price index for the period shows:
1980 = 100
1985 = 141.5
1990 = 188.7

When corrected to constant 1990 prices, the bar chart is rather different:

► Notice too that sales alone are not a sign of progress. To make any judgement, we would need data for profits and net assets.

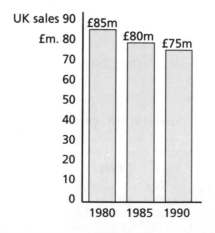

Figure 40.2
A decade of progress?

Causes of Inflation

This is a hotly contested subject, and many theories exist. The major contenders are:

- **cost-push theories** propose that inflation is essentially caused by rises in the market prices for the factors of production. Wage increases, especially when negotiated by powerful unions, are the most important source of cost pressure. Rents similarly may rise sharply. Material costs can also increase rapidly, especially for imports, and movements may be exaggerated by changes in the exchange rate (see Chapter 42). Rising costs from any source drive up prices through pressure on profit margins. Initially, in difficult trading conditions, firms may absorb increased costs. Eventually a target return on capital must be achieved, and prices rise
- **demand-pull theories** consider that price levels rise when aggregate demand approaches the limits of aggregate supply (see Chapter 37). While firms have unused capacity, increasing demand leads to increased output. But with rising output, bottlenecks develop in the economy as more and more firms approach capacity. The result is a slower increase in output and a faster increase in prices. This is because the factors of production – especially labour – run into short supply. Costs are being 'bidded up' by the pressures of demand
- **monetary theories** essentially propose that inflation is caused by the supply of money increasing faster than output. Money depends for its value on the goods and services that it will buy. Assuming that the speed of circulation remains roughly constant, it must follow that expanding the money supply faster than output will mean a fall in the buying power of money. This is exactly the meaning of inflation. Money is created through the extension of credit by the banking system. It is argued that to control inflation the government must target and limit growth in the money supply. This is achieved through the control of interest rates (see Chapter 41), and restrictions on public sector borrowing.

► Since the 1980s, controlling inflation has tended to be the dominant factor in government economic policy.

There is still no agreement over the causes of inflation. The problem has a chicken and egg quality. For example, an existing rate of inflation may cause higher wage increases, which expand demand and increase the rate of inflation. This process is called a **wage-price spiral.** Similarly it can be argued that increases in the money supply are not the cause but the effect of inflation.

Controlling Inflation

Different theories to explain the causes of inflation mean different policies for its control. These include:

1 **Taxes and government spending**
An increase in direct taxation cuts disposable incomes and hence demand. But an increase in indirect taxation, while choking off demand, directly raises the inflation rate (by adding to retail prices),

and may only fuel the pressures for higher wages. Cuts in government spending reduce aggregate demand and also help to avoid growth in the money supply.

2 Incomes policies

This means a public policy to control the growth of incomes and demand. Compulsory and advisory policies ended with serious industrial unrest in the 1970s, and the Conservative government abandoned the whole principle. However control of public sector pay can represent an indirect incomes policy.

3 Control of the money supply

This was most intensively applied during the early 1980s. The government attempts to manage the money supply through setting time-related targets for its growth. However it has proved very difficult to define the money supply, while the nature of its link with inflation has been widely questioned.

4 Interest rates

Increases in the rate of interest are not only important in controlling the money supply. They also reduce demand through their effect on mortgage payments and interest on consumer credit, loans and overdrafts.

 Set up a three-column table. In the first column make notes on the theories of the cause of inflation. In the second column note the kinds of policy which the theory leads to. In the third column write the limitations of the theories and their associated policies.

Impact on Business

▶ Inflation raises the level of risk in business.

Inflation has a number of negative effects on business.

- **planning and budgeting** are undermined by uncertainty over the value of money in the future. A varying inflation rate means that all future financial flows are unknown in real terms. This creates instability and increases the risk of business enterprise
- **investment** may be reduced by a climate of business uncertainty. Real rates of return on investment become very difficult to predict
- **profits** are often depressed by cost inflation as attempts by firms to increase their prices may cause unacceptable reductions in sales
- **pricing decisions** are complicated by inflation. Nominal price increases which are only in line with the general price level may be perceived by consumers as real increases. Frequent price changes meet particular consumer resistance, yet periods of a 'steady' price mean periods of continuous price reduction in real terms
- **export sales** can be badly hit if UK inflation rates exceed those in competitor and customer countries
- **industrial relations** may worsen as the workforce make increasing pay demands to keep up with the rate of inflation. These demands may be unrelated to the financial realities of the business.

Some firms benefit from inflation, since part or all of their costs increase more slowly than the rate of inflation. The result is a fall in real costs and a potential increase in profits. In the medium term many fixed costs do not rise with inflation, leading to an advantage of this type.

 Read the following data and answer the questions below.

Bettabox Ltd manufactures plastic storage boxes in a range of colours. The table below shows average cost and price data for three consecutive years:

	year 1	year 2	year 3
Average total cost	£3.00	£3.15	£3.60
Price	£4.00	£4.20	£4.50
Retail price index	100	105	115

1 How has the firm's profit margin changed between Year 1 and Year 3?

2 How has the real price of a box changed over the period?

Summary and comment

• various governments have tried to 'fine tune' the economy. This means regulating demand so that growth occurs without causing inflation. In practice, adjustments to tax, government spending and interest rates have complex time-lagged effects, and may anyway overshoot their targets
• fairly stable rates of inflation are less damaging to firms than erratic rates which create instability in the business environment
• the effect of inflation on the overall output of business is difficult to judge. The policies to reduce or control inflation often cause sharp falls in demand, that certainly cuts output and investment
• inflation results in winners and losers among consumers. Those on fixed incomes lose, while those within employment gain – especially if strongly unionized or if in a buoyant sector of the economy. Firms whose market is mainly among 'winners' or 'losers' will find their sales affected accordingly.

(41) Interest rates

Chapter objectives

After working through this chapter, you will:

∎ understand the meaning of interest rates and how they are determined

∎ know how consumer demand is affected

∎ understand the relationship with investment decisions

∎ be able to analyse the impact on a firm's sources and uses of funds.

THE MEANING OF INTEREST RATES

► An interest rate is a hire charge for money.

If a firm or an individual wants the loan of a car or a piece of machinery then they expect to pay a hire charge. This is reasonable, since the owner of the car or machine is deprived of its use for a period, knows that the value will depreciate, and risks the borrower's failure to ensure its safe return. Exactly the same principle applies to lending money. A sum of money represents a certain quantity of resources. Indeed, money is in effect an open-access entitlement to resources of the holder's choice. Thus interest is simply the hire charge for money. The rate of interest must be high enough to compensate the lender for:

- the period without the use of their money and the postponement of their consumption
- the likely fall in the value of money caused by inflation
- the risk that the borrower will fail to make repayment.

Demand for Loans

It is attractive to borrow money when the benefits of its use are judged likely to outweigh the cost of borrowing. For example, you might take a bank loan to buy a new car, so that you could accept a new job with a longer journey. The benefits of this job might easily outweigh the cost of interest payments: the car, in other words, is a good investment. A firm makes decisions in the same way, balancing the interest rate on additional funds against the projected rewards.

Tyne Taxis Ltd is operating profitably, but needs an additional car to meet growing demand from railway station forecourts. The firm obtains a business loan after estimating that the return from this investment will comfortably exceed the bank's rate of interest.

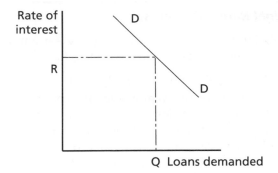

Figure 41.1
The demand for loans

The demand curve for loans is downward sloping. As rates of interest rise, demand for loans falls.

Supply of Loans

Money for loans is made available through savings: i.e. postponement of present consumption. The rate of savings tends to rise with the rate of interest, but also depends on other factors (e.g. financial expectations about the future). However the largest source of loan finance is credit created by the banking system on the strength of its existing deposits. This is also how the money supply expands and is subject to some indirect government control through the Bank of England.

The Rate of Interest

There is no single rate of interest. Instead a range or grid of rates exists, with the actual rate charged depending on such factors as:

- the size of the loan
- the duration of the loan
- the risk factor presented by the borrower
- the security offered to cover any default.

Mortgage finance is relatively cheap since the lender has the security of the house. Credit card finance, by contrast, is expensive, being both risky and costly to administer.

The grid of lending rates rests on a basic rate which is the absolute minimum interest rate payable. When the base rate changes, the whole grid of rates is shifted upwards or downwards. Base rates in turn are effectively determined by the Bank of England, on instructions from the Treasury.

►Base rates.

Real and Nominal Rates of Interest

The nominal rate of interest is that actually charged. As an annual rate however, its real value depends on inflation. Thus:

real rate of interest = nominal rate − inflation rate.

Suppose you borrow £100 for one year at a ten per cent interest rate, during which time the price level also increases by ten per cent. After one year you repay £110, which now has a purchasing power of exactly £100 one year ago. In real terms your lender has received no interest at all. Real interest rates in the UK were actually negative through most of the 1970s, transferring resources from lenders to borrowers. Since 1980 there has been a sharp change, with positive real interest rates varying between four and eight per cent.

► The government seems increasingly inclined to use interest rates as a way of attempting to regulate the level of aggregate demand, and to control inflation.

Impact on Demand

The level of interest rates is a very important factor affecting the demand for goods and services. It works in two ways:

1 Interest payments by households make up an increasing proportion of total spending. The growth of home ownership through easy mortgage availability and the explosion of consumer credit mean that the spending power of many households is sharply affected by the rate of interest.

2 Credit sales of goods and services are affected by the rate of interest charged. This is particularly important for consumer durables (e.g. cars), where a high proportion of total sales are on credit. Firms may offer favourable credit terms as part of their marketing mix (see Chapter 10).

Investment Decisions

The discount rate used by firms in investment appraisal (see Chapter 27) is influenced by the rate of interest for many firms. Essentially, changes in the rate of interest will determine the cost of investment for many firms. Thus an increase in interest rates will make investment more expensive, and rule out previously viable projects. However the benefits of investment usually accrue in the longer term, and large firms may be fairly insensitive to short-run fluctuations in the interest rate.

Sources of Funds

Changes in the rate of interest also affect firms through their gearing ratio (see Chapter 22). Loans to business may carry either fixed or variable interest rates. A highly-geared firm with variable rate loans will be sharply affected by any rise in the rate of interest. The increasing burden of interest charges may come at exactly the time when profits are squeezed. The result is falling interest cover, and the ultimate risk of insolvency. Meanwhile creditors are likely to increase the pressure for prompt payment as the finance of unpaid bills becomes more expensive.

Asset Management

The rate of interest represents the ultimate opportunity cost for all the assets in any business. If the rate is ten per cent, and an asset is earning a return of less than ten per cent, then in theory at least the shareholders would be better off selling the asset and investing the proceeds in a bank. A rise in interest rates should make managers look more critically at every asset category. Typical questions might be:

- could a surplus strip of land be let or sold?
- might the size of the vehicle fleet be reduced?
- can stock levels be cut, especially for slow-moving items?
- should credit control be tightened?
- could cash or liquid assets be shifted into higher interest-bearing investments (financial fixed assets)?

► The minimum opportunity cost of holding non-interest-bearing assets rises with higher interest rates.

 Interest Rates

In less than a year the bank base rate is increased from eight per cent to fifteen per cent. How would you expect the following to be affected and why?

1 A retailer of curtains, carpets and home furnishings.

2 A firm planning to use loan finance for the construction of a new warehouse complex.

3 a) The total number of titles held in stock by a large bookshop.

b) The period of credit allowed to customers by a computer supplier.

Summary and comment

- governments are tending to make increasing use of interest rates as an instrument of economic policy. Changes have powerful effects on aggregate demand and can be used as part of an anti-inflation strategy
- increases in interest rates are effective in reducing demand, but also cut business investment, which may be harmful to future growth prospects
- high interest rates increase the opportunity cost of liquid assets, and put pressure on managers to reduce their working capital
- small firms may find fixed rate loans a safer choice, enabling them to plan realistic levels of interest cover
- rising interest rates depress demand most severely for luxury consumer services and durables. Necessities and single use goods are less affected

- the increase in mortgage finance means that many households are now highly geared. The effect of interest rates on mortgage payments has been a key factor in home-owner spending patterns.

(42) International trade

Chapter objectives

After working through this chapter, you will:

▌ know the advantages of international trade and the reasons why countries may restrict its flow

▌ be able to interpret the balance of payments

▌ understand how exchange rate movements affect business decisions

▌ appreciate the significance of multi-national firms

▌ know how trade and debt affect Third World nations

▌ know the meaning of the following key terms: current account, visible/invisible trade, current balance, external assets.

INTERNATIONAL TRADE

International trade allows international specialization, which is a major source of increased wealth throughout the world. Each country has a unique pattern of comparative strengths and weaknesses in producing the goods and services demanded in the world. The vital benefit of trade is that it enables each country to concentrate its resources on the output combination for which it has the greatest **comparative advantage**. In this way each country can achieve the most efficient allocation of its resources, and the value of every country's output is greatly increased.

► Over the period 1960–90 the volume of world output increased three times, while the volume of world trade rose by nearly five times.

Arguments for Protection

Despite the advantages of international trade, countries often have reasons for wishing to restrict its flow. These chiefly relate to the **protection** of home industry. Countries may want to restrict international trade for the following reasons:

- **new industries** may need time to become established before confronting the full force of foreign competition. In their early stages average costs may still be relatively high and markets only weakly secured. However, once protected, firms may find the transition to full competition very difficult
- **structural change** in industry occurs through shifting patterns of demand and competition. An industry in decline may need protection to allow time for adjustment and investment in restructuring
- **unemployment** may be the direct result of foreign competition as firms close or shed labour through falling market share
- **dumping** can occur where another country exports goods at prices below their cost of production in order to liquidate a surplus or

seize a market share abroad. Such tactics are recognized as fair grounds for protection
- **balance of payments** deficits (see below) may prompt short-term protection while other measures take effect
- **strategic industries** (such as aerospace, steel, electronics) may be protected to ensure national security.

With the exception of the strategic argument, the case for protection is essentially short term. Otherwise the effect is to featherbed inefficient industries and to deny consumers the benefit of competitive world prices.

Barriers to Trade

The main methods of protection are:

- **tariffs** are a tax on imports by value or volume
- **quotas** limit the quantity of an imported product entering the country over a given period
- **exchange controls** limit the availability of foreign currency to buy imports
- **subsidies** involve government financial assistance to home industries
- **voluntary agreements** mean that one country agrees to limit its exports to another
- **administrative restrictions** create technical and bureaucratic obstacles for particular imports
- **counter-trading** means that a country makes certain import orders conditional on the other country buying an equivalent value of their exports
- **buy-back agreements** involve import of capital equipment on condition that part of its subsequent output is bought by the exporter.

The trend since the late 1940s has been a steady reduction in trade barriers, assisting the rapid growth in world trade. The use of trade barriers by any country invites retaliation by others. There is always the risk that retaliatory actions can escalate, causing mutually damaging reductions in the flow of trade.

 The British textile industry has been very severely affected by imports of textiles from cheap labour areas in Asia. Both manufacturers and unions have lobbied Parliament to impose higher import duties on cheap imports. Draw up a case for protection of the British textile industry, and then draw up a case against it.

The Balance of Payments

A country's international accounts, showing a summary of all financial transactions with the rest of the world is called the **balance of payments**. This will be explained by referring to the specimen accounts on p. 319:

▶ In the slump of the 1930s many countries tried to protect home industries by raising tariffs. The results were reduced flows of trade, more factory closures, more redundancies and further twists in the downward spiral.

UK Balance of Payments 1990
Summary Statement

	(£m.)	(£m.)
CURRENT ACCOUNT		
Visible trade		
exports	+102 746	
imports	−120 657	−17 911
Invisible trade		
exports	+117 491	
imports	−113 379	+ 4 112
Current balance		−13 799
CAPITAL ACCOUNT		
External assets		−72 987
External liabilities		+82 709
Net transactions		+9 722
BALANCING ITEM		+4 077

The **current account** is essentially a record of the financial flows arising from exports and imports of goods and services. **Visible trade** refers to tangible goods (e.g. motor vehicles), and **invisible trade** refers to a broad range of services such as tourism, transport, banking and insurance. Also included are interest and dividend payments received in Britain or paid abroad. The **current balance** is simply the net balance of visible and invisible trade.

The capital account shows the inflows and outflows of investment between the UK and the rest of the world. Short-term capital flows represent movements of money between countries to maximize the financial gain – through changing interest or exchange rates. Long-term flows occur when international investment takes place in the purchase of shares or fixed assets, or when governments agree long-term loans. Changes in the UK's **external assets** implies net outflows of sterling (e.g. UK residents buying securities abroad), and it is therefore shown as **negative**. Conversely, changes in the UK's **external** liabilities mean inflows of sterling (e.g. foreign residents buying UK securities), and is therefore shown as **positive**.

► All accounts in the balance of payments record inflows and outflows of money – not literal goods or services. A British family taking a holiday in France create an invisible import – i.e. they have bought a range of services (e.g. accommodation) from France. Their payments involve an outflow of money from the UK.

Balance of Payments and Inward Investment

The Japanese car firm Toyota is building a new car plant at Burneaston (near Derby). The cost will appear as a **positive** item on the **capital account**. Notice however that, once profits begin to be remitted back to Japan, they will appear as a **negative** item on invisibles in the **current account** (check that you understand).

Which item in the UK balance of payments would be affected by each of the following business decisions?

1 A north of England manufacturer sells six heavy electric motors to a firm in Spain.

2 A timber merchant in Hampshire buys a consignment of pine planks from a Swedish company.

3 A Belgium chemicals company takes out fire insurance with a major London firm.

4 A West Midlands steel fastening company sends its sales executives to a conference in Paris.

5 During one year a Japanese-owned car company sells 30 000 vehicles from its UK factory to dealers in Germany.

6 A Californian electronics firm builds a factory in south Wales.

7 A British metals conglomerate buys a copper mine in Zambia.

Taken as a whole, the capital and current accounts must **always balance**. The reason is simple. Any deficit (i.e. a net outflow) must have been financed by borrowing (an inflow), selling assets abroad (an inflow) or using foreign currency reserves (counted as an inflow). The same principle applies to a household. If you spend more than your income, then you must have either borrowed sold off assets or used savings. By the same reasoning a country with a surplus can repay debts, increase its assets abroad or add to its reserves. In practice the accounts do not actually balance, since many transactions inevitably go unrecorded. However the principle is not affected, and the **balancing item** is simply an accounting device to ensure a technical balance.

Clearly a country's current account balance is an important sign of economic health. A deficit in some years, balanced by a surplus in others, is satisfactory. But repeated or increasing deficits mean that a country is either running down its reserves or becoming progressively more indebted. This cannot continue indefinitely without a collapse in the country's currency. Consequently governments adopt policies to keep the pattern of trade in broad balance. These can directly affect business:

► Only structural (long-term) deficits on the balance of payments normally require corrective government policies.

- **trade barriers** (against non-EC countries) may be raised, perhaps increasing the cost of imports, but protecting UK firms
- **aggregate demand** may be reduced by raising interest rates or tax levels. This should cut demand for imports, but will increase unemployment and reduce investment
- **depreciation of the exchange rate** will increase exports and reduce imports, but is now a restricted option due to the membership of the Exchange Rate Mechanism (ERM) (see p. 321).

In the early 1980s Britain had a large balance of payments surplus.

Since 1987 there has been a deficit, which stood at £14.4bn by 1990. This was a factor in government efforts to reduce aggregate demand from 1988–90.

Exchange Rates

When goods or services are purchased by one country from another, it is necessary to settle the debt in the currency of the seller. For this reason a worldwide foreign exchange market exists, with electronic dealing between financial centres. An exchange rate is really the price of one currency in terms of another. These prices vary with the forces of demand and supply like any other price:

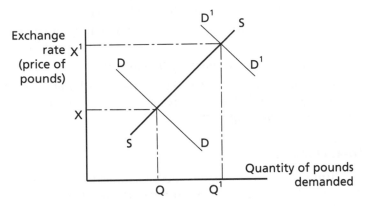

The demand for pounds might increase (DD – D1D1) through growth in UK exports or high UK interest rates attracting investors' funds to London. As a result the equilibrium value of the pound rises from X – X1.

Figure 42.1
Exchange rates and the demand for sterling

From 1971 to 1990 the pound 'floated' on market forces, although there were often government policies to influence its value. Since 1990 Britain has been a member of the ERM. This means that the pound must remain within a narrow range of values against any other EC currency. Any risk of breaking these boundaries is counter-acted by the Bank of England deliberately buying or selling pounds on the foreign exchange market, so adjusting the equilibrium of demand and supply.

The exchange rate has a vital affect on the effective price – and hence volume – of UK exports and imports.

The Effect of Exchange Rates on Demand

Britannia-Marine Ltd sells deep-sea pumps to US oil companies, competing with leading Japanese suppliers. Each basic pump costs £10 000. The exchange rate stands at £1 = \$1.60, so the American importers pay \$16 000 per pump. Sales amount to 1 000 units each year, with an estimated price elasticity of 2. The following year the pound strengthens to an average rate of £1 = \$2. The American importers must now pay \$20 000 for each pump, or a rise in the effective price of 25%. The result is a switch to Japanese suppliers and a slump in sales to 500 units (down 2 × 25% = 50%).

Exchange rate fluctuations are a real hazard to many firms. A UK manufacturer importing components or raw materials will suffer cost increases if the pound falls in value. Of course the mechanism can operate in reverse. For exports, a fall in the pound's value will boost sales. A major argument for ERM membership is that more stable exchange rates assist business planning, and greatly reduce the risks of European trade.

(ACT) Obverse Ltd imports American baseball boots at $27 per pair to sell at a twenty-five per cent mark-up through sports outlets in Britain. The exchange rate has been £1 = $1.50, but suddenly strengthens to $1.80. The mark-up remains the same but sales rise by thirty-three per cent.

1 What was the old and what is the new selling price of boots in Britain?

2 Calculate the price elasticity of demand.

3 If the firm was selling 6 000 pairs per month under the old exchange rate, what is the increase in the total profit caused by the strengthening of the pound?

Multinationals

When a firm owns or controls business facilities in more than one country it is called a **multinational enterprise**. Such firms vary from industrial giants with global operations down to many medium-sized enterprises with a few branches abroad. Multinationals are increasingly important, and include the vast majority of Britain's largest 100 firms. Of these, twenty are foreign-owned, accounting for twenty per cent of total sales and fourteen per cent of employment in manufacturing industry. Significantly, Britain's foreign-owned firms tend to be found in the fastest growing business sectors, and over half are American. Worldwide, multinationals are extremely important – and powerful – in the business world.

The multinational form of business organization has certain distinct advantages:

► The American firms Ford, General Motors and Exxon each have sales values greater than the GDPs of all but fourteen countries in the world. The dominance of multinational firms is still increasing as their output grows at ten to fifteen per cent annually – well ahead of most national growth rates.

- achieving control over raw material supplies in multiple locations (this was the origin of many multinationals)
- exploitation of scale economies, including greater access to capital and ambitious research and development programmes
- attraction, accumulation and full development of technical and managerial skills. These are often supported by valuable patents and trademarks
- ability to place different stages of production in low-cost locations. The use of cheap labour in developing countries is particularly important
- potential to qualify for government assistance (e.g. capital or training grants) in a range of host countries
- capacity to develop international products and yet to produce different versions in different countries with accurate targeting of

national markets
- gaining monopoly power both in buying the factors of production and in selling end-products
- ability to minimize tax liabilities using transfer pricing techniques. This means selling semi-finished goods between subsidiaries at prices which ensure high accounting profits where tax rates are low, and low profits where tax rates are high
- opportunity to avoid trade barriers between countries
- diversification of risk by operating in a range of production centres and markets.

Complex combinations of these factors determine the multiple locations which are actually selected by multinational managements.

There has been heated argument over the rights and wrongs of multinational enterprise from the point of view of host countries. The major advantages are:

- new jobs are created in host countries which are often relatively well paid
- modern investment and new technology is transferred from the home country
- foreign exchange earnings may be considerable and balance of payments deficits reduced
- local management may be improved through the example set by multinationals
- tax receipts of governments are increased and foreign aid may become politically more likely.

However the criticisms are also serious:

- the risk of closures and withdrawal when more profitable locations emerge, or when government grants expire
- some investment is only for assembly purposes (known as 'screwdriver' factories) with limited value added locally
- prestigious and highly skilled functions (e.g. research and development) remain based in the home country
- actual tax payments may be very slight due to transfer pricing
- economic and even political independence is reduced as decisions taken at corporate headquarters may come to overshadow national policy.

Poorer countries usually welcome the employment and investment potential from multinational enterprise, but face particular problems. The company may bring capital-intensive production methods that create relatively few local jobs. Its output may consist of luxuries inappropriate to the country's needs, yet still marketed to the population. Raw materials may be rapidly exhausted with the risk of long-term environmental damage. Traditional ways of life may be undermined and the rural-urban drift accelerated.

 Make notes on the advantages and disadvantages of multinationals to the host country.

►The North-South divide.

Less Developed Countries (LDCs)

The term 'less developed countries' includes many nations in Latin America, Africa and Asia. Despite rich and often vital cultures, they face a range of economic problems, which often include:

- small endowments of natural resources
- a dependence on labour-intensive primary production
- a small industrial base with limited availability of newer technology
- very basic and incomplete infrastructures of power, communications, transport, education and health care
- rapid population growth
- low or very low GDP per capita – usually under $400 per year.

►Ethiopia has a population of 48m. compared with the UK's 57m. yet the UK's GDP is about 150 times greater.

Developing countries often suffer from a cycle of poverty and deprivation from which it is difficult to escape. Low and unstable incomes mean a lack of saving and investment. Governments have limited tax revenues, while export earnings from primary production are overspent on essential imports and interest on debt. The potential for economic growth can thus be very restricted, with constraints on per capita incomes from population growth. Problems are often further compounded by political instability, unfavourable climates and low standards of education, nutrition and health.

The economic problems and achievements of LDCs vary very widely. The least developed countries have the very lowest incomes (less than $400 GDP per capita), and are usually the most severely constrained by the poverty cycle. By contrast the newly industrialized countries (NICs), especially in the Pacific Basin, have achieved high rates of economic growth, and increasingly compete with Western countries in industrial markets.

►South Korea achieved an average growth rate of 9% over the period 1980–8.

Thailand's economy was growing at 12.5% in the late 1980s.

All of the wealthier Western nations have **aid programmes** for LDCs. The official United Nations target is for aid to represent 0.7% of GDP. In practice, aid as a percentage of GDP (1989) varies widely but is a relatively small item in national budgets:

Norway	1.0
France	0.8
Britain	0.4
USA	0.17

(Source: *The Economist* 6 June 1990)

Some of the aid programmes have been immensely valuable, but problems have been:

- the failure of some Third World governments to channel aid towards the poorest sectors of the population
- the tendency to favour urban projects when the greatest needs are in rural areas
- a bias towards large-scale prestige projects (e.g. airports), when small-scale local projects would be more cost effective.

There are two particular areas of difficulty for the developing world in its relationship with the industrial western countries:

1 Primary produce markets

Some LDCs have depended excessively on a single primary product (e.g. coffee from Kenya or copper from Zambia) so that a fall in its price disrupts the national economy. Price instability among primary products generally causes damaging fluctuations in producer incomes. Meanwhile real prices themselves have tended to fall since 1980, yet some essential imports for LDCs have become relatively-more expensive. The developed world's demand for many primary products is in long-term decline as usage becomes more efficient and synthetic substitutes are found for natural materials (e.g. rubber).

2 Debt

Large-scale lending by Western countries to LDCs took place during the 1970s. The subsequent sharp rise in real interest rates left some countries with a vast burden even to service, let alone repay, their debts. The result was that for most of the 1980s the outflow of interest and repayments substantially exceeded the inflow of new loans and official aid. The position has eased somewhat in the 1990s.

► Brazil owed $114.6 billion in 1988.

► African countries exported £2 in interest payments for every £1 received in aid and new loans in 1990.

 Make notes on the problems Third World countries experience in the pattern of international trade.

Summary and comment

• the downward trend in trade barriers since the Second World War has been interrupted by recent recessions. The pressure on countries to protect their home industries against competition increases when sales are falling and unemployment is rising

• often trade barriers only delay inevitable changes in a country's industrial structure. The postponement may actually intensify the consequences of competition by enabling firms to avoid the necessary development of new technologies, new products and new markets

• although the relative importance of manufacturing industry has declined, it remains a vital sector. Services lead proportionally to less exports and are more vulnerable to recession

• economic expansion in Britain is very prone to causing a faster growth in visible imports. This is partly due to the wide range of goods no longer domestically produced. It is also caused by a tendency for consumers of durables and luxuries to prefer imported brands

• inward industrial investment has increased since the late 1980s. Japanese and American firms have been attracted by Britain's relatively low costs and the opportunity to produce inside the single European market

• since the 1980s there has been a rapid growth in joint ventures, where companies enter into partnerships for research, production or marketing purposes. The trend has been strongest within Europe, and between Europe and Japan. Many deals fail, but joint ventures can be the effective way to match differing strengths, or to compete successfully with larger rivals

• despite the very real criticisms of multinationals, it must be remembered that they have sponsored enormous progress in new technology and business techniques. A real part of our living standards depends on their strength and vigour

• British aid programmes often have 'strings attached', in the form of requirements to purchase British goods

• quite apart from moral considerations (see Chapter 44), it can be argued that by raising incomes in poorer countries, Western firms will benefit by finding new markets for their goods and services.

(43) The European Community

Chapter objectives

After working through this chapter, you will:

■ understand the objectives and structures of the European Community (EC)

■ be aware of EC policies as they affect business

■ know the implications of the Single European Market

■ be able to analyse the current response of firms to EC membership

■ know the meaning of the following key terms: European Council, summit meetings.

WHAT IS THE EUROPEAN COMMUNITY?

The Second World War began in Europe and twenty-two million lives were lost. When it ended there was a very strong feeling that the countries of Europe must never go to war with one another again, and instead should build a new unity that embodied their common culture and common goals. A step in this direction was taken in 1951 when France and Germany brought their coal and steel industries under joint control. More radical progress came in 1957 when the **Treaty of Rome** formed a community of six nations: France, Germany, Italy, Holland, Belgium and Luxembourg.

The main economic goals were:

▶ The European Community (EC) was founded by the Treaty of Rome 1957.

* to eliminate customs duties and quotas on trade between member states
* to charge a common external tariff on imports from non-member states
* to ensure fair competition between community firms
* to operate a common agricultural policy
* to achieve the free movement of people, capital and services within the community.

In addition – and as a natural consequence – there was a commitment among members to increasing coordination and unity at a political level.

At first, Britain chose to remain outside these initiatives, given its close links with the Commonwealth (ex-members of the British Empire) and the United States. Instead the European Free Trade Association (EFTA) was formed to include Britain and smaller countries outside the Community. But during the 1960s the economic importance of the Community increased, and Britain applied to join. After initial rebuffs, serious negotiations began in 1969, and membership was achieved with Ireland and Denmark in 1973. The EC has continued to grow. Greece joined in 1981, followed by Spain and Portugal in 1986. The next likely members are Austria, Switzerland and Sweden, while eventual expansion to include Eastern Europe now seems likely.

EC MEMBERS					
Country	Population (millions)	GDP per capita (£)	% Growth (av. annual) 1988–90	Un/employ. early '92* %	Consumer price index 1990 **
Belgium	9.9	9 394	4.0	13.0	111.0
BRITAIN	57.1	8 949	2.0	9.4	133.3
Denmark	5.1	12 745	0.9	10.9	121.2
Holland	14.8	9 189	3.4	4.2	104.2
France	55.9	10 465	3.6	9.8	116.5
Germany	78.1	11 805	4.0	6.3	107.0
Greece	10.0	3 300	2.7	4.7	222.6
Ireland	3.5	6 000	4.1	20.8	117.6
Italy	57.4	9 199	3.1	19.0	131.8
Luxembourg	0.4	10 750	n/a	1.6	109.0
Portugal	10.3	2 718	4.5	6.5	170.9
Spain	39.0	5 949	4.6	15.0	136.8

* = unemployment as a percentage of the working population
** based on 1985 = 100

► For an explanation of a price index see pp. 307–8.

Running the Community

The supreme decision-making body in the EC for setting broad long-term policy is the **European Council**, comprising the heads of state from each country. Their **summit meetings** take place in different European cities three times each year. Because the Treaty of Rome created a community of nations in an evolving and permanent relationship, a number of formal institutions exist:

► The EC incorporates a common market: barrier-free trade between member states and a common tariff against imports from non-members.

- **The Council of Ministers** decides detailed Community policy on each issue. Each member state is represented by its Foreign Minister or minister responsible for the subject concerned. Voting power is roughly proportional to population size, and must be unanimous for major decisions
- **The European Commission** makes proposals to the Council of Ministers, and is responsible for carrying out policy as finally decided. Its headquarters are in Brussels, and the seventeen members must represent the Community as a whole rather than their 'home' nation states
- **The European Parliament** is directly elected by the people of the member states. It has a right to be consulted about Commission proposals, and has an important role in drafting the Community budget. However it does not possess the law-making power of a national parliament

► The last elections for the European Parliament were in 1989. The next are in 1994.

- **The Court of Justice** in Luxembourg has seventeen independent judges, and passes judgement on Community disputes. Its source of authority is the Treaty of Rome, and countries must accept its decisions.

The European Community Budget

The Community is financed by contributions from each country, which include the proceeds of the Common External Tariff, a percentage of VAT receipts and an additional percentage (up to 1.2 per cent) of GDP. Total revenue in 1989 amounted to 4.8bn ECU (European Currency Units).

The ECU is the Community's own currency. The ECU is used to denominate the budget and is of growing importance. Its value is based on placing a quantity of each member state's currency – weighted according to the size of their economy – in a 'basket'. This can then be valued in terms of any national currency, on the basis of current exchange rates. In November 1992 the ECU was worth 92p.

The major items of budget spending finance the following:

- **The Common Agricultural Policy** (CAP) aims to ensure relatively stable and fair incomes for farmers within the Community. The 'guidance fund' attempts to improve agricultural efficiency, and the 'guarantee fund' supports farm produce prices. This involves purchasing any surplus output of farmers at guaranteed minimum prices, causing the accumulation of 'mountains' for some products. The CAP accounts for a dominant sixty-seven per cent of the total budget
- **A Regional Fund** provides grants to finance improvements in the infrastructure of the Community's least prosperous regions (e.g. construction of roads and bridges). These are designed to encourage business investment
- **A Social Fund** provides grants to assist in creating employment with particular emphasis on training schemes. Aid is targeted towards people and areas with special needs.

► Efforts are in progress to reduce the real level of European farm subsidies and to encourage environmentally sensitive farming.

UK Membership of the European Community

In 1951, at the time of the coal and steel initiative, Britain's GDP was higher than those of the Community founder members added together. In 1958 when the Community was established, Britain still had a higher GDP per capita than any major member. Yet by 1973 when Britain finally joined, its GDP per capita was the lowest in the enlarged Community, except for Italy and Ireland. It was partly Britain's economic decline relative to continental countries that spurred the government into joining. Unfortunately the first decade of membership was a period of sharp recession and instability. Many British firms were ill-prepared for the export opportunities of membership, with their export marketing geared towards the Commonwealth countries rather than Europe. In many consumer goods industries there was increasing import penetration of the British market by European firms. Meanwhile, the Community's rules and budget – and especially the support for farming – had been designed without thought for British interests. The result was a long

► Germany and not the USA is Britain's most important trading partner.

► The UK population is only 17% of that of the European Community.

► In 1991 the EC and the EFTA (European Free Trade Association) countries agreed to create a European Ecomomic Area (EEA). This will extend many aspects of the single market to Austria, Finland, Iceland, Liechtenstein, Norway, Sweden and Switzerland.

dispute over fair budget contributions, eventually settled in 1984. More fundamentally, Britain has never shared the continental desire for a progressive political union of member states. However the EC has become increasingly important to the British economy. Over the period from 1972 (the year before joining) to 1990, the proportion of Britain's exports taken by the EC has risen from thirty-four per cent to fifty per cent, and the proportion of imports that are purchased from the EC has risen from thirty-four per cent to fifty-three per cent.

The Business Arguments for British Membership

There has always been overwhelming support from British industry for EC membership. The major arguments in favour of membership are:

* **economies of scale**: the potential is increased by the open European market. The population of the UK is 57 million, while the total Community population is now 340 million. Firms can develop products for a European rather than purely UK market. There are further advantages in combined European research projects and in the growth of joint ventures
* **specialization** of business shifts towards a Europe-wide pattern allowing the theory of comparative advantage to be amplified in its benefits. In theory, market forces drive resources in each member state towards their most efficient use
* **export potential** is increased within the Community by the removal of trade barriers and with other countries through greater efficiency and hence lower prices
* **competition** between firms in Europe should provide a greater spur to both innovation and efficiency
* **investment** is stimulated by competition and the enlarged sources of finance in Europe. Inward investment from non-EC states (e.g. Japan) is made more attractive by a unified market. Poorer regions within EC states gain grants from the Regional Fund
* **synergy** (or the 2 + 2 = > 4 principle) can be generated by the dynamism of an expanding market and the rise in business expectations for the future.

However these arguments are mostly about potential, and not automatic advantages. Economies of scale may fail to materialize, or even become diseconomies. Competition may be obstructed by monopoly power. European export potential may reverse into national import penetration. Investment may flow towards the most prosperous countries and regions, causing unemployment and decline elsewhere.

The Single European Market 1992

All of the arguments above are sharpened in importance by the **Single European Act 1985**. This set in motion a programme of removing the remaining barriers to trade and fair competition within the Community. Although the year 1992 has become a name for this programme, it is actually a complex process requiring 279 separate measures to be agreed over the period 1987 to 1992. This amounts to a final fulfilment of the Treaty of Rome, customs duties and quotas having already been abolished between members. The result is a **Single European Market** from 1993, whose features include:

- **technical regulations** relating to products becoming standard throughout the EC
- **free trade in services** (e.g. banking and insurance) achieved by harmonizing relevant regulations
- **public sector purchasing** opened to competition from all member states (e.g. in defence contracts)
- **elimination of subsidies** by governments for home industries that distort competition
- **indirect tax rates** (especially VAT) broadly standardized to ensure fair price competition
- **free capital movements** between countries by abolition of exchange controls (see Chapter 42)
- **free movement of labour** ensured by agreeing on EC-wide validity of vocational and professional qualifications
- **unrestricted physical movements** of goods and people, through the abolition of border controls and simplification of paperwork for goods in transit.

These changes will not all be achieved by the target date, but progress will continue.

The Single Market provides major opportunities for UK firms to increase their sales and European market share. However it remains necessary to strengthen and broaden management skills, especially in the areas of strategic planning and marketing for Europe. There is also still a need for better understanding of European national cultures and greater proficiency in the main European languages. The '1992' programme needs to be seen in the context of wider plans for monetary and political union. Inter-governmental conferences are currently in progress to consider a range of proposals. In addition a **Social Charter** has been proposed, which would give improved legal rights to all employees and consumers in the Community. Minimum standards would for example cover aspects of consumer protection, health and safety at work, and freedom of movement within the EC.

► Increasingly firms are developing a European marketing mix with modifications for each national market.

Make notes on the opportunities and threats to British firms constituted by the EC.

Kent Conserves Ltd is a medium sized firm producing a wide variety of fruit jams at its factory near Ashford in Kent. With well-established success in the UK, the marketing director now aims for export orders from other countries in the EC.

1 State one important factor that should be considered by each of the following departments before launching the export initiative:

a) production   b) finance   c) personnel

2 Suggest three problems – apart from price – which might arise from the firm's European marketing mix.

Summary and comment

- it can be argued that the EC forms an exclusive and inward looking 'club' for rich nations. However the Community accounts for nearly twenty per cent of all world trade, even when excluding transactions between EC members. It offers favoured trading terms to the poorer countries that were formerly part of the European empires, and provides by far the largest proportion of world foreign aid

- Britain has found it psychologically difficult to identify with European Community membership. Physical separation from the continent, language barriers and historic links with the USA and the Commonwealth have made integration difficult

- opposition to the EC is often based on the belief that membership is eroding the sovereignty of the British Parliament and the independence of national policy. On the other hand, the EC can exert greater influence in world affairs than Britain alone, while the business world is increasingly integrated on a European basis

- it must be recognized that greater economic and political integration in Europe is likely to happen regardless of British objections. Meanwhile the character of the EC may change with the likely accession of new members from both Western and Eastern Europe

- income and prosperity remain very unequal within the EC. The benefits of membership have probably been strongest within a 'golden triangle' linking London, Milan and Paris. On the geographical fringes of the Community, major regional problems continue to exist (e.g. in southern Italy, Northern Ireland and Portugal)

- certain UK business sectors have particular comparative advantages and should benefit from the Single Market. These include electrical engineering, pharmaceuticals, food and precision equipment in the manufacturing sector, and banking, insurance and aviation in the service sector

- the Single Market will also offer opportunities for all EC companies. There is a danger that a new wave of assaults on some UK markets will begin

- the removal of remaining trade barriers will tend to increase the importance of price in the European marketing mix

- with their heavy reliance on equity finance, UK companies will be vulnerable to takeover bids from American and Japanese firms seeking access to the European market.

Business responsibility

Chapter objectives

After working through this chapter, you will:

■ appreciate the meaning of social responsibility in business

■ know the legal basis for consumer protection

■ be able to analyse the differing motives for social responsibility

■ understand the nature and influence of pressure groups

■ understand the concept of finite natural resources

■ recognize the threats that business activity can pose to the environment

■ know the techniques used to measure social and environmental costs

■ know the differing motives firms have for social and environmental responsibility

■ be able to evaluate the response of firms to ethical issues

■ know the meaning of the following key terms: codes of practice, externalities, cost-benefit analysis.

THE IDEA OF SOCIAL RESPONSIBILITY

Social responsibility is the concept that a business has obligations that extend beyond the lawful process of its profit-driven activity. Nearly two centuries of social reform have already brought many responsibilities within a firm's legal operation, but the outer boundary of responsibility is still blurred and subject to much argument. All firms have responsibility towards their shareholders, but they may also be argued to have social responsibility towards:

• employees
• suppliers
• consumers
• the community
• the environment.

Each firm expresses a different degree of responsibility towards each of these groups. A more radical view proposes that all interest groups are 'stake-holders', and the shareholders are only one among others.

For each of the business decisions below, identify the groups towards whom the firm might recognize social responsibility and explain briefly why.

1 A UK brewer plans press and poster advertising for a new brand of high strength lager.

2 A bank mails its customers with brochures that offer personal loans to finance luxury purchases.

3 A large engineering company intends to relocate away from its existing base which is in a small town with high unemployment.

4 A national chain store which has previously stocked British handmade toys hopes to achieve small savings by switching its contract to an overseas supplier.

5 A timber merchant applies for planning permission to locate a sawmill and warehouse on the edge of a picturesque Sussex village.

In most of these situations there will be no simple answers.

Consumer Protection

Historically, business was based on the principle 'caveat emptor', which means 'let the buyer beware'. Consumers were expected to use common sense in their purchases, and it was not for the law to interfere in the process. However there have always been **common law rights** derived from custom and practice, which require reasonable conduct towards customers. For example, a firm cannot knowingly sell a product likely to cause injury or damage. Since the late nineteenth century the law has gradually increased its regulation of the buyer/seller relationship.

Consumer Protection Laws
- **Sale of Goods Act 1979** states that goods for sale must be:
  1 of merchantable quality
  2 fit for their purpose
  3 as described.
  In 1982 the law was extended to include services
- **Trade Descriptions Act 1968** protects consumers against false or misleading statements about goods and services
- **Fair Trading Act 1973** established the Office of Fair Trading (OFT) to monitor trading practices, and to take or recommend legal action where necessary. The OFT is also responsible for controls of monopolies and mergers that might restrict competition against the public interest
- **Consumer Credit Act 1974** requires disclosure of the annual percentage rate of interest (APR), with time for the consumer to cancel a contract if they wish
- **Unfair Contract Terms Act 1977** bans unfair disclaimers or exclusion clauses. Guarantees cannot disclaim responsibility and dis-

► Responsibilities to employees were discussed in Chapter 30.

claimer notes cannot exclude the consequences of negligence
- **Consumer Protection Act 1987** makes it a criminal offence to sell unsafe goods, taking into account any associated marketing material, instructions or warnings. Sellers of defective goods are liable to civil action for any loss, damage or injury caused.

The Director General of Fair Trading encourages trade associations to operate **codes of practice** for their industry. These are not legally binding on members, but could influence court judgments, and are a flexible means to ensure up-to-date regulation.

► Well-known codes are maintained by the Motor Agents Association and the Association of British Travel Agents.

Consumer Protection Agencies
- **Trading Standards Departments** are run by local councils and have the power to enforce consumer protection laws. They also provide an important advisory service on everyday problems
- **Environmental Health Departments** are also council-run and have power to protect public health, especially in relation to the sale of food
- **The Office of Fair Trading** acts for the government in checking and enforcing all laws relating to fair trading
- **The Consumers' Association** has charitable status and carries out extensive research and testing on every type of product. Its findings are published in *Which?* magazine
- **National Consumer Council** is a government funded organization representing the consumer interest, and responsible for research, education services and related campaigning
- **Regulatory bodies for privatized industries** have the task of monitoring the activities of the companies now supplying key public services, and representing the interests of their consumers: e.g. the Office of Telecommunications (OFTEL), or the Office of Gas Supply (OFGAS)
- **Advertising Standards Authority** (ASA) is a voluntary body that operates the British Code of Advertising Practice. This requires all advertisements to be 'legal, decent, honest and truthful', showing proper social responsibility and maintaining principles of fair competition. A similar code exists for sales promotion
- **Independent Broadcasting Authority** (IBA) maintains a Code of Advertising Standards and Practice relating to television and radio
- **British Standards Institute** (BSI) is a voluntary body encouraging health and safety in design, quality standards and environmental protection. Its kitemark logo indicates that a product reaches a BSI safety standard.

 Select any three of the agencies above and use the library or the Citizens Advice Bureau to find out their functions and responsibilities.

► To what extent is environmental impact included in business decision making?

Examples of pressure groups

GreenPeace and Friends of the Earth campaign for improved protection of the environment.

The Health Education Council and Action on Smoking and Health (ASH) campaign for discouragement of smoking and for greater controls on cigarette marketing.

Transport 2000 campaigns for better public transport; the Automobile Association (AA) campaigns on behalf of motorists.

Pressure Groups

A pressure group is an organization campaigning to achieve changes in attitudes and behaviour, and often seeking changes in the law. Most pressure groups directly or indirectly wish to influence business decisions, and often appeal to the concept of social responsibility.

Many organizations that are not specifically pressure groups are still important in campaigning for the interests of their members, e.g. trades unions, employer associations, and chambers of commerce. Inevitably all groups appeal for public support and seek vital publicity. Pressure groups publish many kinds of supporting materials, campaign through advertising and mass media coverage, organize petitions and demonstrations, lobby MPs and represent their views to firms and the government. The business community may be influenced directly through changes in the law, or indirectly through recognition that a significant part of public or local opinion has a point of view that cannot be ignored. This may affect the national policy of companies (e.g. not to sell products tested on animals), or a local decision (e.g. to provide litter bins outside a fast food shop).

 Identify a pressure group which aims to make firms behave in a more socially and environmentally responsible way. Obtain their literature and evaluate it in terms of its quality as promotional material.

BUSINESS AND THE ENVIRONMENT

Business activity involves the transformation of resources into the goods and services demanded by consumers. There are three physical phases in the process:

PRODUCTION → DISTRIBUTION → CONSUMPTION

Driven by the market forces of demand and supply, the physical cycle of production and consumption results in a continuous flow of waste entering the environment. This cycle raises many important questions:

• What are the environmental consequences of different business activities?
• What are their likely long-term implications?
• Can the environmental costs of production and consumption be measured?
• Do a company's accounts include all the costs of production?
• Should renewable and non-renewable resources be treated differently?
• Who should pay for environmental protection?

Back in the 1950s and 1960s such questions were rarely asked. Natural resources were merely raw materials and the free gift of nature. It was the task of business and technology to exploit these gifts as quickly and cheaply as possible. The progress of modern

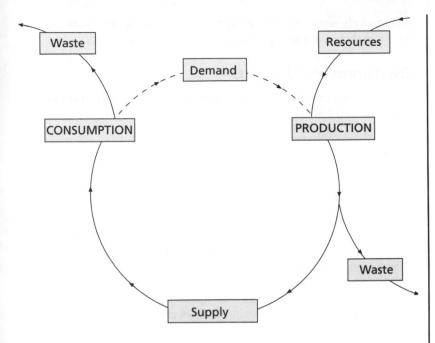

Figure 44.1
*Waste from the production
cycle*

technology and mechanized production was filling the homes of the Western world with an abundance of consumer goods. Nor did waste seem any problem. The atmosphere, the oceans and the areas of 'wasteland' seemed big enough to take everything. While previous generations had bought goods that were carefully made to last a lifetime, the latest products were now 'throw-aways', or had their obsolescence 'in-built'. Oil was so 'cheap' in terms of dollars that some Americans would go away on holiday and leave the central heating running. It took a world oil crisis to change perspectives.

The Motor Car

To manufacture a car requires large amounts of metals, plastics and chemicals. It also needs a major input of energy. Once in use, it converts – hugely inefficiently – non-renewable fossil fuel into mechanical power. In its short life it will burn about 20 000 litres of petrol, releasing into the atmosphere about 50 tonnes of the 'greenhouse' gas carbon dioxide, and 5 kilos of the poisonous gas carbon monoxide. The roads along which it runs cover huge areas of once productive farm land, while scarring sensitive land-scapes, sometimes beyond recognition. Each year in Britain alone about 6 000 people are killed, and 80 000 people are seriously injured by motor vehicles – many of them children or the elderly. The car's life ends prematurely when a repair is regarded as 'uneconomic', and the manufacturer's advertising persuades the driver to buy a newer model.

Of course the car is a very useful and enjoyable possession, but does the showroom tell anyone its true cost?

► The USA has only five per cent of the world's population but produces twenty-three per cent of CO_2 emissions. Its projected forty-six per cent rise in electricity consumption by 2010 will more than cancel out any European attempts to reduce CO_2 emissions.

Increasingly scientific reports appeared, pointing out the dangers of resource depletion and pollution of the natural environment.

Environmental Impacts

All business activity makes some impact on the environment, and this occurs in a wide variety of ways:

- non-renewable resources such as minerals and oil are being depleted
- renewable resources such as timber and fisheries may be exploited faster than they are replaced
- emissions from industrial processes enter water systems and the atmosphere
- the topsoil is affected by chemical inputs and by erosion
- waste enters the environment through production processes and household consumption
- transport systems make demands on energy sources and land space while creating additional gas emissions
- housing and business developments require increasing areas of land.

The environment can absorb these impacts on a moderate scale but today there are signs everywhere that the scale of impact is no longer sustainable. All over the world, business activity poses threats to the environment – threats that are increasingly likely to rebound on human beings. The primary cause is the rapid increase in output and living standards across the richest parts of the world.

Many developing countries are now on the brink of large scale industrialization. Consider the following data:

Country	GDP ($bn)	Population (m.)	GDP per capita ($)
USA	5 208	248	21 000
China	398	1 105	360
India	283	833	340

Source: World Bank

If China and India were even in the future to reach the US living standards of today, then their output would need to expand by 58 times and 62 times respectively. This would impose on the environment the equivalent of 7.8 additional US total outputs of today – or 58.1 UK total outputs.

The Environment and the Market

Market forces (see Chapter 1) are effective in generating wealth and in allocating resources to the production of goods and services. The circular flow of income (see Chapter 37) expands a country's output and consumption as demand increases. All the major economies have experienced almost continuous growth since the Second World War, yet there is no sign of consumer demand being satisfied. Indeed, many priorities such as housing, health and education still represent major wants that are largely unfulfilled. Most political leaders argue that only economic growth will enable these needs to be met. Yet the larger part of any increase in national income is actually spent on luxuries such as cars, videos and foreign holidays. Thus it would require a massive economic expansion to fulfil those more basic needs. Indeed, if demand is insatiable, then the projection of economic growth is presumably infinitely upwards. What does this mean for a fragile environment and finite resources? Jeremy Seabrook (1990) suggests that in its demands on the environment, the market is a highly dangerous ratchet mechanism that knows no safety limit.

Measuring Social and Environmental Costs

A firm counts as the costs of its production those expenses that it is obliged to pay. But in many cases there are other very real costs that arise in society and in the environment.

Unpaid costs

Buxton Quarries Ltd extracts limestone in the Peak District National Park, which it sells to civil engineering firms for use in roadbuilding. The firm's profit and loss account shows those costs that are private and internal to the firm. But it does not reveal other costs that are **public** and **external** to the firm. These external costs might include:
* damage to the National Park landscape
* reduced tourist trade in the locality
* widening of country lanes for the firm's fleet of trucks
* noise and accidents caused by these vehicles.

These social and environmental costs are called **externalities**. However this term also includes any social or environmental **benefits** that arise from business activity. For example, a new reservoir will flood a rural valley, yet create new opportunities for leisure pursuits such as water sports and fishing. Externalities raise a very interesting and important criticism of the market and its price mechanism. We have already met the simple supply curve which relates price to output (see Chapter 10).

► **Externalities** are costs external to the firm.

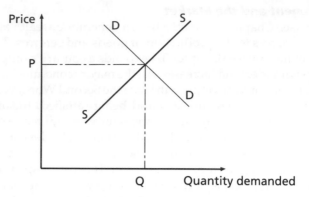

Figure 44.2
Simple market equilibrium

It is clear that the industry will produce Q units at price P.

Look closely again at the supply curve. If the industry's costs were to rise, then there would be a fall in output at each price as profitability was squeezed. This must logically be represented by a shift in the supply curve to the left. In Figure 44.3 below, this movement in the supply curve reflects the addition of social and environmental costs to the usual internal costs of production. Although these externalities are not actually paid by the firm, the model allows us to explore their implications.

▶ Notice that input of social or environmental benefits would cause a shift in the supply curve to the right, with the implication of a lower price and a higher output.

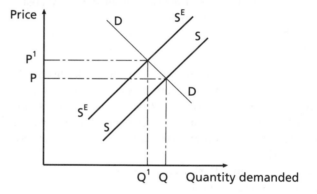

Figure 44.3
Equilibrium including external costs

▶ Externalities such as creating employment or maintaining transport links in rural areas have been important justifications for nationalized industries.

We can now see that if externalities were included in a firm's decision making, then:

- price would be higher, at price P^1
- output would be lower, at Q^1.

▶ Sir Crispin Tickell (scientist and former advisor to Margaret Thatcher) compared the environment with a boat. 'We can remove one, two or ten rivets without apparent damage. But at a certain point – it could be the eleventh or the thousandth rivet – we cause the timbers to fall apart'.

This principle of externalities has potentially great significance. Most production by firms carries external costs which are rarely included in the price. How would the millions of private sector business decisions taken every day differ if their analysis included social and environmental costs and benefits? A product could be highly profitable when its costs ignore its environmental impact. Inject environmental or social costs, and it might well be dropped as unprofitable. Such a business world is interesting to imagine. Many present day products would disappear or be radically re-designed. Others would become far more expensive, and used only when really necessary. Yet others would be cheaper, and presently non-existent products would come into being.

This picture is, of course, improbable! However the price mechanism has already been used very powerfully with the lower duty on unleaded petrol. The future might see taxes on packaging or products that release pollutants or CO_2. Should the use of cars be reduced through taxation, with better facilities for cyclists and pedestrians, together with a policy of subsidies for buses and trains?

Cost-Benefit Analysis

Efforts have been made to include externalities in major public sector projects, using the technique of **cost-benefit analysis** (CBA). This was first applied in Britain during the 1960s to evaluate the Victoria Line Underground project, and later in planning airport development for London. Each external (non-private) cost and benefit is assessed and given a financial value. For example construction of a new rail-freight terminal might cause noise and nuisance to local residents (external cost), but help to reduce road congestion (external benefit). External costs are then added to a project's total internal costs, while external benefits are added to its expected internal revenues. Investment appraisal can then proceed as normal. The valuation of externalities can be highly controversial. What is the value of a rare plant species threatened by a housing project? Or the value of a medieval church facing demolition to make way for a new airport? It can be argued that making such decisions is necessary to give external costs (and benefits) a more effective input to the decision-making process. Fuller use of CBA in the public sector was urged by the Pierce Report (HMSO 1989). Similarly there are moves to develop green accounting techniques that might lead to firms in both the public and private sectors publishing 'environmental audits' showing their net impact on the environment, expressed in financial terms.

► The Pierce Report recommended the calculation of **sustainable income** – the level of income we can enjoy without running down our overall capital stock – including natural resources.

Business Decision Making, Society and the Environment

While formal cost-benefit analysis is confined to the public sector, private sector business decisions are increasingly influenced by environmental factors. Values and attitudes among consumers are shifting to reflect increased awareness of the environmental and moral dimensions to business. Across a range of issues – such as destruction of the world's rain forests or the practices of modern factory farming – consumer concern is growing. It is important to notice how, if market forces created these problems, the market is now responding strongly to the new pressures for change. While green products used to be found only in a few specialist shops, they now crowd the shelves of every supermarket and chain store. This trend is even further developed in parts of Europe, especially in Germany. Some firms, of course, have been cynical in their exploitation of environmental awareness, treating it as little more than a sales promotion tactic.

► In Europe Green Parties have some political influence (mainly in putting the environment on the agenda of other parties).

► The European Community has the authority in all member states to scrutinize major projects with serious environmental implications.

Others take the issues very seriously. Many public companies now include statements of environmental concern in their official objectives, and some are adjusting their production methods and product mix accordingly. Pioneering firms such as Body Shop International or Ecover (a producer of cleaning materials) have made the environment a first priority in their business values and in their marketing mix.

Dart Developments Ltd is planning to site a holiday village on the cliffs of North Devon, close to the existing village of Withycombe. The development would feature a three acre site for caravans and mobile homes plus twenty-five bungalows. A shop, bar and reception centre would be constructed next to the main car park. Plans for a takeaway restaurant, open air swimming pool, and children's playground are also included, together with a café on the beach. The necessary land would be purchased from a local farmer while the South West Coast Path would have to be diverted inland. The lane connecting the A362 with the site would require improvement to cope with the summer traffic. Parking restrictions would be needed in the centre of Withycombe with its narrow street of small shops. The twice weekly bus service to and from Bideford would be increased to twice daily by the development company to attract visitors.

The whole scheme is something of a bombshell to the local community and at once there are strong feelings for and against the granting of planning permission.

1 Identify the likely external costs and benefits of the project.

2 Why would it not be satisfactory to leave all the decisions for market forces to resolve ?

Motives for Social and Environmental Responsibility

Many companies regard their public image as very important in the development of their reputation and market share. Good publicity is often generated by acts of social responsibility and the recruitment of quality staff can depend on the firm's national and local reputation. In addition, new market segments can be reached by responding to trends in public opinion, while the imposition of extra legal requirements may be avoided by socially responsible behaviour. Directors and senior managers may also be acting on the basis of personal moral belief.

THE MEANING OF BUSINESS ETHICS

Business decision-making engages constantly with moral judgement, and ethics is therefore a central issue for management.

All firms are constrained by the framework of **law**, which clearly has an ethical basis: for instance, cigarette advertising regulations. But in many ethical decisions there is either a lack of legal definition or an expectation that the firm will set itself higher standards than those demanded by the law.

► Ethics are moral principles. Morals are judgements regarding what is right and wrong, good and bad.

Legal frontier
Firm A: ethical frontier
Firm B: ethical frontier

Figure 44.4
Legal and ethical limits

Firm A generally stays within the law in its ethical conduct, follows legal requirements, but in some cases will 'cut corners' to serve its own interests. Firm B works to standards well above the legal minimum, and would regard itself as 'ahead' of the law on most ethical matters. In practical terms Firm A might create redundancies without warning and offer only the bare minimum in compensation. By contrast, Firm B might consult its staff over proposed redundancies and then offer generous financial terms, with individual consultations and support.

► Many modern firms have based their reputation on high ethical standards in the treatment of employees, customers, suppliers, the community and the environment. It is hard to imagine a serious scandal at a firm like Marks and Spencer. Companies known for their ethical standards are often among the most successful in commercial terms.

Ethics in Business Today

Increasing educational opportunity and higher living standards are creating a more sophisticated society where higher expectations are projected on to business activity. Many questions are asked about the fundamental purpose of business and the nature of corporate morality. The simple idea of directors acting for shareholders in attempting to maximize their return on capital may be criticized as ethically insufficient. Employees, consumers and the community are beginning to emerge as stakeholders while the concept of **stewardship** towards the environment is gaining ground.

Major failures in business conduct generate worldwide publicity. The illegal tactics of the Guinness directors in the take over of Distillers (1986) emphasized the risk of powerful managers acting without regard for the law. In 1991 the Bank of Credit and Commerce International (BCCI) collapsed, raising questions about the adequacy of legal controls over the operations of multinationals. When the Exxon Valdes released millions of gallons of crude oil off the coast of Alaska in 1987, the ethics of oil companies were criticized for practices

► 'Business is, after all, just another form of human enterprise, so why should we expect less from it, in terms of social ethics, than we do from ourselves and our neighbours?' Anita Roddick in *Body and Soul* (The story of the Body Shop).

that endangered the environment. Meanwhile the Herald of Free Enterprise disaster (1988) highlighted the concept of corporate responsibility for breakdowns in safety systems.

More firms are now issuing written ethical codes that make their moral principles explicit both to staff and the outside world. For example, BP's 'Policy on Business Conduct and Code of Business Ethics' stresses clearly to employees that they must observe both local law and the company code.

 How might ethical principles affect decision-making in the business situations below:

1 A supermarket chain is considering Sunday opening – while this remains illegal.

2 The export manager of an electronics firm is offered a contract to supply security equipment for the police force of a third world dictatorship.

3 A toy manufacturer commissions a series of TV advertisements to cover the weeks before Christmas.

4 A building society offer a routine job to a sixteen year old who had intended to stay in the sixth form to take A levels.

5 A soft drinks company switch from returnable to non-returnable bottles to reduce costs.

6 A civil engineering company know minor breaches of safety policy are occurring yet also knows that costly man-hours are being saved as a result.

Summary and comment

• the impact of business on the environment is a fundamental question concerning human beings and their relationship with nature

• in their decisions, firms have a duty to shareholders in ensuring profitability. This means meeting demand in the market, i.e. the purchasing choices of ordinary people. However it is possible for firms to influence and educate their shareholders, employees, suppliers and consumers in environmental values

• rising environmental standards for business in Europe and the USA can actually increase the environmental threats elsewhere. Firms may decide to re-locate environmentally damaging activities to poorer countries with weaker legal constraints. Some multinational companies are careful in assessing the environmental impact of their business, but others will exploit local environments to the maximum degree permitted by law

• techniques for the measurement of social and environmental cost are still at an early stage of development. It is likely that CBA will be applied more widely in public sector decision making. For the private sector, there may be increasing imposition of taxes to

reflect environmental costs
- the European Community Social Charter (see Chapter 43) is an attempt to make business serve social objectives as well as strictly business objectives. If all companies in all EC countries followed the proposed terms of the Social Charter (for example, by paying a minimum wage), then none would be disadvantaged relative to each other
- an increase in many prices is implied as firms develop environmentally safer products with modified production techniques and materials. This would impose some constraints on the rise in living standards. It is possible that this outcome will become increasingly acceptable to most people
- some researchers and writers are pessimistic about the capacity of a market economy to restrain its impact on the environment. Against this view, it may be argued that the democracy of the market place and the ballot box will jointly modify business activity to ensure environmental protection
- while environmental protection demands constraints on the use of physical resources, future economic growth might occur through higher quality in products and an increased output of human services
- it is worth remembering that serious environmental concern first appeared during the 1960s. Far from being a passing 'fashion', the issue has grown enormously in its influence on public and political awareness and on business behaviour
- ethical debate is often a good predictor of the social changes that later alter the patterns of economic demand
- some firms are initiating change in response to ethical issues that is planned and proactive
- to be effective, ethical standards need the decisive backing of top management
- ethical codes should be developed with the involvement and agreement of managers at all levels. Otherwise subordinate staff may fear the consequences of raising ethical objections to company decisions.

Appendix 1: Inflation table

Year	1966	1971	1976	1981	1982	1983	1984	1985	1986	1987	1988	1989	1990	1991
1967	1.026													
1968	1.074													
1969	1.132													
1970	1.204													
1971	1.318													
1972	1.412	1.071												
1973	1.540	1.169												
1974	1.787	1.356												
1975	2.221	1.685												
1976	2.588	1.964												
1977	2.998	2.275	1.158											
1978	3.247	2.464	1.255											
1979	3.682	2.749	1.423											
1980	4.344	3.296	1.679											
1981	4.860	3.688	1.878											
1982	5.278	4.005	2.039	1.086										
1983	5.521	4.189	2.133	1.136	1.046									
1984	5.796	4.398	2.239	1.193	1.098	1.050								
1985	6.148	4.665	2.376	1.265	1.165	1.114	1.061							
1986	6.357	4.824	2.456	1.308	1.204	1.152	1.097	1.034						
1987	6.623	5.025	2.559	1.363	1.255	1.200	1.143	1.077	1.042					
1988	6.947	5.271	2.684	1.429	1.316	1.258	1.199	1.130	1.093	1.049				
1989	7.488	5.681	2.893	1.541	1.419	1.356	1.292	1.218	1.178	1.131	1.078			
1990	8.196	6.219	3.167	1.686	1.553	1.485	1.414	1.333	1.289	1.238	1.180	1.095		
1991	8.677	6.584	3.353	1.785	1.644	1.572	1.497	1.411	1.365	1.310	1.249	1.150	1.059	
1992	0.000	0.000	0.000	0.000	0.000	0.000	0.000	0.000	0.000	0.000	0.000	0.000	0.000	0.000

To use

For theoretical 1989 price (vertical) at actual 1976 (horizontal), MULTIPLY by 2.893

For theoretical 1976 price (horizontal) at actual 1989 (vertical), DIVIDE by 2.893

Appendix 2: Discount factors

End of year	Discount factors %					
	6	8	10	12	15	20
1	.943	.926	.909	.893	.870	.833
2	.900	.857	.826	.797	.756	.694
3	.840	.794	.751	.712	.658	.579
4	.792	.735	.683	.636	.572	.482
5	.747	.681	.621	.567	.497	.402
10	.558	.463	.386	.322	.247	.162

Appendix 3: Assessment and examination

WRITTEN ASSIGNMENTS

Get Briefed
The requirements for written assignments from subject to subject, course to course, examination board to examination board. If you are asked to complete a written assignment without being given a detailed guidance on how it should be presented, you have every right to complain. This is not something you should be left to guess about.

Understanding the Brief
Study the brief carefully. You can solve a lot of problems at this stage. It might be something as short as an essay title, or a long briefing for a marketing project. Right from the start try to imagine what the finished product will look like. This may well raise questions of interpretation. Make a list of these and ask for guidance from a tutor. If this is not forthcoming, discuss the problem with someone else. You will often find that simply putting your problem into words makes the problem disappear.

Organizing Your Time
For large pieces of work, especially those which require research, it is essential to make a plan showing what you are going to do and by when. All kinds of contingencies may cause problems for you: the book you require is on loan to someone else, the person you want to interview is on holiday, some data you require isn't published until after your deadline, etc. The better you plan, the easier you will find it to adjust to changing circumstances.

Organizing Your Mind
Many people find that the best way for them to organize their mind is to use a spider diagram like the one shown overleaf. Many of the spider's legs will turn out to be irrelevant, but at least you will know which ones are there to be cut off.

  When you have thought around the assignments in this way and as you think further about it, you can start to assemble materials. Look at your lecture notes, activity responses and file cards. Check reading lists. Look at the contents pages and indexes of your textbooks. By the time you have done this you will probably have to draw another spider diagram.

Start Drafting
Unless you are a very skilled writer, you simply won't be able to start writing an assignment at the beginning to reach a successful conclu-

sion at the end. Before it reaches this point, your work will have to go through several drafts. Either keep your early drafts in note form, or if you write them more fully, be prepared to cut them, and reassemble them in a different order. If you use a word processor this is easy.

If You Get Stuck

If you get stuck, the first thing to do is to try to make a list of your difficulties. Say to yourself 'I can't do this because . . . '. A lot of the confusion surrounding your difficulties will then disappear and the real problems should emerge. If you have any left, take the list of difficulties to a tutor or some other source of help. The worse things to do if you get stuck are to stay up night after night getting nowhere, or to give up without seeking advice.

Check Before You Finalize

When you have a draft, check it against the brief. Be tough with yourself. Will this draft, when written up, really meet the requirements? If it doesn't then make a list of the ways in which it fails. Use the list to redraft and repeat.

Sleep On It

If you possibly can, leave the work alone for a few days. When you come back to it you will see its strengths and weaknesses more clearly.

The Final Version

This may be the second or third version. It should be clearly written and correctly spelled and punctuated. Leave wide margins on the page for tutor's comments. Make sure you follow any local requirements for length, line-spacing and structure. It may well require a bibliography. Failing any local advice, references quoted in the text should take one of the following forms:

Either '(Barnes, 1992)' or 'as Barnes says (1992)'. Then at the end list the references in alphabetical order according to author name. For book references the references are: second name, initial or first name, publication date, publisher. For articles: second name, first name or initial, date, title, periodical title, volume, part or part number, page. And where your reference appears in a book edited by someone else: author's second name, initial or first name, date, title, editor's second name, initial or first name, title of book, publisher.

Check the final version and hand it in on time.

REVISION

In an ideal world you would be reviewing your work from the second day of your course. But we don't live in an ideal world and most people leave revision until the last few weeks before the examination. Nevertheless, if you have taken some of the advice offered earlier, you will have been maintaining good, easily retrievable notes and file cards throughout your course and so be off to a flying start when revision time comes.

Work out a revision timetable, with realistic learning objectives at each stage – you will find many of the chapter objectives in this book useful, but you will have to make some up for yourself. Use past papers, but NOT to question spot. Question-spotting is a bad mistake. Use past papers to identify which broad topics and themes the examiner usually asks about and revise them carefully. Analyse past papers for their commands. Make sure you know the differences between 'describe', 'account for', 'analyse', and so on. What you must not do is to revise actual questions and prepare model answers. Model questions rarely come up!

Ask yourself questions and answer them. Try to think like an examiner. As you approach different topics ask yourself, what questions could the examiner ask me about this.

Revise Actively

Make notes and summaries all the time. Make notes of notes, summaries of notes and notes of summaries. Annotate your notes with notes from a textbook and then produce a tidy version. Convert notes in continuous text into notes in diagram or table format, or vice versa.

As your revision proceeds, try to reduce the whole course to a series of trigger words and phrases - just enough to jog your memory. Practise writing your answers under the pressure of time. How much can you get down in the time available? Practise writing answers of that length.

Work in regular sessions with breaks every hour, but get used to working for three hours at a time before taking a longer break.

► Make sure you know how you will be examined. How many exams? How long? What choice of questions? Will there be compulsory questions, essay questions, data-response questions, short answer questions? These all require different skills and different ways of revising.

► Establish how much of your syllabus you should revise.

► Check the assessment objectives which are printed in the syllabus document produced by your board.

► Read the Chief Examiner's reports for previous years. Note well what these reports say. Not only does the Chief Examiner have experience of the mistakes of thousands of students, he/she actually decides what is mistaken and what is correct.

► Taking an active approach to revision is essential. Passive revision, i.e. sitting reading through notes and textbooks is both boring and ineffective.

► Revise with friends, discussing questions and trying to explain things to each other.

THE EXAMINATION

Think of the examination as an opportunity for you to give a performance, with an audience of one – the examiner. You are displaying your knowledge, understanding and skills to someone who wants to applaud you.

Here are some key points to bear in mind:

- make sure you know when and where the examination will be held. If it is an unfamiliar place, try to visit it beforehand and check your travel arrangements
- the evening before the exam. make sure you have all the pens, pencils and other equipment you will need
- arrive in good time, but don't stand around chatting. Go for a walk to loosen up and get the oxygen flowing to the brain
- when the exam starts, read through the whole paper (or those parts which relate to your options)
- do NOT start writing immediately, but settle down, get the feel of the paper, check the instructions and find the questions you feel ok about. Take a few minutes to double check that you are following the rubric correctly
- choose your probable questions, but don't firm up your choice at this early stage
- the marks allocated to each question, or parts of each question are a rough guide to how much you should write on each. If two marks are allocated, make two good points and stop. You won't get more than two marks however many brilliant points you make
- draw up a rough timetable for yourself – 'by 10.35 I should have finished the first question', etc.
- start your first question. Now for the golden rule of exams

> ANSWER THE QUESTION SET:
> DO WHAT THE EXAMINER TELLS YOU TO DO

- for all but very short answers, make a plan
- think all the time. Don't just try to remember things, but think about how to apply what you know to the question set
- don't overrun your time on a particular question. It takes much longer to get a few more marks at the end of an answer than at the beginning of another
- take rests during your exams. Loosen up physically; breathe, stretch, shut your eyes while you are thinking
- leave enough time for checking and polishing your answers. A single additional mark could mean a higher grade

► Give yourself time off, especially on the day before the examinations start.

► Examiners want you to do well. They are instructed to mark your work by giving you credit for everything you do properly, not to penalize you for your mistakes. Your marks start at zero and go on up whenever you do something right. The examiner is looking for opportunities to reward positive achievements, so supply plenty of these and make it easy for the examiner to find them. Examination answers are vehicles for you to display your achievement.

► If you suffer badly from nerves, learn to relax through the use of deep breathing techniques. Don't take pills, except under medical supervision. Don't drink alcohol before an exam. It relaxes the wrong part of your brain.

► The most common reason for candidates failing to get the marks they should is not lack of knowledge or skill, but failure to observe the golden rule. Make sure you do what the examiner asks you to do.

► Presentation and layout are important, because they should help the examiner to find your good points easily. Use short sentences and paragraphs to make your points clearly and concisely.

► GOOD LUCK!

Index